CONFLICTING ACCOUNTS

A TOUCHSTONE BOOK
Published by Simon & Schuster

 TOUCHSTONE
Rockefeller Center
1230 Avenue of the Americas
New York, NY 10020

Copyright © 1997 by Kevin Goldman
Afterword copyright © 1998 by Kevin Goldman
All rights reserved,
including the right of reproduction
in whole or in part in any form.
First Touchstone Edition 1998
TOUCHSTONE and colophon are
registered trademarks of Simon & Schuster Inc.
Designed by Edith Fowler
Picture research by Natalie Goldstein
Manufactured in the United States of America

10   9   8   7   6   5   4   3   2   1

The Library of Congress has cataloged the
Simon & Schuster edition as follows:

Goldman, Kevin.
    Conflicting accounts : the creation and crash
of the Saatchi & Saatchi advertising empire /
Kevin Goldman.
    p.   cm.
Includes index.
    1. Saatchi & Saatchi—History.
2. Advertising agencies—History.   I. Title.
HF6181.S23G65   1997
338.7'616591'0973—dc20   96-32066   CIP
ISBN 0-684-81571-0
    0-684-83553-3 (pbk)

To Arthur E. and Judith Goldman
and
to my three best girls,
Pam, Alex, and Jo

"Who's a busy man? Me? I'm chairman of the board. I have nothing but time."

—Mr. Bernstein, *Citizen Kane*

PROLOGUE

THE ADVERTISING AGENCY on the third floor of No. 60 Kingly Street in London's trendy Soho district was a sham. Behind the reception desk sat two pretty young women hired for just one day; newspapers were carefully set out on a handsome wooden desk; opulent flower arrangements were scattered throughout. There were two huge models in the hallway; one of a British Airways Concorde, the other of a Qantas 747. And, to complete the effect, expensive artwork from the collection of noted London art collector Charles Saatchi lined the office walls. But five minutes after a small delegation from British Airways completed a two-hour meeting there on April 25, 1995, the stage was struck.

The ad agency's actual headquarters was less than one mile away in a tiny nondescript office in a brownstone at 35 Davies Street, just off quiet, elegant Berkeley Square. The puckish sign on the buzzer read "Dress Rehearsal Ltd." The leader of this budding ad agency wouldn't allow any outsiders to his modest headquarters, especially old friends who were also executives of British Airways. The airline's ad account, valued at £60 million, had been up for grabs among advertising agencies since January, and this new shop wanted to snare British Airways for its own.

Orchestrating this vast charade at No. 60 Kingly Street was Maurice Saatchi, the forty-eight-year-old mercurial advertising wizard who four months earlier had been tossed out as chairman of Saatchi & Saatchi Company PLC, the giant advertising holding company he founded with his brother Charles in 1970. After a tense eight-and-a-half-hour board meeting on December 16, 1994, a member of the Saatchi & Saatchi Company PLC board marched into Maurice Saatchi's office and offered him a largely ceremonial position as chairman of Saatchi & Saatchi Advertising Worldwide.

Saatchi, a proud man for whom appearances were everything, was humiliated by his dismissal; indeed, one friend who spoke to him the night of his ouster said he thought he could hear Saatchi weeping into his car phone, though Saatchi himself said he did not cry. Regardless, he was understandably extremely upset.

It turned out to be a brief mourning period. The board of Saatchi & Saatchi had foolishly given Maurice Saatchi two weeks to think the offer over; that was far too long. Once he rejected the notion of actually working for someone else, Maurice Saatchi began scheming.

Now Maurice Saatchi had one purpose: to exact revenge on his old company, to ruin it, rob it of its most valued employees, strip it of its cherished clients, and destroy those who set out to destroy him. His disdain, in particular, ran deep for David Herro, a thirty-three-year-old Chicago fund manager who had spearheaded the drive to unseat him. Herro was a solidly built, handsome Midwesterner with a clear sense of family and business values. In Saatchi, Herro saw only what he viewed as corruption and a total disregard for what Herro would describe as "corporate governance." Saatchi also disliked Charles (Charlie) Scott, the affable and sloppily attired chief executive officer who had saved the company from financial ruin, but kept his head in the sand when it came to confrontations with anyone, especially Maurice Saatchi.

Saatchi's plan was simple: start a rival ad agency and selectively lure allies from Saatchi & Saatchi Company PLC, which owned Saatchi & Saatchi Advertising Worldwide and Bates Worldwide, to his upstart operation, which Charles Saatchi cleverly dubbed The New Saatchi Agency.

In advertising, image is everything. Maurice knew that by establishing his fledgling agency as New Saatchi, he was, in a single stroke, positioning his former company as old and passé. Months later, a marathon peace session to halt endless legal wrangling between the two sides would almost disintegrate over the name of Maurice Saatchi's new venture. There was much at stake for both sides. Saatchi is one of the most recognizable brand names in advertising, along with J. Walter Thompson; McCann-Erickson; DDB Needham, which is made up in part of the former Doyle Dane Bernbach; and D'Arcy Masius Benton & Bowles—as famous in advertising as some of the brands it represented: Pampers for Procter & Gamble, Wendy's fast food chain, Schweppes beverages, and, of course, British Airways.

At its height in 1987, Saatchi & Saatchi was the number one ad company in the world; it achieved that status by gobbling up ad agencies and related businesses at alarming speed and at foolish prices. But the plan fit with Maurice and Charles's motto: "Nothing Is Impossible." That mission was capped on May 8, 1986, when the brothers audaciously purchased Ted Bates Worldwide, then the third-largest American advertising agency, for $400 million down and another $50 million in 1988. But the acquisition would come to unravel Saatchi & Saatchi Company PLC.

Saatchi & Saatchi's swift ascent to the top of advertising vexed many Madison Avenue executives, even though some were getting obscenely wealthy because of their association with the Saatchis. Advertising was considered a uniquely American profession. And buying some of the venerable names along Madison Avenue were these two odd brothers of Iraqi-Jewish descent—one of whom, Charles, the so-called creative brother, made it a policy never to meet with clients nor, for that matter, with his own employees after the company's first, say, four years. Maurice, the financial expert, was clearly a snob and spendthrift who boasted of two raspberry-colored Bentleys, a home in Cap Ferrat, and a spectacular country house in Sussex, England, named Old Hall. He lived with his second wife, Josephine Hart, author of the sex-laden novel *Damage*, later made into a movie starring Jeremy Irons.

The Saatchi brothers, known in London simply as "the Brothers," embarked on an unprecedented shopping spree with one goal in mind: to be the largest ad agency group in the world. They achieved their extravagant goal in 1986 in part with the purchases of three U.S. agencies: Dancer Fitzgerald Sample ("Where's the Beef?" for Wendy's), Backer & Spielvogel (which coined "Tastes Great, Less Filling" and launched Miller Lite), and Ted Bates Worldwide ("Melts in your mouth, not in your hand" for Mars's flagship M&Ms candy).

By 1986, Saatchi & Saatchi had acquired thirty-seven companies, thirteen in 1985 alone. By the time the brothers stopped, they had parlayed a \$40,000 investment in 1970 into a giant empire of eighty subsidiaries with billings exceeding \$3.2 billion. All told it owned seventeen ad agencies as well as several management consultancies and media buying companies.

But hard times hit Saatchi & Saatchi Company PLC in 1989 because of a slowdown in advertising and disappointing performances in its consulting business; its nineteen-year unbroken record for sustained profit growth ended. Then, its pretax earnings fell to £21.8 million (\$36.8 million) in the fiscal year ended September 30, from £138 million (\$244.4 million) the previous year. Saatchi & Saatchi Company PLC fell to the world's second-largest ad company, behind WPP Group, headed by, of all people, a former Saatchi & Saatchi executive, Martin Sorrell, who had masterminded many of the company's early acquisitions. Eventually, Interpublic Group of Companies, which owns McCann-Erickson Worldwide, and Omnicom Group, which owns BBDO Worldwide and DDB Needham, would pass Saatchi & Saatchi Company PLC as well and exile it to fourth place. In the end, it would slip to fifth place.

Maurice Saatchi, as one senior management consultant would later recall, never lost his obsession to regain Saatchi & Saatchi's number one position. Maurice, said the consultant, "was obsessed with market dominance. It was his favorite, old, and in many ways his only strategic imperative. And that was size. He was never able to achieve size in any permanent way by growing companies. He got there temporarily by acquiring them." Maurice Saatchi never outgrew two mantras of the late 1980s: to be number one is wonderful, number two is terrific, number three is threatened, and number four is failure; to be big is good, to be good is better, and to be both is best.

At the time of Maurice's removal as chairman on December 16, 1994, Saatchi's clients included Mars, the candy and pet food manufacturer; Procter & Gamble; Mirror Group, which owns the *Daily Mirror* in the United Kingdom; General Mills, makers of Cheerios; Sara Lee's Hanes division; Toyota; Avis Rent-a-Car; and Warner-Lambert.

Now, Maurice Saatchi wanted only to win British Airways, thereby launching his nascent agency and, more importantly, crippling "Old Co.," as he dismissively called Saatchi & Saatchi Company PLC, for whom British Airways was a flagship account since it won the business on September 14, 1982. He despised the reality that the world was now occupied with two companies named Saatchi. Maurice Saatchi wanted to rid the planet of Saatchi & Saatchi Company PLC and its onerous unit Saatchi & Saatchi Advertising Worldwide. He wanted either to acquire it or to shut it down.

THESE WERE AMONG THE THOUGHTS that occupied Maurice Saatchi's mind on April 25, 1995, as he strolled into a huge conference room filled with twelve video monitors along one wall as well as two television sets and a horseshoe-shaped desk. Accompanying Saatchi was Tim Duffy, a tall, boyish-looking thirty-one-year-old account director, one of the first to defect from Saatchi & Saatchi and sign on with the new venture. Duffy recalled he was smitten with the ad business almost from the moment in 1987 that he walked into Saatchi & Saatchi Advertising headquarters at 80 Charlotte Street in Fitzrovia, a nondescript London neighborhood. A contagious energy infected the place back then, as if working for Saatchi & Saatchi meant working for the best.

And, for a magic period, it did: Saatchi & Saatchi Advertising created some spectacularly effective ads. In 1978, hired by the Tory party, it produced a poster of a seemingly endless line of unemployed individuals. The caption: "Labour Isn't Working." The ad ran at only twenty sites, but the message was startling and pervasive. The Tories won and Margaret Thatcher was propelled to power. Another famous ad, created in the company's first year of existence, for Britain's Health Education Council, showed a glum-looking man with a haircut shaped like that worn by the Beatles, his belly bulging. The caption: "Would you be more careful if it was you that got pregnant?" That ad became such a powerful icon that when the agency opened a pub in its headquarters, it was named the Pregnant Man.

Saatchi & Saatchi's most noteworthy commercials were for British Airways, including one in which the island of Manhattan lifted off into space. It was Saatchi & Saatchi that coined the British Airways slogan, "The World's Favourite Airline." Now, Maurice Saatchi and Tim Duffy had to work the magic once again and convince British Airways executives to award the prestigious account to this untested agency. One British Airways executive attending the meeting at No. 60 Kingly Street that April day was Sir Colin Marshall, the airline's chairman, who had twice written in support of Maurice Saatchi.

Other British Airways executives in attendance that day were Robert Ayling, the forty-nine-year-old group managing director and heir apparent to Sir Colin; Derek Dear, general manager, marketing communications; and Val Gooding, general manager, business units. The Australian airline Qantas, of which British Airways owns 25 percent, was also represented at the pitch by Geoff Dixon, managing director, and Ken Ryan, a marketing executive. Unknown publicly at the time was the weight of Qantas's opinion over an agency selection.

After Maurice Saatchi resigned in January 1995, Peter McLaughlin, a Qantas marketing executive, called Bill Muirhead, the former chief executive of Saatchi & Saatchi Advertising North America, who had resigned shortly after Maurice's departure, and asked, "Who is going to look after us?" When British Airways decided to speak with other advertising agencies about the account, Qantas followed.

Accompanying Maurice Saatchi and Tim Duffy was Maurice Levy, chairman of Publicis SA, a French advertising group. Maurice Saatchi had allied himself with Levy in order to handle British Airways' demanding worldwide media buying and planning operations. At the opening of the presentation, Saatchi referred to himself as "Maurice the Brain" and to Levy as "Maurice the Mechanic," alluding to Levy's money and ad agency network.

Maurice Saatchi was unmistakable in his oversize tortoiseshell eyeglasses. Uncharacteristically, he wasn't wearing the jacket to his dark Comme des Garçons suit. He welcomed everyone and assured them the presentation would last only two hours. Maurice is tall and thin and usually has a cat-swallowing-the-canary grin. His face, while framed by the large eyeglasses, is also punctuated by thin lips. In one-on-one conversations he speaks softly so that the listener is forced to strain and pay close attention to what is being said.

The British Airways contingency was to see four ad agency

finalists that spring day—Saatchi & Saatchi Advertising on Charlotte Street, Bartle Bogle Hegarty, a well-respected creative hotshop on Great Pulteney Street in London's Soho district, The New Saatchi Agency, and J. Walter Thompson on Berkeley Square. Of the four, Bartle Bogle was considered New Saatchi's major competition: it created eye-catching ads for Levi's, Audi, NatWest Bank, and Sony. Saatchi & Saatchi was said to have virtually no chance to retain the business. New Saatchi was considered a favorite because of the close association between Maurice Saatchi and Sir Colin.

"We have entitled the presentation Encore," Maurice began, speaking slowly and deliberately, looking at each person in the room eye-to-eye. "An encore is when you have a pleasant experience and want more. But do you want the same song or a new song? . . . Do you want to say, 'Jolly good show. Well done everybody. It's obviously worked. We need more of the same,' or do you want to say, 'Jolly good show. Well done everybody. It's obviously worked but the world has changed and we need something different'?" Maurice Saatchi and Tim Duffy were there to assure British Airways that New Saatchi wasn't going to sing the same old tune.

Duffy laid out the problems facing British Airways: "It's difficult to disentangle one airline from another. Our challenge is to ensure British Airways can sustain a premium in the new world of leisure." A solution, continued Duffy, is to "break the rules again. Harness the 'masterbrand' of business and leisure."

After a while, Maurice Saatchi turned to a device that had worked effectively for him in the past: surprise guest stars, albeit on videotape. Playing off the slogan "The World's Favourite Airline," Saatchi promised British Airways that if it signed with The New Saatchi Agency, it would be aligned with the world's favorite media deal maker, Rupert Murdoch, chairman of News Corp.; the world's favorite composer, Andrew Lloyd Webber, who said he would write the airline's new jingle; the world's favorite airport, Gatwick, outside London and operated by British Airports Authority; the world's favorite lottery, represented by Victor Markowitz, chairman of G-Tech, which operated 75 percent of the world's lottery games. For a presentation of the world's favorite employees, Maurice Saatchi secured the services of former Monty Python player John Cleese, who personified the stiff-upper-lip British character. On video, Cleese performed a moderately amusing bit about motivating the British Airways troops.

After Maurice Levy made a somewhat stilted and rambling presentation about how the British Airways account would be serviced by Publicis around the world, the group was treated to a videotape showing three former Saatchi & Saatchi executives, wearing suits and ties, not laboring in an ad agency, but relaxing in a rambling garden. The joke was immediately clear to everyone in the room. On the tape were Jeremy Sinclair, forty-eight years old, former acting chairman of Saatchi & Saatchi Company PLC; Bill Muirhead, forty-eight, former chief executive officer of Saatchi & Saatchi North America; and David Kershaw, forty, former chairman of Saatchi & Saatchi's U.K. operation.

The three had resigned January 9, 1995, six days after Maurice Saatchi had officially left the company, to join him in his new venture. Combined, the three executives were with Saatchi & Saatchi for more than sixty years and their loyalty to Maurice Saatchi was unquestioned. The three amigos, as they quickly became known, were still under contract to Saatchi & Saatchi Company PLC and couldn't work for anyone else until complex legal wrangles were sorted out. In London, the three were on what is known as Garden Leave. They planned to join Maurice Saatchi as equal partners with Charles Saatchi at The New Saatchi Agency as soon as it became legally possible. Until then, at full salary, the three set up shop off fashionable Regent Street in a tiny office nicknamed the Garden Shed and the Potting Shed, sometimes even known as the Plotting Shed. They were forbidden to speak to Maurice Saatchi about the business or anyone connected with his new agency, which, of course, was ludicrous, and which went basically unmonitored. Hence the tongue-in-cheek video; intercut with footage of the three executives loafing among the flowers with classical music in the background were worker bees at The New Saatchi Agency frantically setting about their nerve-wracking work to the accompaniment of Dolly Parton's hit tune "9 to 5."

What followed the tape was vintage Maurice Saatchi, an Elmer Gantry act that was to disarm and charm the gathering. "I must have woken up every morning for the last few weeks wondering what to say to you at this stage of the proceedings," he began, clearing his throat in the same affected, staged way Woody Allen has perfected. "I decided that it boils down to only two things. Firstly, we owe you an apology. Because if it weren't for certain events on our side we would not be taking this time out. . . . We owe you an apology. The second thing is you owe us nothing. Whatever happens today, we will always be grateful for what we've done together. And I want you to know that there will always be a group of people in the world, mainly this group, who are on your side.

"Now you've got to choose a new partner for the next stage of your growth. I haven't known or observed a better business relationship than we've had over the years. . . . Any agency will give you the right requirements. . . . The only question is what more you're going to get. I hope you would not expect me to let you out today without giving you some compelling reasons for appointing us. And I will try to spell out six."

Using the video wall again, Saatchi began to list the reasons: Experience—"We have spent fourteen thousand hours" in British Airways' London offices since Saatchi & Saatchi Advertising became the agency, Saatchi reminded them; New—"Through some miraculous divine intervention, all these experienced hands find themselves in a new young and fresh setting," he went on; Creative; Organised—"We are ready to go," Saatchi assured British Airways; Rational; Emotional—"We are not cold, calculated machines." The letters then formed the word "Encore."

The presentation concluded with a British Airways design icon—a red line below the word "Encore." As the line was drawn, it was accompanied by the sound of an airliner taking off, the same sound effect that ends each British Airways television and radio ad.

Executives from British Airways and Qantas left and then the torturous waiting began. British Airways was a must-win for The New Saatchi Agency; without it, the budding venture would never escape boutique status.

The next day, April 26, Duffy was awakened at 9 A.M. by a call from Derek Dear, British Airways' general manager, marketing communications, someone with whom Duffy had a close relationship. Without betraying any indication as to how the other agencies had performed in their presentations, Dear told Duffy that he needed to see him immediately and alone. "It's urgent," Dear said. Dear said someone else from British Airways would come: Mervyn Walker, director of purchasing. Duffy delicately suggested they meet for lunch at Maurice Saatchi's posh mews house on Bruton Place, off Berkeley Square.

The issue that brought the two sides together again was money: The New Saatchi Agency was charging a lot. "We were expensive," Duffy said, "but that's because we knew how much it cost to run the business."

After Dear and Gooding left, Saatchi and Duffy were joined by Maurice's wife, Josephine Hart. "We said this is absolute torture," Duffy said. The decision was expected by the end of the week. By April 29, nothing happened.

Meanwhile, Bill Muirhead, an immensely likable Australian native who had been part of Maurice and Charles Saatchi's inner circle since 1972 and who, more than anyone other than Maurice, gambled his future by walking out of Saatchi & Saatchi, was finding the waiting hard. He didn't shave; he took to wearing a T-shirt with the saying "Losing Is Not an Option." He never cleaned it. He called everyone for gossip, for a sign that he wasn't foolish to resign, as his wife, Jeanne, had privately believed. Unlike the others, Muirhead spent what he made, had no stock in the company and very little, if any, savings.

Monday, May 1, came and went. Then, on May 2, while Maurice was in his green Toyota Camry on the way to lunch, his mobile phone rang. It was Robert Ayling asking to see him at 3:30 in the airline's Berkeley Square office.

Duffy heard of the meeting on his cellular phone while having a beer at Ye Grapes, a pub in Shepherd's Market. On his way back to the office, he ran into Muirhead and Kershaw, who were imbibing beer from cans. At 4:15, when no one on Davies Street had heard from Maurice—the meeting at British Airways had concluded by then—Duffy called Josephine Hart a few blocks away on Bruton Place. She hadn't heard from her husband, either.

At 5:30, without any hint of what was to come, Maurice Saatchi returned to 35 Davies Street. He asked the staff to gather for a meeting. Speaking slowly and theatrically, he said, "British Airways has awarded its entire business to" (long pause) "us."

Pandemonium swept the place. The three amigos and others guzzled warm Champagne. The first outsider through the door was Andrew Lloyd Webber. Charles Saatchi, keeping in character, was nowhere to be found.

Maurice Saatchi failed to provide an important detail of the meeting with British Airways, however. "It was a tight competition," Ayling had told Saatchi.

Maurice Saatchi later learned how tight. Several British Airways executives had wanted Bartle Bogle to be awarded the assignment. Saatchi & Saatchi had been eliminated quickly because the airlines thought the agency's strategy was adrift. "Is this the same group of people who have been working on the account for ten years?" one Qantas executive said to a British Airways official after the Saatchi & Saatchi pitch. J. Walter Thompson wasn't considered exciting enough from a creative standpoint. Bartle Bogle's flaw was that it wanted everything to originate from London and resisted opening satellite offices. That was unacceptable to Qantas, which drafted a letter to Ayling asking him to consider the situation rationally.

On Davies Street, no one was paying attention to one line in the British Airways press release: "The contract has been awarded to New Saatchi for one year." That was unusual. When companies select an ad agency, contracts are never publicly mentioned. Agencies can get fired on a moment's notice for no reason whatsoever. The belief was that British Airways was putting its new agency on the tight leash of a twelve-month tryout.

The party continued at the Atlantic Bar & Grill. Eventually, Maurice Saatchi slipped away from the festivities and went home for a quiet dinner with his son, Edward, and stepson, Adam. British Airways was his now and Maurice Saatchi wouldn't rest until his former company was on its knees. He had little regard for any senior executive left at Saatchi & Saatchi; they were spineless toadies who carried out the orders of David Herro, a snotty upstart from Chicago, of all places. With British Airways under his belt, with Jeremy Sinclair, Bill Muirhead, David Kershaw, Tim Duffy, and other defectors from Old Co., Maurice Saatchi was ready to strike. Maurice Saatchi had the British press in his corner; through the years, he and Charles Saatchi spent hours charming reporters and selectively leaking headline stories. Charles Scott, Saatchi & Saatchi Company PLC's acting chairman and chief executive officer, was an accountant, someone more comfortable with a balance sheet than a storyboard. Certainly, he was no match for the Saatchi publicity machine.

FEW WOULD ESCAPE Saatchi & Saatchi vs. Saatchi & Saatchi unscathed. Reputations would be ruined, huge sums of money would be spent on legal maneuvers, and an unpleasant odor would engulf both camps. Advertising is an industry that sells image. Odd, then, that both sides would publicly torture each other to such an extent that the images of both Saatchi & Saatchi Company PLC and The New Saatchi Agency would be sullied. Rival agencies would cringe at the level of discord. It was harming the entire advertising industry: "I wish these people would go away and let us do business," said Martin Puris, chairman, chief executive officer, and chief creative officer at Interpublic Group's Ammirati Puris Lintas, an agency respected for its creative output. "They've done more harm than we've managed to do in the last hundred years. Industry critics who say the advertising business is flaky and catastrophe is around the corner will say, 'Aha!' "

What is clear is that Saatchi & Saatchi and The New Saatchi Agency vastly underestimated each other: Maurice Saatchi misread the depth of resentment bubbling in David Herro, the stockholder. And Herro, Charles Scott, and countless Saatchi & Saatchi executives—with one notable exception—failed to heed warning signs that Maurice Saatchi wouldn't leave quietly.

More than anything, the creation and crash of Saatchi & Saatchi—Maurice Saatchi and the advertising agency holding company—underscored the delicate nature of the advertising industry. Advertising is a business built entirely on the smoke and mirrors of individual reputations, personal salesmanship, and the charisma of those involved. Basically, there is no difference between the itinerant patent medicine salesman of the nineteenth century and the smart-looking advertising salesman in the late twentieth century. Both weave a spell and tell a tale.

Advertising is an industry in which the amount of money to be made rivals the fortunes made by the investment banker robber barons. Indeed, one man, Charles Saatchi, made so much money in advertising that he was able to control the world's contemporary art market. In advertising, there is no genius beyond the genius to invent yourself. Of course, one must remember that if you can reinvent yourself today, someone—perhaps a David Herro—can reinvent you tomorrow. But then, if you are as clever and diabolical as Maurice Saatchi, you can then turn around and invent yourself a second time.

CHAPTER
ONE

MAURICE AND CHARLES SAATCHI are Iraqi Jews born in Baghdad. Their father was Nathan Saatchi. "Sa'aatchi" translated from Arabic means "watchmaker" or "watch dealer," although Nathan Saatchi was a successful textile merchant. Like many of his peers, Nathan used a matchmaker in order to meet a wife. He was told to walk past a certain house at a certain time and a girl, Daisy Ezer, would be standing there. Daisy had been educated at the Alliance School for Girls, which was sponsored by the French government, and had a middle-class background. When they married in 1936, Nathan was twenty-nine and Daisy was seventeen. One year later, David, the first of four sons, was born in Baghdad. Eventually, David would settle in New York, become a successful commodities broker, and eventually live in the fashionable summer resort of the Hamptons on eastern Long Island as a sculptor. Charles Nathan Saatchi was born June 9, 1943, and Maurice Nathan Saatchi on June 21, 1946, both born in Baghdad like their older brother. The fourth and youngest brother, Philip, would be born in London in June 1953. He would become a singer and songwriter.

Although their parents spoke Hebrew and Arabic, the Saatchi children were ordered to speak only English at home. Nathan was an elder of the Sephardic and Portuguese Synagogue on Lauderdale Road in Hampstead. Maurice Saatchi remembers his upbringing in a "very religious home" but "all the four sons have lost their religion, which is a pity."

In 1947, after purchasing two textile mills in north London, Nathan Saatchi moved his family to London, settling into a house in Ossulton Way, in an upscale neighborhood near the Hampstead Golf Club. Eventually the family would settle into a house with eight bedrooms on Hampstead Lane in Highgate, one of London's most expensive areas. As it turned out, Nathan and Daisy Saatchi left Iraq just ahead of a massive exodus; within a few years, 120,000 Jews fled Iraq, leaving only 15,000 behind. The *Jerusalem Post* reported in 1986 that "No other exodus in Jewish history, except the exodus from Egypt, was comparable in terms of its drama and spontaneity to the story of the Iraqi Jews." Shortly after the end of World War II, the attitude of Jews in Iraq fundamentally changed. There were reductions of the number of Jews in civil services. Also, restrictions were placed on the teaching of Hebrew. Contact with Palestine was forbidden. Jews were forced to include Muslims as business partners. Zionism, the government in Iraq said, was "poisoning the atmosphere." Then, Jews were prohibited from purchasing land. Any Jew leaving the country had to deposit a guarantee of £1,500 and Jews were no longer accepted into government schools.

After a shaky start, Nathan Saatchi, mainly through contacts in the Middle East, established a successful textile business in London. At twenty-seven, David, his oldest son, finally succumbed and joined the family business, which he hated. In 1967, he joined the Israeli army to fight in the Six-Day War. The war was over before David actually had a chance to join the combat, but it accomplished one goal: he got away from his father. From Israel he went to the United States, where he was still living in 1996.

Charles Saatchi attended Christ College, Finchley, before giving up at age seventeen. Charles was a handsome young man who sported a mop of long dark curly hair before the mop top was made fashionable by the Beatles in 1963. Like his siblings, he was tall, over six feet, and towered over his father. Like his older brother, he did not excel in school. As a child and later as an adult Charles Saatchi adored playing board games, such as Scrabble and chess. Even when he was president of Saatchi & Saatchi, Charles spent part of some days with his office door closed as he and several pals, including Michael Green, a childhood friend who is now chairman of Carlton Communications in the United Kingdom, pored over a game.

Charles's career had false starts. When he left school, there was a period when he did little more than party and ride around

London on a motorcycle in leather attire. He spent a year in the United States simply seeing the country and doing little else but observing the popular culture, including advertising. He devoured television and popular culture and he had an insatiable appetite for sports cars. But when it came to a profession, Charles Saatchi was adrift. He tried college again, this time to study design, though it was a short-lived attempt. It was not until Charles was twenty-two that he landed a job that finally seemed to interest him.

In 1965, he was hired as a junior copywriter in the London office of the giant United States advertising agency Benton & Bowles. Even though he quickly earned a reputation as a talented copywriter, Charles was not placed on any first-tier accounts; he was too young and considered a junior member of the agency. But after only two and a half months, Charles would meet someone who would have great influence on his professional life: Ross Cramer, twenty-seven, senior art director at Benton & Bowles. The two met one day when Saatchi stood behind Cramer while at his drawing board. "I like that," Saatchi told Cramer of the piece he was working on. They hit it off and Saatchi quickly asked to be paired with Cramer.

While at Benton & Bowles, Charles Saatchi would become attracted to Doris Lockhart Dibley, a copy group head. Tall, blond, and decidedly cool, Doris Dibley, the daughter of a Memphis newspaper editor, could have been cast as the heroine in an Alfred Hitchcock movie. Smitten as Saatchi was, there was little he could do; Dibley, seven years older than Charles, was a newlywed, married to a racing car driver named Hugh Dibley.

Ultimately, Benton & Bowles was not the place for the talented pair of Saatchi and Cramer. Some agencies nurture creativity; others want advertising that takes no chances. Benton & Bowles fell into the latter category. So Saatchi and Cramer resigned and joined Collett Dickenson Pearce, a fledgling agency with a reputation for creative excellence. Already at Collett Dickenson were future film producer David Puttnam, whose credits would include *Chariots of Fire*, and future film director Alan Parker, whose credits would include the 1996 film version of *Evita*, starring Madonna.

It was at Collett Dickenson Pearce that Charles Saatchi

soared as a copywriter. He let his hair grow, connecting to the Swinging London of Freddie and the Dreamers, the Rolling Stones, and Herman's Hermits. It was here he honed a love of cars, driving around London in a Lincoln Continental. He also owned a Jaguar, a Mercedes-Benz, and a Ferrari.

Charles Saatchi continued his partnership with Ross Cramer and in 1967 won an award for advertisements produced for Selfridge's, the London department store. One said, "A warning to the under 12s. Be on your guard when your parents volunteer a trip to Selfridge's toy department. It could be a bribe to get you inside our barber shop." Another read, "The most valuable things shoplifters get off with in Selfridge's are the girls at the cosmetic counter."

The duo also worked on the Ford account. It was here that Charles Saatchi made his first significant contribution to British advertising. The year he had spent in the United States paid off for Charles Saatchi with the Ford assignment. He was a fan of American advertising in which a company could show a rival's product in a commercial or in a print ad. The rules of Britain's Institute of Practitioners of Advertising forbid the practice, which in the United Kingdom was known as "knocking copy." For the Ford Executive model, Charles Saatchi and Ross Cramer produced an ad that showed a Jaguar, a Rover, and a Mercedes. The headline read, "The Ford Executive compares quite favorably with these grand cars." Another ad said, "With some 2 liter cars you pay for the name. Ford only charges you for the car."

Despite their success, Saatchi and Cramer left Collett Dickenson in 1967, briefly working at John Collins & Partners, a small agency. Partly because of size and partly because of internal politics, Saatchi and Cramer departed after only six months, this time deciding they had had enough of working for others. Why not simply open a consultancy that would be hired on a project-by-project basis by anyone who cared to tap into their creative juices?

CramerSaatchi opened on Goodge Street in 1967. It was a small but potent agency; in addition to Saatchi and Cramer, there was John Hegarty, whom the pair met at Benton & Bowles and who later joined them at John Collins & Partners.

There was also Jeremy Sinclair, a literate bald-headed man

with gentle eyes who speaks in a whisper while chain-smoking Cuban cigars. Sinclair was born in London on November 4, 1946, went to school in Scotland, and eventually settled in Paris when his father, a management consultant, relocated there. At an outdoor book kiosk along the Seine in 1966 Sinclair by chance picked up the book *Confessions of an Advertising Man* by David Ogilvy, co-founder of the great advertising agency Ogilvy & Mather. Ogilvy hit hard the theme of building brands, that consumers would purchase more expensive items if they were drawn to a well-executed marketing plan. Kellogg's cereal, for instance, costs more than so-called private label brands, yet Kellogg's generally outsells brands such as President's Choice. Advertising is a major factor.

At the time, Sinclair was twenty-one, unmarried and intrigued by the advertising profession. He purchased a copy of *The* (London) *Times* and wrote to Watford Art College, which was advertising a course in copywriting. Having sent the letter, Sinclair then left for Algeria for a few months. Upon his return to Paris, he found two letters from Watford. One contained an examination for admittance, another was a note inquiring why the school hadn't received the exam; nevertheless, he was invited for an interview. He borrowed the plane fare to London from his mother, completing the exam on the flight. He was accepted.

While in school, Sinclair worked nights shifting scenery on weekends at a local theater. Armed with his portfolio from school, Sinclair made the rounds of various London agencies. One person who saw him, Dan Levine, a copywriter at Collett Dickenson Pearce, telephoned his old friend Charles Saatchi. Charles liked what he saw. The applicant's assignment was to do a first-person ad, and Sinclair chose Ayds, a weight-reduction product. Sinclair's was the only whimsical ad submitted; the headline in Sinclair's was, "Two men offered me their seats on the bus. I needed them both."

Charles offered Sinclair, who had graduated from school by this time, a job at £10 a week. Sinclair, recalling in 1995 accepting the offer, said, "I took one look at Charles and said, 'Yeah, he'll do.'"

One of the ads CramerSaatchi devised was for the launch of *Cosmopolitan* magazine in the United Kingdom. The agency proposed a commercial showing a couple on a lovely vacation. "Where did you get the idea of coming here for the holidays?" the man asked the woman. The answer: *"Cosmopolitan,* Page 42." The next scene showed a couple in bed. The man said, "I don't believe it. Where did you get the idea of doing that?" The reply: *"Cosmopolitan,* Page 144."

The self-regulating British ad industry objected. Sinclair negotiated. "Could you show a couple in bed?" he asked. "Yes, if they're married," came the answer. "But you can't have the man asking the question." So the ad ran with only the woman saying, *"Cosmopolitan,* Page 144." "You didn't need to ask the question," Sinclair said. "You knew what was being asked. The government had infinitely improved the script." Sinclair liked to boast that the commercial was written before he ever saw a copy of the magazine.

Such eye-catching ads in the rather staid world of advertising in the United Kingdom resulted in publicity not only for the client but for CramerSaatchi as well.

The consultancy business was not limited to advertising. It also flirted with the film industry by writing scripts. Charles Saatchi and David Puttnam developed a script about an eleven-year-old girl who ran off with her boyfriend to get married. Originally called *Melody,* it was changed to *SWALK,* or *Sealed with a Loving Kiss.* Alan Parker wrote the actual script and the film was made but quickly disappeared.

CramerSaatchi continued to do well in advertising with three-quarters of the top twenty agencies hiring the consultancy. In early 1970, CramerSaatchi broke its own rule and took on a client directly instead of being the conduit between the advertising agency and the client. In this instance, the client was the Health Education Council, and it came to CramerSaatchi through Ross Cramer. He knew a woman who worked for the HEC because their children attended the same school. It was the same time that the Royal College of Surgeons released a detailed report linking cigarette smoking and cancer. There was pressure on the Labour party to drive down the sales of tobacco products and the assignment was given to the HEC, which turned to CramerSaatchi for help.

It did not matter that Charles Saatchi smoked with enthusiasm. He relished the assignment. One ad was produced that showed a liquid tar being poured into a glass saucer. The caption read: "No wonder smokers cough." Below that the line read, "The tar and discharge that collects in the lungs of the average smoker." The ads generated even more publicity for the consulting firm.

Then came the pregnant man ad, one of the most memorable in London advertising history. Jeremy Sinclair thought one morning that it might be more effective to show a man appealing for help because of a pregnancy instead of the woman. A pregnant woman, after all, is wholly predictable. Sinclair then wrote the line that would accompany the ad: "Would you be more careful if it was you that got pregnant?"

Saatchi endorsed Sinclair's advertisement. The HEC, which normally followed a conservative approach to its advertisements, also blessed Sinclair's efforts. Within weeks, it was the most discussed ad in London, and soon after *Time* magazine published it, giving it international exposure.

While Charles Saatchi was firmly established, Maurice Saatchi began to emerge professionally as well. Maurice was less outgoing than Charles but a far superior student; at Tollington Grammar, he consistently made the honor roll. He transferred to the London School of Economics in 1964. Maurice felt he could have been a top-flight cricket player; he was the star number three bat on the team, but he was struck in the head during a game and had to be carried off the field. He graduated with first-class honors in 1967.

Maurice's job choice would have great ramifications for the brothers for years to come. Maurice Saatchi wound up at Haymarket Publications, which owned several periodicals, including *World Press News* and *Campaign,* a weekly magazine that in 1996 remained the leading advertising trade journal in the United Kingdom. Haymarket was controlled by Michael Heseltine, who, in 1995, was Deputy Prime Minister to John Major, and Lindsay Masters.

It was Masters who offered Maurice his first job as his junior assistant. Before accepting, Maurice asked, What is the salary? Masters was taken aback. Salaries generally weren't discussed, much less negotiated by recent graduates. One thousand pounds a year was the standard and Maurice would receive the standard. Maurice politely declined the offer, saying he had considerable expenses, including a Stingray, a fancy sports car. Masters inquired as to what Maurice would need. Two thousand pounds, came the swift reply. He was hired.

Maurice would make many acquaintances at Haymarket, including that of a colleague in the classified advertising department, Josephine Hart. Hart would remain with Haymarket for fifteen years and become a board member. She would also marry Paul Buckley, a Haymarket director who also began his career as a personal assistant to Masters.

Maurice Saatchi remained with Haymarket for three years, working closely with Masters; the two became involved with the launch of *Accountancy Age* and Maurice sold advertising space for the magazine.

Haymarket was on the prowl to purchase established magazines and no one was a better observer of the attempts than Maurice Saatchi. He would study Heseltine's technique of writing to virtually every publishing house offering to buy their magazines. Hundreds of letters were sent annually. Heseltine believed that if Haymarket managed to snare two magazines each year, that was fine.

Although Charles and Maurice Saatchi were established professionally and in their mid-twenties, they continued to live at home with their parents. Such an arrangement enabled the two brothers to engage in detailed discussions about their respective businesses. Charles was justifiably impressed with Maurice's ability to digest and analyze sophisticated business plans.

When Charles hatched the idea of forming a new ad agency, Ross Cramer's reaction was surprising. He opted to bow out of the plans in order to pursue his ambition of directing feature films. That never happened; instead, Cramer became a well-regarded director of commercials, a profession he enjoys in 1996.

So in May 1970 Charles Saatchi told his employees in a rapid-fire speech that the consultancy was evolving into a full-fledged advertising agency, that more people would be hired, that Ross Cramer was leaving, and that his replacement would be Maurice Saatchi.

The announcement wasn't well received; Maurice had never worked at an ad agency. But that's all right, Charles said of his brother; what Maurice lacked in ad skills he more than made up for in financial depth.

It would be a partnership fraught with tension. Charles Saatchi would never let his younger brother know exactly his place in the family. Charles would throw things at Maurice in fits of pique.

"Charles would panic if there was a problem," said Martin Sorrell, a former Saatchi & Saatchi financial executive. "He had tremendous fear."

Once, a clairvoyant told Charles, "By the time you're twenty-five, you will be down and out."

On the day Saatchi & Saatchi won the highly sought-after British Airways account in September 1982, Sorrell was sitting in Maurice's office relishing the victory. Charles joined them and Maurice said, "Isn't it wonderful?"

"Can you imagine what's going to happen when we lose it?" Charles responded.

Charles would often recite to Maurice what came to be known in the executive suite as the gutter speech. "But for me, Maurice, where would you be?" Charles said. "You'd be in the gutter somewhere."

Charles and Maurice did share one vexing trait: impatience.

IN MAY 1970, when Charles Saatchi announced to the staff of CramerSaatchi that the consultancy would become an advertising agency, the brothers already had held private discussions among themselves as to what the name of the new enterprise should be. Quickly, Charles Saatchi decided upon Saatchi & Saatchi. "It's a bloody good name," he said. "No one will forget it because it is so bizarre." Actually, Charles Saatchi was not convinced of the acceptability of the Saatchi moniker in the advertising marketplace. But he concluded that it was the name they were stuck with. "Let's make it an asset," he said.

Charles also decided the company had outgrown its offices on Goodge Street. After a brief search, the brothers were shown office space at No. 6 Golden Square in the city's Soho district. It was a beautiful square near the bustle of Piccadilly Circus. No. 6 was one of the most elegant buildings in the square with carved stone pillars. The Saatchis rented the ground floor and basement. The agency was designed with an emphasis on open space; employees scurried about and a high sense of energy invaded the place. Some CramerSaatchi-produced advertisements were hung like posters, which was unusual in London ad agencies at the time, although it became an accepted practice a few years later. There was a spiral staircase leading to the basement, which housed a projection room and a conference room.

Other than the HEC, a second client was the Citrus Marketing Board of Israel, which sold its oranges and lemons around the world under the name Jaffa. It wanted to launch a major marketing effort in Britain in order to take advantage of the boycott of oranges from South Africa. The ad produced included the line "And the Lord saith: let there be oranges . . ." It ended with the line "Jaffa: the Chosen Fruit." Ultimately, the ad was not used because the client deemed it "anti-Jewish." Yet the client liked the irreverence and kept the agency.

By the end of the summer of 1970, Charles and Maurice Saatchi had attracted a staff and they wanted to officially launch their new advertising agency.

ON SUNDAY, September 13, 1970, a full-page ad appeared on page seven of the *Sunday Times* of London. The headline: "Why I think it's time for a new kind of advertising." The ad was trumpeting the arrival of a new agency: Saatchi & Saatchi Advertising. The ad said that a campaign "only succeeds if it ultimately helps create new sales for a client, and does so efficiently and economically." But advertising didn't accomplish this; rather, its objective was to improve a company's image or brand awareness: "Images and brand awareness are meaningless, if they fail to achieve greater turnover; the test is cash in the till." Account executives, the ad said, are "the middle-man between the advertiser and the people who are paid to create the ads."

One person who read the ad was Bill Muirhead, who resembles in appearance and manner the brash and attractive Paul Hogan character in *Crocodile Dundee*. At the time, Muirhead was working at Ogilvy & Mather in London, and it was while eating a sandwich in a park that he happened upon the ad. "I was an ambitious account executive just starting out," he said. "And I'm reading that I may soon be, or should be, obsolete."

Indeed, the ad promised that the account executive would be eliminated at Saatchi & Saatchi Advertising; the position would be replaced with a "co-ordinator who is not briefed by the client, does not brief the creative people, does not pass judgment on ads, and does not present ads to the clients, but works with the creators as a day-to-day administrator."

As with many facets of the Saatchis, this was pure boast. Within six months, Saatchi & Saatchi Advertising would hire six account executives. The reason was simple: copywriters and art directors are ill-equipped to deal with clients in the way the Saatchis wanted them to. Creative individuals didn't want to coddle clients. They just wanted to create ads.

The ad also contained a proposal meant to startle the advertising industry: Saatchi & Saatchi Advertising would not seek a 15 percent compensation on billings, the traditional industry standard. The Saatchis described it as a "dying system," so they would charge clients 22 percent.

The compensation formula traces its roots to 1841, when Volney B. Palmer opened an agency in Philadelphia that represented newspapers wishing to sell space to out-of-town advertisers. There were over five thousand newspapers in the United States, all with different circulations and ad rates. Placing the ads in each newspaper was a laborious task. In exchange for doing this service, Palmer charged the newspapers 25 percent of their space rate, plus costs of postage and stationery.

By 1849, he not only had offices in New York, Philadelphia, Boston, and Baltimore, but he had competition as well.

Until the 1990s, here was how the advertising media buying game worked: if an agency placed an ad and it cost $10,000, it demanded and received a 15 percent discount, meaning it cost $8,500 to place it. However, the agency still charged the client $10,000; it pocketed the $1,500. The agency had an interest in looking for the highest possible rate. (The 15 percent compensation is no longer a given; rather, the rate is negotiated.)

In exchange for the higher fee, Saatchi & Saatchi promised

clients "the cheapest possible buying of space and time." That proposal, too, was soon and quietly abandoned.

Maurice and Charles Saatchi spent £6,000 on the ad in the *Sunday Times*, which was written by Robert Heller, an editor of *Management Today* and columnist of the *Observer* in London. Although he boasted that it was the easiest assignment he had ever received, Heller got cold feet as the ad got closer to publication. He didn't want his name associated with it. After all, he was an editor, and here he was endorsing a new agency. So, at the last minute, he asked that his name be withdrawn. It was replaced by the name of Jeremy Sinclair, a creative executive with the new agency.

CHARLES WAS twenty-seven and Maurice twenty-five when they registered Saatchi & Saatchi Advertising in August 1970. The new agency was financed with approximately £100,000, including £1,000 of ordinary shares and £9,000 of preference capital, which was to be repaid within three years. Among the backers of the new agency was the designer Mary Quant, who made the miniskirt fashionable. Quant and her husband, Alexander Plunket-Greene, became involved through their friendship with Lindsay Masters. Quant agreed but on one odd condition: that Masters too would invest in Saatchi & Saatchi Advertising. This was dicey since Masters was a part owner of *Campaign* magazine, which reported on the advertising business.

But Masters did invest, and for years *Campaign*, an excellent publication with an eye-catching layout and interesting, snappy writing, was labeled, usually with envy, as Charles Saatchi's house organ. Newly hired editors would routinely receive cases of Champagne from Saatchi & Saatchi. And Charles would spend a great deal of time on the phone with *Campaign* editors planting the next positive story about Saatchi & Saatchi.

And why not? Advertising agencies are unusually adept at conveying the positive attributes of a client. They traditionally fall short in promoting themselves. But Charles Saatchi mastered the art of the telephone call. Yes, he could be portrayed as shy, elusive, and unavailable. But the truth was quite the opposite. He knew how to craft an image for himself and for the agency. Certainly reporters covering the advertising business in London didn't think of Charles as aloof and shy.

At *Campaign*, the calls from Charles would start on Monday and continue until deadline time; the publication now hits newsstands on Thursday, though then it was published on Fridays.

Charles Saatchi hit upon an obvious but unique idea: to brand an advertising agency in the way a company tries to brand a product. In the same way Sony made televisions, General Motors made automobiles, and McKinsey was a brand name for consulting, Saatchi & Saatchi would be equated with great advertising.

Cannon Holdings (which held the Masters, Quant and Plunket-Greene investment) had 15 percent of the working shares. The rest were divided among four working directors: Charles, 42 percent; Maurice, 38 percent; John Hegarty, 2.5 percent; and Tim Bell, 2.5 percent.

Tim Bell, a tall, handsome, charming individual, was hired as media director on September 12, 1970, from Geers Gross, a new London agency. Bell was born and raised in London by his Australian mother and her second husband, an alderman and mayor of Marylebone. Bell wanted to be a jazz musician, but his mother disapproved. At nineteen, he was sent to Stella Fisher Employment Agency on Fleet Street, the famous London thoroughfare that was once home to many of the city's newspapers. He worked for several years for ABC Television performing the unglamorous job of a paper pusher in the advertising department. From there he went to Colman, Pretis & Varley, then to Hobson Bates, both ad agencies, and finally to Geers Gross.

When Charles Saatchi decided the agency needed a media director, an individual who bought space and time from newspapers and television stations, he approached two executives in the corporate world, one from Campbell Soup and the other from H. J. Heinz, and was rebuffed twice. It seemed no one wanted to work for two young Iraqi Jewish brothers with a strange name, even though one, Charles, had a reputation for creative excellence. When still other candidates fell through, Bell was mentioned as one of the best media specialists in the city.

"Charlie rang me up and said, 'I understand you're the best

and would you like to come join us?' " Bell said. "He was quite irresistible." Bell, mistakenly, thought Charles had written the pregnant man ad, which he considered the best ad ever produced. So he was already a fan.

Charles would run the creative department, Maurice would handle the clients, and Bell would be media director. He was twenty-eight. There were three copywriters, three art directors, Charles, Maurice, and Bell.

"Because I was there at the beginning," Bell said, "I emerged into doing everything. I was the new business man, client handler department, production department, research department, and media buying department."

Bell would also become the so-called third brother, worshipping Charles and Maurice until he was tossed aside in a particularly messy professional public divorce that would take years to heal. By the end, he would refer to himself as the ampersand in Saatchi & Saatchi.

SAATCHI & SAATCHI ADVERTISING at No. 6 Golden Square officially opened for business on September 14, 1970, one day after the full-page ad describing the agency ran in the *Sunday Times.* But the news was out before the *Times* ad; on September 11, *Campaign*'s lead story carried the headline, "Saatchi Starts Agency with One Million Pounds." As was custom among advertising agencies, the Saatchis overstated their billings; they were nowhere near one million pounds. Charles was described as the "copywriting partner of the highly respected CramerSaatchi creative consultancy." Maurice appeared in the fourth paragraph as "marketing the agency." The *Campaign* article also said the company was backed by "a City financial group plus considerable investment from the elder brother." (The City is the financial community in London. In reality, there was not a single "City financial group" involved.)

The agency began humming along. Maurice Saatchi would hone his charm on potential clients. His pitch would go along these lines: "Hello, my name is Maurice Saatchi and we have a new advertising agency. Although you are probably very happy with your present advertising agency, I think we have found a way for you to make more money and sell more products." When the chief executive of the company asked for specifics, Maurice would say only to stop around the agency to view a presentation.

Once again, Saatchi & Saatchi was breaking the rules. It was heretofore considered taboo to approach another agency's clients. Traditionally, agencies wait to be invited to pitch the account by the client or a headhunting firm. But Maurice Saatchi believed rules simply didn't apply to him. He never had. It was a curious, if not infuriating, characteristic. Wendy Smyth, Saatchi & Saatchi's tough-as-nails finance director, described Maurice as "the lovable puppy who comes in and craps all over the carpet and then licks your hand."

Disregarding the conventional way of doing business was working for Maurice Saatchi in 1970; those cold calls to potential clients didn't result in instant business, but they accomplished a significant goal: they got executives into the agency for a face-to-face presentation and the agency received top-of-mind recognition. If an account came up for review, then, more than likely, Saatchi & Saatchi would be asked in to the pitch.

One of the first ads produced by Saatchi & Saatchi Advertising was for the Health Education Council, the same client for which the pregnant man ad was created. Again, Jeremy Sinclair created the television commercial: lemmings jumping off a cliff intercut with people walking across Waterloo Bridge in London. The voice-over said, "There's a strange Arctic rodent called the lemming which every year throws itself off a cliff. It's as though they want to die. Every year in Britain thousands of men and women smoke cigarettes. It's as though they want to die." The ads got the much needed publicity and the client roster grew to include British Leyland, the automobile manufacturer, and Associated Newspapers, publishers of the *Daily Mail*, among others.

Saatchi & Saatchi was in the news a great deal, a fact credited to Charles's keen intuitive dealings with reporters. A journalist covering a specific beat likes to feel he is the most important individual to the executives he is covering. Charles Saatchi had the knack for instilling that feeling. But the attention and stories that became part of the Saatchi legend gnawed at the agency's employees. "We were out to make great and memorable ads," said Jeremy Sinclair. "We didn't care about all the stories."

The tales included Charles throwing a chair at Maurice out

of frustration that Maurice was not grasping a point quickly enough. After heaving the chair, Charles shouted, "I can't believe we came from the same womb." Often, Charles would hit his brother, causing Maurice to bleed.

Add to this equation the fact that Saatchi & Saatchi Advertising fundamentally was a mean place to work.

Nasty, petty comments were made by senior Saatchi & Saatchi executives (interestingly, Charles and Maurice were not involved) about virtually everyone at the agency. Everybody had what Bill Muirhead described as a "foul nickname." Some were original, others not. Maurice Saatchi, for instance, was called "Four Eyes." Charles Saatchi was Carlos, "the Jackal," named after the infamous assassin who was finally to be caught in the Middle East in 1995. John Hegarty was known as the "Anorexic Albino." Tim Bell was nicknamed "Tom Bell" because that is how he once was referred to by a client.

Jeremy Sinclair was called "Red Fire Engine." Sinclair would teach once a week at the School of Economic Science. Colleagues imagined the class repeating a chant and the agency executives cruelly imagined Sinclair and others sitting in a corner chanting "Red fire engine, red fire engine" over and over until an inner peace was achieved. The exact reason why the employees chose to ridicule Sinclair by referring to a fire engine has been lost over the decades. Roy Warman, who joined in January 1971 from Geers Gross to be Bell's number two on the media side, was called "Swamp." And Bill Muirhead was known simply as "Blockhead."

"It was a very competitive environment," Muirhead said. "It was so bad that if you woke up with a pimple, you didn't dare go to work that day. You called in sick because you were so scared you would be made fun of."

Early in 1972, Muirhead resigned from Ogilvy & Mather to join Dorland Advertising. On his third day on the job, Muirhead received a call from Maurice Saatchi. "Why don't you come work for us?" Maurice inquired. The brothers, looking to expand their agency and, finally, realizing they needed a bona fide account executive, had heard terrific things about Muirhead.

"I didn't see how I could considering I had been at Dorland for only three days, but I was fascinated," Muirhead said. And so he went off to No. 6 Golden Square and was immediately impressed with the surroundings and hectic atmosphere. While waiting in the reception area to be summoned by Maurice, Muirhead noticed a man peering over the partition and staring at him. The individual never identified himself. He just glared for a time and then disappeared. Muirhead later learned that it was Charles Saatchi. Since the name Saatchi & Saatchi was on an impressive brass nameplate outside the Golden Square offices, Muirhead incorrectly believed the agency rented the entire building, a belief no one at Saatchi & Saatchi tried to correct.

The agency had other assets Muirhead and others in the all-male club admired: two beautiful secretaries who made the waiting room all the more appealing. One female wore see-through tops and another, recalled a senior executive, "looked as if she didn't wear any knickers."

Muirhead was impressed with what he saw and decided to take the plunge. He had found Maurice charming and was also struck by Bell's marketing skills. He joined and began working on his first account, the *Daily Mail*.

SAATCHI & SAATCHI ADVERTISING was immediately profitable. In its second year, it had profits of £90,000, after expenses, salaries, and taxes. In 1973, its third year, profits rose 11 percent to £100,000.

By then the brothers also had acquired domestic lives. Charles married Doris Dibley. He had continued to be smitten by this sophisticated woman who spoke several languages and knew a great deal about art and wine. She was graduated from Smith College and spent a year at the Sorbonne in Paris. Shortly after Charles left Benton & Bowles, he returned for an office Christmas party in 1967. Dibley's marriage was in trouble but she rebuffed an overture to date Charles. That changed shortly after she separated from her husband, and she and Charles lived together for six years before finally getting married in 1973. Doris would introduce Charles to the art world, which would become and remain one of his greatest passions.

At first, Charles had not been enthusiastic about getting married. Annoyed, Doris went off to Paris. Charles, unsure whether she traveled with another man or not, enlisted Jeremy Sinclair to phone her in Paris. "We haven't seen Charlie in about a week and we were wondering whether or not he was with you," Sinclair said in a game of bluff he would do for only the closest of friends.

Doris was sufficiently worried to place a call to Charles. Shortly after, she returned and he proposed.

A year earlier, in 1972, Maurice Saatchi married Gillian Osband, a children's book editor and writer who was the daughter of a wealthy north London property executive. The couple had known each other since childhood.

Their circle of friends included Paul Buckley, a Haymarket director who began as an assistant to Michael Heseltine, and Buckley's wife, Josephine Hart.

IT WAS IN 1973 that the Saatchi brothers began to make acquisitions. The reason was simple. Maurice Saatchi had a single, audacious ambition: to be the largest advertising agency company in the world. He had little choice in how to achieve his goal: Saatchi & Saatchi had to begin acquiring companies. Eventually, the company came to be nicknamed Snatchit & Snatchit. Maurice's approach to rival advertising agencies and other related companies mirrored the way Michael Heseltine of Haymarket solicited competing publication companies to investigate whether there were magazines for sale.

Maurice would begin each letter the same way: "I am sure this will be the last thing on your minds, but I wondered if you felt it would make sense to dispose of your company." In 1973, Charles Saatchi leaked a story to *Campaign* that Saatchi & Saatchi would soon buy an agency in the United States. Nothing happened. Then *Campaign* dutifully printed another Charles Saatchi–delivered story: that the agency would create a subsidiary in Paris. Again, nothing materialized, although the buzz had its desired effect: Saatchi & Saatchi was an agency with large global plans. Saatchi & Saatchi did make its first acquisition in 1972, of a property company called Brogan Developers. This purchase was used to house Charles Saatchi's growing art collection. In 1973, Saatchi & Saatchi made another acquisition: E.G. Dawes, a Manchester ad agency. The brothers merged Dawes with its own Manchester office, which it had established to serve a client, Great Clewes Warehouse, a unit of Great Universal Stores. Saatchi & Saatchi also acquired Notley Advertising, which practically doubled the agency's size. Because of the sudden influx of newly acquired employees, Saatchi & Saatchi in 1973 moved to Lower Regent Street from Golden Square.

Another acquisition during the period wasn't as successful. The brothers purchased George J. Smith, a small London agency, for £90,000. But the money the company said it was owed by outsiders, it turned out, was greatly exaggerated. George J. Smith was virtually bankrupt.

After getting more business out of existing clients—a smart strategy in order to weather an advertising industry recession—Saatchi & Saatchi recorded profits in 1975 of £400,000. This was accomplished despite the fact that the agency had lost one of its key clients, Singer, the sewing machine company. The expanded assignments were the main reason.

In the early days, virtually all of the unsolicited offers were rebuffed, including one to Boase Massimi Pollitt, a successful agency that didn't feel the need to sell to these upstarts.

The Boase Massimi rejection aside, that was soon to change.

CHAPTER
TWO

S.T. GARLAND ADVERTISING, opened in 1928 by Sidney Garland, a former *Daily Mail* sales rep, was independent until 1960 when Compton Advertising in New York decided it wanted a major presence in the United Kingdom. Compton in the United States first forged the relationship with S.T. Garland Advertising in 1960 because Procter & Gamble, Compton's largest client, wanted to expand into the United Kingdom. Compton was under orders from Procter & Gamble to open an office in the United Kingdom prior to the time when the giant packaged good manufacturer would begin selling its products, said Milton Gossett, then-president of Compton. Compton purchased 49 percent of the Garland agency with an option for another 2 percent, allowing Compton Advertising to control a new company called Compton U.K. Partners that owned 100 percent of Garland-Compton.

Garland-Compton had offices on Charlotte Street and a strong client base, starting with Procter & Gamble, the world's largest advertiser, and later adding Rowntree Mackintosh and United Biscuits. Saatchi & Saatchi became involved with Garland-Compton in 1975. Maurice Saatchi, on the prowl for a business manager, approached Ron Rimmer, Garland-Compton's managing director. Rimmer had no intention of leaving, but informed Ken Gill, Garland's president, of the inquiry. What neither Rimmer nor Maurice knew was that Gill, according to Milton Gossett, was "desperate in looking for someone who could follow himself." Gill wanted someone who could add pizzazz to the somewhat stodgy agency. After some consideration, he figured this relatively new agency named Saatchi & Saatchi might contain just the spark of creativity that his agency needed.

This time, Gill contacted the Saatchi brothers and negotiations began. To help solicit support for the deal, which was bound to be complex because it was a reverse takeover—in which the smaller company essentially took over the larger entity—Gill phoned Gossett, an old friend, and asked about the possibility of acquiring Saatchi & Saatchi. Gill wanted Gossett to come to London to meet the two brothers.

"Ken was in love with them," Gossett said. "And I quickly grew fond of them. I love rascals and rogues and I saw them as out of the mold and different."

That was praise coming from Milton Gossett. A soft-spoken, dignified man, Gossett joined Compton as a secretary in 1949 after ignoring the recommendations of an aptitude examination that said he would have a future either as a newspaper reporter or as a park ranger. He rose through the ranks of Compton, from traffic manager to copywriter to head of the copy department; he later became president and then chief operating officer, chief executive, and chairman.

Although Gossett enjoyed the brothers, Stu Mitchell, Compton's then-chairman, did not. Their meeting lasted only a matter of minutes. "The brothers and Stu, who was a straightforward kind of person, took one look at one another, and all Stu saw were these emotional brothers and all they saw was this straitlaced executive, and the brothers and he both said no way," Gossett said. But after hearing pleas from Gossett as to how powerful the creative work of Saatchi & Saatchi was, Mitchell reconsidered and the talks resumed.

Gill also asked one other close associate to look at the deal: James Gulliver, an investor and takeover artist who owned his own firm as well as about 10 percent of Compton shares. He, in turn, gave the assignment to one of his associates, Martin Sorrell.

Sorrell, a short, intense man with a mischievous streak, is the son of a businessman who operated England's largest retail consumer electronics chain. Sorrell grew up well in north London's Jewish business community. He studied economics at Cambridge and wrote for *New Cambridge*, the university's alternative journal, instead of *Varsity*, the mainstream publication. Sorrell covered the 1964 Democratic National Convention in Atlantic City for *New Cambridge*. He described himself as a frustrated journalist and, indeed, he was at ease with reporters and relished advertising industry gossip. Sorrell attended Harvard Business School and chose not to join the family business upon graduation. Instead, he remained in New England, settling upon a marketing consultancy in Connecticut. He returned to England five years later and joined Gulliver.

When Gulliver mentioned to Sorrell he ought to take a look at Saatchi & Saatchi, Sorrell recalled seeing the company's name on Regent Street and thought it was a Japanese hi-fi company.

By the end of 1975, a deal was struck. The brothers would sell their business to Compton for shares. They would own 36 percent of the combined equity of the enlarged group; Compton in New York would own 26 percent after the reverse takeover, down from 49 percent; the balance of the shares were held by public shareholders.

There was one non-negotiable point: the name Saatchi & Saatchi couldn't be eliminated. Although Gill and Gossett resisted, they eventually caved in and the merged agency with the unwieldy name Saatchi & Saatchi Garland-Compton was created. Of course, the brothers knew what they were doing in that positioning. No one, including newspaper headline writers, would consistently say or write out that lengthy name; instead, they would, and did, shorten it to Saatchi & Saatchi.

Gill and Gossett wanted the announcement to be of a merger, not an acquisition, but that was not to be with the Saatchi brothers orchestrating the behind-the-scenes nuances of the news. *Campaign* magazine set the tone with its headline in September 1975, "Saatchi Swallows Up the Compton Group." Charles Saatchi's close relationship with the respected publication had paid off once again. The headline had a devastating psychological effect on Garland-Compton. Although the beginning was rocky, the relationship between the two agencies actually worked out quite well. "It was a good marriage," said Milton Gossett.

The merger was hardly noticed in the United States mainstream press; the *New York Times* issue of September 26, 1975, for instance, included it as a minuscule addendum to a large Advertising column on Chevrolet's new 1976 Chevette. "Saatchi & Saatchi & Co., a British ad agency, has agreed to merge with Compton

Partners, the holding company of the Compton group of ad agencies in the United Kingdom. When that happens the holding company will change its name to Saatchi & Saatchi Compton and the group to Saatchi & Saatchi Garland-Compton with billings over $70 million." The writer added: "With that kind of scratch, why not change your name?"

With the Garland-Compton deal, Saatchi & Saatchi rose to the fifth largest agency from number thirteen. More important, Compton U.K. Partners had a public listing. The brothers would use the stock market to propel their acquisition binge. Saatchi & Saatchi also gained three international clients: Rowntree, United Biscuits, and Procter & Gamble. But the celebration didn't go on for long. All three companies told their "new" agency that it was being put on notice: Rowntree gave a three-week deadline and United Biscuits and Procter & Gamble gave six months each. That meant Saatchi & Saatchi had to pitch the accounts again and rewin the business. Remarkably, it did.

Ken Gill was the managing director and those executives who worked at the combined agencies remembered Gill as a father figure to the Saatchi brothers. Like children, Maurice and Charles delighted in teasing Gill, but they usually wound up listening to him, several recalled.

Milton Gossett, meanwhile, grew close to Maurice Saatchi. Gossett introduced Maurice to executives at Procter & Gamble, where he would establish relations that would figure heavily twenty years later. Maurice Saatchi stayed with Gossett and his wife and the couple would often visit Maurice's London home where they would admire his large toy collection and where they shared a common interest in horticulture. (Gossett's family owns a nursery in South Salem, New York, named Gossett Brothers.)

If Garland-Compton lost one critical aspect of the skirmish, they won another: Saatchi & Saatchi had to move into Garland-Compton headquarters on Charlotte Street. When they did, it was not only to top offices, but to senior positions as well. Tim Bell became managing director of the merged agencies. Ron Rimmer, the person who served as a catalyst between the two companies, left shortly after the merger for McCann-Erickson. Jeremy Sinclair became creative director, and Roy Warman, media director.

Saatchi & Saatchi Compton Ltd.'s annual report for the year ended September 30, 1976, speaks to the company's accomplishments and its frustrations: page 10 was titled "Some of the Year's Success Stories," and showed stills of several major campaigns. The clients included British Leyland ("the first time saturation TV was used in a sales promotion for British cars—widely considered to be the most effective sales drive seen in the motor industry in recent years"), Schweppes (the campaign convinced consumers to imbibe tonic water straight), Brutus Jeans (the jingle the agency created went to number two on London's hit parade and Brutus "went to brand leadership"), and Gillette-Braun ("introduced in February 1975, the Braun electric shaver had reached the number two position in the dry shaver market just one year later").

In the Chairman's Statement, Kenneth Gill said that only one client, Bass, moved its account because of a conflict based on the merger (Harp's new lager). The combined agencies gained more business from a large number of existing clients. "This performance," Gill wrote, "made Saatchi & Saatchi Garland-Compton the fastest growing of Britain's top ten agencies in 1976."

The report also included a headline, "How We Run Our Agency as a Quoted Company." It said: "We are often asked whether the fact that our Company is quoted makes a difference to the way we run our advertising agency business. The answer is—hardly at all. As a Quoted Company we run our business as any business should be—in business-like fashion. . . . We write a financial plan, we monitor achievement against that plan and we try to signal trouble ahead—with a large flag!"

The report also included a fact that Saatchi & Saatchi uncovered and wanted to exploit: Britain's largest agency, J. Walter Thompson, had clients that had been with it for years—Kellogg's, Gillette, and Kodak were with the agency for thirty-nine, eleven, and thirteen years, respectively. Procter & Gamble and Rowntree Mackintosh "between them have been our clients for over 60 years! These stable relationships have meant increasingly secure and stable agencies at the top of British Advertising.

"As more and more sectors of the economy have come to see advertising as a major force in their business, this has meant that large agencies have become more and more broadly spread in terms of their sources of income, and increasingly less dependent on any one sector of the economy." Television advertising, the company said, no longer relied on detergent and food as the major contributor. Many new categories emerged, including records, films, cars, and financial institutions.

However, the Saatchi brothers were bothered that, despite the relative youth of their agency, it still had less than 5 percent of the total British advertising market.

IN 1978, THE BROTHERS' flashy style attracted another client, who would further propel the reputation of Saatchi & Saatchi as being on the cutting edge of creativity. The client was Margaret Thatcher, the Conservative party's candidate for Prime Minister in Britain's upcoming general election. The Conservative party faced an uphill battle in trying to wrest control from the ruling Labour party. But Gordon Reece, the Conservatives' newly appointed director of communications, had the unorthodox idea of hiring an advertising agency to devise a colorful and hard-hitting campaign that would take shots at the Labour opposition. Prior to 1978, the political parties in the United Kingdom did not select ad agencies to head up their campaigns; rather, they relied on pro bono work from volunteers.

Reece was a television producer and, until contacted by Thatcher, was advising Armand Hammer of Occidental Oil on publicity. Having spent time in America and having seen hard-sell techniques used in some American advertising—the majority of British ads remained tame despite Saatchi & Saatchi's efforts—Reece believed the brothers' agency could give the Conservative party a jump start. The take-no-prisoners approach to political advertising, especially in the campaigns of Presidents Lyndon B. Johnson and Richard M. Nixon, had not gone unnoticed by Reece.

Reece had definite criteria for what he wanted in the ad agency for the Conservative party. It had to be big, yet hungry, with strengths on the creative side.

Reece recalled working with Charles Saatchi briefly in the 1960s on a commercial for the *Daily Mail* newspaper. He also knew the reputation of Tim Bell and Jeremy Sinclair. Although Reece had been scheduled to meet Charles Saatchi on Charlotte

Street, when he arrived, the selectively elusive and shy Charles wasn't around; Reece would have to settle for the less flashy, but equally impressive Maurice.

Tim Bell, on vacation in Barbados, spoke with Charles Saatchi and urged him not to take on such a time-consuming and high-profile client. But Bell's opinion wasn't even considered. In fact, when he returned to Charlotte Street, the brothers handed Bell the assignment.

Bell became deeply involved in the campaign and to this day he includes Margaret Thatcher among his closest friends. He became Sir Tim Bell after she knighted him in 1991. And with this campaign, Bell and the agency became trailblazers in British political advertising. Reece got what he wanted: an entire campaign that spoke not to issues but to voters' emotions.

The first ad came in the spring of 1978. Saatchi & Saatchi ran a teaser ad in the tabloid newspapers warning that if the public missed an ad that would run at 9 P.M. that evening, they would regret it forever. Again, Jeremy Sinclair was the chief creative force behind the commercial, which showed everything in Britain going backward, including people walking backward across Waterloo Bridge. The voice-over announcer said, "This country was once the finest nation on earth. We are famous for our freedom, justice, and fair play. Our inventions brought the world out of the Middle Ages to industrial prosperity. Today we are famous for discouraging people from getting to the top. Famous for not rewarding skill, talent, and effort. In a word, Britain is going backwards. Backwards or forwards because we can't go on as we are. Don't just hope for a better life—vote for one."

The ad didn't go unnoticed by the public, nor by the Conservatives' opposition. A memo dated April 4, 1978, written by Edward Booth-Clibborn, the Labour party's adviser on political advertising, and sent to party leader James Callaghan, said, "Saatchi & Saatchi are not only London's fastest-growing and most successful agency in financial terms, they are also a force to be reckoned with in the execution of the work they undertake."

That summer, a copywriter named Andy Rutherford submitted a billboard for the agency to consider showing to Thatcher. His assignment was to focus on the economy and industry. Unemployment was on the rise, so Rutherford designed a poster that showed a large, seemingly never-ending line outside an unemployment office. The headline: "Labour Isn't Working." Under the snakelike line, Rutherford had written, "Britain's Better Off with the Conservatives." That slogan echoed a 1959 slogan, "Life's better with the Conservatives."

Although Saatchi & Saatchi executives weren't enthralled by the ad, Thatcher loved it. The billboard received a huge amount of publicity, becoming as famous as the pregnant man ad, although it appeared in only about twenty sites.

There were other billboards as well: one with the headline "Britain Isn't Getting Any Better" was illustrated with a line outside a hospital. Another, in a child's scrawl, said, "Educashun Isnt Wurking."

On May 3, 1979, Thatcher and the Conservative party won, defeating Labour by a 5.2 percent margin. In 1995, Maurice Saatchi would credit Margaret Thatcher as the catalyst in establishing Saatchi & Saatchi in the world. "The victory in 1979 was the basis of our expansion, particularly in the U.S. Mrs. Thatcher was respected in America and she made us." A victory party was held at 10 Downing Street and virtually everyone who worked on the campaign attended, including Maurice Saatchi, Jeremy Sinclair, and Tim Bell. Charles Saatchi, as was his custom, chose to stay away.

The campaign would be the height of Tim Bell's profile with Saatchi & Saatchi. And he would revel in his role at Charlotte Street.

But there was something wrong. Tim Bell's office was in the belly of the agency on Charlotte Street on the first floor. The brothers and Martin Sorrell were on the sixth floor. That was where the power resided. Maurice and Charles had enticed Sorrell to join in 1976 by giving him a 20 percent stake in a subsidiary called Saatchi & Saatchi Developments. "I was to build Saatchi & Saatchi horizontally to other areas," Sorrell said. "The charter for the development unit was to take them outside advertising. But it never happened. I was a bit conned by them because I don't think the brothers ever had any intention of allowing me to do it." Nevertheless, some properties were considered, including a small British publishing company.

It was Sorrell who replaced Bell as the so-called third brother.

It was Sorrell's brilliant financial strategic and analytical mind that was behind the aggressive expansion of Saatchi & Saatchi. Bell was an ad man, period. Like many creative types, Bell needed almost constant stroking to reassure his frail ego that all was well. The brothers no longer had time for such indulgence. Worse, Bell was against many of the brothers' plans to expand. "We began clashing," he said. Bell would ask, "Why are you doing this?" to virtually every acquisition the Saatchis wanted to make.

Bell said the relationship vastly deteriorated in March 1982 when Saatchi & Saatchi acquired Compton Communications Inc. in New York. "That left things unclear as to who was running what," Bell said. The ambiguity was only pronounced to Bell; Milt Gossett was appointed chairman and chief executive of the worldwide agency and Bell now had to report to Gossett, instead of Maurice and Charles. "I had the impression that I ran the agency and really worked for no one," Bell said. "I was the operating manager, the brothers ran the holding company, and Gossett ran the American company."

Further, Bell said he wasn't rewarded for the agency's fortunes; he wanted his name on the door. Instead, the brothers appointed Bell the international chairman of Saatchi & Saatchi Compton Worldwide.

Bell needed to be replaced at Charlotte Street not only because of the increasing tension between him and the brothers, but also because of his erratic behavior, which everyone attributed to a combination of drinking, cocaine, and the everyday pressures of the ad business. (After a dark period, Bell sobered up, and to this day he remains clean, sober, and happy.) Bell was recruited to help choose his own successor.

When it came to choosing a replacement, Bell embarked on an unorthodox method: he hired a psychoanalyst to compile profiles of the candidates, which included four senior Saatchi & Saatchi Advertising executives: Jennifer Laing, Bill Muirhead, Roy Warman, and Terry Bannister. Warman and Bannister were among the original members who joined Saatchi & Saatchi in the early 1970s. Warman came aboard in 1971, defecting from Geers Gross, as Tim Bell's media director; Bannister came in 1973 after working for Fison's, a pharmaceutical company and a Saatchi & Saatchi client. Bannister joined as an account supervisor.

"Saatchi was growing so quickly back then," Bannister said, "the agency was basically taking on everyone they knew who could speak properly, and even some who couldn't."

So, Warren Lamb, a psychoanalyst, was introduced at an executive meeting as an industrial psychiatrist who specialized in team building. He told the startled group that he could judge an individual by the way he or she made decisions. Lamb would spend about three days with each of Bell's candidates. "He was like a fly on the wall," Bannister said. "It was odd and I don't even think the brothers were aware of this system."

Even though everyone scoffed and protested, they went along with Bell's wishes. Several weeks later, when they were each given their profiles prepared by Lamb, they were surprised that they recognized themselves. Warman and Bannister received complementary reports; that is, everything Warman wasn't good at, Bannister was, and vice versa. So Warman and Bannister took over for Bell as joint chief executives of Saatchi & Saatchi on Charlotte Street. But Bell had wanted a significant role in the Saatchi & Saatchi public company. For several years, Bell tried to make the best of it, but he hated the job of heading the international division. Instead, his entire role, he said, was seeing people who didn't want to see him. Bell supervised Europe, Australia, and the Far East, but he had no authority in the United States or London. Bell said he began seeing less and less of Maurice and Charles and, in turn, "They began to share less with me. They didn't seem to be very interested in what I was doing. I felt I ceased to be the favorite person." Bell felt betrayed. "We had built something together," he said, "and I was being cut out. I wound up reading what they were up to in the newspaper. I think they got fed up with me."

Yet Bell pressed onward at Saatchi & Saatchi. He continued to win new business, including Mattel toys in 1983 as well as the Gillette Europe account. But he wasn't aware when Saatchi & Saatchi—the brothers and their close-knit circle, as opposed to the agency—pitched, and won, what would become a flagship account, British Airways. Indeed, Bell was told of this victory by the public relations director of the former state-owned airline, which was then headed into the private sector.

Oddly, when Bell asked Charles Saatchi about this, Charles denied winning the account. The news that British Airways awarded Saatchi & Saatchi the prestigious account was announced a week later.

Tim Bell would work intensely for Saatchi & Saatchi in 1983 when Margaret Thatcher called for elections. Again, the agency, anchored by Bell, was pressed into service. One memorable ad, written by Charles Saatchi and Jeremy Sinclair, compared the Communist Manifesto to the policies of the Labour party and found they were similar. "Like Your Manifesto, Comrade," was the headline. Thatcher scored another decisive victory.

At that time, Bell confronted Charles Saatchi. Bell wanted a single reward for everything he had done for the brothers: he wanted to be named to the board of the holding company. The board consisted of only five directors: the brothers, Martin Sorrell, Kenneth Gill as chairman, and a company secretary named David Perring. Charles Saatchi's reply was swift and final: "You never, ever go on the board of the public company," he screamed at Bell. Charles's logic was that the board would become crammed with advertising executives if, after every acquisition, they had to place on the board the head of the company being bought. Bell couldn't believe it. Now, Bell was being lumped into a group, not a special case of someone who had nurtured the agency.

Charles, sensing that Bell would most likely go, made an overture to a close friend he hoped would replace Bell: David Puttnam, who ultimately decided against it, choosing instead to head Columbia Pictures in Hollywood.

In the fall of 1984, Bell was feeling particularly depressed because the prestigious *Financial Times* had published a story that said he had gotten a lot of new business for Saatchi & Saatchi and that the brothers should have been more grateful. Bell called Charles at home and said, "I hate this and I can't bear it anymore." Charles replied, "You had better come see me."

Bell phoned Charles after first being offered another job from Frank Lowe, a tall, lanky executive whose frail physical appearance belies a relentlessly tough personality. Bell and Lowe had gotten to know each other again while working on ads for the National Coal Board. Coal miners had gone on strike in March 1984 and Bell had asked whether the board wanted his help in persuading the public that the strike was wrong-headed. Bell was doing this out of friendship and loyalty to Margaret Thatcher. Saatchi & Saatchi didn't even have the account. Lowe Howard-Spink & Marschalk did. Lowe admired Bell and heard through the gossip mill all about Bell's misery with the brothers. Lowe offered Bell what he knew Bell wanted: his name on the door and role as a member of the board.

In the meeting with Charles, Bell informed him of the offer. "If that's what you want, go ahead," Bell recalled Saatchi saying. "It had come to this; from sitting between Charles and Maurice in the same office to holding my hat in my hand looking for attention."

It would have been a safe assumption that news of Tim Bell's resignation would receive banner headlines, especially from the advertising trade press. But *Campaign*, because of a request from Charles Saatchi, placed it on page three. Tim Bell, the savvy advertising and public relations executive who knew about image, called it the final insult.

After his departure, Tim Bell would have no contact with Charles and Maurice for three years. "I never saw Maurice when I left the agency," Bell said. "He wouldn't talk to me. When you leave Saatchi & Saatchi, they black you out. You die."

Martin Sorrell would also learn this. In the spring of 1985, while still working at Saatchi & Saatchi, Sorrell began investing in a publicly traded company called WPP Group, or Wire & Plastic Products, which manufactured wire shopping baskets among other products. "I wanted to do my own thing," Sorrell said and told Maurice of his intention. Saatchi's reaction was to say, "What a good idea. Charles and I are thinking of doing the same thing [investing in another company]. Could you please have a look at this company and tell us what you think?"

The company the Saatchis said they were thinking of investing in was a successful stationery company called Stat-Plus. That is, until Sorrell came along with WPP. The brothers wanted to buy 20 percent of WPP, a testament not only to their regard for Martin Sorrell, but also of how much they wanted to continue to control him.

Sorrell said no, he had discussed it with the board and his partner and it was agreed that the Saatchis would be allowed to buy only 10 percent, which the brothers promptly did. "Eventually they got upset once they saw what I was doing with WPP and realized that it wasn't a passive investment for me," Sorrell said.

When Sorrell was leaving Saatchi & Saatchi to work at WPP full-time in 1986, the *Financial Times* wanted to write a profile of him. "It's not time," Sorrell told the editor. But the *Financial Times* was going ahead with the story with or without Sorrell's involvement, so he cooperated. On the day the story ran on page two, the *Telegraph* in London ran a long story and profile on Sorrell's successor at Saatchi & Saatchi, Andrew Woods, an attorney. Sorrell felt outmaneuvered, once again, by Charles Saatchi. "I thought to myself, why did I resist doing this story?" Sorrell said. "I should have made a bigger deal out of this."

As for Tim Bell, he would resurface unpleasantly in the life of the Saatchis in 1987 when Margaret Thatcher called for another election. Her popularity was such that a third victory appeared likely. Saatchi & Saatchi liked to hedge all bets, and kept Bell on a retainer. Despite that, however, they froze him out of the Conservative campaign.

Then, trouble began with Thatcher's own leadership. A battle over the Westland helicopter firm and who would rescue the nearly bankrupt company—an American company, or one from Europe —divided her cabinet. Her poll ratings dropped, and in true form when a client saw trouble, the first one blamed was the advertising agency.

Advertising is, in many ways, a demeaning and unstable way to make a living. All too often clients don't appreciate break-through work even though they say that's what they want. Also, an ad agency's fate is unresolved every time the management of a client changes. A marketing manager usually wants to make his or her mark known and that can be swiftly done by simply firing one ad agency and hiring another.

And when sales dip, the first scapegoat is the ad agency.

Political advertising is no different, and in the election of 1987 Margaret Thatcher didn't like what she was seeing coming out of Saatchi & Saatchi and, specifically, the minds of Maurice Saatchi and Jeremy Sinclair. This time, it was the agency, not the client, blamed for not taking chances with the ads. Finally, Thatcher decided to do something about the situation: she called in a competing advertising agency for additional help. Young & Rubicam, founded in the United States in 1924, used research over creativity and came to the Prime Minister's attention through Geoffrey Tucker, a campaign adviser. Young & Rubicam conducted a statistical analysis of the Prime Minister's ratings.

Meetings between Saatchi & Saatchi executives and Thatcher did not go well. Finally, Thatcher demanded that Jeremy Sinclair come to 10 Downing Street. Negative ads should be dramatically decreased, she told senior Saatchi & Saatchi executives in a dressing down neither side would ever forget. She wanted the ads to be two parts positive to every one part negative. And, while she was demanding she get her way, Thatcher had a question that had been gnawing at her: "Where is Tim Bell?"

Maurice Saatchi explained that the election in 1987 would have no role for Bell. He was gone. "If you want him, Saatchi & Saatchi will resign the account," Maurice told Thatcher.

She needed the agency, but was furious with Maurice Saatchi's hardball tactics. A day after the meeting, Thatcher called Tim Bell herself. "She asked me what she should do," Bell said. "I said it would be foolish to have them resign since they are very good and I don't have the resources to do what they can do."

A compromise was struck: Thatcher wanted Bell to work for her "privately." Bell said Thatcher wanted him "to come see her every morning and every evening and I'll show you their work and you tell me what you think."

Bell said that Maurice and Charles Saatchi "never believed me, but it's true. I supported every campaign that was shown to me."

Nevertheless, some of Bell's work was used over the strenuous objections of Maurice Saatchi. For instance, Bell and Frank Lowe devised the line "Britain is great again. Don't let Labour ruin it." This echoed the 1959 campaign slogan, "Life's better with the Tories. Don't let Labour ruin it."

When Saatchi & Saatchi, which had been ordered to work the slogan into its campaign, finished with it, the slogan was "Britain is great again, don't let Labour wreck it."

The campaign ended with the election June 11, 1987, and the third victory for Margaret Thatcher.

But Maurice and Charles Saatchi fixated on the misconception that Tim Bell and Frank Lowe were taking credit for the win. What followed were threats of lawsuits, leaks to the press about Bell's personal life, and, finally, actions that would cause the shares of Lowe Howard-Spink & Marschalk to collapse.

Tim Bell would be fully resurrected by the Saatchi brothers seven years later, in late 1994, for what many would say was his greatest challenge: recasting the image of his old friend turned nemesis Maurice Saatchi.

Tim Bell would succeed and, together, Tim Bell and Maurice Saatchi would deliver a shot across the bow of Saatchi & Saatchi Company PLC that few would ever forget.

CHAPTER
THREE

By 1981, SAATCHI & SAATCHI COMPANY PLC was enjoying tremendous fortune. It was awarded new assignments from Cadbury Schweppes for Typhoo Tea, from Procter & Gamble for the launch of Pampers and Ariel Automatic, from United Biscuits for K.P. Foods, from Associated Newspapers for the launch of the *Mail on Sunday,* and from other clients including Campbell Soup, Black & Decker, and Allied-Lyons.

Maurice and Charles Saatchi wanted their company to be number one. While they had a goal, they lacked a cohesive business strategy. Nor did they ever consider the possibility that advertising spending might begin a free fall. The Saatchis assumed, wrongly it turned out, that ad spending would increase with double-digit growth forever.

The primary motivating force behind the brothers' hunger to be the largest advertising agency holding company in the world may well have been the immigrant status of their family. Britain is a class society that barely tolerates immigrants. No matter how high an immigrant rises in society, that person is still regarded as an outsider. A former senior-level Saatchi & Saatchi associate said, "They are first and foremost, no matter how they tried to disguise it, Iraqi Jews. They look at everything as an open-air market. Just grab everything," said the associate, himself Jewish. That is too simplistic, however. For one, consumers at market usually try to hold out for the best deal. All too often with the Saatchis, however, that was not the case. Saatchi & Saatchi usually paid top dollar, an ill-fated strategy.

And Maurice and Charles Saatchi's goal might not have been misguided had there been a business plan to back it up. But once the Saatchi brothers acquired a company, they lost interest in it.

Sometimes Maurice and Charles simply wanted to acquire an agency for no reason other than it existed. In the spring of 1981, on the very day that Frank Lowe announced in London that he was leaving Collett Dickenson Pearce to start his own agency, Lowe Howard-Spink & Marschalk, he happened to be having lunch with Maurice at Odins on Devonshire Street.

"Charles and I would like to offer you one million pounds in exchange for 30 percent of your agency," Maurice told Lowe shortly after the two were seated. It took a minute for Lowe to dismiss the offer. In that short period of time, Lowe thought how "droll" it would be to make one million pounds without producing a single ad from an agency that had not yet opened. "We'd never clash," Maurice added. "If you have any ambition, Frank, it is to be the best creative agency. Our ambition is to be the biggest." Lowe politely, but firmly, declined the offer, coming away from that lunch believing that the seeds of the brothers' downfall were already sown; the Saatchis, Lowe felt, had sacrificed their creative edge in favor of size.

The course was set with the reverse takeover of Compton. Procter & Gamble, Compton's biggest client, did not encourage creative breakthrough advertising. With the exception of the flagship office on Charlotte Street, creativity was swept aside as Saatchi & Saatchi grew larger. To grow larger still, Saatchi & Saatchi had to come across the Atlantic.

By 1981, Madison Avenue was just a concept. Few ad agencies remained on the street that had become synonymous with advertising. But to be number one, a company had to have a major presence in America.

However, America was not waiting with open arms for someone to come in and chip away at its dominance in what has been since the late 1800s a true American institution. The American advertising industry was epitomized by the three-martini lunch, the commuter whose train took him (a male, rarely a female) home to Greenwich, Connecticut, or Larchmont, New York, in Westchester County. The names of the agencies were J. Walter Thompson, Doyle Dane Bernbach, Young & Rubicam, and McCann-Erickson. Prior to the Industrial Revolution and the mass manufacturing of goods, demand for goods exceeded supply; there had been no need for advertising.

With the onset of the Industrial Revolution, more goods were produced than customers wanted. Manufacturers had to distinguish their products from those of their competitors, so companies began to give names to their products, as opposed to just letting the generic name carry the day. Customers, therefore, had to be convinced to go into a store and ask for a product by asking for the specific brand name. Consumers had to be made aware of these brands. And consumers had to be convinced to buy not only new brands coming to market, but also long-established products that, one would think, did not need to be sold aggressively. Thus, advertising was created. It was through advertising that companies hoped to persuade the public. And not only did the advertising have to announce the name of the product, it also had to explain why someone would select the product being advertised over similar competitors.

Consider corn flakes, the most basic of cold cereals. There is little difference between corn flakes manufactured by, say, Kellogg's and President's Choice, a cheaper generic brand. Kellogg's spends $25 million annually to advertise its corn flakes with the icon of a rooster. President's Choice spends a fraction of what Kellogg's spends and pitches its lower price. But Kellogg's and Leo Burnett in Chicago, its corn flakes advertising agency, capitalize on the insecurity of people. The perception is that if you serve someone President's Choice corn flakes instead of Kellogg's, you will be thought of as cheap, instead of as a savvy shopper. Advertising's persuasive powers win.

Claude C. Hopkins, the president of the Lord & Thomas agency (which would evolve into Foote, Cone & Belding), wrote in 1923, "We know what is most effective, and we act on basic laws." The law, as written by Thomas Rosser Reeves, the chairman and chief creative force at the Ted Bates Worldwide advertising agency, was the Unique Selling Proposition. "The consumer tends to remember just one thing from an advertisement—one strong claim, or one strong concept," Reeves said. In other words, an advertiser should make a claim of a single product attribute that its rivals could not. That is where "Melts in your mouth, not in your hand" came from for M&Ms candy and "Helps build strong bodies 12 ways" for Wonder Bread.

Of all the towering figures in advertising, including David

Ogilvy ("What you say in advertising is more important than how you say it"), Charles Saatchi was most inspired by Bill Bernbach. Bernbach was born in the Bronx, became research director of the New York World's Fair in 1939, director of public relations for the William Weintraub Agency, an advertising agency, in 1943, and in 1945 moved to Grey Advertising as creative group head. Two years later, Grey promoted him to vice president in charge of all creative work, but he chafed under the cut-and-dried research methods at Grey. He really wanted to produce clever ads. In 1949, Bernbach left Grey along with Ned Doyle, an account executive, and Maxwell (Mac) Dane and together they co-founded Doyle Dane Bernbach. It was at this agency that Bernbach practiced the craft of advertising the way he wanted to with creativity as the crucial ingredient. At the 1961 American Association of Advertising Agencies annual convention, Bernbach said, "Properly practiced, creativity can make one ad do the work of ten." Bernbach also said, "Research can tell you what people want, and you can give it back to them. It's a nice, safe way to do business, but who the hell wants to be safe. . . . Advertising isn't a science, it's persuasion. And persuasion is an art," words that rang true with Charles Saatchi.

When Doyle Dane opened, ad spending in the United States was $5.2 million. It would steadily build through the 1950s as consumer spending rose 98 percent during the postwar boom, from $5.7 million in 1950 to $11.3 million in 1959. An important part of the image of the affluent society was advertising.

Doyle Dane made its mark in 1959 when it was awarded the Volkswagen account. Prior to Doyle Dane's unorthodox approach, car advertising generally featured drawings of the car in print and shots of an auto speeding along country roads. Bigger was better when it came to car models. But Doyle Dane embraced the odd-looking Volkswagen Beetle. "Think Small" was the headline of one ad. Another ad showed a Volkswagen being pulled by a tow truck and a headline that read, "A Rare Photo."

Volkswagen would remain one of Doyle Dane's most venerable clients until 1993 when the account was moved to a boutique agency created by Doyle Dane, which had then been merged with Needham Harper Worldwide to form DDB Needham. Needham spun off a small agency called Berlin Cameron Doyle, with $80 million in annual billings, headed by its former New York president, Andy Berlin, to service the account. But the tiny agency would lose the account within sixteen months to be replaced by Arnold Fortuna Lawner & Cabot, a midsize Boston agency. Its well-received slogan, "Drivers Wanted," would recall the whimsical approach of Doyle Dane.

While Saatchi & Saatchi was associated with great advertising in the United Kingdom, the type of advertising that Bill Bernbach could admire, the agency remained virtually unknown in the United States. Through the mid-1990s, Saatchi & Saatchi Advertising failed to be equated with creative ads. "They never got over the fact that in the United States it was Saatchi who?" said Milt Gossett.

The Maurice Saatchi who approached ad agencies in the United States in order to buy them was a quintessential Englishman in his thinking. Britons are brought up with no idea of how to extend beyond the reach of the island. What's more, the ad community in Britain believes that an advertisement is exactly the same as any other commodity, that is, it can easily be exported.

In *The Act of Creation,* author Arthur Koestler writes that "emphasis and implication are complementary techniques." On the one hand, emphasis "bullies the audience into acceptance." On the other hand, implication "entices it into mental collaboration." And advertising in the United States and in the United Kingdom differ in that American advertising resonates with Koestler's emphasis; think of the Crazy Eddie ads in the 1970s where a manic actor shouted at the audience that the electronics retail chain's prices were "insane!" British advertising slyly uses implication, including subtle humor epitomized by the appearance of John Cleese in commercials for Schweppes tonic water. The British ad industry believes that implicit advertising is easier to export around the world because humor is universal. A screaming Crazy Eddie and other emphatic techniques aren't.

It is against this backdrop that Maurice and Charles Saatchi decided that "Nothing Is Impossible," and began shopping for American advertising agencies. The Saatchis would have been unable to complete a single purchase if theirs hadn't been a public company listed on the London Stock Exchange. When Saatchi & Saatchi wanted to raise money for acquisitions it would simply issue new stock for investors who were only too willing to ride the gravy train.

The process by which the company issued more stock is a rights issue—issuing new stock and giving existing shareholders the "right" to purchase it first—and isn't employed often in America. But Saatchi & Saatchi perfected it. On the surface, a rights issue has an immediate drawback: it dilutes the worth of the shares already held by stockholders. But the rights issue also has a built-in corrective measure: it gives shareholders the right to purchase shares at a discount, so the percentage they own in the company doesn't change. The money raised in a rights issue can be used for several purposes, including the acquisition of new companies or to pay down debt.

Maurice and Charles Saatchi believed that the company's stock was so highly valued that it could issue more stock and use the proceeds to buy companies at a lower multiple of earnings. Maurice and Charles, as always, aimed high. By the time Saatchi & Saatchi began scouring Madison Avenue in the late 1970s, Charles Saatchi had retreated from public view; Maurice Saatchi, along with the financial genius Martin Sorrell, orchestrated the sales.

In 1977, Bob Gross, the president of Geers Gross, told Maurice that he knew of an American agency that was quietly for sale: Cunningham & Walsh. Maurice and Sorrell spent time in New York, locked in negotiations with Cunningham & Walsh. It didn't take long for word of Saatchi & Saatchi's interest to reach Milt Gossett. He was horrified at the news. Cunningham & Walsh and Gossett's agency, Compton Advertising in New York, shared something in common: Procter & Gamble. If Saatchi & Saatchi were successful in its acquisition of Cunningham & Walsh, that could anger Procter & Gamble, which wanted its huge ad assignments spread throughout different advertising agency networks. Gossett contacted Maurice and told him the implications of such an acquisition. "They didn't care much about conflicts," said Gossett. "And that made us very nervous. This was a big, big problem."

The talks with Cunningham & Walsh were dropped, however,

as Saatchi & Saatchi, led by Martin Sorrell, went after Wells Rich Greene, founded by Mary Wells, one of the legends in advertising. Others agencies came across their radar screen as well, including Doyle Dane Bernbach and Foote, Cone & Belding.

Meanwhile, despite Gossett's uneasiness about the Saatchis' carefree attitude toward client conflicts, he loved the company of the brothers. But Gossett wanted control of Saatchi & Saatchi Compton in London in order to rein in the brothers and their acquisition ambition. With Gossett in control, he could steer the brothers away from anything that might endanger the Procter & Gamble account.

Gossett proposed that Compton raise its stake from 26 percent to 40 percent. "Maurice said okay," Gossett said. "The deal was practically done when, at the last minute, Charles said no."

"Why don't you buy all of us?" Charles asked Gossett.

"I would never buy all of you," Gossett told Charles Saatchi. "Then the two of you could go off and start another advertising agency. Then I'd really be in trouble."

The brothers could hardly keep a straight face.

While this dance was going on, Gossett began separate negotiations of his own with the purpose of acquiring another agency in London just in case any conflicts arose with Procter & Gamble. This would be Gossett's own agency in London and his insurance for retaining Procter & Gamble in case any acquisitions made by the Saatchis angered the global packaged goods client. "I wanted to make sure I had a place for all our conflicts," said Gossett.

The agency Gossett purchased was KMP, founded in 1964 as Kingsley Manton and Palmer. The three partners had been directors of other firms: David Kingsley at Benton & Bowles, Michael Manton at Crawfords, and Brian Palmer at Young & Rubicam. The agency had fallen into financial disrepair in 1974 when one of its clients, Brentford Nylon, went bust. The management was eventually bought out by Guinness Morison International, a subsidiary of Guinness Brewing. The management bought back its independence in 1979 and kept it until 1982 when Milt Gossett and Compton came along.

After finalizing the deal, Gossett had lunch with Ken Gill, chairman of Saatchi & Saatchi, to tell him about KMP. "Milt," Gill said, "I want you to take a look at this memo." It was a proposal for Saatchi & Saatchi to pay $50 million for Compton Advertising in New York. Gossett was furious. He had rebuffed one offer from Maurice Saatchi and now, on the heels of Gossett purchasing another London agency, the brothers were going after him again.

"We were a privately held company," said Gossett. "I could have agreed to that proposal, but I was so angry I just put the note in my desk and didn't look at it again."

Somehow, the other Compton managers found out about the note. In all likelihood, Maurice Saatchi initiated well-placed phone calls and asked why Milt Gossett never mentioned to his own managers the fact he had the note, the contents of which could make them all rich.

One day Maurice telephoned Milt Gossett and said, "Why don't we buy all of you? We're a public company and we can raise the money." But Compton was still twice the size of Saatchi & Saatchi. Gossett refused the offer.

Finally, after six months, Gossett telephoned Maurice. "Okay, we can learn a lot from you and we should try and get together." Gossett placed Bob Huntington, Compton's chief financial officer, in charge of the deal. He made one peculiar request, however: please keep Martin Sorrell out of the negotiations. Gossett was not a fan of Sorrell, whom he blamed for a lot of the unhappiness between Compton in the United States and Saatchi & Saatchi Company PLC in London. Sorrell, Gossett said, "could be a terror when taken off his leash." Instead, he wanted Maurice Saatchi and Huntington to negotiate directly.

"I knew that if Maurice made the deal sound good to Bob, it would sound good to everyone, since Bob was so skeptical about it," said Gossett.

Charles Saatchi made an unusual appearance in New York as the talks were heading for a successful conclusion. He came with a specific request: he wanted Saatchi & Saatchi, as opposed to a single Saatchi, in the title of the agency. At first Gossett bristled, but then he realized what a brand name Saatchi & Saatchi had become in London. The deal was signed in March 1982 at the Rye Town Hilton Hotel in Rye, New York. The name would be Saatchi & Saatchi Compton; the deal provided the agency with its independence and made Milt Gossett chief executive. Maurice Saatchi couldn't come to the agency to break open Champagne, however, until one critical detail was worked out. Gossett wanted $10 million to give agency executives the equivalent of what their stock would have been. Maurice initially said no.

Maurice was staying at the Lowell Hotel, a quiet establishment on East 63rd Street off Madison Avenue favored by British ad executives.

To this day, the Lowell operates its telephone system through a switchboard. Gossett's multimillion-dollar demand necessitated that Maurice place many calls to London from the Lowell. The hotel kept demanding Saatchi pay every few hours because he was running up such a high telephone bill. Finally, Maurice Saatchi gave in to Gossett's $10 million demand.

The deal was announced on March 15, 1982, one week after Maurice Saatchi had laughed during a transatlantic telephone conversation with the advertising columnist of the *New York Times* when it was suggested such an acquisition was in the works. Saatchi & Saatchi paid $29.2 million in cash and another $27.6 million to be paid over ten years if the agency achieved after-tax profits of $4.07 million.

Such a formula was the cornerstone of a Saatchi & Saatchi financial structure for acquiring companies: the Saatchis, having been stung by the dismal purchase of George J. Smith in 1974, no longer paid full price unless absolutely necessary. Instead, Saatchi & Saatchi would pay a portion of the purchase price, usually less than half, then insist the balance be earned out over a period of time. The deal accomplished an important goal in that the executives and managers who made the company so attractive in the first place, and were the company's most valued assets, would be forced to remain in place and continue to work hard if they wanted the balance. And the formula protected Saatchi & Saatchi from paying the full amount if a company fell apart or was a lemon, as was the case with George J. Smith.

In order to raise the $29.2 million, Saatchi & Saatchi had a rights issue of £26 million. Until that moment, the brothers owned 36 percent of the business. The rights issue would reduce their holdings by exactly half. It was Sorrell who had to explain the deal to the brothers: "Are you prepared to own 18 percent of Saatchi & Saatchi plus Compton or 36 percent of Saatchi on its own?" Maurice and Charles Saatchi chose the former option. Their prize was $810 million in billings in 1981 and a ranking of sixteen worldwide and nineteen within the United States. The two agencies shared ten multinational clients. Also included in the deal was KMP, Gossett's "insurance" agency.

Saatchi & Saatchi continued to ask agencies if they "ever considered selling." Most said a polite no. Then Maurice began calling David McCall, the chairman of McCaffrey and McCall, a successful midsize agency with such blue-chip clients as Mercedes-Benz, the ABC network, Canadian Club whisky, Norelco razors, Pfizer pharmaceuticals, and the JC Penney retail chain. The agency, founded in 1933, was originally named C.J. LaRoche & Company and held the Hiram Walker spirits account. McCall and James J. McCaffrey bought the agency in 1963.

As a midsize agency, McCaffrey and McCall was having some difficulties attracting new accounts because it lacked an international network. "We either didn't get the account after pitching the business, or we weren't asked to pitch," said David McCall. For instance, although the agency was chosen by a team from General Foods for the account, the business went to Ted Bates Advertising because the client didn't believe McCaffrey and McCall could handle a global assignment.

To persuade McCall, Maurice turned on the charm. "I liked Maurice immediately," McCall said. "I especially liked the fact he is European." McCall and his wife began to socialize with Maurice and Josephine Hart, whom Maurice married in October 1984, the same year as his divorce from Gillian Osband.

When the negotiations began, McCall and the agency's treasurer would huddle with Maurice. McCall also consulted his outside attorney, Morton Janklow, who is also a well-known and highly regarded literary agent. "David, the Saatchis' ancestors were doing deals in the streets of Baghdad while your family was painting themselves blue," Janklow told him by way of reassurance. McCall also met Charles Saatchi and already knew his then-wife, Doris. She had worked for McCall at Ogilvy & Mather when she was a copywriter and he was a copy chief.

On June 24, 1983, Saatchi & Saatchi agreed to pay $10 million down for McCaffrey and McCall and another $10 million to be earned out against profits over three years.

"They were impeccable and left us alone," McCall said. There was one thing that bothered McCall about the whole process, however. Once the deal was done, he never heard from Maurice Saatchi again. He didn't hear from Charles either, but McCall expected that. "I thought Maurice and [Josephine Hart] were our friends," McCall said naively. "I didn't realize they were only after our bottom line." Once agencies such as McCaffrey and McCall were purchased, Maurice and Charles Saatchi ignored the executives and the employees, an ill-advised move since it only alienated the very people who made the companies valuable in the first place. Eventually, McCall and others involved in the Saatchi & Saatchi deal took their handsome sums of cash and left; the agency didn't fare well once they departed. Many accounts left, including Mercedes-Benz and ABC. In February 1994, McCaffrey and McCall, its agency a shell of its former self, was folded into another Saatchi & Saatchi agency.

But Saatchi & Saatchi wasn't satisfied with gobbling up advertising agencies. The brothers hit upon another acquisition gimmick: they wanted to buy research companies, management consulting companies, and other marketing service entities, such as public relations companies. The justification for this audacious business plan was that Saatchi & Saatchi would be able to offer its clients a full complement of services, a type of one-stop shopping that heretofore was unavailable. Saatchi & Saatchi would become a full-service company offering clients not only advertising, but public relations, research, sales promotion, direct marketing, corporate image and design, strategic planning, systems for employee recruitment, and financial services.

Through computers and sophisticated telecommunications, the world had shrunk, and Maurice Saatchi keenly recognized the fact.

In 1984, the brothers purchased Yankelovich, Skeely & White/Clancy Shulman and McBer & Company, two polling and market research specialists. Saatchi & Saatchi made its largest purchase ever at the end of 1984 when, for $100 million, plus an earn-out of another $25 million, it acquired the Hay Group, an international management consultancy with one hundred offices in twenty-seven countries. Hay was founded in 1943 in Philadelphia by Edward Hay, although it was mostly run by Dr. Milton Rock, who would eventually head the consultant division of Saatchi & Saatchi. Now Saatchi & Saatchi had a foothold into a potentially lucrative business that already had two giants, Arthur Andersen and McKinsey.

As the world shrank through affordable transportation, computers, and advanced telecommunications, companies expanded into different countries. A main ingredient to the success of any product introduction into a new market was, of course, advertising. And companies were pressuring their ad agencies in an unprecedented way to become experts in selling products in countries they previously ignored.

It was this issue that piqued the interest of Maurice Saatchi, an issue that one day would contribute to his ruin at Saatchi & Saatchi.

One of the periodicals to which Maurice subscribed was the *Harvard Business Review.* In an issue published in 1983, he was drawn to an article titled "The Globalization of Markets." It was written by a respected Harvard professor, Theodore (Ted) Levitt, a cranky and highly intelligent man who resembles the convicted Watergate figure G. Gordon Liddy.

At the time the article was written, Levitt was a professor of business administration and head of the Marketing Department at the Harvard Business School. Levitt believed world markets were becoming homogenized by low-cost transportation and communications. Therefore, a worldwide convergence on common products satisfying common needs was being produced. By the late 1980s, eighty-seven of the hundred largest advertisers in the United States were multinational companies.

Advertising agencies became international when their clients insisted on it. In 1899, for instance, J. Walter Thompson, founded in 1864, opened a London office to service clients. McCann-Erickson, founded in 1902, expanded outside the United States because of Standard Oil. Leo Burnett in Chicago, founded in 1935, expanded because of Philip Morris's Marlboro brand.

The Marlboro Man, the lone cowboy, was perhaps the most international icon in advertising. It worked unaltered in all countries but two: Japan, where the poster had to include more than one cowboy because a man alone is assumed to have been ostracized, and Colombia, because a cowboy there is a man who cleans the stables.

Not all the expansions were immediately successful; Stanley Resor, chairman of J. Walter Thompson, closed its London office in 1916 to save costs. It was reopened in 1923 when Henry Ford started selling cars made in European factories.

One of Ted Levitt's former students, Robert Louis-Dreyfus, learned well. In the spring of 1995, Louis-Dreyfus, seated in his father's offices in Paris, would fondly remember Levitt. "He was the best professor I ever had. A great showman in class. But, let me tell you, he was a lousy businessman."

In his *Harvard Business Review* article, Levitt said, "Companies must learn to operate as if the world were one large market—ignoring superficial regional and national differences."

Coca-Cola, for example, was becoming a worldwide brand. It could be marketed to people all over the world. And, Levitt argued, that could be done with a single message. For its part, Coca-Cola estimated that on its worldwide ad budget in 1987 of $300 million, it saved $8 million in creative expenses by using one global advertisement.

"By translating these benefits into reduced world prices, they can decimate competitors that still live in the disabling grip of old assumptions about how the world works," Levitt said.

The large multinational companies, in order to keep profits climbing, had to find new markets in which to sell their products because the existing markets were being saturated with competitors.

"The globalization of markets is at hand," Levitt wrote. "With that, the multinational commercial world nears its end, and so does the multinational corporation. . . . The global company will shape the vectors of technology and globalization into its great fecundity. It will systematically push these vectors toward their own convergence, offering everyone simultaneously high-quality, more or less standardized products at optimally low prices, thereby achieving for itself vastly expanded markets and profits. Companies that do not adapt to the new global realities will become victims of those that do."

And in the Saatchi & Saatchi Company PLC annual report for the year ending September 30, 1983, Levitt was quoted as saying, "The global corporation operates at low relative cost—as if the entire world (or major regions of it) were a single entity; it sells the same things in the same way everywhere."

Maurice Saatchi, who treated Levitt's word as gospel, now did what Maurice Saatchi always did when he found something he became enchanted with: he set out to acquire Ted Levitt. Saatchi flew to Cambridge, Massachusetts, for a meeting with Levitt. The two immediately liked each other.

Levitt was establishing new ground in advertising, which had its roots in the 1850s as a service confined to retailers who were buying space in local newspapers. Ad agencies not only produced advertisements, but they also bought media space for the client in newspapers and magazines and on television, radio, and billboards. The account executive, or "suit," would be placed in charge of coordinating the activity.

For such a volatile and creative industry as advertising, the field is relatively stable. About 95 percent of clients stay with their agency year-in and year-out. It is front-page news when a split occurs, such as when Anheuser-Busch fired D'Arcy Masius Benton & Bowles after seventy-eight years on its flagship Budweiser account on November 13, 1994.

Levitt, a complete gentleman, grew increasingly disturbed by what he felt were flagrant transgressions by Maurice. But it would take a while before the Saatchi charm wore off.

Maurice came away from the initial meeting as impressed with Ted Levitt as he had been with Levitt's writing. Virtually immediately Saatchi & Saatchi Advertising began implementing the Levitt theory of marketing. In March 1983, a team of British Airways executives, led by Lord John King, who was appointed to take the near bankrupt airline private and out of the ownership of the state, gathered in Saatchi & Saatchi Advertising headquarters on Charlotte Street.

Also in the room were Maurice Saatchi and Bill Muirhead, the account executive on the British Airways business. British

Airways needed an overhaul in its services and in its marketing. The joke in the U.K. was that BA stood for Bloody Awful.

Muirhead, a dedicated account executive and tennis enthusiast who once forced himself to learn to tolerate opera because many of his clients liked it, discovered a fact that British Airways heretofore hadn't exploited. It flew more passengers to more international destinations than any other airline in the world.

That led to the agency presenting a single campaign with the universal slogan, "The World's Favourite Airline." Muirhead also discovered another interesting factoid: British Airways carries more passengers across the Atlantic Ocean each year, 1.2 million, than live in Manhattan.

That led to the commercial "Manhattan Landing," which was presented to the British Airways executives on that March afternoon on Charlotte Street.

The spot opens with a man walking his dog late at night. Suddenly the dog stops and looks at the sky. A woman peers out of her door. "Roger, Manhattan, continue to two thousand feet," says a voice-over. As a crowd gathers, Manhattan island, with its soaring skyline, lifts up and appears on a flight path for Heathrow Airport in London. The announcer says, "Every year, British Airways flies more people across the Atlantic than the entire population of Manhattan." More than anything, the film resonates with *Close Encounters of the Third Kind*, the 1977 Steven Spielberg movie about aliens landing on earth.

The commercial would be launched in the United States, Canada, Australia, and Britain on the same day; it would be seen in twenty-five other countries shortly afterward. British Airways would spend £25 million on placing the ad in the first year alone, a whopping figure for an airline.

The British Airways ad did more than boost the image of British Airways; it enhanced the reputation of Saatchi & Saatchi Advertising. It was the first ad produced on Charlotte Street and seen by Americans.

The "Manhattan Landing" television ad was accurately described as a major triumph of Ted Levitt's credo of global advertising. It whetted Maurice Saatchi's appetite to capitalize on globalization and expand.

IN EARLY 1985, Kenneth Gill wrote a letter to Maurice and Charles Saatchi informing them that he wanted out. Gill had suffered a heart attack and he thought the pace was too much. In his letter, Gill wrote that he wanted Maurice to take over as chairman.

His reply came via a frantic phone call from the brothers. Maurice didn't want the chairman's seat. "The chairman takes all the flak," Gill recalled Maurice saying. Gill said he convinced Maurice to do it and, in return, Maurice asked Gill to remain on the board. On March 25, 1985, Maurice Saatchi, thirty-seven, who never had a corporate title other than company director, was named chairman of Saatchi & Saatchi Company PLC.

Although the brothers never stopped prowling around for advertising agencies to buy, they began gobbling communications companies at breakneck speed. Typical was the relatively small acquisition of Siegel & Gale, a corporate communications consultancy with worldwide clients including 3M and TRW. Siegel & Gale, founded in 1970, was approached by a broker for Saatchi & Saatchi in 1984. The growing global network established by the brothers intrigued co-founder Alan Siegel. "Having the capability of a global network and tying together with a really good advertising agency system would be an interesting thing to do," Siegel said. "And I needed capital to grow."

So Siegel called around the industry and found that Saatchi & Saatchi was willing to pay ten times earnings for Siegel & Gale, whereas the American agencies were willing to pay only three to five times earnings. Negotiations commenced, but were subject to fits and starts. "I didn't know it at the time," Siegel said, "but they were talking to many companies and trying to do deals all over the place." When Maurice Saatchi did turn his attention to Siegel & Gale, Siegel said, "he didn't focus on the work. He was purely interested in numbers, in financial projections." When Maurice visited Siegel & Gale's offices on Avenue of the Americas in New York before the deal was done, he curtly declined to see a slide presentation of the agency's work and had no interest in meeting any of the employees.

Alan Siegel recalled the day in April 1985 when the acquisition was finalized at the offices of White & Case, Saatchi &

Saatchi's U.S. attorneys, "one of the more upsetting days in my business life." The representatives from Saatchi & Saatchi kept leaving the room suddenly, coming back in and leaving again in regular intervals. It was only a day later that Siegel realized what had been going on: Saatchi & Saatchi were closing other deals with other companies simultaneously, including Marlboro Marketing, a sales promotion company. In the press release, Siegel & Gale was lumped with other companies purchased by Saatchi & Saatchi. "You spend twenty-plus years building a company and then you see you're not treated special when you're bought," Siegel said.

Siegel quickly realized his company was in trouble. "I just saw they were buying things indiscriminately," he said. "They didn't have management skills or depth to put this thing together." Such was the immediate dislike and mistrust of Saatchi & Saatchi that Siegel & Gale never placed the Saatchi name in any of its corporate literature or ever volunteered its association with Saatchi & Saatchi to any potential client. Alan Siegel would, like so many others associated with the brothers, ultimately get his revenge; his would be particularly sweet, but he would have to wait a decade.

Maurice Saatchi next placed a call in 1985 to Herb Rowland, chief executive of Rowland Company, a well-respected public relations company founded in 1961. It boasted such blue-chip clients as DuPont, Procter & Gamble, Toyota, General Mills, and Hasbro. "As you would imagine," Maurice said to Herb Rowland, "we are interested in acquiring your PR unit to go along with the businesses we have." Saatchi indicated that he had scouts in New York looking for such a business. "I've looked at your client roster," he continued, "and this is the kind of agency we want. There's a dazzling necessity about you and your company becoming part of our operation." Rowland replied that he already had turned down feelers from Ogilvy & Mather and Ted Bates Advertising. "Please don't take this the wrong way," Rowland continued, "but I can't imagine putting a public relations agency in with an advertising agency. We need to be independent."

Martin Sorrell then called and said he and Maurice would fly over to New York on the Concorde to discuss the matter. Once in

Rowland's office, Sorrell laid out the plan. "There is no problem about remaining independent," he said. "Rowland will be acquired by the holding company and will remain autonomous." Much to his own surprise, Rowland found himself saying, "I'm interested." The purchase price was $10 million down with an earn-out.

By the time of the Rowland acquisition, the Saatchi empire had grown so large, the company divided itself into two major units: communications services, which included advertising, sales promotion, design and corporate identity, direct marketing, and public relations; and consulting services, including management consultancy, information and research, and recruitment. Dr. Milton Rock headed up the consulting services division.

To lead its communications services division, Saatchi & Saatchi went outside its ranks, something the brothers were loath to do. Through a headhunter they found Anthony Simonds-Gooding, then chief executive of Whitbread Brewery. Simonds-Gooding is a jovial, barrel-chested, friendly executive who looks uncomfortable squeezed into expensive pin-striped suits. He has a full head of gray hair and a smile that never leaves his face. Like everyone at Saatchi & Saatchi, he was assigned a nickname: "Tony Christmas Pudding."

At Whitbread, Simonds-Gooding was quite comfortable with his life. Whitbread was a classy operation. Each afternoon, he was served tea on a silver tray by servants wearing white gloves. Then, Maurice Saatchi came calling.

The two first met about fifteen years earlier when Saatchi & Saatchi was getting started. Simonds-Gooding was working at Lintas, the then-in-house ad agency for Unilever originally known as Lever International Advertising Service. Simonds-Gooding was advertising manager of Birds Eye Foods when he received a telephone call from Maurice Saatchi. "We're starting an advertising agency," Saatchi had said, "and I would very much appreciate fifteen minutes of your time." Partly out of curiosity and partly out of courtesy, Simonds-Gooding had gone to Golden Square. There was no small talk; just Maurice Saatchi saying, "I'm really worried about your peas advertising." Simonds-Gooding appreciated the audacity of the pitch, but turned down the offer to fix the Birds

Eye peas ads. Not too long afterward, another overture came from Maurice Saatchi: would Simonds-Gooding be interested in joining as marketing director of the fledgling agency? "Luckily for them I turned it down," said Simonds-Gooding. Instead, the brothers eventually recruited Tim Bell.

Simonds-Gooding was still uninterested in Saatchi & Saatchi when Maurice contacted him in 1985. This time, however, he appealed to Simonds-Gooding's "finer nature, my ambition, and creative side."

"My brother and I have hardly begun," Maurice told Simonds-Gooding. "We like to think and strategize. We'd like to buy companies and we'd like you to run them."

This pitch appealed to Anthony Simonds-Gooding. For one, he believed he wouldn't be second-guessed by Maurice and Charles Saatchi. "I always said they couldn't run a bath," Simonds-Gooding said of the brothers. Just how much distance Maurice and Charles would keep from their new chairman and chief executive of the communications services division is something Simonds-Gooding would soon find out and never forget.

In September 1985, Simonds-Gooding strolled into 80 Charlotte Street for his first day at work and gave the receptionist his name. "Where are you from?" she asked. "I'm actually from here," Simonds-Gooding said, somewhat perplexed. "I'm the new chief executive." There was no record of his appointment; and Maurice and Charles Saatchi had each gone on an extended holiday.

An administrative officer appeared in the reception area and sheepishly told Simonds-Gooding there was no office in the main building, although there was one in the annex a few blocks away. It was evident that the only two individuals who were clued in on Simonds-Gooding's arrival were Maurice and Charles Saatchi. So Simonds-Gooding was dispatched to what was called Death Row on Maple Street, where Tim Bell was isolated before departing. Awaiting him in his out-of-the-way office was a huge flower arrangement with a card from the Saatchi brothers welcoming him to the company.

After a few days, Simonds-Gooding decided there was something terribly wrong with the New York operation, such as the proposal to build an expensive office at 375 Hudson Street in an unattractive, industrial neighborhood in lower Manhattan. So Simonds-Gooding informed Milt Gossett he was coming and wanted to see senior staff. Gossett incorrectly thought Simonds-Gooding had authority only over the U.K. agencies and brushed Simonds-Gooding aside. Simonds-Gooding reacted uncharacteristically with anger. Gossett quickly complied. When Simonds-Gooding entered a New York restaurant expecting to meet with Gossett, he was greeted instead by Gossett's attorney. He was there to explain Gossett's employment contract. Simonds-Gooding soon learned that every executive was tied to an expensive, long-term contract.

Over breakfast in New York, Compton executives told Simonds-Gooding to forget his proposal to scuttle the building on Hudson Street and fire its architect, Richard Rogers. Simonds-Gooding said if the building was going to be erected, it should be by another architect. Rogers, he said, knew nothing of building offices; his expertise was in large spaces, not conducive to an office environment. "Forget it," said one executive to Simonds-Gooding. "This building is being built by a friend of Doris Saatchi. Charles wants to build this to make a statement for Doris." At the time, Maurice Saatchi was in New York, staying at the Mayflower Hotel on Central Park West. Simonds-Gooding tried to call him, leaving word that he wanted to discuss 375 Hudson Street. Maurice refused to answer his calls. Finally, David Perring, the company secretary, called Simonds-Gooding. "This is something Charles wants to do," Perring said. "Don't offend Charles."

Simonds-Gooding quickly realized he wasn't a popular figure. For the first time in the brief history of Saatchi & Saatchi, there was a layer between senior executives and Maurice and Charles Saatchi and Simonds-Gooding was the buffer.

Simonds-Gooding, employed by Saatchi & Saatchi for less than two months, flew to London over the weekend, walked into Charles Saatchi's office on Monday, and resigned. "You have undermined my position," Simonds-Gooding said.

Charles's reply was, his associates said, typical: "What has my stupid brother done now?"

Then, Maurice and Charles Saatchi had to seduce Simonds-

Gooding all over. He was assured he would never be blindsided again. Please stay, they begged, although telling him to forget any changes at 375 Hudson Street. That was a done deal.

Simonds-Gooding agreed to stay. And for a while the brothers were true to their word.

CHAPTER
FOUR

"WHERE'S THE BEEF?"

The ubiquitous slogan for Wendy's fast-food chain, at first amusing, then increasingly annoying—presidential candidate Walter Mondale brought the house down with it in his 1984 campaign against Democratic rival Gary Hart—was the brainchild of Dancer Fitzgerald Sample. Dancer Fitzgerald Sample was founded in Chicago in 1923 as Blackett-Sample-Hummert and moved its headquarters to New York in 1948 in order to be closer to the exploding television broadcasting business. In 1986, Dancer Fitzgerald was the thirteenth largest advertising agency in the United States with billings of $876 million and clients including Procter & Gamble, General Mills, Toyota, Sara Lee, and Nabisco.

Dancer Fitzgerald appealed to Maurice Saatchi for two reasons: it had an impressive client roster as well as an admired creative output. On February 24, 1986, Saatchi & Saatchi agreed to acquire Dancer Fitzgerald for $75 million. On the day the purchase was announced, Saatchi & Saatchi also said Dancer Fitzgerald would be combined with Dorland Advertising, which the company had acquired in 1981 for £7 million and which had clients such as British Telecommunications and Guinness. Dorland, despite its deep roots in Britain, was actually founded in Atlantic City in 1886 by John Dorland; it opened its first U.K. office in London in 1905. The merger satisfied several objectives, including the fact that Dorland, with $325 million in billings, had a strong base in London, and Dancer wanted one. The new company, DFS Dorland Worldwide, would be the sixteenth largest advertising agency network in the world and would be operated independently from Saatchi & Saatchi Compton Worldwide.

Now the brothers set their acquisition radar on Backer & Spielvogel, an agency with a stellar creative reputation. Formed in June 1979 by Bill Backer and Carl Spielvogel, two former executives of McCann-Erickson, and McCann's owner, Interpublic, respectively, the agency was first located in the Gotham Hotel on West 55th Street and Fifth Avenue in Manhattan with only the two founders, a secretary, and Paul Spielvogel, Carl's fourteen-year-old son, as a gofer. Spielvogel, a Brooklyn-born son of a raw-fur processor, was the first advertising columnist of the *New York Times*. At the *Times*, he caught the attention of Marion Harper, an advertising executive who was to launch Interpublic: he hired Spielvogel as his assistant and Spielvogel had a magnificent run for two decades. He is quiet, measured, generous, a smart businessman and elegant. Bill Backer is considered a witty and creative standout in advertising. He composed the "I'd Like to Teach the World to Sing" jingle for Coca-Cola and came up with the slogan "It's Miller Time" for Miller Brewing's flagship brand.

Two months after hanging out a shingle, Spielvogel was having lunch at the "21" club on West 52nd Street when he was summoned to the phone. Larry Williams, the marketing director at Miller Brewing, was calling to inform Spielvogel that his fledgling agency was awarded the entire Miller Brewing business.

By 1984, the agency was billing $550 million with clients such as Miller Brewing, National Cash Register, Campbell Soup, Quaker Foods, Xerox, and Philip Morris.

Spielvogel first became acquainted with Charles and Doris Saatchi through their mutual love of art. Shortly after a dinner with the couple in 1985, Spielvogel received a call from Martin Sorrell. Saatchi & Saatchi was interested in acquiring Backer & Spielvogel. For once, there was little resistance. The timing of Sorrell's call was fortuitous. Miller had just transferred its Miller High Life and Löwenbräu accounts to J. Walter Thompson. One reason was the agency's lack of a global network.

Sorrell set up a lunch between Spielvogel and Maurice Saatchi in London at the Connaught Hotel, Saatchi's preferred place to dine. "I told Maurice that it is very important we have total autonomy for five years and he agreed," Spielvogel said. "We ended up doing the deal, I think, because Charles is the decision maker and he wanted it done."

Spielvogel is an utterly charming and amusing man. Perhaps because of his humble origins in Brooklyn, or perhaps because of his modest financial beginnings as a reporter for the *New York Times,* Spielvogel, now a fantastically wealthy man, likes to believe he possesses an innate ability to instantly and accurately size up people; he can. Spielvogel is generous and charitable. He has not only spent vast sums of money on himself, but also on philanthropic and political causes. Perhaps that was why the honeymoon period between the two men with the towering egos would last less than six months.

Because he was once a reporter and was concerned about leaks to the media, Spielvogel labeled the discussions to be acquired by Saatchi & Saatchi "Project Japan." The name came from a casual remark by Bill Howell, Miller's president. While meeting with Backer & Spielvogel executives one day in the Miller Brewing project room in Milwaukee, Howell had said, "By the way, I've gotten a call from that Japanese agency Saatchi & Saatchi. They want to pitch our business. I told them we are very happy with Backer & Spielvogel."

When, in Maurice's estimation, negotiations dragged on too long, he made mention of this fact to Spielvogel. Maurice, lighting a cigar at the end of a lunch with Spielvogel in the Grill Room of the Four Seasons restaurant in New York, put on his little-boy charm, and said, "Carl, we've met three times and you still haven't said yes." Spielvogel, who was used to calling the shots, answered evenly, "Clearly you have never wooed a woman in your life. There is a little wooing that goes on before you get into bed."

Spielvogel, even more fearful of leaks once the acquisition proposal was in its final stages, insisted that he not enter Saatchi & Saatchi offices in London to sign the deal, for fear he would be seen, but the brothers demanded he show up there. Sure enough, Spielvogel was spotted in the lobby by someone he knew who inquired why he was there. "As you know," he said with a straight face, "I'm the chairman of the business committee of the Metropolitan Museum of Art and I'm here to get money from Charles Saatchi." When Spielvogel went upstairs, he said to Charles, "You'll have to give me a check for $1,000 and join the business committee," which he did.

After the final contract was drawn up, but before it was signed, Spielvogel said he would take the proposal to a small number of clients that Spielvogel felt particular loyalty to. The clients gave their blessing. Spielvogel then said to Maurice Saatchi that there was one more piece of business that needed to be addressed: "There are rumors you are going to acquire Ted Bates Advertising. Quite honestly, we believe our philosophy of the business is quite different from the Bates philosophy of the business. If you are going to acquire Bates, you can't acquire us." "No," Maurice replied, "we're not going to acquire Bates. We've had some discussions, but those discussions are over."

Spielvogel took Saatchi at his word, a rare lapse in his otherwise acute judgment.

There was another part of the agreement that, even today, few people know about. Maurice Saatchi insisted that a clause be included that said Backer & Spielvogel would agree within a two-year period to merge with Compton. Backer & Spielvogel was the hot agency and Compton was still considered lackluster.

When the deal was finally done, Saatchi & Saatchi would make an initial payment of $56 million for Backer & Spielvogel with the balance of about $45 million in an earn-out over the next six years.

On balance, it was to be an unhappy marriage between Backer & Spielvogel and Saatchi & Saatchi. Spielvogel felt he was constantly lied to by Maurice; he had little, if anything, to do with Charles. One of the largest affronts to Carl Spielvogel was an episode involving AdCom, which started its life in Chicago as the in-house agency for Quaker. Spielvogel wanted his agency to have a cereal account, so when Quaker said in 1986 it would sell AdCom, Spielvogel jumped at the opportunity. In discussions with Gary Bayer, the head of AdCom, Spielvogel assured him the agency would be autonomous. Although Backer & Spielvogel's bid wasn't the highest, Bill Smithberg, chief executive of Quaker, told Spielvogel, "We're going to permit you to buy AdCom. I think you'll take the best care of our [fifty-five] people. This is not based on money. But you're running the type of shop where our people will be happiest."

Six months after Saatchi & Saatchi acquired Backer & Spielvogel and assured its management it would remain independent, Maurice Saatchi telephoned Spielvogel. "I'm sorry," Maurice began the conversation, "but you're going to have to resign the Quaker account."

"How can I resign the Quaker account when I gave the AdCom people my word they would not be affected by our acquisition?" Spielvogel countered.

"We fished out a letter from our files which said our commitment is to General Mills [a Dancer Fitzgerald client] in the breakfast category," Saatchi said.

"Fine," Spielvogel said, "that may be Saatchi & Saatchi's commitment, but it's not our commitment. We have autonomy. Going into this deal you said there were only two clients we had to clear the system for, Procter & Gamble and Mars. This is outrageous. These people have put their lot in with us. I gave my word. We're not going to resign this." Then, Spielvogel threw down the gauntlet: "If you insist on this," he said, "I want to buy back the company."

As soon as Spielvogel uttered that sentence, a wall came down between the two headstrong executives. "I had all of Maurice's telephone numbers, including the car phone, the country home, everywhere," Spielvogel said. "But I could no longer reach him." Spielvogel then said he would fly to London that week to meet with Maurice. Maurice Saatchi refused to meet with him. In his place, Saatchi dispatched Anthony Simonds-Gooding. Saatchi & Saatchi was unyielding: Backer & Spielvogel would have to resign the Quaker account. After six more months of haggling, Spielvogel finally relented. "We sold AdCom to itself for the price of the fixtures and furniture," Spielvogel said.

EVEN IN THOSE HEADY TIMES, the brothers wouldn't always get their way. One prize that eluded Saatchi & Saatchi Company PLC: Doyle Dane Bernbach.

Doyle Dane had fallen on hard times since the death in 1982 of its legendary founder, Bill Bernbach, and was actively looking for partners. But Doyle Dane immediately rejected overtures from Saatchi & Saatchi and, specifically, Anthony Simonds-Gooding. The Saatchis had made one earlier run at buying Doyle Dane when Sorrell had been the point man. The discussions hadn't gone well and Doyle Dane executives remembered that.

Instead, the agency chose to be one-third of one of Madison Avenue's first megamergers: Doyle Dane, the twelfth largest agency in the United States, would be joined with BBDO (originally Batten Barton Durstine & Osborn), the sixth largest agency, and Needham Harper Worldwide, ranked number sixteen. The merger would form the foundation of a new ad agency holding group, Omnicom, which would become the number one advertising agency conglomerate in the world. Allen Rosenshine, chairman of BBDO and now designated chairman of the newly created holding company, declared that Omnicom was number one "but maybe for only ten minutes."

Maurice and Charles Saatchi still wanted their company to be number one. With the earn-out formula, Maurice believed he hit upon a way to achieve this goal. And, in theory, it was a winning formula; by 1986, when the share price traded at a high of £56.22 ($78), the Saatchis had spent more than $461.5 million to acquire a half-dozen agencies, including McCaffrey and McCall, Compton, and Dancer Fitzgerald Sample. Along the way, they also purchased management consultant and design firms, among other businesses. Compton, for example, was financed with an earn-out.

For a while, the covers of the Saatchi & Saatchi Company PLC annual report had an unattractive design—steps in the form of elongated rectangles, each larger than the next. For the 1988 annual report, the steps were filled in. The first one, the smallest, said simply "Advertising." The next had "Advertising" with "Design" underneath it. And so on until the fifth and final column, which had an impressive seventeen compartments: "Advertising," "Design," "Direct Marketing," "Sales Promotion," "Public Relations," "Market Research," "Corporate Identity," "Display and Merchandising," "Conference Management," "Media Buying and Analysis," "Recruitment," "Management Consulting," "Human Resources," "Distribution Logistics," "Information Systems," "Remuneration and Pensions," and "Litigation Counselling."

TO ACCOMPLISH THE GOAL to be number one, Maurice, with Charles in the background, in mid-1986 revived negotiations that had faltered in the first few months of 1986: to acquire Ted Bates Worldwide. If there was a precursor to the Saatchi & Saatchi acquisition binge, it was Ted Bates, and specifically, its headstrong, workaholic chairman, Robert E. Jacoby. His heroes were Generals Erwin Rommel and George S. Patton Jr. He kept a revolver in his wall safe, taking it with him to meetings.

In his seven years as chairman, Jacoby had overseen the acquisitions of international agencies as well as Campbell-Mithun in Minneapolis, which had the General Mills account, Stern Walters/Earle Ludgin in Chicago, Conill Advertising, Cole & Weber, Sawdon & Bess, McDonald & Little, and William Esty. When it was done buying, Bates had billings of $2 billion.

Theodore (Ted) Bates, an aristocratic native of Maine who attended Yale University, left Benton & Bowles in 1940 to form his own agency. Bates took with him two large accounts, Continental Baking, which made Wonder Bread, and Colgate-Palmolive. Along with him and his cherished accounts came the agency's critical architect, Rosser Reeves, who would promote Bates's signature Unique Selling Proposition theory.

Reeves, the son of a Virginia minister, was a reporter at the *Times-Dispatch* of Richmond before he turned to advertising, becoming a copywriter at Blackett-Sample-Hummert. His onetime brother-in-law was advertising legend David Ogilvy. Reeves had an opulent life-style, racing yachts, owning part of the Half Moon resort in Jamaica, and participating in high-stakes international poker games. He also dabbled in politics. In 1952, he would create and write the television ads for presidential candidate General Dwight D. Eisenhower.

It was Reeves who correctly asserted that most advertising failed to meet the criteria of the Unique Selling Proposition. For instance, Colgate toothpaste advertised itself as "ribbon dental cream, it comes out like a ribbon and lies flat on your brush." It failed to move the product off the shelf. Bates changed the slogan to "cleans your breath while it cleans your teeth." No one had placed a breath claim on toothpaste before. Reeves also came up with one of the most memorable television ads. The client was Anacin. To show the effectiveness of the product against a pounding headache, Bates created a commercial showing hammers hitting the inside of a skull. Once Anacin was taken, the hammers disappeared one at a time.

Despite his accomplishments and despite the fact that Reeves was the largest Bates shareholder, he was voted out by his board in 1965. Senior Bates executives had become convinced that Reeves was a liability because he would use the company stock whenever he needed money, which was often. The agency so wanted Reeves out that it paid him $80,000 annually for ten years to keep him away. At the end of his forced retirement, he contacted Bob Jacoby, who was then chairman of Bates, and asked to see him. Jacoby brought to the "21" club a trusted associate, Donald M. Zuckert, who was president of the agency.

In his southern drawl, Reeves said, "Well, boys, you know, Theodore paid Martin Mayer to write a history of Ted Bates. When he read about the sixteen original partners and saw the scandalous behavior they were involved in, he told me to pay Martin the $75,000 fee, get a release from him, get the manuscripts and destroy them. Of course, I have one in my safe deposit box. My forced retirement is almost up and if you would be willing to make an arrangement with me, I would be willing to give you the manuscript."

Jacoby politely put Reeves off, saying he would have to consider the offer.

Once alone with Zuckert, Jacoby asked his opinion.

"Let him release it," Zuckert said. "All sixteen people are dead."

Reeves left empty-handed, never followed through on his threat, and the manuscript has never been seen. Reeves opened his own agency, wasn't successful, and died in 1984 at age seventy-three.

Reeves was replaced by Archibald McG. Foster, a close ally of Ted Bates himself. Succeeding Foster in 1973 was Bob Jacoby, who joined Bates in 1962 after nine years at Compton Advertising, where he had worked as an account executive on the Procter & Gamble business. Jacoby, a native of Bogota, New Jersey, in Bergen County, began his career at Shell Oil as an economist after graduating from Princeton University in 1951. But the advertising business interested him more than the oil industry, so after less than a year at Shell, he moved to Compton.

Although he is mellow at age sixty-eight in 1996 and enjoying his post-Bates afterlife in Ponte Vedra, Florida, near Jacksonville, Bob Jacoby was anything but calm and endearing during his reign at Bates.

Saatchi & Saatchi's prolonged, painful, and misguided acquisition of Bates in 1986 was dubbed Macbates by *Advertising Age,* the weekly trade publication. Bob Jacoby was its chief protagonist and made $111 million in the deal. Jacoby became the Michael Milken of the advertising industry, despised, in part, because of the personal wealth he gained through the sale of Bates.

Saatchi & Saatchi and Bates needed one another: Saatchi & Saatchi wanted Bates in order to attain its goal of being number one. Bates wanted Saatchi & Saatchi, or whatever suitor was desperate enough to meet Bates's outlandish demands for selling, because its executives were reaching retirement age and buying their stock back would cost upward of $150 million. No private company, Jacoby deduced, would want to raise that much capital.

In addition to its impressive client list and its worldwide network (it had 108 offices in forty-eight countries), Bates was also attractive because it was one of the most profitable advertising agencies in the world. In the fiscal year ended March 1986, Bates recorded pretax profits of $64.5 million; its ratio of pretax profit to income was 16.8 percent compared with an industry average of 10 percent.

On agency president Donald Zuckert's fiftieth birthday in 1984, Jacoby presented his friend with a gold money clip and $50. Over dinner, Jacoby said, "I'm going to sell the agency and I'm going to make $100 million." Beginning in January 1985, he set out to do just that. Jacoby and John Hoyne, Bates's international agency chief, met at the Helmsley Palace in New York with Maurice Saatchi and Simon Mellor, Saatchi's point person on acquisitions.

In 1995, Jacoby would recall that Mellor contacted Hoyne and said he wanted to discuss an acquisition. During the meeting at the Helmsley, Maurice spoke at length of the state of the advertising industry, how it was drifting to a global structure and 75 percent of the large clients would prefer one global agency to handle their accounts. Then Maurice embarked on one of his favorite lectures, that clients wanted more from their ad agencies than simply campaigns. They wanted public relations, strategic planning, and corporate design, among other services.

"How much do you want to spend?" Jacoby asked, puffing on a cigar.

"A good price is $250 million," Maurice said, incorporating, of course, the familiar earn-out formula.

The price Jacoby had in mind was $500 million, cash, up front. "I just doubled the price as a way of discouraging him," Jacoby said later. "In January 1985, I wasn't sure I wanted to sell the entire agency. So the conversation sort of deteriorated from there." But Mellor continued to call Hoyne through 1985. "A deal was forming as if it were real," Jacoby said. "But we didn't say we were going to sell it and they didn't say they would buy it."

Finally, it appeared as if Saatchi & Saatchi would give in to all of Jacoby's demands for the sale, except buying the agency entirely for cash. Saatchi & Saatchi wanted some of the payment to be in stock. "No," Jacoby said. "I already have Bates stock. I want some of that green stuff finally."

In January 1986 Mellor told Hoyne that Saatchi & Saatchi agreed to most of those conditions. All that was left, Mellor said, was for Jacoby to come to London to meet with Maurice. (Bob Jacoby would never meet Charles Saatchi.)

On January 9, 1986, in Claridges Hotel in London, Jacoby, Hoyne, Maurice, Mellor, and a Saatchi & Saatchi Company PLC executive in charge of negotiations, Andrew Woods, met in a suite. Maurice Saatchi began by saying the company had been thinking about its price proposal and it had another one in mind. "It became apparent that this conversation was baloney," Jacoby said. "I stopped him immediately and said Hoyne and myself would like to go to the lobby and talk this over." When they got to the lobby, Jacoby turned to Hoyne and said, "This is insane. What am I doing here on a fool's errand? I'm not going back upstairs. John, go get my coat." And Jacoby wanted Hoyne to do one more thing: present Maurice Saatchi with a note written on a hotel card on which Jacoby scribbled the words "$500 million cash." Hoyne retrieved the coat and left the startled Maurice Saatchi with the note.

On April 27, 1986, when Omnicom became the largest ad agency holding group, Jacoby told Hoyne, "Maurice Saatchi has the biggest ego in the ad world. We're going to hear from him." Within days, he did.

Meanwhile, Milton Gossett at Compton was deeply concerned about the rumored talks between Saatchi & Saatchi and Bates. If the two got together, Gossett told anyone who would listen, Procter & Gamble would be displeased since Bates had Colgate-Palmolive as a client. He tried to speak with Maurice Saatchi, but, typically, Saatchi had little time for such a discussion since he never saw any validity in the client conflict argument.

Saatchi & Saatchi wanted to do the deal on Jacoby's terms, even though the price would be more than twice what it had spent on all thirty-seven acquisitions the agency made previously. The company didn't have the money, so it initiated a rights issue of 57.6 million new shares of stock that netted $560 million.

What Saatchi & Saatchi didn't know was that at the same time it was negotiating to buy Bates, Zuckert was conducting parallel discussions with Interpublic Group and its chairman, Phil Geier, and chief financial officer, Eugene Beard. "I don't trust the Saatchis after the last time," Jacoby told Zuckert. But Interpublic wanted to use stock to buy Bates, and Zuckert dismissed that proposal immediately. Interpublic proposed putting out a secondary issue—shares sold to the public—with a guarantee that within ninety days it would buy out the secondary and Bates would get the funds.

"No paper deal," Jacoby said.

"It's guaranteed paper. And it's $10 million more than Saatchi is willing to pay," Zuckert said.

"No cash, no deal," Jacoby said, unmoved.

Zuckert contacted Geier and Beard and said, "You better get the money somehow or else you're going to lose."

Jacoby didn't wait. Four days after the Saatchi & Saatchi deal was signed—but one day before it was made public—Geier and

Beard called Zuckert in his Connecticut home and said, "We've got the money. Let's go."

"You're a day late and a nickel short," Zuckert said. "It's over. We signed with Saatchi."

In the end, Zuckert said, the Interpublic deal was much better. "We would have remained autonomous. No matter what Jacoby said, Saatchi told us that because they're paying all this money up front, we weren't also going to have our autonomy."

With the cash in hand and Jacoby's demands unwavering, the contract was signed in four days. It was announced on May 12, 1986, at Bates headquarters on the twenty-seventh floor of 1515 Broadway in Times Square.

"Saatchi & Saatchi was offering us twenty-two times earnings instead of the market value of agencies, which was ten times earnings," Jacoby said in 1995, recalling the size of the sale. Jacoby would receive $70 million plus another $40 million for his voting shares in the agency. He was also signed to a five-year contract to continue as chairman of Bates that would pay him $1 million annually. At the time of the sale, there were about two hundred stockholders at Bates, with Jacoby the largest. On May 22, 1986, he presented them with great news: Bates's stock book value was $390 a share; Saatchi & Saatchi Company PLC price was $853.02.

Although Jacoby had privately referred to the Saatchi acquisitions as a "Ponzi scheme," he said to reporters when the deal was announced, "I want to thank Maurice and Charles Saatchi for their good taste and foresight." Full-page ads announced the deal in the *New York Times* and newspapers in London. The headline: "The Hardest Sale We Ever Made." The copy said, "As the British know all too well, Americans don't give up their independence easily. So it's with great pride that Ted Bates Worldwide looks forward to becoming part of the world of Saatchi & Saatchi." At the bottom was Ted Bates's signature.

Unnoticed in all the hoopla, sadly, was the single-word response Ted Bates once gave to the question whenever he was asked whether the agency would go public or be acquired: "Never."

On May 16, 1986, Jacoby, still reveling in his new power and wealth, was elected chairman of the American Association of

Advertising Agencies. But the celebration was to be short-lived for everyone: Bob Jacoby, Maurice Saatchi, and Anthony Simonds-Gooding, whom Jacoby described in 1995 as a "nice guy, but nothing more than a beer salesman who never should have been put in charge of the U.S. advertising operations of an advertising company." Milt Gossett was prophetic about the devastating fallout of a Bates acquisition by Saatchi & Saatchi.

Jacoby had kept the negotiations to sell the agency secret from virtually everyone, including some of Bates's longtime clients, who felt betrayed. On June 24, two such Bates clients, Warner-Lambert, with billings of $68 million, and RJR Nabisco, with $96 million, pulled their accounts. And that was only the beginning. Gone by August were Michelob, $38 million; Ralston, $12 million; and McDonald's, with $8 million. Bates also lost about $100 million in Colgate-Palmolive assignments. Procter & Gamble also punished the Saatchi network for the Bates deal by pulling four brands from Saatchi & Saatchi Compton and DFS Dorland Worldwide.

Bates was not only being rocked from the outside, however. A civil war was causing crippling damage internally. Leading the charge against Jacoby were two of his top lieutenants: Donald M. Zuckert, Jacoby's number two at Bates, and Lawrence (Larry) Light, executive vice president and multinational managing director, who had a particularly close relationship to the Mars account and, specifically, to Forrest Mars Jr. Meanwhile, the night before the acquisition was signed, Light refused to sign a Saatchi & Saatchi employment contract, a move that would have jeopardized the entire deal. The price of Light's signature was steep: he wanted the position of president of Bates International. Jacoby acquiesced, tossing aside the person already in the job, John Hoyne, who had negotiated the Bates sale.

Zuckert, who has a law degree from New York University, was widely popular at the agency, which he joined in 1960 as a twenty-five-year-old account manager working on such Warner-Lambert accounts as Trident gum and Certs breath mints. He rose through the ranks to eventually become president of Bates's New York office. After the sale to Saatchi & Saatchi, Zuckert traveled to London for a quick meeting with Simonds-Gooding and to attend the Wimbledon tennis matches. He hadn't yet met either Saatchi brother. "But Jacoby thought I went to London and ratted on him to the Saatchis," Zuckert said in 1995. "For what? To this day, I have no idea." Zuckert can't recall exactly when or why Jacoby turned against him, although he offers one explanation: liquor. Jacoby loved to drink beer or Canadian Club. "Then you'd never know what would happen," Zuckert said.

On the evening of September 3, Jacoby handed his secretary a memo addressed to Zuckert and Light. Then, Jacoby departed for a camping vacation in a remote area of Colorado. He would be, he told his secretary, unreachable. The memo was an announcement of sorts: John Hoyne was named president of Ted Bates Worldwide, senior to Light, and Zuckert was replaced as New York president by John H. Nichols, a forty-nine-year-old tall Texan who had joined the agency in 1985 from Leo Burnett in Chicago. Zuckert hated Nichols and had often ridiculed his suggestions.

Shortly after the memo was circulated to the principals, Nichols entered Zuckert's office. "I'm taking your office," Nichols said. "I want you out of here and on another floor."

"John, you're not doing anything," Zuckert said. "The board of directors hasn't met yet. And Jacoby may have said he is going to do it, but it means nothing."

In an extraordinary example of bad timing, Simonds-Gooding was at Bates on September 4 and ran into Don Zuckert in the hallway. Zuckert let fly a slew of accusations about the agency and about Bob Jacoby. "You guys have done a terrible job in investigating this agency before buying it," Zuckert shouted. "You have a man here [Jacoby] who is disrupting the whole agency, and who is so drunk every afternoon that whatever he told you in the morning changes. He could come back next week and change this memo.

"I'm sick and tired of covering up for him," Zuckert continued, "and of patching things up for him. You can deal with my lawyers. I'm quitting."

(Jacoby would admit that he drank, but not to excess. Advertising, even in the enlightened 1980s, involved drinking. "But I was always able to function," Jacoby said in 1995.)

Simonds-Gooding next walked into the office of John Hoyne

and repeated what Zuckert told him. "Is this true?" Simonds-Gooding asked Hoyne.

"Well, you didn't buy a monastery," Hoyne replied straight-faced.

Simonds-Gooding returned to Zuckert's office, deeply depressed. "I guess this is all true. Why didn't we know this?"

"You didn't do due diligence," Zuckert said. "If you're diligent enough, you'll find doo-doo."

Please give us a week, Simonds-Gooding said to Zuckert. When, after a week, nothing happened, Zuckert packed his belongings from the agency into his car and left. As he drove on the Henry Hudson Parkway heading north out of Manhattan, his car phone rang. It was Light asking Zuckert to meet with him and Simonds-Gooding at the Mayflower Hotel. It was there that Zuckert was offered Jacoby's job as Bates chairman.

Zuckert said he would accept, but he had several conditions: he wanted his appointment approved by the Bates board and not just shoved down its throat, and he demanded that Hoyne and Nichols walk the plank. Simonds-Gooding had no problems with those conditions. Meanwhile, he wanted Zuckert and Light to stay out of sight in the Lowell Hotel and not speak to anyone.

What got Saatchi & Saatchi to move on the Bates affair? After all, Maurice Saatchi wanted to be involved with Bates as much as he wanted to be involved with any of the businesses his company acquired over the years, meaning not that much at all. But then his phone rang. On the line was Forrest Mars Jr. "I guess you don't want our business," Mars said. "We don't like John Hoyne and yet you put him in charge of our business. He never showed up when he was in charge of the international business. And we don't want anything to do with Jacoby. The last time he showed up here, he was drunk. You only want to get rid of the two people we like the best and who have improved our business. I guess you don't want our business." Then Mars hung up.

When Jacoby finally resurfaced on September 10 at the American Association of Advertising Agencies Western Region Convention in Lake Tahoe, Nevada, he called Simonds-Gooding, knowing nothing of the turmoil engulfing his cherished Bates. Simonds-Gooding did nothing to enlighten him. Instead, he said

Saatchi & Saatchi wanted to merge Bates with Compton and Milt Gossett would be in charge.

"You have to be kidding," Jacoby replied. "We have client conflicts. This is a lousy idea. The cultures are also completely different. I worked at Compton for nine years before coming to Bates and I know." Jacoby also reminded Simonds-Gooding that the Bates contract with the Saatchis specifically guaranteed Bates its independence.

The Saatchis could care less what any contract said. Saatchi & Saatchi now owned Bates and it would do what it wanted with its properties, Simonds-Gooding said. "So we're going to do it," Simonds-Gooding continued. "Bates is moving to Hudson Street."

Finally, Jacoby asked the central question: "What am I going to do?"

Nothing at Bates, he was told. Instead, Jacoby would join Simonds-Gooding at Saatchi & Saatchi Company PLC in a senior position. And one more thing: Zuckert and Light would be reinstated and Nichols and Hoyne would be demoted.

The size of Bob Jacoby's ego was epitomized by the portrait of him that hung in the front hallway of Ted Bates. Austere portraits of chief executives and chairmen are not unusual. Jacoby may have sold Saatchi & Saatchi the Bates company, but he would draw the line at his portrait.

Upon his return to New York, Jacoby said, "They're sure as hell not going to hang my portrait on Hudson Street." He bought it, sending a check for $7,000 to Saatchi & Saatchi in London, and gave the painting to one of his daughters. He also declined the offer from Simonds-Gooding. But Simonds-Gooding was true to his word: Jacoby was finished at Bates. Zuckert was named chairman and chief executive officer. Jacoby would spend the next few weeks avoiding Zuckert and Light.

Jacoby left Bates on September 21, 1986, but in the Saatchi & Saatchi tradition, he didn't go quietly. He sued the company for breach of contract and he won, receiving $5 million in damages. A three-member panel of the American Arbitration Association said Jacoby's actions "were not acts having the purpose and effect of materially injuring the reputation, business or business relationships" of Ted Bates Worldwide. The only immediate result for Jacoby was that he had to resign as chairman of the American Association of Advertising Agencies for the obvious reason that he no longer worked for an advertising agency.

In 1986, Maurice and Charles Saatchi were discussing Bob Jacoby, his payment, and the fact that Jacoby was a problem: Charles Saatchi said, "He's got $100 million of our money in his pocket. Cash! God, I'd kill for $100 million. I'd do anything for $100 million."

Maurice replied, "Would you really, Charles? Would you run down Charlotte Street naked for $100 million?"

"I'd do that for $10 million," Charles replied.

Without skipping a beat, Maurice Saatchi said, "I'd do it for a million."

Jacoby may have been a bully and an ingrate, but he was straightforward about his plans for the agency. In this regard, his dismissal may say more about Maurice Saatchi than Bob Jacoby. On August 7, almost a full month before Jacoby wrote the memo making the executive changes, he wrote to Maurice: "Zuckert is a housekeeper and I would have changed his role whether you bought us or not." As important, Maurice not only didn't seem to mind, but verbally patted Jacoby on the back: "We have not come across anyone quite as dynamic and determined as you have been," Maurice wrote to Jacoby. "It is a new experience for us and a very pleasant one."

The Bates affair had a devastating psychological impact on Simonds-Gooding. He wasn't prepared for the bare-fisted rough-and-tumble the Saatchi acquisitions were causing. He had become a traffic cop and parental figure, always having to calm egos of grown children, all of whom were making vast sums of money. Even when the Bates situation was settled, however, the turmoil didn't end for Simonds-Gooding. Since Maurice and Charles Saatchi didn't have a corporate strategy for all the companies they bought, it fell to Simonds-Gooding to make sense of it all. It was out of this need for order that the Big Bang was conceived.

Simonds-Gooding wanted to merge all the agencies, including Compton, Dancer Fitzgerald, Bates, and Backer & Spielvogel to form one huge ad agency under the Saatchi & Saatchi name. The vexing subject of client conflicts would be resolved, Simonds-Gooding told a contentious meeting at the Pierre Hotel on Fifth Avenue in Manhattan. All the clients had to see was that the agency executives endorsed the plan.

But the agency heads didn't endorse the plan. Far from it. And when Milt Gossett and Ed Wax, head of Saatchi & Saatchi Advertising Worldwide, flew to Cincinnati to meet with Procter & Gamble executives, they returned saying the giant package goods company was dead set against the proposal.

That was good news for Gossett and Wax, who weren't pleased that the plan, as outlined by Simonds-Gooding, would have placed Carl Spielvogel as the chief executive of the giant agency. "Gossett held out for co–chief executive," Spielvogel said. "I said that I have never heard of such a position, with two individuals sharing the chairman's role. I said that wasn't acceptable. And he said the proposal was unacceptable. The talks came to a screeching halt." The problem of agencies adrift remained.

Then, in January 1987, Simonds-Gooding called on Spielvogel at Backer & Spielvogel's offices at 11 West 42nd Street. Simonds-Gooding looked completely devastated and exhausted, Spielvogel said. "Carl," he said, "we have a problem. You have to merge with Bates."

"What?" Spielvogel answered. "There's no way we're going to merge with Bates. They're completely different from us. We're creative and Bates is more interested in strategy."

Simonds-Gooding received a similar response from Donald Zuckert. "It's a bad idea," Zuckert said. "But you own us. If that's what you want to do, I'll support you." Further, Simonds-Gooding said Spielvogel would be chairman and Zuckert would be president. Zuckert said he wouldn't stay, however, but he would help with the merger. "Please," Simonds-Gooding said, "we can't stand the bad press of a second chief executive leaving Bates. If you put the merger together and don't speak to the press, we'll pay you everything we owe you." Simonds-Gooding persuaded Spielvogel by basically renegotiating the Backer & Spielvogel acquisition and, Spielvogel said, "upping the ante to make it worth our while."

Seven months after the initial conversation, on July 16, 1987, Ted Bates Worldwide and Backer & Spielvogel merged. Although

Bates was far larger and known around the world, the name of the agency became Backer Spielvogel Bates, much to the dissatisfaction of Bates employees. The resentment over the agency's combined name would continue to fester for seven more years. Carl Spielvogel was named chairman and chief executive of the merged agencies with 104 offices in forty-six countries and $2.7 billion in billings. Donald Zuckert, who was chairman and chief executive of Bates, became president and chief operating officer. Zuckert left Backer Spielvogel Bates on December 31, 1987. "Saatchi & Saatchi was true to its word," he said in his first public remarks since leaving Bates. "They paid me everything they owed me. And I was true to my word."

The month before the merger, on June 21, Dancer Fitzgerald Sample merged with Saatchi & Saatchi Compton to form a combined U.S. unit called Saatchi & Saatchi DFS Compton. It would be the largest agency in New York with billings of $2.3 billion. The consolidation ended Dancer Fitzgerald's relationship with Dorland Advertising, the number-three-ranked London agency.

Some of the characters in Macbates tried a comeback on Madison Avenue. Bob Jacoby, with John Hoyne and John Nichols, attempted a takeover in June 1987 of J. Walter Thompson, America's second oldest agency. But the trio was outbid by Martin Sorrell, the financial genius who left Saatchi & Saatchi in 1986 for Wire & Plastics Products. In May 1985, while still at Saatchi & Saatchi, Sorrell bought a stake, along with stockbroker Preston Rabl, in WPP Group; the two invested £400,000 in exchange for 29.9 percent of WPP. WPP paid $566 million for J. Walter Thompson, or approximately $60 million more than Saatchi & Saatchi paid for Bates. Jacoby, Hoyne, and Nichols also bought shares in Ogilvy & Mather, but ultimately sold them when they encountered resistance to a takeover. WPP Group later paid $825 million to acquire Ogilvy & Mather.

Hoyne would die young, at age fifty-five, on the operating table at the American Hospital in Paris while undergoing treatment for a severe stomach ulcer on May 25, 1993. Nichols retired and in 1995 was living quietly in the southern region of the United States.

Jacoby said he wanted to reenter the advertising industry in large part to seek revenge against the Saatchis. But he never did. He grew to enjoy retirement as an extremely weathly man. "The Saatchis' problems began with their mind-set," Jacoby said in 1995. "They weren't good businessmen. They were flashy self-promotion Barnums. The one thing I found out was that they really didn't like clients.

"They should have bought a widget company where you didn't have to care about the people. The product was important and it would come out the same no matter who produced it. That's not the way it is in advertising."

Zuckert agreed with Jacoby: "[The brothers] had only one goal," he said. "To be number one. They thought client conflicts would be okay just so people could get to work with Saatchi. They had no Americans who knew the American market." Saatchi & Saatchi was never able to transport the creative brilliance they had in the United Kingdom to any of their other shops.

"Carl Spielvogel learned quickly and went public with his opinion that they were amateurs. He wanted to buy the agency back. I'm sure he wanted to be a good soldier and to salute the flag. But there was no flag to salute."

Because of all the activity of merging agencies in the United States, Simonds-Gooding moved along with wife and children to New York from London. But he was seeing far too little of them and he wasn't enjoying his work. In eight of the first nine months of 1987, for instance, Simonds-Gooding clocked sixty-six transatlantic flights. Once the complex and delicate mergers were complete, Simonds-Gooding said he had had enough. On September 23, 1987, he resigned at age fifty to become chairman of British Satellite Broadcasting, a private consortium that planned to provide satellite-delivered programming to the United Kingdom. The project was short-lived and he returned to advertising after a short period. In 1995, Simonds-Gooding was chairman of Ammirati Puris Lintas in London, an agency that is part of the Interpublic Group of Companies, a holding company that also owns McCann-Erickson and Lowe & Partners/SMS. The relationship was short-lived. He quietly left the agency in early 1996.

Analysts said at the time that Simonds-Gooding's departure would have little effect on Saatchi & Saatchi. Said Alan Gottesman, who was then an analyst with L.F. Rothschild, Unterberg, Towbin, "He was a hired gun. They'll hire another gun."

SIMONDS-GOODING said his sudden resignation had nothing to do with a highly secret meeting Maurice Saatchi held in the City on September 9 that would become public September 13 and prove highly embarrassing to Saatchi & Saatchi, the company and the brothers, especially Maurice.

The events of September 9 would have reverberations for months, exposing Saatchi & Saatchi Company PLC as financially vulnerable and making it the subject of unprecedented ridicule.

It would also force Maurice and Charles Saatchi to take inactive roles, moving into the background of the company they cofounded.

CHAPTER
FIVE

IN 1987, SAATCHI & SAATCHI Company PLC recorded its seventeenth year of consecutive growth. Its profits before tax were £124.1 million, up from £70.1 million from the same period a year earlier. Its London agency ranked number one in profits in the United Kingdom. Saatchi & Saatchi Company PLC obtained listings on the Paris Bourse and the New York Stock Exchange. By the end of September, the turmoil involving Bates was subsiding, an achievement credited to Bob Jacoby's removal from the agency and his subsequent departure. The company said its consulting business was poised for growth. The company estimated that by 1990 the total consulting market would be worth approximately $230 billion. Saatchi & Saatchi Consulting established the Center for Competitive Advantage in Washington, D.C.

Still, the brothers weren't satisfied.

Maurice and Charles Saatchi had achieved what they set out to do; now the brothers wanted to enter into a new business, one that they believed would fit perfectly into their advertising and consulting units.

Maurice and Charles Saatchi wanted to buy a bank.

They saw a bank acquisition as a logical extension because, Maurice believed, banking was nothing more than financial services. Saatchi & Saatchi had reached the limit of what advertising could achieve. If one examined the services that companies needed, they would include finances as well as communications.

Steven Winram, an acquisitions manager at Saatchi & Saatchi, answered his telephone one day in June 1987. It was Maurice calling from his home in Cap Ferrat in the south of France. "I want you to do some research on a company," Maurice said, "and if word leaks out on this, you'll lose your job." The company was

Midland Bank. Winram told Saatchi he thought it was an odd establishment for Saatchi & Saatchi to research.

"Don't ask," Saatchi replied.

In fact, Midland wasn't the first financial services institution that Saatchi & Saatchi hoped to acquire. The company had previously considered bidding for Phillips & Drew before Union Bank of Switzerland acquired the British stockbroker in 1985.

Working closely with Winram was Michael Dobbs, a thirty-eight-year-old graduate of Oxford and Harvard, where he earned his Ph.D. In the early 1970s, he worked as a news editor for the *Boston Globe.* He returned to London in 1975 and was hired as a researcher in the Conservative party's central office. Although many in the party admired his skills, Dobbs didn't impress Margaret Thatcher, who felt Dobbs had dispensed less than valuable advice. After the 1979 election, Tim Bell offered Dobbs a job at Saatchi & Saatchi Company PLC as director of corporate communications. In an unusual move, Dobbs worked at the agency, but continued to advise the Conservative party chairman, Norman Tebbit. Dobbs's office was in the company's Lower Regent Street headquarters and it was here that Maurice greeted him on his first day on the job. "We're going to buy Midland Bank," Maurice said.

Midland Bank, the fourth-largest British bank, with 2,100 branches in the United Kingdom and assets of $77 billion, was in bad shape. Its previous international expansion efforts foundered, including its purchase in 1980 of a 57 percent stake in Crocker National Corp. Midland had bought the balance of the California bank holding company shortly after, but sold it to Wells Fargo. Midland also had trouble with Third World loans.

While the Saatchis were considering a run at Midland, Hanson Trust PLC said it purchased a 5.8 percent stake in Midland. Although Hanson said it was an investment, others saw the stake as the beginning of a possible takeover.

The chances of a Saatchi & Saatchi win in a Midland bid were slight, if only considering the numbers. Saatchi & Saatchi stock was valued at less than £1 billion; Midland was capitalized at £2 billion. It would cost Saatchi & Saatchi £4 billion to acquire Midland.

Saatchi & Saatchi's adviser was David Clementi, a merchant

banker with Kleinwort Benson. Clementi said it would be possible for Saatchi & Saatchi to raise that amount by issuing £3 billion of new Saatchi stock and a credit line of another £1 billion.

Clementi, along with Maurice, sought tacit approval from the Bank of England, guardian of the banking sector, and from the Treasury for Saatchi & Saatchi to go ahead with its bid. One person involved with the plan said Saatchi & Saatchi was "given an amber light by the Bank of England because Maurice Saatchi had spoken to the right politicians." A great deal of the work had been done by Touche Ross, which was not the usual accounting firm employed by Saatchi & Saatchi.

In a meeting with two executives at the Bank of England, George Blunden, deputy governor, and Rodney Galpin, director in charge of the banking sector, Maurice and Clementi outlined their plans. Blunden and Galpin were poker-faced. They did not approve or disapprove of the proposal, but said Saatchi & Saatchi should discuss the offer with Midland itself.

There were obstacles on the horizon. New rules were about to take effect that allowed the Bank of England to limit any shareholding in banks to 15 percent; anyone who exceeded that cap without first getting approval from the Bank of England would be determined "not fit and proper" to run a bank. Further, the rules were to be retroactive. Simply put, a hostile takeover of a bank would not be tolerated.

Maurice Saatchi began preparing for his discussion with Midland Bank with an intensity exceeding that of a business pitch to a potential advertising client. It was hard to conceive of the audacious nature of the plan: it was as if the head of an advertising agency in the United States decided to make a bid for Chemical Bank. After Maurice informed the Bank of England of his intentions, the Bank of England briefed Midland's chairman, Sir Kit McMahon. McMahon had decided he wouldn't endorse a bid by Saatchi & Saatchi, but agreed to grant a meeting with Maurice. The meeting was scheduled for September 9, two days before a full Midland board meeting at which McMahon planned to inform the board of Saatchi & Saatchi's interest. He would recommend it reject any interest from Saatchi & Saatchi.

Maurice Saatchi showed up at Midland on the morning of

September 9 and bypassed the main entrance, having been told to go in a small entrance and take a tiny elevator up four floors. Saatchi and McMahon met alone. Saatchi told him of the £1 billion of new capital his company would put into Midland. He also informed McMahon that there would be no changes at the top once the acquisition was completed, that McMahon would continue in his role.

McMahon listened and then told Maurice that some of Midland's depositors "don't want us to be livened up or made more exciting." As far as those companies were concerned, "the duller [Midland] was, the better," McMahon said. "My managers and customers would not find it easy to understand why they were part of an advertising agency." There was also something troubling McMahon about Saatchi's responses. Saatchi offered few details.

Finally, McMahon asked Saatchi a question that would expose all of Saatchi's weaknesses: "What are you going to do about all the Third World debt we have?" Saatchi was stumped. He left Midland shortly after that, depressed and worried. He knew Midland was slipping away.

Two days later, as McMahon had predicted and hoped, the board rejected Saatchi & Saatchi's offer. Maurice tried to talk McMahon into another meeting, but McMahon, fearing a second face-to-face would trigger leaks in the City, politely declined.

Maurice Saatchi, as usual, hadn't followed a policy of full disclosure. Saatchi didn't tell Kit McMahon that on the day of the Midland board meeting, Friday, September 11, he telephoned Sir Robert Clark, chairman of Hill Samuel Group PLC, a merchant bank. Saatchi asked to meet with Clark at once. Clark said through his secretary that he didn't see the need to meet Saatchi; Hill Samuel was satisfied with its advertising. Then, David Clementi, the merchant banker, called and specified what Saatchi wanted: to take over the bank. Hill Samuel was ripe for a takeover. It had earlier put itself in play by conducting merger talks with Union Bank of Switzerland, but those negotiations went nowhere.

Late in the afternoon of September 11, Saatchi and Clark met in the office of David Davies, Hill Samuel's chief executive. The two men listened while Saatchi spun his tale of how beneficial an acquisition by Saatchi & Saatchi would be. As Maurice had told

Midland, the company didn't want to change management at Hill Samuel. Saatchi & Saatchi would put in £200 million in capital and pay a premium close to 20 percent. The offer sounded good.

Over the weekend, news of the Midland offer by Saatchi & Saatchi leaked to the press and the brothers quickly became the subject of unprecedented criticism and ridicule. A Midland spokesman was quoted as saying that the Saatchi proposal carried a "lack of commercial or strategic logic." A British banking analyst said the brothers "appear to be believing their own press clippings. They won't be treated very seriously." Another analyst, Neil Blackley with James Capel & Co., said, "I can't even pretend to see any synergies" between Midland and Saatchi & Saatchi. Emma Hill, an analyst with Wertheim & Co., said, "Here they had just paid a ridiculous sum for Bates, had had difficulties with their consulting, and the next thing you know, Maurice wants to buy a bank." The *Financial Times*'s Lex column concluded that Saatchi & Saatchi "smacked of a firm which had run out of ideas."

The City's reaction was swift. Saatchi & Saatchi share prices fell 6.2 percent in two days. "After news of the bid was leaked, it was a difficult situation," Dobbs said. "It was a painful, confusing time."

In truth, Saatchi & Saatchi Company PLC should have been talked out of the Midland Bank bid by its advisers. But Maurice purposely did not use either of the company's usual advisers, Warburg and UBS. Vanni Treves, the company's attorney at Macfarlanes and the only noncompany employee on the board, said in 1996 that fees, and not prudent advice, were driving advisers. "It was seductive to think of myself as a humble lawyer sitting on the board of Midland Bank. But everyone, early on, should have said, 'Forget it, this ain't going to work.' "

As news broke on the wire services, two of the company's senior executives, Terry Bannister and Roy Warman, received calls from Charles Saatchi. Bannister and Warman were co–chief executives of Saatchi & Saatchi Advertising International, a curious division consisting of everything except the United States.

"Want to pop around, boys?" Charles asked. The two went to his office on Charlotte Street, where Maurice was also waiting.

"What the fuck are you doing?" Bannister said.

"Don't you think it's brilliant?" Charles responded.

"No," Bannister said. "It's crazy."

News of Hill Samuel hadn't leaked out yet and Charles Saatchi informed the two of the plans.

"Who are you going to get to run it?" Bannister asked.

"You two," Charles answered. "You've handled everything we've thrown at you so far."

In 1995, Bannister said that he never believed the brothers would have given the responsibility of running a banking division to himself and Roy Warman. "They just wanted to try out the idea," he said.

On September 17, Hill Samuel's board formally rejected the offer from Saatchi & Saatchi. David Davies said the proposal was "lacking clear commercial advantages to Hill Samuel and terms which the board felt able to recommend to shareholders."

On October 19, the stock market crashed.

Saatchi & Saatchi shares fell by one-third in twenty-four hours. The stock dropped to 548 pence (there are 100 pence in a British pound) in mid-October from 670 in mid-September. Its high in 1987 was 705. There was a drain on cash flow because of the run of acquisitions and that began to eat away at profits.

The fourth quarter of 1987 saw several other troubling events. Anthony Simonds-Gooding left in late September. His successor was, it would turn out, a particularly poor choice: Victor E. Millar, the fifty-three-year-old chairman and chief executive of the Saatchi & Saatchi consulting division who had joined the company in December 1986 from Arthur Andersen & Co., the consulting company, where he was one of the two worldwide managing partners and a member of its executive committee. He had worked at Arthur Andersen his entire adult life, arriving there in 1958. He led the way for Arthur Andersen in the fastest growing area of the industry, information consulting.

"Consultants aren't like normal advertising people," Maurice Saatchi said to Millar in 1986 when he was courting him. "We need someone with a consulting background."

After Simonds-Gooding's sudden departure, Charles Saatchi asked Millar to take over as chairman and chief executive of both Saatchi & Saatchi's consulting and communications groups. "I wasn't anxious to do it," said Millar, who in 1995 was president of AT&T Solutions, the systems-integration and outsourcing business. "But Charles can be very persuasive. He sent about three or four dozen red roses, promised a raise in salary and all that. I said this isn't what I want to do for long, but if it makes sense, I'll do it."

Millar's plans at Saatchi & Saatchi were to build a $1 billion consulting business by acquiring top brand-name consultants such as Bain and Boston Consulting Group. Millar quickly alienated the advertising, or communications, side of Saatchi & Saatchi. "Maurice must have believed that anyone who was in an exalted position at Arthur Andersen must have known something about everything," said Terry Bannister. "But he didn't."

In early 1988, Millar summoned the chief executives of the Saatchi & Saatchi ad agencies in Washington, D.C. He told the group that advertising had stopped growing. It was going to stabilize or decline. It was an unattractive area to invest in. But it did generate cash. The role of the agencies now was to provide the cash to enable him to invest in high-growth industries. Mainly, consulting.

Clearly, this was a serious miscalculation on Millar's part. He had summarily dismissed an entire industry, one from which everyone else in the room made their livelihood. Millar's attitude and philosophy particularly annoyed Roy Warman and Terry Bannister, who had spent their entire professional lives in or connected to the advertising industry. Millar didn't see a difference between the consulting business, which he was so familiar with, and advertising, about which he readily admitted his ignorance. The two businesses made money differently: in consulting, a company spends money, trains individuals, and attracts clients on that basis. In advertising, however, an agency cannot afford to hire employees until after it wins accounts. Worse, Millar told Warman and Bannister that part of his job at Arthur Andersen had consisted of spending £700 million in training and developing employees each year. That kind of budget would kill any advertising agency.

Millar also changed the budgeting process in the advertising agencies to be compatible with that of the consulting companies; that meant revenues were to be projected on the number of personnel in a unit and margins managed by adjusting costs in line with those revenue forecasts. It was, said Millar's detractors, of which there were many, a formula for disaster.

Around this time, Charles Saatchi decided to move Warman and Bannister to the communications division within Saatchi & Saatchi Company PLC and out of Saatchi & Saatchi Advertising International.

"But we need more time here," Bannister told Charles.

"You're wasting your time on a potty little network," Saatchi answered. "Come here and do something important."

The remark shook the two advertising executives. "Charlie Saatchi should have remembered this potty little network, as he called it, accounted for 90 percent of the holding company's profits," Roy Warman said in 1995.

Of course, there was no appeasing Charles Saatchi except by saying yes. Warman and Bannister felt they could at least postpone the inevitable, telling Saatchi they couldn't consider the offer immediately.

In May 1988, Warman and Bannister left for a Saatchi & Saatchi Advertising meeting concerning Pacific Asia. They were just starting a meeting in Singapore on May 12 when the telephone rang. It was Jeremy Sinclair, the leading creative executive at Saatchi & Saatchi, and he was speaking quickly. "I'm sorry, I'm sorry," Sinclair blurted into the phone. "I tried to stop him. I couldn't stop him. He's done it."

"What?" the two wanted to know.

"He's done it," Sinclair said again. "Charlie's done it. He issued a statement appointing you both to the PLC [public company] board."

After telling Sinclair to fax them the press release of their appointment as chief executive officers of the communications division of Saatchi & Saatchi Company PLC, Warman and Bannister considered their next move. They could have refused, which would have made the company look foolish. Instead, they chose to acquiesce to Charles Saatchi's demands. Sinclair denied their recollection, adding that he never apologized.

DAVID NEWLANDS, Saatchi & Saatchi's finance director, who had taken over for Martin Sorrell in October 1986, was the company's Chicken Little, except Maurice and Charles Saatchi hadn't been listening.

"We're going to run out of money, we're going to run out of money," Newlands told Warman and Bannister in 1988 after their appointment to Saatchi & Saatchi Company PLC. "You have to get this through Maurice's head."

The free-spending acquisition binges by Saatchi & Saatchi had caught up to it. The blueprint for disaster had several parts: Saatchi & Saatchi had completed almost every acquisition with the ultimately ill-advised earn-out formula, so the executives of the companies Saatchi & Saatchi were acquiring received handsome payments, usually for five years. But the incentive had been to generate profits and hit a level that had been agreed upon for a larger cash settlement at the end of the earn-out. The Saatchis felt this would be advantageous to them because the executives would have to stay for a defined period of time under Saatchi & Saatchi rule. But once the earn-out was achieved, there was no longer potent motivation for the agencies to perform at a level and pace they had previously.

The company's bottom line was also hurt by over $1 billion in client defections connected to the series of agency acquisitions, including Ted Bates.

Another factor contributing to the financial woes at Saatchi & Saatchi was the slowdown in ad spending in the United States. Throughout the early 1980s, ad spending increased at a predictable double-digit rate. Then, in 1986, it grew to $109.65 billion, up just 7.8 percent from 1985. In 1989, growth would slow further, to 5 percent, with spending totaling $123.93 billion. In 1990, spending would rise only 3.8 percent, well below the gross national product level, to $128.64 billion, and in 1991, ad spending would decline for only the second time in fifty years, according to figures supplied by McCann-Erickson, to $126.40 billion. At the same time, clients began cutting the standard 15 percent compensation received by advertising agencies to as low as 11 percent, and a majority of agencies willingly went along. They had little choice. The acquisitions by Saatchi & Saatchi and other worldwide ad agency holding companies highlighted how much money the agencies were making and clients felt it was excessive.

By 1988, the City had turned on Saatchi & Saatchi; the company couldn't issue the stock it wanted in order to continue its acquisitions.

On June 17, 1988, Saatchi & Saatchi, under the advice of S.G. Warburg, one of its bankers, made a Faustian pact when it agreed to raise money through a method known as the convertible preference share, or Europreference, named for the international investors it targeted. The deal involved a £176.5 million ($316 million) convertible preference share issue. It looked like equity on Saatchi & Saatchi's balance sheet, but it more resembled interest-paying debt to foreign investors. The company immediately used $77.4 million to make a bid for Gartner Group Inc., a Stamford, Connecticut–based research firm known for its computer market forecasts.

At the time, Lorna Tilbian, an analyst with Sheppards in London, said, "It will appeal to a completely new universe of investors, rather than the London investors who are fed up with Saatchi, people like Belgian dentists and Swiss gnomes. Saatchi is as novel in its forms of finance as it is in laying out its strategy."

The Saatchi issue would pay a 6.75 percent annual dividend and was convertible into Saatchi & Saatchi common shares at a price of 441 pence a share starting October 1, 1989. These are called rolling put options, which are designed to encourage investors to retain the shares and eventually convert them into common Saatchi & Saatchi shares. While complex, the consequences of the Euroconvertible were straightforward: if Saatchi & Saatchi's share price didn't go above 441 pence by July 15, 1993, whoever purchased the Euroconvertible had the right to "put" the stock back to the company. Saatchi & Saatchi would be forced to buy the stock back at its original selling price plus a 25 percent bonus. Saatchi & Saatchi potentially owed Europreference holders more than £211 million, or more than $300 million. The seeds were planted for Saatchi & Saatchi to slip into bankruptcy.

The atmosphere resembled the Mad Hatter's Tea Party, said John Perriss, who headed Saatchi & Saatchi's media buying operation. Meetings weren't conducted on the executive floor of Lower Regent Street, the Saatchi & Saatchi Company PLC office. Instead, David Newlands, Roy Warman, and Terry Bannister would retire many afternoons to the Royal Automobile Club, or RAC, where, over beers and a game of snooker, business would be discussed. "Costs were spiraling away and profits disappeared like snow in the spring," said Perriss.

Yet the good times continued in the executive suite: nine of the company's twelve directors received big increases in their stock options. Maurice and Charles more than doubled their share options to 490,909 on September 30, 1988, from 213,529 at the beginning of the fiscal year, October 1, 1987. Maurice's salary was boosted 25 percent to £625,000, or $1.08 million, from £500,000.

All told, Saatchi & Saatchi spent approximately £6.5 million annually on the expenses of Maurice and Charles Saatchi; one year, Maurice alone spent $60,000 on taxis; he threw a party costing $50,000 for the premiere of *Damage*, the movie directed by Louis Malle, based on Maurice's wife Josephine Hart's first novel. The company also took care of costs resulting from such luxuries as Charles Saatchi's penchant for automobiles: he had seventeen, many of which the company maintained.

Saatchi & Saatchi Company PLC was a costly venture itself. It had offices in London, New York, and, because of the consulting unit, Washington. Roy Warman estimated that it cost £30 million annually to operate the holding company.

All these factors contributed to, for the first time, the tarnishing of the Saatchi name. "We were referred to so often as 'troubled Saatchi & Saatchi' that I felt we should have changed the name so that it started with Troubled," said Terry Bannister.

Warman and Bannister approached the brothers with a suggestion: change the name of the holding company from Saatchi & Saatchi to anything else. The reasoning was clear: there was confusion among the agencies, the clients, and the media over Saatchi & Saatchi Company PLC and Saatchi & Saatchi Advertising. And there were other agencies within the Saatchi network, after all. Whenever the holding company got into financial difficulties, its name would be blasted across headlines, thus tainting the reputation of Saatchi & Saatchi Advertising, which continued to do well and satisfy clients. Maurice and Charles would not hear of it, despite the fact that a major client, Procter & Gamble, also wanted a name change. "I will never be chairman of this company while its name changes," said Maurice Saatchi, a declaration he would make over and over in the coming years.

Toward the end of the 1980s, Maurice and Charles Saatchi attempted to renegotiate their employment contracts and pump up their golden parachutes, if the time came for their departure. According to three individuals closely involved in the negotiations, Maurice and Charles Saatchi wanted a revised contract stipulating that if they left the company, they would be paid £1 million apiece for fifteen years in order to prevent the brothers from competing with Saatchi & Saatchi. Vanni Treves, the company attorney and a member of the board, said no. "There is a line in the sand," Treves said in a rare interview in 1996. "You come to a point where you have to say, 'I'm not prepared to go beyond that line. Don't push me as to why I put the line there. I know it is the right place for the line.' " The brothers, their critics said, believed the line could always be moved.

MEANWHILE, OTHER DEVELOPMENTS in the advertising industry were attracting Maurice Saatchi's attention in late 1987 and 1988. Martin Sorrell was making his name as an advertising baron in his own right at WPP. There, Sorrell embarked on a course of action that, at first, didn't threaten the Saatchis: he chose to acquire so-called below-the-line companies, those specializing in all marketing services not covered by traditional print, broadcast, and cable advertising. The rationale to Sorrell's thinking was that companies were beginning to spend less on advertising and more on promotional vehicles such as free samples, in-store discounts, and coupons. Within eighteen months of Sorrell's arrival at WPP in 1986, the company made fifteen acquisitions and its price per share shot up to £11 from about 50 pence.

On June 10, 1987, Sorrell made an unexpected, yet wholly predictable, change in his strategy: he proposed to buy J. Walter Thompson, one of the oldest ad agencies in the United States, and the JWT Group, the parent company. The initial bid was valued at about $460 million and ultimately became Madison Avenue's first hostile takeover. WPP had already accumulated 4.98 percent of JWT stock. Only a week earlier, Don Johnston, JWT chairman and chief executive, said, "We believe it is in the best interest of our people, our clients, and our shareholders to remain independent."

In fact, Thompson was ripe for a takeover, and Sorrell was familiar with Thompson since he and Maurice Saatchi had considered making an offer before. The agency's best days were behind it. Profit margins were 4 percent, well below the industry average. (They were one-third of Bates's profit margins, for instance.) In 1986, JWT had revenue of $641 million and was the fourth-largest ad agency in the United States. There was also instability in Thompson's executive ranks. Joseph O'Donnell, chairman of the Thompson unit and heir apparent to Don Johnston, chairman of the JWT Group, which included entities other than the advertising agency, and the J. Walter Thompson Company, the actual agency, had openly questioned Johnston's ability as an executive.

On the day O'Donnell was supposed to get his seat on the JWT board in February 1987, he met individually with board members and said Thompson could be profitable, if Johnston was no longer involved. O'Donnell also said that the senior management of JWT should take the company private through a management buyout. The board met to consider O'Donnell's proposal, which included ten criticisms of Johnston. Johnston was given a chance to present his side. Within an hour, Joe O'Donnell was fired by the board.

O'Donnell was ultimately correct in his assessment of Johnston. The executive had left JWT vulnerable to a takeover. On June 26, 1987, after two weeks of negotiations, JWT signed a definitive agreement to be acquired by WPP Group for $566 million, or $55.50 per share. But six months after the deal, some of Thompson's problems had only worsened. More than two hundred employees were laid off and the agency lost prestigious accounts, including Burger King, Goodyear Tire & Rubber, Hyatt International, Chevron USA Inc., PepsiCo's Slice brand, and Sears, Roebuck & Co.'s Discover card. WPP's total market capitalization then was $262 million, less than half of the price it paid for JWT.

Sorrell, like the Saatchi brothers, was not about to stop. Two years later, on May 15, 1989, WPP agreed to acquire Ogilvy & Mather for $54 a share, or $864 million, the largest price paid for an advertising agency. The final price was set after offers from

WPP of $45 a share and then $50 were rejected. Ogilvy dismissed the initial offer as "a sales pitch which suffers from serious flaws in business logic."

Kenneth Roman, Ogilvy's chief executive, took the unusual measure of releasing to the media a letter he sent to Martin Sorrell in which he said Sorrell's public characterization of the discussions as friendly was "inaccurate and disingenuous. . . . My conversations with you over the past several months have been the direct result of your persistence and not my interest in your grand scheme." Roman and Sorrell had first met in a New York restaurant in February 1989 at Sorrell's request.

The media didn't embrace what was correctly perceived as the latest British invasion. The *Wall Street Journal* wrote that Sorrell, "along with two fellow Britons named Saatchi, is hammering the final nail in the coffin of the country-clubbing martini-drinking Man in the Gray Flannel Suit," a reference to the 1956 movie starring Gregory Peck as Tom Rath, a suburbanite and war veteran coping with the postwar pressures of family, money, and a new Madison Avenue job.

In order to woo Ogilvy & Mather, co-founded in 1948 by Madison Avenue legend David Ogilvy, WPP considered changing its own name to Ogilvy. But that idea was quickly abandoned because it would have raised the same issue that was a constant source of friction at Saatchi & Saatchi: whether an ad agency should be owned by a holding company with the same name.

Although David Ogilvy retired in 1975 and was living in a twelfth-century château south of Paris, he still commanded the attention of his former agency. And David Ogilvy's wish was to keep that agency independent. "It took me forty years to build this damn thing up," Ogilvy said at the time the acquisition talks surfaced. "I got my clients and this little jerk buys them." Ogilvy was even more emphatic about Martin Sorrell when he spoke with the *Financial Times:* "God," he said, "the idea of being taken over by that odious little shit really gives me the creeps. He's never written an advertisement in his life." (The *Financial Times* altered Ogilvy's remark to "odious little jerk," a change Ogilvy would later complain about.)

That assessment was quite a departure for Ogilvy, who had a reputation for unequaled class. Educated at Oxford, Ogilvy had been an assistant chef in the Hotel Majestic in Paris; he later sold stoves door to door in his native Scotland. Because he was the biggest stove seller in the company, he was asked by management to write a sales manual. He was good at it and thought advertising would be the next logical step. His first advertising job was at Mather & Crowther, who liked him so much that they, along with S.H. Benson Ltd., put up the capital for Ogilvy's own New York agency in 1948.

In the end, Sorrell courted Ogilvy himself, the executive who created the "man from Schweppes" ads, and whose agency invented the Hathaway man, a model who would wear a patch over one eye. Ogilvy was offered the position of nonexecutive chairman of WPP, a job he accepted; he then blessed the acquisition. At the final board meeting on May 15, 1989, many Ogilvy board members wore red suspenders, a trademark of the agency's founder.

Meanwhile, Charles Saatchi was growing increasingly concerned over WPP Group's growth and ability to deftly acquire ad agencies. Before the Ogilvy & Mather deal was approved, Charles telephoned his former colleague Martin Sorrell and said they should get together. The two met for afternoon tea at Fortnum & Mason, the renowned emporium on Piccadilly. Saatchi arrived wearing a bulky leather outfit; Sorrell was dressed in his usual suit and tie. Saatchi asked Sorrell if he was "wired" and Sorrell replied that if anyone would be, it was Charles since his attire could easily mask such a device.

Saatchi next got down to business: he wanted to merge WPP Group with Saatchi & Saatchi, drop the WPP name, but have Sorrell run the business. Sorrell instantly declined the offer, citing, among other reasons, client conflicts. Saatchi & Saatchi represented Procter & Gamble and Toyota; WPP's clients included Unilever and Ford. Besides, Sorrell said, "I've grown attached to the business."

And Charles Saatchi and Martin Sorrell would have virtually no contact after that lunch. That is, until the fall of 1995 when Charles telephoned Sorrell in a rage; Saatchi had been told that Sorrell had been whispering sinister stories to the *Wall Street Journal's* Advertising columnist concerning the financing of Saatchi's art collection. Saatchi told Sorrell to cease. Sorrell was more amused than intimidated.

CHAPTER
SIX

By MARCH 1989, Chicken Little had had enough. David Newlands, Saatchi & Saatchi's finance director, who would tell anyone who would listen, which meant nobody, that Saatchi & Saatchi Company PLC was about to run out of money, resigned on March 2 to join General Electric Co. PLC in London, a company that has no connection with General Electric in the United States. Newlands, who was respected in the City, had argued to the brothers that he should become chief executive of the group following the resignation of Anthony Simonds-Gooding. But there was no chance Newlands would receive the top position. By then, Newlands was openly dismissive of Maurice Saatchi and the job went to Victor Millar. (Others said Newlands resigned because he could not deliver profits he had promised.)

And with his solid relations with the banking community, Newlands was thought of by the brothers as a threat, someone who could possibly take their company away from them.

Newlands knew what he was leaving. He told at least one associate privately that there are usually three telltale signs a company has hit bottom: it takes on a lease in a new building that it names after itself, it signs all board directors to long-term contracts, and it buys a corporate jet. In truth, Maurice and Charles Saatchi didn't care for traveling, so a corporate jet was never anything on the brothers' acquisition list. But after Newlands left, the financial state of the company was so precarious that Charles Saatchi actually attended his first board meeting.

After Newlands's departure, Maurice and Charles didn't appoint a permanent replacement as finance director. The brothers weren't looking for strength when it came to filling Newlands's role: "If we bring in a strong finance director, we will lose the company," Charlie Saatchi said to Terry Bannister. Instead, Andrew Woods, chairman of Saatchi & Saatchi Holdings (USA), was made Newlands's temporary replacement. Woods was a forty-two-year-old former merchant banker hired by Saatchi & Saatchi from County Bank in 1985. At the time, he worked in an office Saatchi & Saatchi had established in the General Motors Building on Fifth Avenue in Manhattan. His mission had been to seek out companies for Saatchi & Saatchi to acquire.

Woods's tenure in his position wasn't pleasant. Time after time, he tried to get the brothers to focus on the financial morass. "If you don't want to listen and begin to act responsibly," Woods told them more than once, "then fire me." Woods would resign from the company eight months after succeeding Newlands.

Newlands's departure, meanwhile, caught the attention not only of the City, but of finance executives within the company, including Wendy Smyth, a management accountant. Smyth, a petite, serious individual with strong convictions and a disdain for Maurice Saatchi, joined Saatchi & Saatchi in December 1982 in the United States when she was twenty-nine. Prior to that, she had been an accountant with KMG Thomson McLintock. She was brought on board by Martin Sorrell when Saatchi & Saatchi was working its deal with Compton "because I was the only U.K. person in the U.S. who worked on the account side." Smyth worked for Compton for a year in New York and then Sorrell brought her back to London in 1986 as finance director of Saatchi & Saatchi Advertising International; in 1989, Smyth began to see what Newlands was talking about. "The communications businesses were doing okay," she said, "but not providing the sort of growth that was needed for profits."

Each year the annual report opened with a Chairman's Statement from Maurice Saatchi and each year the chairman was pleased to report another year of growth for Saatchi & Saatchi Company PLC, its "fill in the blank" year of uninterrupted growth. Until, that is, the annual report for the fiscal year ended September 30, 1989.

In 1988, profits before tax increased 11 percent to £138 million. In 1989, they plummeted to £21.8 million. Losses were mounting. In 1988, the company paid $115.4 million in deferred payments and reorganization costs related to the merger of its agency networks. In fiscal 1989, the amount was £78.3 million. In fiscal 1989, purchases, less sales of tangible fixed assets, registered a cash outflow of £58.6 million, compared with a cash outflow of £79.4 million a year earlier; acquisitions of subsidiaries resulted in a cash outflow of £24.8 million, compared with £129.1 million a year earlier; and deferred consideration and reorganization costs paid resulted in a loss of £78.3 million, compared with £115.4 million in the year-earlier period.

Saatchi & Saatchi's low point came at Claridges on Brook Street in London at noon on March 21, 1989. The setting was Saatchi & Saatchi's annual shareholders meeting. It was, Maurice said later, "the very worst moment of my career."

He began with the good news: Saatchi & Saatchi Advertising, with worldwide billings of $10 billion, was doing fine. It remained the number one advertising company in the world.

Then, Maurice delivered a profit warning, something he had never done before. "Total group profits," he said early in his address to shareholders, "will be below those of last year."

After eighteen consecutive years of profit growth, the ride was over. Reaction was swift. Within one hour of the news out of Maurice's mouth, Saatchi & Saatchi's share price dropped 60 pence, to £3.20.

Shortly after Maurice Saatchi delivered the bad news, Kemper Financial Services in Chicago, a major institutional investor, sold approximately 500,000 shares of Saatchi stock. In less than two weeks after the shareholders meeting, Saatchi & Saatchi's American Depository Receipts—negotiable instruments traded on U.S. exchanges that represent shares of foreign stocks—fell to $14.50 from $20.

If there was going to be a bright spot in the widening Saatchi & Saatchi Company PLC portfolio, it probably was not going to come from the unpredictable advertising industry, despite the solid performance of Saatchi & Saatchi Advertising. Instead, it would come from a decidedly less glamorous area.

Quietly, Saatchi & Saatchi had tapped another profitable market and amassed an envied and respected division within its communications unit: media buying. Clients not only need advertisements to be created, they also need the ads placed throughout the media, which requires a different kind of expertise. A company needs to know where best to put ads and how to negotiate the best rates. After Ted Bates was acquired, John Perriss, a deputy managing director at Saatchi & Saatchi Advertising in London whose background was media planning, suggested in a note to Maurice dated June 9, 1986, that all the media buying units of the disparate agencies merge to form a single giant division. The advantage, Perriss said, was that the giant unit, packed with blue-chip, large-spending clients, would have greater clout negotiating rates. The theory was sound, since increasingly clients were splitting accounts between advertising agencies and outside media buying companies, such as Western Media International in Los Angeles or DeWitt Media in New York. To counter the loss in business, advertising agencies began establishing their own, separate media buying companies.

Perriss's suggestion wasn't immediately embraced. Carl Spielvogel said, "If you think this is such a good idea, why not leave us out of it and fuck up your own backyard?" Eventually, Spielvogel was won over and on October 14, 1988, Zenith Media opened for business in the United Kingdom with clients from Saatchi & Saatchi Advertising and Backer Spielvogel Bates. Zenith wasn't the first choice for a name, especially since individuals still associated the name with television sets and radios. Meridian had been rejected, as was Paramount. "We wanted something that sounded global and at the top," Perriss said.

Zenith resonated well to Perriss. The only problem was a television production studio in London named Zenith that was objecting to Saatchi & Saatchi using the name. Fortunately, Perriss discovered, it was owned by Michael Green, one of Charles Saatchi's oldest and closest friends. Perriss telephoned Charles and asked him to intervene.

"Why aren't you calling it Saatchi & Saatchi Media Buying?" Charles asked.

Perriss explained he purposely wasn't using Saatchi because he wanted to attract non-Saatchi accounts.

"I think your idea sucks," Charles shot back. "It's outrageous that you're not calling it Saatchi . . . I don't care the fuck what you call the company if you don't call it Saatchi."

In the end, Green, without the help of Charles Saatchi, put aside his objection. Zenith Media was an instant success.

The same couldn't be said for the moribund consulting businesses. The consulting unit's revenues had been expected to increase 80 percent, but they were up only 32 percent in 1989 to $248.5 million from $188.4 million for the same period a year earlier. Costs, meanwhile, were skyrocketing. The Hay Group, once considered the crown jewel in Saatchi & Saatchi's consulting arena, was "significantly underperforming." Hay invested heavily in training and methodology, gearing up for new business before it had any.

Maurice Saatchi would need better news by September 1989 when the company released its interim results.

It was against this backdrop that he asked to see Roy Warman and Terry Bannister in his office on Lower Regent Street. Layoffs had to be carried out, he told them. But each dismissal had to be carefully considered. In order for the procedure to make any sense financially, those being let go had to make "above average salaries," Warman said. "That meant we had to carefully consider each person before sacking them."

It was a long, arduous, and painful process for Warman and Bannister. Others said the duo fired no one; the task instead was carried out by Bill Muirhead, chairman of Charlotte Street, and Paul Bainsfair, managing director. For Maurice, however, it was merely taking too long. So he summoned Warman and Bannister for another meeting. Maurice began by telling the two executives that he had recently read a book by then–Chrysler chairman Lee Iacocca. When the former Ford Motor executive arrived at Chrysler, he found costs out of control and had to institute cost-cutting measures, including layoffs. Iacocca, Maurice said, carried out this unpleasant task by having subordinates stand at the doors of Chrysler and fire every tenth person. "I want you to do that here," Maurice said.

Warman and Bannister were astonished. "Don't be ridiculous," Warman responded. "What if we're in the lobby of Charlotte Street and one of your buddies like Jeremy Sinclair or Bill Muirhead happens to be the tenth person? Should we sack them?"

Of course, Sinclair and Muirhead and every other senior Saatchi & Saatchi executive were spared being fired. Nevertheless,

Saatchi & Saatchi, between January and May 1989, laid off 6 percent of its workforce, eight hundred out of fourteen thousand employees. It would be the first in a series in layoffs that would ultimately reach seven thousand.

There was some grumbling within Saatchi & Saatchi that the outside world was overreacting to events within the ailing company. Victor Millar, chairman of Saatchi & Saatchi's communications and consulting divisions, said publicly, "When you're a high-profile company and you take some pride in crowing about your achievements, you have to be able to take some blows. . . . I'm not griping. I just want to make it clear that we're not in a desperate situation."

Less than one month after Millar's statement, Saatchi & Saatchi shuffled top management. Millar was removed from the position of chairman and chief executive of the communications unit, although he remained chairman and chief executive of the consulting unit. The company gave Andrew Woods, Saatchi & Saatchi's finance director, the additional role of deputy chairman of the consulting division. Publicly, Millar said he was "very supportive" of the move. He didn't want to run both divisions anyway. "I came . . . to run consulting; that is my first love," he said. "My background is not in advertising." Roy Warman and Terry Bannister, joint operations directors at the communications group, became chief operating officers of Saatchi & Saatchi with overall responsibility for communications and consulting. Warman and Bannister were hardly fans of Millar. "Victor was of the view that the consulting business was going to be the entire company," Warman said.

Shortly after the disastrous March shareholders meeting, Warman and Bannister traveled to New York with Millar to have breakfast with an analyst at Merrill Lynch, which was then a large investor in Saatchi & Saatchi. Although the three Saatchi & Saatchi executives hadn't rehearsed, they had decided that the answer to the analyst's predictable question, "Was the company still interested in doing diluted acquisitions?" would be an unqualified no.

Over coffee, the analyst laid out a favorite theory: a doomsday scenario caused by a global recession. He wondered if Saatchi & Saatchi had planned for such a possibility, which, predictably, it hadn't.

Then the analyst asked, "Are you still interested in diluted acquisitions?"

"Yes," Millar responded.

Merrill Lynch sold its investment in Saatchi & Saatchi by noon. Referring to Millar, the Merrill Lynch analyst later said to Warman and Bannister, "I feel sorry for you guys. I don't know what you're going to do."

Neither did Maurice Saatchi, although everybody else appeared to know a way out of the financial morass that the company had become: above all, Saatchi & Saatchi was an advertising company; it should return to its roots and sell off the consulting division. Maurice would not hear of it even after he was told that if the consulting division weren't sold, the company would run out of money a lot sooner.

Maurice told investors that the company was number one in advertising and that the acquisition phase was over. Not surprisingly, he said, costs had been growing ahead of revenue and the costs were too high. In fact, the 1989 fiscal first-half interim results were awful, showing pretax profits plunging 57 percent to $36.6 million from $85.6 million a year earlier. Earnings in the consulting business in the first half of the fiscal year fell 13 percent to $11.6 million from $13.3 million for the same period a year earlier. In November 1989 Maurice Saatchi finally conceded, "Consultancy, from the stock market's point of view, proved to be a liability from day one."

Since the March annual meeting, the company was reviewing strategy for the consulting business in order to enhance shareholder values. "Although the good growth prospects in the consulting industry have been confirmed by increased revenues this year," Maurice told investors, "we believe it is inappropriate under current market conditions to maintain our aim for world market leadership in this sector." On June 14, 1989, without first informing the employees of Saatchi & Saatchi, the company announced it would sell its entire consulting division. Having spent a total of $250 million for the consulting businesses, Saatchi & Saatchi hoped it would fetch $420 million to $458 million.

Even then, Maurice Saatchi wouldn't let go entirely. Although the company hoped to sell the businesses within six months, Maurice said he wouldn't "exclude the possibility" that Saatchi &

Saatchi might continue to hold minority stakes in the businesses. The first consulting company to leave the Saatchi & Saatchi umbrella was Gamma International, a small French concern specializing in information software; it was sold to Le Group André for $11.9 million.

Andrew Woods was removed as finance director after only three months on the job and was assigned the task of working with the Blackstone Group, an investment banking firm, on floating the consulting unit as a separate company. Maurice said, "In due course, a new finance director will be appointed."

Amidst the tumult, Maurice and Charles Saatchi made their boldest move yet: in June 1989, they moved Saatchi & Saatchi Company PLC from shabby and ordinary offices on Lower Regent Street to a luxurious granite building called Lansdowne House on the south side of Berkeley Square. The company was signed to a twenty-five-year lease that actually took effect in 1988. Berkeley Square, within walking distance of the Ritz Hotel and Caprice, one of Princess Diana's favorite eateries, was truly one of the most charming spots in Mayfair. Quiet, bordered by so many two-hundred-year-old plane trees the sky was barely visible, Berkeley Square commanded some of the highest real estate prices in London.

Lining the square were showrooms for Rolls-Royce and Bentley as well as the Clermont Gambling Club. In the building's basement was Annabel's, a discreet private nightclub.

Though Saatchi & Saatchi Company PLC only occupied one floor—the seventh, which was, of course, the top floor—the brothers negotiated to have the name Saatchi & Saatchi adorn the front of the building in big black block letters. Critics of the brothers resented this act of audacity for several reasons: for one, it cost the company a onetime payment of £70 million for the name placement. Another reason was the name itself. Only on Berkeley Square would the name merely be Saatchi & Saatchi; excluded were "Company PLC" and "Advertising." It was as if the building were a monument to the brothers themselves. The holding company wasn't even the building's principal tenant. That was Glaxo, a pharmaceutical company, which was locked out of having its name over the building's entrance.

It was, of course, a ludicrous and ill-timed move, hitting some employees in Saatchi & Saatchi's vast network as a slap in the face. Others, however, saw it as the ultimate sign of confidence that all was well in the company. Maurice and Charles continued to treat the public company as a small family-run business. The company was on the skids, yet its two founders, along with the holding company employees, decamped in the most expensive real estate in the West End.

There was another proposal that could have softened the blow and helped the company's ailing bottom line. The Canadian real estate developer Olympia & York held intense and protracted discussions with Saatchi & Saatchi Advertising about moving the Charlotte Street office to Canary Wharf, a huge development on the Thames in southeast London that is a stark departure from London's skyline. Sleek, with soaring towers, the Canary Wharf complex resembles the World Financial Center in New York. At the time of the discussions, Olympia & York, owned by the Reichmann family in Toronto, was having difficulty attracting tenants. In a city that already suffered permanent traffic gridlock, Canary Wharf was quite a hike. Eventually, companies such as the *Telegraph* and the Mirror Group, which owns the *Daily Mirror* and *The Independent* newspapers, and Ogilvy & Mather, the advertising agency owned by Martin Sorrell's WPP Group, moved to Canary Wharf.

Olympia was so anxious to sign Saatchi & Saatchi that it agreed to take over the company's surplus office spaces in New York, including old offices of Bates, Rowland Company, Dancer Fitzgerald Sample, and Backer & Spielvogel.

Bill Muirhead, who then was chairman of Saatchi & Saatchi Advertising on Charlotte Street, was dispatched to Canary Wharf, which was still under construction. "In the year 2000 this may be the place to be," Muirhead told his associates and superiors. "But now, getting here would be a hardship on many of our employees, and some may quit rather than be forced to come here every day." Saatchi & Saatchi then extracted a commitment from Olympia to pay each Charlotte Street employee one year's salary after two years of working at Canary Wharf. It was agreed by Terry Bannister and Roy Warman and virtually all of the senior executive staff that the company had to agree to this deal; it was too rich to pass up.

The Saatchi brothers also endorsed the deal. "We were going to be paid a lot of money, thirty million pounds up front, and we needed that money," Maurice Saatchi said later. "I was very enthusiastic about it. But the Charlotte Street employees were against it. In the United Kingdom, the clients come to visit the agency, not the other way around. We thought we would lose a lot of people if we moved to Canary Wharf."

As if to ensure that Saatchi & Saatchi Advertising would stay put, an article appeared in the London *Sunday Times* detailing the incentives Olympia was generously giving to Saatchi & Saatchi to snag it for Canary Wharf. Although it could not be proven, it was pretty much assumed that Bill Muirhead had had a conversation with the paper regarding the Canary Wharf situation.

The following day, representatives of the Reichmann family walked into the offices of Saatchi & Saatchi and said, "We don't do business this way." The deal was off. Talks resumed several weeks later, only to finally fall apart for good because the Reichmann family grew nervous over the financial health of Saatchi & Saatchi and feared the company would go bust.

The scuttling of the advantageous deal for Saatchi & Saatchi coincided with a painful and inevitable decision: for the first time the company had to bring in an outsider in order to get out of its financial morass. Maurice held regular meetings in Berkeley Square with David Binding, the company secretary, Wendy Smyth, Roy Warman, Terry Bannister, and Tim Jackson, the head of investor relations, to review the company's financial performance and how to get costs down and improve operating margins. It was understood that Saatchi & Saatchi Company PLC needed someone with international experience; the brothers needed to install a chief executive quickly, before the banks imposed one.

During this period, Charles Saatchi called Tim Bell, his old-friend-turned-nemesis. Over coffee, Saatchi told Bell that the company had hit a rough patch and new management was needed. Would Bell consider coming back and running the show as chief executive of the entire company?

Bell considered the offer—it was what he wanted all along—but he had one condition: he might take the job if Michael Dobbs were tossed out and "hung by his toenails from a lamppost in

Berkeley Square." By this time, Dobbs was a best-selling novelist, and in his first book, *House of Cards*, a character who seemed to be modeled after Tim Bell was found dead in the bathroom of a highway rest stop with a hypodermic needle protruding from his arm. (Dobbs was only working part-time at Saatchi & Saatchi by then in order to concentrate on his fiction writing.)

The talks eventually led nowhere, not because of Dobbs, but because Bell discovered the brothers were talking to other candidates, including Sir Christopher Bland, a respected executive with London Weekend Television. Finally, Maurice focused on Robert Louis-Dreyfus, a forty-three-year-old entrepreneur who is a member of one of the wealthiest families in France and who, until 1988, ran the pharmaceutical market research concern IMS International. Saatchi & Saatchi had previously tried to buy IMS and Maurice remembered its impressive chief executive. Maurice reached Louis-Dreyfus in Davos, a ski resort in the Swiss Alps, and, during one telephone conversation, said, "We have good assets. My brother and I want to pull back and focus on the clients."

Only one-third of that was true. Under the proper financial guidance, Saatchi & Saatchi Company PLC could recover and maintain its position as a potent force in advertising. But Maurice, at least, wanted to pull back on a temporary basis only. He wanted a sophisticated financial executive to fix what he, his brother, and their strategy had wrecked; then he wanted the company back. And, of course, Maurice and Charles still didn't care to focus on clients, although they each had favorites they would lavish attention upon. Maurice kept close tabs on Procter & Gamble, British Airways, and Mars, while Charles reviewed all the creative work on Silk Cut, the cigarette brand, and British Airways.

Maurice's secret desire to snare Saatchi & Saatchi once it was put back on a sound financial track was one factor that made Robert Louis-Dreyfus the preferred candidate. Louis-Dreyfus is a sprinter, not a marathon runner. Once Louis-Dreyfus made it clear he didn't intend to stay long after he completed his mission at Saatchi & Saatchi, Maurice lunged.

"It was always clear that Robert was a Mr. Fix-It," said Wendy Smyth, Saatchi & Saatchi's financial officer.

Louis-Dreyfus was a Paris-born, Harvard Business School–educated executive, with a keen sense of humor and an equally honed perception of human nature. Tall with a crop of curly brown hair and eyes that sparkle and crinkle when he smiles, which is often, Louis-Dreyfus epitomized French charm, frequently groping for the proper English word that fit what he was trying to convey. He possessed a self-deprecating manner, often mocking his lack of business skills and the damn good luck of his successes. He eschewed suits and ties, preferring jeans and colorful plaid flannel shirts. He dated Kim Basinger for a brief time.

Louis-Dreyfus, born June 14, 1946, left an upper-class home at age seventeen. His father was the second-generation owner of S.A. Louis-Dreyfus et Cie, once France's largest private firm and one of the world's largest grain trading companies. In 1995, at age eighty-eight, Jean Louis-Dreyfus took the Metro to the office every day near the Arc de Triomphe.

The senior Louis-Dreyfus refused to invite his son into the business upon his graduation from the Harvard Business School, but Robert found work at S.G. Warburg, an investment firm. After that, he joined his father in 1974, staying there eight years before moving to IMS, where he was appointed chief executive officer in 1984 and negotiated its sale to Dun & Bradstreet in 1988. Within four years of Louis-Dreyfus's arrival, IMS grew sevenfold. When he joined IMS, its market capitalization was $230 million. In 1988, Dun & Bradstreet purchased IMS for $1.7 billion. Louis-Dreyfus walked away with $10 million.

The first contact Robert Louis-Dreyfus had with the brothers was when Saatchi & Saatchi was on one of its acquisition binges and tried to buy IMS in 1987. Martin Sorrell, who conducted all the financial deals for Saatchi & Saatchi Company PLC, met Louis-Dreyfus at the Connaught Hotel. He later met with Maurice Saatchi a few times at Saatchi & Saatchi Company PLC headquarters, which was housed at 15 Lower Regent Street.

But he wasn't interested in selling because Louis-Dreyfus, a shrewd business professional, didn't like the looks of the Saatchi & Saatchi financials. Then, in June 1989, Louis-Dreyfus received a call at his home in Zurich from Maurice. Louis-Dreyfus was retired then, having completed the sale of IMS, and wasn't interested in an overture from the Saatchi brothers. "But the problem with retirement," said Louis-Dreyfus, "is that all your friends aren't retired. So if you want to play tennis, you have to play the coach."

And playing tennis with the coach wasn't what Louis-Dreyfus had in mind when he retired from the professional world. So he was ripe for seduction when the courtship by Maurice Saatchi began. There was no more ardent suitor than Maurice Saatchi. In one year alone, he spent close to $9,000 on flowers. Not only to clients, mind you, but to government ministers who happened to change jobs, and to staff for birthdays.

By the time the brothers set their sights on Robert Louis-Dreyfus, they had moved the offices of the holding company, Saatchi & Saatchi Company PLC, to Berkeley Square from Lower Regent Street. Robert Louis-Dreyfus was thus invited to the company's Berkeley Square headquarters. He walked on the marble floor through the soaring atrium to the exposed elevator and into a world of white.

Maurice and Charles Saatchi are minimalists when it comes to office decor. The walls were a startlingly bright white. The floor was divided: half for the brothers and a conference room, the other half for the sixty or so employees who worked as the holding company staff.

The brothers "talked with charm about a partnership," Louis-Dreyfus said. They had to. They were desperate. Saatchi & Saatchi Company PLC had fallen into deep financial trouble. The culprit was Maurice. Whereas Charles was content with supremacy in London, Maurice had grander designs; he wanted to be the largest in the world. And while Charles was satisfied focusing on advertising, Maurice wanted to expand the portfolio. Everything became fair game for the Saatchi empire, including consulting firms. Globalization was the buzz word of the time.

It took close to a dozen face-to-face meetings at Berkeley Square to come to an agreement, and on October 12, 1989, Robert Louis-Dreyfus was named chief executive officer of Saatchi & Saatchi Company PLC, succeeding Maurice, who remained as chairman. Charles would continue on the board, which hardly mattered; Charles never attended a board meeting. It was part of the well-orchestrated mystique to portray Charles Saatchi as a recluse when, in reality, he led quite an active social life. Steve Martin, the actor and playwright, was one of his closest friends, as was Mick Jagger.

Louis-Dreyfus, however, didn't do his homework. "I didn't check with the auditors," he said. "I took the brothers at their word. I thought the job would be fun." He would be proven horribly wrong on both counts.

Louis-Dreyfus brought with him an old friend and colleague from IMS, Charles Scott, to be finance director, filling a crucial position that had been vacant for months. Scott wore baggy, unkempt suits, drove a modest Toyota, and loved playing soccer. His grandfather Charles and father, Charles, were officers in the oldest Scottish regiment, the Black Watch. Charlie Scott says with some pride that his grandfather is one of the few who got "to go out at the start of World War I and return at the end. That's unusual. Most were killed."

Scott, a large man whose head was topped by a small, neat crop of gray hair that made him look older than he actually was, and who had a wide grin that made his otherwise shy personality appealing, described himself as an "army brat." He was born in Scotland but his family quickly relocated to Germany, where he spent the first five years of his life. He then moved with his family, including a brother, to Scotland, to Africa, and to Cyprus.

From his very early years, Charlie Scott gravitated to numbers. "I always did well in math on intelligence tests," Scott said, "and I found numbers quite enjoyable. There was always something to solve. And the answers were tangible and measurable."

Yet accounting wasn't Scott's first choice. Professional soccer was. But early on Scott realized he was kicking at windmills and chose a safer profession. Although in disarray on the outside, Charlie Scott had sophisticated taste in some things, such as food. He loved Clark's, for instance, a tiny restaurant in Hampstead, in walking distance of his apartment in Camden Hill, that each evening served the same meal to everyone. And he loved wine. He could consume almost an entire bottle by himself during dinner.

Scott was admirable in that he was incapable of telling a lie;

indeed, he would probably break out in hives if he did. That was in contrast to Maurice Saatchi, who perfected the art of conjuring up a whopper in a matter of seconds that would not register on a lie detector.

Scott was a simple man; he found tremendous pleasure in getting together with pals for a tennis match or spending the evening with a small circle of friends. But he wasn't an executive to run a worldwide advertising agency. Scott was basically uncomfortable with people, a characteristic that was at odds with what was needed to run what was in effect a people business.

Advertising executives perfected the three-martini lunch for a reason. Other than to create ads, their main function was to entertain and appease clients, to take them to lunch, to socialize, to take their psychological temperature.

Once, Burt Manning, chairman of J. Walter Thompson, was stranded with dozens of advertising executives at a remote airport in Virginia because a jet had engine problems. It would take an additional seven hours to return to New York. Manning marched into the airport's only office and emerged minutes later having chartered an eight-seater private plane to fly him and his wife—and selected guests—back to New York. Why the hurry? Manning was scheduled to take a client and his wife to the theater that evening.

But Scott would rather toil in the background and allow others to schmooze clients. Little wonder. Scott personifies the textbook image of an accountant, a likable nerd, but little match for sophisticated business executives such as Maurice Saatchi. Scott was trained as an accountant and worked in the United Kingdom for Itel Corp., eventually becoming its finance director. In 1977, he joined IMS International, where he became chief financial officer.

It was at IMS that Scott met Robert Louis-Dreyfus.

On October 12, 1989, Robert Louis-Dreyfus agreed to join Saatchi & Saatchi Company PLC along with Charlie Scott, who was named finance director. The appointments were effective January 1, 1990, and the three-month lag concerned analysts, who felt the company needed immediate attention. Scott, too, thought Saatchi & Saatchi would be fun. But, while "popping in" on the company shortly after he decided to quit IMS, Scott bumped into

Maurice (left) and Charles Saatchi in the early days of Saatchi & Saatchi. Maurice was the front man, while Charles played the recluse, once pretending he was a janitor and dropping to his knees to polish a doorknob in order to avoid an introduction to a client.

Michael Heseltine, a partner in Haymarket Publications, one of Maurice Saatchi's first employers. Lindsay Masters, one of Heseltine's partners, was an early investor in Saatchi & Saatchi Advertising, as were Mary Quant, the designer of the miniskirt, and her husband, Alexander Plunket-Greene. Heseltine wanted to invest but couldn't, since he had just become a government minister.

Would you be more careful if it was you that got pregnant?

Anyone married or single can get advice on contraception from the Family Planning Association
Margaret Pyke House, 27-35 Mortimer Street, London W1N 8BQ Tel. 01-636 9135

Two of the advertisements that put Saatchi & Saatchi Advertising on the map. The so-called pregnant man ad, written by Jeremy Sinclair in 1970, became an icon of sorts for the agency. The "Labour Isn't Working" ad for the Conservative party was credited by many with propelling Margaret Thatcher into power as Prime Minister. It was the beginning of a longstanding relationship between Maurice Saatchi and the Conservative party. In the late summer of 1996, Maurice was rewarded with the title Lord Saatchi by Prime Minister John Major.

LABOUR ISN'T WORKING.

BRITAIN'S BETTER OFF WITH THE CONSERVATIVES

© KEITH McMILLAN

FINANCIAL TIMES PHOTO BY BRENDAN CORR

Sir Tim Bell was once considered the third Saatchi brother, or the ampersand in "Saatchi & Saatchi," but by 1984 he and the brothers had had a bitter dispute over the chain of command and he left. Maurice rehired him in late 1994 when Maurice was removed as chairman.

Martin Sorrell orchestrated many of the acquisitions made by Saatchi & Saatchi Company PLC. In 1986, he joined WPP Group, a small company that made supermarket wire baskets, and turned it into a worldwide advertising force with bold acquisitions not unlike those he had made for Saatchi & Saatchi. In 1987, he paid $566 million for J. Walter Thompson, one of the most respected names on Madison Avenue.

© 1995 JIM HARRISON

Donald Zuckert was one of the senior executives at Ted Bates Advertising when it was purchased by Saatchi & Saatchi Company PLC. Zuckert, a popular and powerful figure at Bates, left after a civil war broke out involving his boss, Robert Jacoby. The upheaval put Bates in a tailspin; the company has never recovered.

Carl Spielvogel was an executive at Interpublic Group before cofounding Backer & Spielvogel, one of the fastest growing and most respected ad agencies in the business, which was bought by Saatchi & Saatchi in 1986 and merged with Ted Bates Advertising. Carl Spielvogel retired and started a new career as chairman of United Auto Group.

Anthony Simonds-Gooding was recruited to be Saatchi & Saatchi's chief executive officer and put together all the agencies Maurice and Charles had acquired. He left in 1987 to run British Satellite Broadcasting.

Robert Louis-Dreyfus, a millionaire native of France, was brought in to save Saatchi & Saatchi Company PLC by Maurice and Charles under pressure from the company's banks. "Once you have fixed the company," Louis-Dreyfus was warned, "the brothers will want their train set back." Louis-Dreyfus left the company before it was fully healed financially and now runs Adidas.

Charlie Scott succeeded Louis-Dreyfus as chief executive officer. Because the company was still ailing, he forced the brothers to cut back on expenses. Maurice retaliated with a harsh campaign against Scott in the London press.

TWO PHOTOS: CORDIANT PLC

REX USA

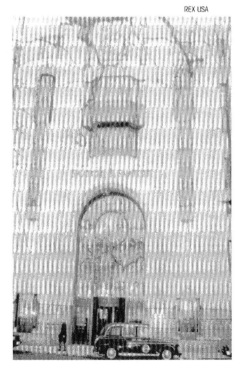

Saatchi & Saatchi Company PLC headquarters in Berkeley Square, the most expensive real estate in London. This became the battleground where Charlie Scott fought the brothers. Long after the entire company had moved to more modest offices, the brothers and their small staff remained here until Scott forced the board of directors to order them out.

Roy Warman and Terry Bannister, two of the senior executives of Saatchi & Saatchi Company PLC, were often criticized by Maurice Saatchi loyalists for not doing much work and spending their time golfing, criticism Warman and Bannister felt was unjust.

A rare photo of Charlie Scott, Robert Louis-Dreyfus, and Maurice Saatchi together at a company shareholder meeting. At one point, the stock had lost 97 percent of its value. Critics say Maurice was insensitive to the plight of shareholders; one board member was saddened to see older shareholders stuffing sandwiches in their pockets at Saatchi shareholder meetings.

LEOPARD LTD.

SPOONER/GAMMA LIAISON

© KEITH McMILLAN

Robert Louis-Dreyfus so hated confrontation that he sent his secretary with a letter telling Richard Humphreys, a skillful Saatchi & Saatchi Company PLC financial executive, that he was fired, even though their offices were only feet apart. Humphreys became a part-owner of N.W. Ayer, the oldest advertising agency in the United States, and later submitted a bid to Maurice for Bates Worldwide days before Maurice was forced out.

David Herro, a thirty-three-year-old fund manager at Harris Associates in Chicago, began investing in Saatchi & Saatchi Company PLC because it was undervalued. Herro came to the conclusion that Maurice Saatchi was working not in the best interest of the shareholders but of himself and became obsessed with removing Maurice as chairman.

HARRIS ASSOCIATES

Suzanna Taverne, an independent consultant whom Maurice brought in to conduct a review of how the company was structured, quickly concluded that Maurice was a problem.

RICHARD A. CHASE

Theodore (Ted) Levitt, a respected Harvard Business School professor and a member of the Saatchi & Saatchi board of directors recruited by Maurice, pioneered the theory of globalization in advertising. Levitt, too, would soon tire of Maurice and believed he should be removed as chairman. In the end, Levitt became Saatchi's most vocal critic on the company's board.

Sir Peter Walters, a respected London businessman, was one of Maurice Saatchi's longtime supporters. When it became clear that the board would vote against Maurice, Walters gave in and the friendship was over.

Tim Jackson, director of investment relations at Cordiant PLC, as Saatchi & Saatchi Company PLC was eventually renamed, had a ringside seat for all the financial problems that plagued the company. He too realized it would be best for Maurice to step aside. Jackson and Suzanna Taverne helped David Herro with information.

Above left, Josephine Hart, the author of the controversial novel *Damage,* first met Maurice Saatchi in 1967 when they both worked at Haymarket. The two developed a friendship that turned into romance after they divorced their respective spouses. They married in October 1984.

Above right, Charles Saatchi and his second wife, Kay, a native of Little Rock, Arkansas, who once worked as an ad rep for *GQ.*

Below left, Doris Lockhart-Saatchi, a native of Memphis, Tennessee, was Charles's first wife; they were married in 1973. It was Doris who inspired Charles to amass the largest private collection of contemporary art and to open the Saatchi Gallery in St. John's Wood.

Below right, Charles Saatchi taking a break from his latest obsession, go-cart racing. He races several times a week and organizes marathon tournaments not unlike the Tour de France.

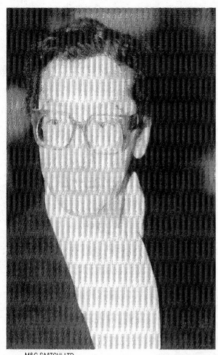

Maurice Saatchi was removed as chairman of Saatchi & Saatchi Company PLC by angry shareholders in early 1995. In less than a month, he, along with his brother and three others, would start a rival company.

Charles Saatchi left his position as honorary president of Saatchi & Saatchi Company PLC a few months after Maurice was forced out.

THE THREE NON-SAATCHI PARTNERS IN M&C SAATCHI:
Above, Jeremy Sinclair, considered a creative genius by his peers and competitors, joined Charles Saatchi in 1968 at CramerSaatchi, a forerunner to Saatchi & Saatchi Advertising.

Below left, Bill Muirhead, considered the ultimate "client" executive, became Saatchi & Saatchi's first account director. By the time he resigned in 1995, he was head of Saatchi & Saatchi Advertising North America.

Below right, David Kershaw was head of Saatchi & Saatchi Advertising on Charlotte Street in London, the agency's flagship office. When M&C Saatchi was forming, one partner suggested that Kershaw, the youngest of the five partners, not be an equal partner, a suggestion that was short-lived.

CORDIANT PLC

Robert (Bob) Seelert, a former General Foods executive, was recruited to be Cordiant's chief executive officer in 1995. He is the polar opposite of Maurice Saatchi: he has no flair and little interest in the spotlight. Ironically, Cordiant critics say that Seelert actually earns more than Maurice would have if he had been allowed to remain with the company.

© KEITH McMILLAN

Ed Wax, a former executive of Compton Advertising, is chairman of Saatchi & Saatchi Advertising North America. Bill Muirhead once said that Teflon doesn't stick to Wax, so immune is he to criticism. The dislike is mutual.

Michael Bungey, head of Bates Worldwide, was resented upon his arrival in the United States. He was viewed as another British import who knew little about the way the American advertising industry worked. When senior Saatchi & Saatchi Company PLC executives were contemplating the fallout from clients if Maurice Saatchi were dismissed, Bungey incorrectly asserted that longtime Bates client M&M/Mars would not leave. It did.

CORDIANT PLC

TWO PHOTOS: CORDIANT PLC

OPPOSITE:

Top, Wendy Smyth, Saatchi & Saatchi Company PLC's finance director, refused to sign a letter of support for Maurice the week of the board meeting held to decide his fate. She once described Maurice as a puppy who "craps all over the carpet and then licks your hand."

Bottom, Jennifer Laing, a longtime Saatchi & Saatchi executive who was once lured back to the company with a red Ferrari, was asked to return a second time by Ed Wax. Laing replaced David Kershaw, her longtime friend, as head of the agency on Charlotte Street. She turned out to be a tireless foe to Maurice and his partners and had a large say in what their new agency would be called.

Above right, Johan Eliasch was brought in by Charles Saatchi to serve as a go-between in the peace process and to settle complex legal battles between Cordiant and what was then being called The New Saatchi Agency.

Below right, Maurice Saatchi and Prime Minister John Major in June 1996 celebrating the first birthday of M&C Saatchi at a gala held at the Saatchi Gallery. Naturally, Charles Saatchi did not attend, the only one of the five partners not to.

© KEITH McMILLAN

NEW LABOUR
NEW DANGER

One of Labour's leaders, Clare Short, says dark forces behind Tony Blair manipulate policy in a sinister way. "I sometimes call them the people who live in the dark." She says about New Labour: "It's a lie. And it's dangerous."

M&C SAATCHI LTD.

M&C Saatchi's advertisement for the Conservative party in the summer of 1996. It depicted Tony Blair, head of the Labour party, as a devil. The ad, which ran only once in select newspapers, was immediately denounced by the Labour party and Britain's advertising guidance board banned it. No matter. Stories about the controversy appeared around the world and, of course, many publications ran reprints of the now-famous advertisement. Free of charge.

Christopher Bunion, Saatchi & Saatchi's treasurer. "We're about to break our bank covenants," Bunion told a startled Scott. "You better get aboard quickly or else you won't have a job to come to."

What followed was, for Scott, "the worst time in my business career. Just months of sheer hell." And that was before Maurice Saatchi turned against him.

The brief handed to Louis-Dreyfus and, therefore, Scott by the Saatchi brothers was precise: sell the consulting businesses and repair the company's horrendous financial state. "I was intrigued," Scott would say later. "We took a look at the company's 1988 annual report and spoke to a few people who understood the company. We came to the conclusion that this didn't sound like too big a problem. It was a company with top-quality business, which had diversified and gone wrong."

"I will have the final say," Louis-Dreyfus said publicly at the time of his appointment. "If I didn't think that was the case, I wouldn't have come to the company."

Ominously, two days before the appointments of Louis-Dreyfus and Scott were announced, Saatchi & Saatchi's largest shareholder, Southeastern Asset Management, a Memphis investment firm that held a 10.24 percent stake in the company, said it had been approached by unnamed third parties about restructuring the group. The translation was abundantly clear: maybe a bidder for Saatchi & Saatchi would emerge. Mason O. Hawking, Southeastern's president, said the talks were not initiated by his firm and, further, Southeastern supported Maurice and Charles Saatchi and the steps they were taking to resuscitate the company.

Throughout the courtship and even in the moments leading to the announcement of the appointments of Louis-Dreyfus and Scott, Maurice and Charles deliberately kept two executives out of the loop: Roy Warman and Terry Bannister, the co–chief executives of the company's advertising operations. Warman and Bannister were part of the close-knit Saatchi circle and had among the longest tenures of anyone: Warman had joined at the beginning in 1971 and Bannister had arrived in 1973. "Maurice and Charlie hadn't even told their own chief executives," Louis-Dreyfus said. "I met [Warman and Bannister] one day in Maurice's office. Their reaction to me? Rather cool."

Roy Warman conceded he and Bannister were distant to Louis-Dreyfus, "but our reaction wasn't to Robert. It was the way Maurice and Charles presented him to us. We had already been through Anthony Simonds-Gooding and Victor Millar as the great saviors. To us, Robert was the latest genius passing by the window." Neither Warman nor Bannister believed he would ever be in line to be chief executive of the entire company because, Warman said, Saatchi & Saatchi needed "a senior financial person and that's what we were advocating."

As soon as Louis-Dreyfus settled in, he began turning the company into his own. That meant removing some of Maurice and Charles's closest friends from lofty positions. In particular, he focused on Warman and Bannister. Louis-Dreyfus proposed the advertising unit be divided into three parts: Saatchi & Saatchi Advertising, Backer Spielvogel Bates, and the slew of other, smaller agencies. Warman and Bannister would each head up a unit, and Jeremy Sinclair, who was then an executive in the holding company, would take charge of a third unit.

Warman and Bannister hated the idea and told Louis-Dreyfus so. They presented a counterproposal in which Saatchi & Saatchi Advertising, the Rowland Co., and Kobs & Draft, which accounted for 42 percent of the company's business, would be put together and run, not surprisingly, by Warman and Bannister. Sinclair could run the rest. Louis-Dreyfus found the plan appealing, but sheepishly said he couldn't do it, since he had already agreed to let Jeremy Sinclair become the new head of Saatchi & Saatchi Advertising Worldwide.

Louis-Dreyfus began roaming the halls of the Berkeley Square offices in stocking feet and blue jeans. One of the first tasks he tended to was selling off the consulting businesses. Looming over him was the clock ticking on the Europreference, the convertible preference stock, that was coming due in mid-1993. If the stock price couldn't be raised to 593 pence (it was then around 90 pence), the company would be forced to pay Saatchi & Saatchi convertible holders £211 million in cash, funds the company simply didn't have. Hopes of selling the consulting unit as a single entity were dashed when no buyers surfaced.

Louis-Dreyfus soon realized how much resentment there was

against the brothers when he attended meetings with the executives of the consulting companies owned by Saatchi & Saatchi. "The only thing damning I will say about [Maurice and Charles Saatchi] is real and is pretty damning," Louis-Dreyfus said in 1995. "Most of the people who sold the Saatchis their businesses never saw them." The brothers' attitude, he said, was that the worker bees, including the executives, were peasants. Maurice and Charles created a mystique of superiority about themselves. "Everyone wanted to fuck us when we were trying to sell the consulting businesses," Louis-Dreyfus said. "The heads of the companies were vindictive."

Charlie Scott found morale in the companies that Saatchi & Saatchi owned appalling. "People felt they were sold a bill of goods with grand plans for the future," Scott said. "But no one ever saw Maurice or Charles."

In late 1989, Louis-Dreyfus and Scott flew to Chicago from London to hold discussions with Peterson & Co., a company specializing in trial litigation advice, which Saatchi & Saatchi had purchased for $123 million three years earlier. Peterson & Co. netted Saatchi & Saatchi a $3 million loss after intercompany loans had been written off. "When we said we wanted to resell it, they came in with an offer of $1 million," Louis-Dreyfus said. "They hated us. Not Charlie Scott or me. But the company."

The fiasco continued. Information Consulting Group, in which $31 million was invested, sold for $12 million. The Hay Group, purchased for $132 million, went for $75 million. When the entire group was finally sold, the consulting division brought £80 million to Saatchi & Saatchi; it had invested more than £125 million.

On December 1, 1989, Victor Millar resigned. Originally, Millar had hoped the consulting division would remain intact and he would be tapped to run it. For Millar, it was an unpleasant ending; he and the brothers had stopped speaking to one another, communicating instead through Jeremy Sinclair. "It was an unfriendly, but clean, break," Millar said in 1995 of his departure from Saatchi & Saatchi.

ALSO IN 1995, Maurice sounded philosophical over what he referred to in 1995 as "the most difficult period in my life." He thought the company in 1989 had gone through "the bottom of the cycle. But in a bizarre way [1989] has been a good thing. It had to happen, it's a maturing process." Maurice and Charles figured they would slip into the background and allow sound, responsible businessmen to handle the affairs of the company.

Louis-Dreyfus described his job as "boring. I cut costs and tried to reorganize. Maurice was to tend to clients." Maurice clearly did not relish this assignment of spending time with more than a handful of select clients and trying to woo prospective accounts. Once, Alan Bond, an English-born entrepreneur raised in Australia and head of Bond Corp., a Saatchi & Saatchi client, wanted to meet one of the Saatchi brothers. Bond had said to Warman he would not bother the Saatchi brothers again, "but I can't go back to Australia and tell my associates I gave the company the business without meeting either Maurice or Charles." Bond was told to come back the following week when he would indeed meet one of the brothers. Warman didn't even consider asking Charles, so he told Maurice he had to meet Bond. Warman had even made it easy on him: Maurice could pop into Warman's office wearing his coat and scarf, shake hands with Bond, who would be duly impressed, and, after speaking to him for a few minutes, could simply say he had an important lunch, and depart.

The day arrived and Bond showed up filled with anticipation. Noon came and went and there was no sign of Maurice. Warman excused himself to an outer office and called Maurice. "Where are you?" he asked. "I'm coming, I'm coming," came the impatient reply. Minutes later, there was still no sign of Maurice. Warman, getting increasingly uncomfortable, excused himself again and went to Maurice's office.

Warman was accompanying Maurice when, on the way to Warman's office, Maurice said he forgot something and he would be right there. Warman followed Maurice with his eyes, as the chairman of the company ducked into an elevator. Deeply embarrassed, Warman rejoined Bond and explained what happened. Bond was offended and surprised, and did not give Saatchi & Saatchi the business. In 1996, when asked about this incident,

Maurice Saatchi did not deny it took place: "It sounds totally plausible," he said.

Louis-Dreyfus was being less than candid, of course, in describing his job as "boring." At times, he and Charlie Scott were borrowing money for forty-eight hours at a time to keep the company afloat. One morning, Scott was driving to work when he heard on the radio that six Saatchi & Saatchi directors had bolted. He couldn't believe it; that meant two-thirds of the board resigned.

As it turned out, it was a false alarm. Six senior and mid-level executives of Saatchi & Saatchi Advertising in London, led by Paul Cowan, a group account director, had resigned. They said they were the "true keepers of the Saatchi creative flame" and opened their own ad agency. "Directors" were in abundance on Charlotte Street; there were over a hundred.

On March 13, 1990, Maurice Saatchi addressed the annual shareholders meeting held at the London Marriott Hotel on Duke Street with an announcement he thought would appease investors who smelled, and wanted, blood. He told the shareholders that he and his brother were cutting their $1 million salaries by 30 percent and that other directors of Saatchi & Saatchi Company PLC were taking 10 percent pay cuts.

Robert Louis-Dreyfus felt he had to defend the brothers and told shareholders at the meeting: "My first seventy-two days have convinced me that Maurice and Charles have a vital role to play in the future of this company and we have quickly established an excellent working relationship." Charles Saatchi was "the keeper of the creative flame" and Maurice Saatchi "has a leading role in guiding the direction of the group over the long term and insuring that there is a proper management structure in place." In truth, the banks wanted Louis-Dreyfus to fire Maurice and Charles, but Louis-Dreyfus thought that was too drastic. "We always had a charade of how important [the brothers] were," Louis-Dreyfus said in 1995.

Prior to the shareholders meeting, Louis-Dreyfus had a meeting with Maurice and Charles in Maurice's Berkeley Square office. "Look, with the shit that we're in we're not going to run this company without outside board members," Louis-Dreyfus told them. Saatchi & Saatchi was now listed on the New York Stock

Exchange, which called for its member companies to have independent, outside board members.

There certainly was room. In 1989, David Newlands, Andrew Woods, Victor Millar, and David Perring, the company secretary, had all resigned and left the Saatchi & Saatchi board. There was one outside, or non-executive, director, Vanni Treves, a senior partner with the law firm Macfarlanes, on the board, but Treves barely qualified since he was the chief lawyer for Saatchi & Saatchi. Treves's tenure would be brief, however. "I fell out in a substantial way with the brothers before I resigned from the board," Treves, who had previously not spoken publicly about Saatchi & Saatchi, said in 1996. "As the only non-executive director, I did nevertheless have my own ideas of what was appropriate for the directors of a public company to do.... They were leading a lifestyle I thought was completely inappropriate at the company's expense. They were riding roughshod over all accepted practices of good corporate behavior." Treves, a handsome, distinguished-looking gentleman with a fine head of perfectly combed gray hair, said that when he was on the board there were no board meeting papers, and in fact, there were no board meetings. "The whole thing was run on a wing and a prayer as the brothers' personal fiefdom," Treves said.

Treves's assessment of the Saatchi brothers began to sour when he was charged with approaching Cazenove & Co., one of the leading brokerage houses in the United Kingdom. "Maurice was then and now canny enough to know to be represented by the right people and to be seen in the right company," Treves said. Phillips & Drew, the company's current advisers, were fine, Treves said, "but Cazenove is the best." So Treves called a Cazenove senior partner and to his "astonishment" the firm declined to represent Saatchi & Saatchi. "They are gentlemen of the highest subtleties," Treves said, "and they said they had conflicts of interest. It later became clear that was bullshit. They did have conflicts of interest, but they had conflicts of interest in every field." Instead, Treves believed that Saatchi & Saatchi Company PLC failed to pass the "smell test," meaning that Saatchi & Saatchi did not emit confidence that all was right with the company.

Finally, on Christmas Eve 1989, Treves met with Jeremy

Sinclair and David Binding. "It was agreed that conflicts upon which I found myself, apart from being distasteful, were irreconcilable and that I would resign," Treves said. He did so effective March 15, 1990, with the condition that, although he would no longer perform any legal work for Saatchi & Saatchi personally, the company would not fire Macfarlanes. Asked why Treves would want to set such a condition considering his opinion of the Saatchi brothers' business practices, Treves responded: "They were an excellent client. There was a great deal of first-rate legal work still to be done."

So, to fill the vacant board seats, Louis-Dreyfus in early March brought to the board Thomas Russell, whom Louis-Dreyfus had met while the two were at IMS. Russell had founded and managed Bio/dynamics, which was acquired by IMS in 1973. He was named IMS chairman fourteen years later.

Maurice Saatchi's handpicked board member was Ted Levitt, the Harvard Business School professor whose globalization theory had so affected Maurice's strategy. But if Saatchi thought Levitt would be another crony of the brothers, he was sadly mistaken. "Nobody has ever accused me of being an extension of anybody," Levitt said.

On May 4, the new Saatchi & Saatchi board got down to business and fired Roy Warman and Terry Bannister. It was seen as a victory for Robert Louis-Dreyfus in his power struggle with the two longtime Saatchi executives. Since rejecting Louis-Dreyfus's proposal in reconfiguring the company, which would have significantly diminished their role, it was evident there was little for Warman and Bannister to do. And Louis-Dreyfus had pledged to cut costs at Saatchi & Saatchi Company PLC, where expenses were estimated at $33 million to $41 million annually, compared with $8 million at rival WPP Group. If Warman and Bannister were gone, the company would save $1.7 million annually in their salaries alone, not including their regular dinners at tony London establishments such as the White Tower. And the two weren't close to clients, a death knell in the advertising business. Senior Saatchi & Saatchi ad agency executives, most notably Carl Spielvogel, resented the duo. Once, Spielvogel, no stranger to opulence, was told by his executive assistant, Evelyn Cook, that Warman and

Bannister were coming to New York and that they wanted her to arrange a stretch limousine, complete with the customary bar and color television, to meet them at Kennedy Airport. Spielvogel countered to Cook that a Lincoln Town Car would have to do.

Before the May 4 board meeting, Louis-Dreyfus strolled across the expansive seventh floor in Lansdowne House and told Maurice and Charles what he intended to do concerning Warman and Bannister once the board convened. Maurice decided not to attend the meeting; Charles, of course, kept intact his near-perfect record of never showing up. "These were two loyal guys [Warman and Bannister] who had been with them since the beginning," Louis-Dreyfus said. "You would think the brothers would have asked me why or was I sure I wanted to do this." They didn't. All Maurice and Charles did was say, "Go ahead."

In the meeting, Louis-Dreyfus made a statement, outlining figures for the communications division. The message was clear: Warman and Bannister weren't doing their jobs effectively. Warman and Bannister then made their case. They correctly argued that the company needed senior executives schooled in advertising. But the die was cast. "Maurice wanted us out," said Bannister. "He knew we thought of him as a disaster."

In an unusual move, the two didn't leave the company after the board meeting. Instead, Warman and Bannister showed up for work each day for months as consultants. On May 7, they were in their offices when they received a call from Charles Saatchi. "Pop around," he said.

Warman and Bannister went to Charles Saatchi's office where Charles and Maurice were waiting for a bizarre session.

"Well, boys, what are we going to do now?" Charles asked.

"What?" stumbled Bannister.

"Well, we've done advertising. Take a look at this," Charlie said, tossing a document outlining a radio station operation. "Radio is a good idea."

In 1995 Bannister would recall, "Charlie wanted us to believe there were no hard feelings. We told him to stop. It was over between the four of us." They were just biding their time until they were ready to leave.

Meanwhile, Charlie Scott was dealing with a dizzying array

of financial details and trying to meet the payroll each week. One of the first tasks he assigned himself was hiring a comptroller. The urgency to do so was brought to light after a company employee approached Scott to sign a check for $15.5 million. "Am I authorized to sign this?" Scott asked.

"You're the finance director, you must have the authority," said the anxious check holder.

Scott asked to see the company manual that would detail such matters. "The company what?" was the reply.

"That's when I decided to go out and hire a comptroller, David Weatherseed," said Scott. "And his first job was to write a bloody corporate manual telling employees what they can and cannot do."

Scott worked seven days a week, plugging up the mess that had accumulated over the years. The company, he said, was sitting on a time bomb. It had no money. "Every accountant is taught that the most important thing in a business is cash flow," said Scott. "In the real world, people don't pay attention to that. They look at the income statement instead. Until you come to a company that is on the edge. Then, boy, cash is king." Saatchi & Saatchi Company PLC was just about to go over the edge.

In June, Scott called a meeting of Saatchi & Saatchi's banks. He was late by several minutes and was greeted with hostility. "I just remember a dark room, dark suits, and serious faces," Scott said. While he fumbled to open his briefcase, some contents fell out, including a golf tee, which rolled across the table. Scott, apologizing profusely, was stopped by one banker, who finally broke the tension when he said, "Things over there can't be that bad."

Between January 1990 and April 1991, Scott and Louis-Dreyfus made hundreds of presentations to banks and shareholders detailing the massive restructuring plan. During this frenzied period, another crisis emerged, this one putting the spotlight on Robert Louis-Dreyfus, the man responsible for restoring the company's credibility with the banks and stock markets: in February 1991, Louis-Dreyfus was charged with insider trading by the Securities and Exchange Commission in Washington, D.C. The charges stemmed from the 1988 acquisition of IMS International by Dun & Bradstreet, during which, it was alleged, he passed illegal information to a friend, Andina Cohen, about the impending sale. The

SEC charged that three days before IMS announced it would be acquired, Louis-Dreyfus, while in New York, told Cohen about the deal and she then traded on the information while also recommending the stock to her sister, brother-in-law, and two friends.

His attorney, Robert Myers, said Louis-Dreyfus settled the case so he could concentrate fully on saving Saatchi & Saatchi. He was forced to disclose his dealings, including those of Saatchi & Saatchi, with the SEC in public filings, until 1996. Louis-Dreyfus neither admitted nor denied wrongdoing and agreed to pay a civil penalty of $213,750 and not to violate securities laws in the future. Five others, including Cohen, also settled SEC insider-trading charges.

Meanwhile, the restructuring plan hatched by Louis-Dreyfus and Scott had few allies at first. The initial proposal drew the ire of shareholders, whose holdings would have been severely diluted, since shares outstanding would have ballooned to 492 million from 162 million. The plan called for a $49 million cash infusion as well as the new share issue. The result for Southeastern Asset Management, the company's largest shareholder, would have been severe: its 14.9 percent stake would have plunged between 4 and 5 percent.

But Louis-Dreyfus and Scott needed to pacify the holders of the Europreference shares. Those investors would be owed £211 million in 1993, which would choke Saatchi & Saatchi Company PLC, whose market capitalization was only £36 million. Under the plan, the Europreference holders would receive approximately 50 percent of Saatchi & Saatchi's common shares. They wanted more.

In February, a revised proposal was issued, increasing the number of shares outstanding to 1.5 billion. The proposal would convert the Europreference and United Kingdom preference shares into common shares; the previous plan would have given those holders a combination of common and new preference shares. The Europreference holders would receive 65 percent of the company, and two of the largest holders, ESL Partners, which owned 17 percent of the Europreference shares, and St. James's Place Capital, with about 20 percent, would each also get a seat on the board. ESL's investors include Laurence A. Tisch, who, until December 1995, was chairman of CBS Inc., and his brother, Robert Preston Tisch, owner of the New York Giants football team.

The proposal also called for a £55 million rights offering allowing existing shareholders to buy new shares for 10 pence apiece, along with a £5 million management investment in new shares. Robert Louis-Dreyfus personally underwrote that investment, which was later offered to senior management. Saatchi & Saatchi also received a £25 million increase in bank facilities, as well as an extension on paying off current loans until 1996. Also, Saatchi & Saatchi switched its financial reporting to a calendar year from a fiscal year in 1990.

All of Saatchi & Saatchi's banks were willing to go along with the extensions except for Mitsubishi Bank, its Japanese bank. Mitsubishi wanted full repayment. In one meeting, Louis-Dreyfus, exhausted and disgusted with the bank's position, threw his keys onto the table and said, "Fine, you run the company," and walked out. He returned only after receiving a call from the Japanese bank requesting him to continue negotiating.

Shareholders approved the plan on March 27, 1991. After that, Louis-Dreyfus on his own invested $1.5 million in the company and asked Tom Russell, his close friend from IMS, to put in $1 million. "Does this make business sense?" Russell asked.

"No," Louis-Dreyfus replied.

Russell did it anyway. "We believed in the team that was there," Russell said. "I thought Maurice could sell refrigerators to the Eskimos. Charlie was watching the operations. It was a perfect management team."

Scott, too, was pleased. "We were finally on stable financial footing," he said. "Life was very pleasant and things were going well. Robert and I were feeling pretty smug."

Louis-Dreyfus was feted in Saatchi style at a luncheon held where the brothers presented him with a gold platter with an engraving that read, "We Who Were About To Die Salute You."

But the public gratitude toward Louis-Dreyfus belied a deep, seething resentment he felt on the part of the brothers, particularly Maurice. Saatchi & Saatchi, they believed, was still their company; never mind that it was a public company belonging to stockholders.

MAURICE SAATCHI described the period that placed him in the background of Saatchi & Saatchi Company PLC as "painful

. . . I wore sackcloth and ashes every day." He said he arrived at the company's Berkeley Square office daily, "but I was a lost soul."

Saatchi & Saatchi was reappointed by the Conservative party in 1991, but Maurice Saatchi was purposely left out of the loop, according to several individuals close to the situation. The party felt he was too closely associated with Margaret Thatcher. And in case Saatchi did not get the point, *Campaign* magazine published a story saying as much.

What followed was a month in which Maurice Saatchi had no involvement in John Major's campaign for Prime Minister. But ultimately Saatchi worked tirelessly for the party. It was one of several clients for which Maurice actually did work.

During the election campaign, Saatchi & Saatchi produced an election poster: John Major smiling surrounded by three happy schoolchildren. The caption: "The Best Future for Britain." When the poster was shown to two senior party officials, they were uncomfortable with the finished product. Something did not look right. In fact, the photo was two pictures stuck together. The children and Major were never actually together. The ad agency, and Maurice, argued that the poster was meant to be symbolic, but the Conservative leaders would not go along with the production values. Maurice Saatchi reluctantly agreed to reshoot the advertisement. Not only did Major have to show up, but the agency had to locate the same schoolchildren. When the weather continued to be less than ideal for an outside shot, Saatchi & Saatchi suggested an indoor shoot against a backdrop of a photograph of mountains. But that raised the dishonesty factor again, so everyone waited for the sun to emerge. When it finally did, the ad was shot and the poster was produced and distributed.

Three years later, Maurice Saatchi was talking with the two Tory leaders who had ordered the poster reshot. "Well, I suppose I can tell you now," Saatchi said over coffee. "We didn't use any of that second batch of photos taken in Downing Street. None of them were any good. The picture we used for the poster was a scissors and paste job after all—and you never knew."

The involvement in the Conservative party's campaign was virtually all that lifted Maurice Saatchi's spirits in the period of exile from his own company. The house in Sussex, the house in

Cap Ferrat, the Bentleys, the mews off Berkeley Square did not fill the void. The only component of Saatchi's life that radiated success was his wife, Josephine Hart, who was enjoying the publication of her first novel, *Damage.* "Josephine's career was rising," he said, "and that was a good thing."

By 1991, Maurice felt out of place in the company he co-founded. Of Robert Louis-Dreyfus and Charlie Scott, Saatchi said in 1996, "Certainly they didn't think I had any contribution to make. I didn't have a public persona, nor a persona inside the company. It was a very lonely period. However much I tried to put myself in the background, and no matter how much Charles did as well, no matter how insignificant and humble we tried to be, it was not going to be enough. I got the impression pretty clearly that [Louis-Dreyfus and Scott] would rather I was dead."

CHAPTER
SEVEN

ROBERT LOUIS-DREYFUS was forceful, opinionated, and knew when an insult was meted out. To Louis-Dreyfus, Saatchi & Saatchi Company PLC's offices at Berkeley Square were an affront to its employees who were laid off in order to reduce expenses, and a slight to those workers left behind to mop up. The logical solution was to vacate Berkeley Square for offices on the top floor of Charlotte Street, the London headquarters for Saatchi & Saatchi Advertising. Louis-Dreyfus hated his own idea: he had a small apartment within walking distance of Berkeley Square and the surroundings at Berkeley Square were much more to his liking than the more pedestrian location of Charlotte Street. Actually, the corporate address was Whitfield Street, an equally unimpressive thoroughfare running parallel to Charlotte Street. Those going to the corporate offices entered through the modest Whitfield Street entrance. The hard part was telling the brothers they would have to leave their Xanadu.

Louis-Dreyfus found it difficult to confront the Saatchi brothers on anything unpleasant. For one, he had grown fond of Charles. Louis-Dreyfus was one of the few guests invited to his second wedding in August 1990, to Kay Hartenstein, a native of Little Rock, Arkansas, an art dealer and former sales representative for *GQ* magazine. And Saatchi attended a party in Madrid that Louis-Dreyfus had thrown for his marriage on May 15, 1992, to Margarita Bogdanova, a Russian translator whom he met during one of many flights to London from Zurich, where he lived on weekends. Louis-Dreyfus was also a regular at Charles Saatchi's Tuesday night poker game, which was made up of longtime friends, including Michael Green, for instance. The games were held in hotels or friends' homes, since Kay Saatchi didn't care for poker games. (Louis-Dreyfus didn't share the same feelings for Maurice, however, who he felt had no warmth or loyalty to anyone but himself. "With Maurice, everything is fake," Louis-Dreyfus said.)

In June 1991, Louis-Dreyfus, with Charles Scott attending, held a meeting with the brothers. "We can't stay here," he said, referring to Berkeley Square.

Saatchi & Saatchi executives, Louis-Dreyfus told the brothers, berated him every time they had to fire employees, accusing the holding company of speaking with a "forked tongue." "Everybody spoke to those guys about the situation," Louis-Dreyfus said in 1995. The bankers also wanted the holding company to leave Berkeley Square, which cost £64 a square foot for the fourteen-thousand-square-foot headquarters. The move would follow the strategy outlined by Charlie Scott: "Once the financing is sorted out, you have to concentrate on the costs. Berkeley Square was an obvious way."

The brothers ignored the request.

No matter how often the drumbeat sounded to move the holding company out of Berkeley Square, Maurice and Charles would simply shrug off the suggestion. And a suggestion, after all, is all it ever was; never was there a hint of an order or showdown. Maurice felt the company had grown and was emitting too much class to go back to offices that suggested humble beginnings. And the Saatchi & Saatchi name was on the building in large black block letters above the entrance. What would the Saatchi & Saatchi building be without Saatchi & Saatchi? It became a matter of pride, particularly to Maurice.

In a clear show of audacious behavior, by clinging to their cherished corporate headquarters, Maurice and Charles Saatchi had refused to adopt a bunker mentality. To the brothers, Louis-Dreyfus said, Berkeley Square "was their world. It was the image they wanted to give themselves."

So, Maurice and Charles stayed behind, enacting their own version of *Great Expectations* turned on its head. Like Miss Havisham, who kept everything the way it had been on her wedding day before she was abandoned by her fiancé, everything at Berkeley Square was preserved, but nothing was quite the same. It was an office built for in excess of sixty employees. Now, it only housed the brothers, a receptionist and her dog, a secretary, and a handful of other support staff, including a chef.

There was another issue nagging Louis-Dreyfus: the name of the holding company. Others before Louis-Dreyfus tried to broach the subject, only to be quickly and firmly rebuffed. Louis-Dreyfus's suggestion was just the latest in a long-running series. "I was troubled about it from the beginning of the joining," he said. "It was a disservice to Backer Spielvogel Bates." Saatchi & Saatchi Company PLC had become an albatross to the company's agencies. Executives from Charlotte Street in London and Hudson Street and Lexington Avenue in New York were forced to defend their agencies in new business pitches with potential clients who heard Saatchi & Saatchi, the holding company, was floundering. Of course, any change in the holding company name from Saatchi & Saatchi was an insult to the brothers.

But Louis-Dreyfus was flexing his muscles throughout the company and soon earned the reputation of being hardworking, smart, and adroit financially. Richard Humphreys would also describe him as cold-blooded. In August 1991, Humphreys, a pleasant-looking man with sleepy eyes, was named president and chief operating officer of Saatchi & Saatchi Advertising. Humphreys was an oddity within Saatchi & Saatchi. Not only was he an employee, but through peculiar circumstances, Humphreys was also the largest individual Saatchi & Saatchi shareholder with 18.2 million shares, or just under 1.2 percent.

Humphreys wasn't hired by Saatchi & Saatchi; like so many other components of the vast empire, he was acquired. In 1985, the company bought Humphreys Bull & Barker, where Richard Humphreys was the largest shareholder. His career had begun in 1968 at Garland-Compton where he had helped run a Compton U.K. Partners spin-off, Roe Humphreys. After the 1975 merger with Saatchi, Roe Humphreys was merged with another unit and Roe Downtown was created and Humphreys left, but he remained a small shareholder in the public company, which eventually became Saatchi & Saatchi. He kept accumulating shares as an investment while his agency, Humphreys Bull & Barker, began winning business. When his company was acquired by Saatchi &

Saatchi, it was merged with its KMP subsidiary to form KHBB. He sold for shares, not cash, resulting in his huge stake in the company.

Humphreys fit well into the Saatchi culture; he was ambitious and cared little whom he offended on his way to the top. His promotion in August 1991 was an attempt to better integrate the United States and international operations at Saatchi & Saatchi Advertising, which had largely been run as separate companies. Ed Wax, the affable, back-slapping, and client-catering chief executive of North American operations, was named chairman at the same time.

Robert Louis-Dreyfus quickly sensed that Humphreys fancied his next job would be chief executive of the holding company, which was precisely the post Louis-Dreyfus held. Humphreys had little regard for the French executive, who he felt had no vision for a company that was crying out for leadership. At one point, Humphreys asked Louis-Dreyfus, "What is your strategy for the company? Do you want to combine Saatchi with Bates? What is the strategy for building revenue?"

"The recovery," Louis-Dreyfus said. "The economic recovery."

Humphreys was disappointed. He didn't want to passively await a pickup in the economy. The lack of a blueprint for Saatchi & Saatchi was further evidence in Humphreys's mind that when it came to Louis-Dreyfus, there was less than met the eye. He felt Louis-Dreyfus was an invention of Saatchi & Saatchi, a sentiment echoed by Jeremy Sinclair, the creative executive. In 1995, Sinclair said Louis-Dreyfus "doesn't know anything about the ad business. Don't forget, we made Robert. We deliberately set out and created that persona through public relations. We built him into a personality. And he grew to love the limelight." Humphreys was even more dismissive, characterizing Louis-Dreyfus as a "front man who would be useful and then disappear, but who began to drink the power and wanted to be more famous. He was smitten with the Saatchi name."

Humphreys once asked several Saatchi & Saatchi executives, including Ed Wax, to get together and make an offer to buy the company. Humphreys had access to the money. Several years earlier, while looking to establish a Saatchi network in Korea, Humphreys had become acquainted with W. Y. Choi, a multimillionaire who owned an agency and was looking to invest in foreign advertising businesses.

Wax begged off by telling Humphreys, "My pension isn't vested until next year."

Choi initially thought he would invest in Saatchi & Saatchi and met with Maurice and Louis-Dreyfus. But the two sides couldn't agree on terms.

In January 1992, Louis-Dreyfus and Humphreys again disagreed over the future of Saatchi & Saatchi Company PLC. Humphreys took a gamble by telling Louis-Dreyfus that he wouldn't stay if Louis-Dreyfus left and Charlie Scott was his replacement. Scott, in Humphreys's estimation, was fine for finance director; but Humphreys said he was the only executive who could take over.

Humphreys then left Louis-Dreyfus's office and picked up the telephone in his own office about a hundred feet away. He wasn't there a few minutes when Louis-Dreyfus's secretary walked in and placed a sealed envelope on Humphreys's desk. In it was a note from Louis-Dreyfus, who wrote that although he admired Humphreys's candor, he had no intention of leaving Saatchi & Saatchi "in the foreseeable future." Therefore, since there was no position for Humphreys, Louis-Dreyfus suggested he leave the company.

Which is exactly what Humphreys did. Without speaking to anyone, Humphreys gathered a few personal possessions, and departed Saatchi & Saatchi forever.

Louis-Dreyfus felt he had made the right decision in jettisoning Richard Humphreys. Indeed, he said no clients complained about Humphreys's abrupt departure. It wasn't taken as well by senior managers within Saatchi & Saatchi, who demanded a meeting with the chief executive, complaining that the agency was being taken over by "axe-wielding American accountants." Humphreys was replaced by Robert E. Kennedy, Saatchi & Saatchi Advertising Worldwide's chief financial officer.

Humphreys's relatively quiet departure began a new, albeit brief, period at Saatchi & Saatchi. Senior executives began attacking operating issues and taking the business back to its core. One executive said, "We started to run it as a more professional company." The brothers, meanwhile, were supposed to behave, tend mainly to their own interests, and, above all, stop their infuriating habit of speaking off the record to reporters. Maurice and Charles relished calling reporters and chatting about news that was about to happen to Saatchi & Saatchi, although the brothers insisted they never could be quoted directly, a demand reporters all too willingly went along with, sometimes in absurd situations.

In this manner, Maurice always got his way. It was naive to think otherwise, just as it was for Louis-Dreyfus to expect Maurice to accept his orders to confine his involvement with the company to tending to clients and casting about for additional business.

Charles Saatchi's role, meanwhile, was murky. He dutifully reported for work each morning to Berkeley Square, closed his door, and played board games. Some said he did it throughout the day; others said it was confined to lunchtime. He occasionally reviewed advertisements for select clients, such as Silk Cut cigarettes. But this was precisely what Louis-Dreyfus and Scott wanted him to do.

Then, on February 16, 1992, a curious article appeared on the front page of the business section in the London *Sunday Times*. Louis-Dreyfus, the *Times* reported, "has told Charles Saatchi to shape up or face the consequences. Unless he makes a greater contribution to the agency empire . . . he is likely to lose his executive responsibilities. . . . It has been made clear at board meetings that Saatchi . . . will have his wings clipped if he does not spend more time on agency business." The article, by Rufus Olins, a close friend of at least one Saatchi & Saatchi Advertising executive, described a "lavish drag party" Charles hosted on a yacht in the Caribbean. Saatchi himself appeared in "a little black cocktail dress, black net stockings and slinging a rhinestone handbag."

Louis-Dreyfus told anyone who would listen that the *Times* story was "complete rubbish. . . . This story is totally untrue as we told the paper on [February 14]. . . . Unless the *Sunday Times* publishes a full retraction next weekend, there will be no alternative but to sue for damages."

One week later, the *Times* published a follow-up story in which Louis-Dreyfus reiterated the comment he made at the March 1990 shareholders meeting; he referred to Charles as the "creative flame," and conceded that although his role was "difficult to explain" to outsiders, Saatchi remained "one of the company's most vital assets." Louis-Dreyfus said he was pleased with Charles's work output and salary (£312,500) and that "he has an incredible touch on products. He reviews all our important output and always brings something new to it." The public about-face fooled no one. Everyone suspected Louis-Dreyfus was the source of the original *Times* story. Clearly, he had learned what others had picked up at Saatchi & Saatchi: how to orchestrate a leak to the press.

At the same time, Charles was complaining to friends that the fun had gone out of advertising and that he was looking for something else to occupy his time. In fact, virtually all of his attention was turned to his love of art. Charles Saatchi and his first wife, Doris, had amassed one of the most impressive collections of contemporary art in the world, at one point estimated to be worth over $250 million. Few pieces in the vast Saatchi collection, exceeding eight hundred works by over fifty artists, were produced prior to 1965.

Since childhood, Charles had been a collector, first of Superman comics, then jukeboxes, then cars, and then art. In 1969, at age twenty-six, Charles Saatchi had purchased his first work of art by Sol LeWitt, a New York Minimalist. Charles and Doris had started slowly. Then he came upon the Lisson Gallery in Marylebone, near Regent's Park in London. Lisson specialized in American Minimalist art and Charles bought it in bulk. Nicholas Logsdail of Lisson said Saatchi once purchased an entire show by Robert Mangold. One former Saatchi & Saatchi executive said Charles was actually dealing in art, not just collecting it. Eventually, that belief would be proved accurate.

At its height, the Saatchi collection contained eleven works by Donald Judd, twenty-one by Sol LeWitt, twenty-three by Anselm Kiefer, seventeen Andy Warhols, and twenty-seven by Julian Schnabel. In the 1980s, Charles Saatchi had a £100 million credit line from Citibank to buy art.

Predictably, a sale to Saatchi had a profound effect on the artist. Sculptor Richard Artschwager's early work was bought by Saatchi, who at one point owned nineteen Artschwagers. New York gallery owner Leo Castelli said Artschwager "has become considerably more famous for being included in the collection." Mary Boone, owner of a New York SoHo gallery, once said, "Dealers use [Charles Saatchi] as a seal of approval."

In the early 1980s, Charles and Doris Saatchi bought a cement-floored, steel-girded converted paint warehouse containing five rooms with thirty thousand square feet combined at 98A Boundary Road in the residential London neighborhood of St. John's Wood, near Abbey Road, where the Beatles recorded. Architect Max Gordon transformed it into the Saatchi Gallery. The site was originally a market garden, which was replaced by a series of individual garages. As with most aspects of Charles Saatchi, the gallery is a bit of a mystery. Odds are a visitor will miss the entrance at first. The building itself is behind a row of ordinary single-story stores. The only evidence of the gallery is a tiny buzzer and the words "Saatchi Gallery" etched in white letters on a tiny pane of glass. There is a long driveway that leads to the gallery's entrance and a seventy-foot-by-eighteen-foot reception gallery. When the Saatchi Gallery opened to the public in February 1985, Richard Francis, curator of the Tate Gallery in London, said the Saatchi Gallery "will make an enormous difference to London, and to the art public everywhere."

Any purchase by Charles Saatchi made news. In 1991, he turned his back on the New York art world with two major acquisitions by new British artists. Saatchi was instrumental in launching the career of Damien Hirst in 1992 when he bought *The Physical Impossibility of Death in the Mind of Someone Living,* which was an embalmed fourteen-foot tiger shark afloat in a glass-sided tank of formaldehyde. Also that year, he brought Marc Quinn to the forefront of the art world by buying and showing *Self* at the gallery. *Self* was a cast of Quinn's head in dental alginate, sitting in eight pints of blood—the contents of an average human body—which he had siphoned out of his veins over five months.

Saatchi & Saatchi Company PLC executives said it was difficult to ascertain which artworks were paid for by the company, and therefore its property, and which were purchased by Charles and Doris Saatchi. The couple was spending $1 million annually on art by 1985. Charles was also buying art for Saatchi & Saatchi Company PLC; anything bought by company funds, however, was owned by the company.

Critics derided Charles as nothing but a market manipulator, one who would flood the market with an artist's works, thereby causing the value to plummet. Sandro Chia was one artist who believed his reputation and status were hurt because of Charles Saatchi. The artist, born in Florence in 1946, had begun showing his figurative paintings with other young artists such as Enzo Cucchi and Francesco Clemente at the Sperone Westwater Gallery in SoHo in New York, owned by Gian Enzo Sperone and Angela Westwater. After Charles began purchasing Chia, others followed and soon Chia was commanding $60,000 to $90,000 per painting.

In early 1984, Charles Saatchi telephoned Angela Westwater with a proposal: wanting to increase his Warhol collection, Saatchi offered a respected 1982 Chia work, *Melancholic Camping*, for Warhol's silk-screen *Blue Electric Chair*, which was more expensive. Saatchi said he would make up the difference with cash or additional art. A deal was struck; shortly afterward, Gerry Elliott, a Chicago collector, saw a transparency of the Chia painting while speaking to Westwater. He made an offer on the spot and placed a $10,000 deposit.

But the Museum of Modern Art wanted the Chia painting to include in the inauguration of its expansion. Saatchi tried to telephone Westwater, presumably to call off the swap. He couldn't reach her. When Saatchi found out he no longer had a prized Chia painting, the theory in the art world was he then soured on his work and began selling the bulk of his Chia collection. Supply outstripped demand and the work was perceived as less valuable.

In 1988, Chia told Anthony Haden-Guest in *Vanity Fair*, "Mr. Saatchi told me he collects in depth. 'In depth' means collecting the work of favored artists in quantity over a period, like, for instance, twenty Salles and thirty-two Schnabels."

Chia asked Saatchi to allow him to buy the paintings back, but negotiations were already under way with Chia dealers. Saatchi was selling the Chia work he had. Chia wrote a telegram, Haden-Guest reported, denouncing Saatchi as a negative influence in the art world. In a subsequent letter to *Artnews* magazine, Chia wrote, "I believe the result of that telegram was Mr. Saatchi's campaign to publicize his sales of my work as a 'dispersal,' with all the resulting innuendoes, rather than the purely profit making operation that it was." Julia Ernst, the curator of the Saatchi collection, wrote a letter in response, saying that the Chias were sold to galleries who had dealt with Chia previously. This, wrote Ernst, showed that "care was taken to avoid offending Mr. Chia or publicizing the 'dispersals.'"

Sperone Westwater sold six of Saatchi's Chias to Erich Marx, a German collector, for six figures, then sold two others and absorbed the remaining two in stock. The action taken by Saatchi, however, had a profound effect on the perception of Chia: "Those ambulance-chasing fashion victims have got the guts of earthworms," Robert Hughes, art critic of *Time* magazine, told Haden-Guest. "They got out of Chia."

"At that moment I understood the power of this guy," Chia said. "I thought, I might as well go and paint in Alaska. My telephone was ringing constantly and from that moment no one was ringing anymore. It was unbelievable, like you see in the movies."

Charles Saatchi had made a considerable living out of clients' need to advertise. When it came to his art collection, he was no different. Whenever one of his works was on loan, the public knew it was "from the collection of Charles and Doris Saatchi." Visitors to an exhibit provided by the Patrons of New Art at the Tate in 1981 saw eleven paintings by Julian Schnabel, all but two on loan from Saatchi. Charles had by this time agreed to join the Patrons of New Art. The next Tate exhibit featured works by Jennifer Bartlett, one lent by Charles and Doris Saatchi.

Critics began accusing Saatchi of only lending works by artists he wanted to hype in order to increase their value. Charles claimed that full disclosure was the most prudent strategy because Saatchi & Saatchi Advertising was responsible for the Tate and other art institutions in London.

Critics also complained that the Tate had fallen under the spell of Charles Saatchi by incorporating into so many shows the work of Julian Schnabel, the then thirty-year-old American, instead of other artists from Britain. The resentment spilled over in January 1984 when the Tate offered an exhibition to Hans Haacke, a German artist. Haacke created the painting *Taking Stock*, described by Don Hawthorne in the May 1985 issue of *Artnews* as a "sly, well-researched catalogue of the political and artistic involvements of the Saatchis and their advertising empire." At the center of the painting is Margaret Thatcher. Henry Bates's sculpture of

Pandora opening her box is on a table next to her. Behind Thatcher are bookshelves with volumes containing the names of Saatchi & Saatchi clients, including Allied Lyons, the Conservative party, the Royal Academy, the National Gallery, and Wrangler jeans. On the table is a document listing Saatchi & Saatchi's art holdings and naming Brogan Developers, the subsidiary that once sold unwanted artworks. On the top of the bookcase, two cracked plates bear the images of Charles and Maurice Saatchi, a reference to a Schnabel show two years earlier that included paintings that used broken plates.

In February 1984, one month after *Taking Stock* was placed on exhibit at the Tate, Charles Saatchi resigned from the gallery's Patrons of New Art. One year later, the Saatchi Gallery opened. The first exhibit featured two rooms of Warhol, one dominated by the fifteen-foot-high portrait of Chairman Mao. The other room contained portraits of Elvis Presley and Marilyn Monroe. Other artists in the inauguration exhibit were Brice Marden, Cy Twombly, and Donald Judd. (Saatchi renewed his relationship with the Tate in 1992 and gave it nine works by British artists and sculptors, valued at £100,000.)

Saatchi, of course, had his defenders, including Gary Hume, who, in the late 1980s, was one of Britain's younger artists. Hume's work, including oddball paintings depicting wooden doors, had been bought in bulk by Saatchi. "I think Charles Saatchi is really great," Hume said. "Without him, the young contemporary art world here wouldn't happen. And, although he takes your work and makes money out of it, although he is the biggest dealer in Britain, Saatchi is the saving grace. His purchases early on enabled me to live for six months. He bulk-buys when he buys. It's good for the people because they make more money."

In 1987, Charles and Doris Saatchi decided to divorce. It is difficult to ascertain why, however. Charlie Saatchi told friends that Doris was the most intelligent and wonderful woman he had met and that it was "sad" that two people who loved each other could not make each other happy. After the divorce, Charles continued to buy, sell, weed, and prune his immense art collection. In 1989, at the height of the art boom, Saatchi sold off a hundred works of contemporary art, covertly at first, then openly. The tightly knit and gossipy art world deemed this an act of treason. Many artists had sold large blocks of their work to Saatchi at a discount with the clear understanding that he would keep the pieces as part of a massive permanent collection.

In November 1992, Saatchi unloaded fourteen major works from the Saatchi collection in a most public way: they were auctioned at Sotheby's in New York. The paintings went for less than expected: Warhol's *Marilyn × 100* was expected to fetch more than $4 million; it sold for $3.74 million. Roy Lichtenstein's *Girl with Piano* was sold for $1.65 million, but it had a sale estimate of over $3 million. A painting by British artist Malcolm Morley, estimated at $700,000, was sold for $400,000. The sale of art accomplished two goals: to refine the Saatchi collection and dispose of pieces that may have been overvalued. More important, however, the sale gave Saatchi & Saatchi Company PLC a much needed cash infusion. The 1992 company annual report recorded "sales of art" at £1.8 million, compared with £1.6 million in 1991, for example. In previous annual reports, the sale of art, which began in 1988, was listed as "investment trading profits."

Art remained a constant in Charles Saatchi's life. In 1994, Charles would still make news whenever he purchased new art. In June 1994, newspapers dutifully reported Saatchi's acquisition of two works by an unknown twenty-nine-year-old Scottish artist named Kerry Stewart. "It's quite exciting," she said of Saatchi's purchase, which cost him £2,105. Four months earlier, he had bought three works by Tony Oursler, an American video artist. The three pieces were roughly made figures with squarish pillows for heads. On the pillows Oursler projected a video image of his own or someone else's head, accompanied by a soundtrack, which ran for approximately twenty minutes.

Charles Saatchi also had plenty of time for his growing circle of close friends, including Mick Jagger; Bryan Ferry of the rock group Roxy Music; David Stewart of Eurythmics; Alan Yentob, comptroller of BBC1; and theater producer Michael White.

Friends cautioned individuals who might cross Charles Saatchi with the story of James Tennant, a next-door neighbor of Charles and his second wife, Kay, at 26 St. Leonard's Terrace, a six-floor Georgian terrace house for which Saatchi paid £1.75 million in 1989. The Saatchis renovated the house, changes that Tennant, at 25 St. Leonard's Terrace, complained in a London newspaper resulted in "continual noise pollution and harassment. Saatchi said he was planning a modest extension that would last three months. In fact, he gutted the entire house . . . the drilling has been going on all day, seven days a week." When the work was finally done, Charles dispatched flowers to Tennant, a trademark Saatchi gesture, but Tennant nonetheless sued Saatchi for £100,000, charging that the renovations caused structural damage to his house. There was a bit of a class conflict between the two: Saatchi was a self-made millionaire, whereas Tennant, sixty-two, was educated at Eton and Cambridge before becoming an officer in the Royal Horse Guards.

Saatchi countered that it was he and Kay who were wronged. His builders, he said, were sprayed in the eyes with a macelike substance and then pelted with eggs. After the renovations were completed, Saatchi said Tennant refused to allow his construction crew to examine Tennant's home for damages. Instead, Saatchi said, he had anti-Semitic notes pushed through his mailbox, including one that read, "Go home, Jewboy." In May 1991, Saatchi woke up one morning to find his green Rolls-Royce Corniche convertible set afire. Tennant said he and his wife, Elizabeth, were in the country at the time.

Saatchi's friends facetiously said Tennant had the Saatchi curse placed on him, and in February 1992, a few hours before he was to meet with his attorney to discuss the case against Saatchi, Tennant died of a heart attack.

The construction of the Saatchis' home was a matter of dispute as well. The cost escalated to £1.1 million from the original £600,000. When the work was completed, Charles offered half of what the builders wanted; the matter went to court.

LIFE WAS FAR LESS DRAMATIC for Maurice Saatchi during the period of exile from the day-to-day running of Saatchi & Saatchi, which he called "very painful." Maurice had a great many pleasant distractions, including Old Hall, his estate in Sussex outside London, a home in Cap Ferrat about a half-hour drive outside the Nice airport in the south of France, and a Riva Aquarama, a twenty-four-foot mahogany speedboat, as well as two raspberry-colored Bentleys.

While art was Charles's passion, gardening was Maurice's love. Visitors to Old Hall, the name given to the house built in 1842, are usually first shown around the vast gardens before embarking on a tour of the house. When first planning his gardens, Maurice secured every book on the subject. He visited estates in the area to see what others had done. He build a conservatory to house semitropical plants and he designed a garden with sections for different colors and seasons.

The house resembles a castle and in the summer is draped with wisteria, jasmine, and old pink and white roses. Maurice had bedrooms in the house removed to create a great hall. Three rooms were turned into one huge living room. A Catholic chapel was renovated into a dining room that seats forty.

Old Hall was the subject of a beautiful display in the January 1995 issue of *Architectural Digest*. Outside, there are sixty acres of parkland and ten acres of enclosures of flowers, trees, and lakes. Maurice, the magazine reported, "flooded thirteen acres of pasture to make a lake with three islands, a swimming jetty and a boathouse, complete with rowboats and a classic 1955 mahogany Thames riverboat with blue leather seats."

In September 1995, Maurice Saatchi appeared on *Desert Island Discs*, a long-running BBC Radio program. The guest is asked what luxurious item he would take to a desert island. Saatchi spoke of the love of his gardens at Old Hall. Through modern technology, Saatchi said, he would have a virtual reality headset.

"My stepson Adam, ably assisted by my son Edward, who are both computer wizards, would preprogram a virtual reality headset. . . . I would be able to step out onto my virtual reality terrace in Sussex. . . . Look at the beautiful wall of my house and marvel at the inspired plantsmanship which involved juxtaposing Paul Himelasa's Musk with the fading flowers of Wisteria. I would then carry on my walk, get into my virtual boat, go across my virtual lake, and arrive at my virtual reality jetty. Josephine would arrive and get into the boat and lie down beside me. . . ."

It was a good thing Maurice had Old Hall to occupy his time. His professional life took a back seat to that of his wife, Josephine

Hart, whom he married in 1984, following his divorce from Gillian Osband, the children's writer. (In 1991, Osband would have a hit with a pop-up book titled *Castles,* which explained the evolution of England's castles beginning in 1066.)

Hart is an enchanting, caring individual and the couple's genuine love and devotion to each other is one of Maurice's most attractive qualities. The couple met while working at Haymarket Publications. Saatchi, Hart, and their respective spouses became quite a foursome in London. No one believed that Saatchi and Hart began their relationship until they were each separated from their spouses. Even though she confided in colleagues that she wasn't initially attracted to him, Hart soon found herself drawn to his charm, quick wit, and humor.

When Saatchi and Hart began seeing each other, her husband, Paul Buckley, was crushed and said as much to John Hegarty, the London advertising executive who knew the two couples. "Paul," Hegarty said to Buckley, "this sometimes happens. People don't gradually fall in love with total strangers."

Hart's life was full of horrific events. She was seventeen when her sister and brother died within eight months of each other. Another brother had died a decade earlier. Her family came first and it wasn't until she was in her twenties that she left Mullingar, a small town in the Irish midlands. She stayed at Haymarket for fifteen years and married Buckley, a Haymarket director. Her passion was poetry and she created a series of public evenings in which well-known actors read poetry.

Her marriage, which produced a son, Adam, was floundering, and Maurice accompanied Josephine to poetry readings, although he was lukewarm at best on the art.

Shortly after their separate divorces came through, they married in a small ceremony in the register office in London. A year later, their son, Edward, was born. He was the first grandchild of Nathan and Daisy Saatchi. Another of Maurice's attractive qualities is that he is a devoted father and stepfather who is deeply involved in the lives of his sons.

Maurice is also the most ardent supporter of Hart's career. At Haymarket, she was given a magazine, *Engineering Today,* to manage, but the publication failed. Maurice saw this as an opportunity for Hart to do something she truly had a drive for: the theater. He urged her to establish a theater management company, so in 1986 Josephine Hart Productions Ltd. opened.

Maurice suggested novels that could be staged, including *The Black Prince* by Iris Murdoch, and actors who could be cast. Hart became known internationally in 1991 with the publication of her first novel, *Damage,* about a British doctor who becomes a member of Parliament and has a dangerous obsessive passion for his son's fiancée. Upon publication, Hart said, "Sexual realization is the key to profound peace." Hart's subsequent two novels, *Sin* and *Oblivion,* have not met with the same success. In fact, *Oblivion,* published in 1995, was universally panned. In May 1995, during a rainstorm outside Old Hall, Hart and Saatchi predicted *Oblivion* would receive negative notices and they each composed mock headlines, including "Hart Heads for Oblivion."

Even though Maurice had a lot going on beyond Berkeley Square, he, like Charles, appeared in the offices daily. There were conflicting accounts on what he did once he got there. Louis-Dreyfus said Maurice entertained in expensive restaurants and in Berkeley Square. In 1995, the company had occasion to review Maurice's guest list of the early 1990s. The guests included the Archbishop of Canterbury as well as journalists, not exactly the lunchtime crowd that would toss Saatchi & Saatchi new business. But Maurice dismissed any allegation that he wasn't doing exactly what the company asked him to do. He regularly spoke with clients, including Mars, British Airways, and Procter & Gamble, giving them advice and holding their corporate hands.

The Berkeley Square offices were used for another purpose as well: running the 1992 Tory reelection campaign of John Major for Prime Minister. Berkeley Square provided the security that the Saatchi team wanted for the sensitive assignment. Maurice Saatchi, Jeremy Sinclair, Bill Muirhead, and about thirty others from the Charlotte Street agency used Berkeley Square to orchestrate the campaign. As it had in the past, the Labour party handed the Tories an election issue: taxes. Sinclair correctly said that the way to win was to exploit Labour's intention to raise taxes. Saatchi & Saatchi created ads with the headline "Labour's Tax Bombshell." Major won and Sinclair and Muirhead were able to finesse Maurice inside 10 Downing Street, which he visited regularly.

EVENTUALLY, MAURICE and Charles Saatchi left Berkeley Square, but they didn't go willingly and it took a cantankerous board meeting to accomplish the goal. Neither Maurice nor the company was prepared for the destructive fallout.

It was one thing for company skirmishes to be fought internally. As with everything involving Saatchi & Saatchi, the civil war that erupted was on an unprecedented scale in the advertising industry. It took months to simmer and explode and when it did it caught the particular attention of one major American shareholder in Saatchi & Saatchi: David Herro.

CHAPTER
EIGHT

DAVID HERRO'S modus operandi was to look through garbage stocks. "We don't look in the penthouse of companies to invest in," he said. "We look for companies that may be overlooked." He was rummaging through what he called the trash heap for possible investments in the fall of 1990 when he came upon a real stinker: Saatchi & Saatchi Company PLC.

Herro was a fund manager at the State of Wisconsin Investment Board when he began buying shares in Saatchi & Saatchi Company PLC. He would excel again several years later when he joined Harris Associates to manage mutual funds. Mutual funds were becoming increasingly popular in the early 1990s, their numbers soaring to 3,800 in 1995 from 1,800 in 1987. Assets in mutual funds were estimated at $1.5 trillion, an increase from $114 billion in the mid-1980s.

A mutual fund is a commingling of the assets of individuals, institutions, and other parties; the assets are overseen by an investment manager. In return, the investment manager charges a fee. The mutual fund is basically an investment company that is guided by federal regulations. Some mutual funds are open-ended funds, which means that as more people invest additional money, the fund grows.

Managing such funds was a role that suited Herro, an affable, ruggedly built Midwesterner with a close crop of dark curly hair whose uncompromised integrity was refreshing, especially when it came in contact with advertising, an industry that was by nature disingenuous. David Herro epitomized the solid family values conservative America was advocating in the mid-1990s. He was also unswayed by charm, lyrical talk, and seductive surroundings.

He was born on December 17, 1960, in Milwaukee and raised in nearby Fond du Lac, a farming and industrial community of 35,000, where his mother was a nurse and his father a financial officer at Ahern, an engineering company. Herro was the fourth of six children, five boys and one girl. Even as a youngster he had a reputation for being obstinate, one who wouldn't retreat from a verbal battle. That characteristic earned him the nickname "FS," pronounced Fess, which stood for "Fight Starter."

Herro was a self-described poor student—"My first six or seven years in school were pretty shaky," he said, "with Cs and Ds and the occasional B." His intellectual curiosity was dormant until the end of junior high school, when he began excelling in the social sciences. Then, at St. Mary's Springs, his Catholic high school, he became "thrilled" by history. Perhaps because of his father's profession, Herro was also attracted to economics and finance: he began following the stock market when he was only twelve years old and was a voracious reader of the *Wall Street Journal.*

Herro was the consummate team player. He attributed that to two factors: a large family meant he was expected to pitch in and help for the greater good, and he was also a star football player on the St. Mary's team, the Ledgers. "Everyone has to work together on a team," Herro said. "You can never quit. These are things you learn from playing sports. Even though you're tired and exhausted, you keep going. Then it'll be over and you can rest." When Herro ultimately became aware of Maurice Saatchi, he couldn't comprehend Maurice's reluctance to toe the company's line; in fact, Saatchi's personal interests seemed to be continually at odds with those of Saatchi & Saatchi. Maurice Saatchi, said Herro, played for himself.

As with everything Herro applied his concentration to, he tackled football with his wild enthusiasm. The result was costly: hopes for a college football scholarship were dashed after a series of injuries, including being knocked unconscious during one Ledgers game.

In order to pay for the University of Wisconsin, Herro took several jobs, including one as a caddie at a local golf club and another as a dishwasher at Schreiner's Restaurant. When he entered the university, teaching economics was Herro's ultimate goal.

Upon graduation, Herro decided he needed one year off before entering graduate school, "in order to cleanse my brain." He chose to do that as a salesman at the Hormel Company, a meat packager. As it turned out, Herro had an aptitude for the business and was promoted four times within one year. Hormel executives were surprised when Herro, characteristically, kept his word and departed to begin graduate school at the University of Wisconsin in Milwaukee. "If I stayed at Hormel, I never would have left," Herro said. Shortly after entering the graduate program, Herro realized what it took to become a professor of economics: "I'd have to publish all these stupid papers all the time. I can't spend all my time doing that and enjoy it."

Herro then turned to his other passion, investing, and began looking for a job. In 1986, five months after graduating, he started an international fund, the International Equity Program, at the Principal Financial Group in Des Moines. Three years later, he was lured to the State of Wisconsin Investment Board in Madison, which wanted to start its own international fund. He was in charge of investing $400 million of public-employee pension funds in international markets. His reputation as an above-average international manager was spreading and in time headhunters began calling.

Herro made his first investment in Saatchi & Saatchi Company PLC while at the State of Wisconsin, accumulating 8.03 million shares, representing 4 percent of the company. Saatchi & Saatchi had been a darling stock on Wall Street and in the City in London, but the company didn't catch Herro's financial antenna until the plunge in the Saatchi & Saatchi stock price; between 1987 and 1990, it lost 93 percent of its value and new senior management, specifically Robert Louis-Dreyfus, had come on board. The ingredients were ripe for a garbage picker such as Herro to come along.

It was during a day trip to New York from the Midwest that Herro attended a road show presented by Saatchi & Saatchi Company PLC, one of hundreds of dog-and-pony presentations that companies make to analysts and potential and current investors. He was dutifully impressed with the new Saatchi team and shortly afterward Herro and the State of Wisconsin pension fund "began dabbling" in Saatchi & Saatchi. The fund invested in the recapitalization of Saatchi & Saatchi. "We did it on the basis that although the franchise had been battered, it was still a strong franchise with Saatchi & Saatchi Advertising and Bates," Herro said. "And you had two very capable people turning the business around." The full recovery of Saatchi & Saatchi would take time, Herro knew, but that was fine. "We're long-term investors and we were more than happy to stick with it," he said.

But it was in a private meeting in New York with Louis-Dreyfus and Scott that Herro heard the clincher in deciding to invest in the ailing advertising company: Maurice and Charles Saatchi, Herro was told, were "out of the picture." "To be honest," Herro said later, "if the brothers were in the picture, we wouldn't have touched it. They destroyed the company, so why give them a chance to do it again?"

Once he became an investor in Saatchi & Saatchi, Herro, as he did with other companies, met with the management several times each year. The conversation frequently turned to Maurice and Charles. Maurice, he was told, was working with clients, and Charles was reviewing select creative work. When Herro asked about their expenses, he was told truthfully by Tim Jackson, the company's director of investor relations, "That is still a problem." With salary and expenses, the brothers each were costing the company in excess of £1 million annually. "That's a lot of money for a company that wasn't making any money," Herro said. In 1989, the brothers cost Saatchi & Saatchi £2 million in direct compensation and another £3.5 million in other expenses, including secretarial and domestic staff and entertainment. In 1993, costs associated with Maurice's role as chairman came to £1.04 million; in 1994, £772,000. In addition to his £356,000 salary, there were costs related to the running of his two Bentley Turbos, £87,000 for meals, accommodation, and travel (Maurice insisted on flying the Concorde), and £46,000 for entertainment, including £5,600 for flowers.

After Robert Louis-Dreyfus became chief executive of Saatchi & Saatchi, one particular target for cost cutting was the compensation of senior employees. Saatchi & Saatchi had long been considered top-heavy with senior employees making above-average salaries. Approximately three hundred employees earned more than £150,000 each in 1991 and thirty earned more than £312,000. The compensation committee recommended that Maurice's and Charles's salaries, which had been £625,000, be cut as well. The brothers had contracts and could have forced the issue to retain their higher pay, but instead they agreed to the reduction to £437,500 in fiscal 1990 and £312,500 in 1991 and 1992.

In 1991, the company lost $67 million and had debt of $273 million. The company had 12,800 employees in 455 offices in 65 countries, down from 18,000 staff members when Louis-Dreyfus arrived; 75 percent of the revenues came from the advertising networks; revenue distribution was 44 percent in the United States, 17 percent in the United Kingdom, 27 percent in Europe, and 12 percent in the rest of the world. But not all was going well; clients were firing Backer Spielvogel Bates at an alarming rate, including Prudential Insurance ($60 million in billings), Fisher-Price ($15 million to $20 million), Jhirmack ($13 million), and Xerox ($25 million). It would also lose Miller Lite, one of its flagship accounts, and Magnavox.

In the midst of the rebuilding and account defections, Louis-Dreyfus decided to call it a day at Saatchi & Saatchi Company PLC. Toward the end of 1991, Louis-Dreyfus discussed his succession with Maurice and Charles, who remained in Berkeley Square. "I said I wanted an orderly transition and then I would leave," Louis-Dreyfus said. Later, he admitted that the constant battles to rid Berkeley Square of the brothers and the resistance over changing the holding company name contributed heavily to his desire to resign.

"How do you wish to organize the company when you leave?" Maurice asked Louis-Dreyfus.

"Continue to do what you're doing," Louis-Dreyfus answered. "And maybe you need Charlie Scott."

Later, Louis-Dreyfus said he was somewhat surprised that neither Maurice nor Charles tried to talk him out of leaving. "I was a bit naive," he said. "They started thinking about taking the company back as soon as I said I would leave. They were a bit afraid of me because I had a reasonably strong personality. I knew reporters, I knew other people. Ultimately, they were happy I went away."

The next day, the brothers summoned Louis-Dreyfus to

Berkeley Square from Whitfield Street; they had made a decision and agreed that Charlie Scott should succeed Louis-Dreyfus as chief executive; they asked Louis-Dreyfus to remain on the board. They also asked that the news of Louis-Dreyfus's resignation not be made public yet. In fact, Maurice and Charles wanted to wait until the annual shareholders meeting in June 1992.

Louis-Dreyfus agreed and went to tell Scott the news. Scott was in his cramped, drab office at Whitfield Street, directly opposite the ladies' toilet, a location he chose on purpose. Clearly, he didn't see his role in a people-oriented industry as one requiring him to meet with many people outside the company.

Scott saw that his part was to manage operations and he didn't need much of an office to accomplish that. In fact, Scott made it a point never to meet a client. A shy person by nature, Scott preferred to crunch numbers and allow the more gregarious Maurice Saatchi to handle the clients.

Sitting in Scott's office, Louis-Dreyfus initially told him only of his plan to leave, including keeping it secret until the shareholders meeting in June. "I really don't care when I leave, so that's okay with me," Louis-Dreyfus told Scott. Then, Louis-Dreyfus confided that he was beginning discussions to become chief executive of Adidas A.G. The German sportswear manufacturer was in trouble and Crédit Lyonnais, a beleaguered French bank, was trying to recruit Louis-Dreyfus to sort out the mess at Adidas. Immediately, Scott wondered what this meant for him. Would he follow Louis-Dreyfus a third time, this time to Adidas? Louis-Dreyfus never offered Scott a job. Instead, the two talked in generalities.

Joining Adidas would mean relocating to Germany, Scott was told. That wasn't a move Scott was sure he wanted to make. For one thing, he now had a wife, Janet McKenna, whom he had met while she was at Saatchi & Saatchi Advertising as a long-term planner in the finance department. Further, he liked London and thought he would be in line for Louis-Dreyfus's chief executive position, which would soon be vacated. The Saatchis had not yet offered him the position. In truth, Louis-Dreyfus wanted to bring Scott with him, but, he said later, "I didn't do it because I thought the brothers wanted him to run Saatchi. I thought it would be unfair to the company to take him away with me."

Convincing Scott, who was promoted to chief operating officer from finance director in 1991, to take the job of chief executive wasn't an easy sale, however. "Having learned from my introduction into Saatchi," he said, "I thought carefully about what I would need to happen in order to take the job." As good a job as Louis-Dreyfus and Scott did in getting Saatchi & Saatchi back to financial stability, it still wasn't a healthy company. Scott wanted to make sure Saatchi & Saatchi "was in good shape with the banks" and he wanted the company to issue yet another rights offering so the company could reduce bank debt and invest in its operating companies.

Maurice and Charles readily agreed to Scott's terms. But the brothers, and Maurice in particular, had a deeper motivation for allowing Scott to succeed Louis-Dreyfus. Maurice believed that whereas Louis-Dreyfus was assertive and flamboyant, Scott was shy and dull. He was just the candidate to be pushed around by Maurice. Others warned Scott to tread carefully. Michael Bungey, chairman and chief executive officer of what is now called Bates Worldwide, said, "Once their toy is fixed, the brothers will want it back."

However, Saatchi still needed Scott, too. It emerged that Saatchi & Saatchi Company PLC was so financially ill when Louis-Dreyfus and Scott arrived that it had been within days of going bankrupt. Although the company was at least on the road to recovery, it wasn't there yet. It still needed an executive who was respected in the City and Maurice's credibility in that sector remained nil.

With Charlie Scott on board, Louis-Dreyfus then focused on Wendy Smyth, who had been the company's chief financial officer since July 1991. He offered her a promotion to finance director. Perhaps because she had been with Saatchi & Saatchi since 1982 and knew its Machiavellian inner workings, Smyth, like Scott, hesitated. "I was very concerned in accepting the offer," Smyth said. "I wanted to make sure it was being done with the support of the whole board. I was very concerned the brothers wanted the company back. From having known them for a long period of time, my belief was they only gave up the reins because they absolutely had to. They still regarded it as their company."

Robert Louis-Dreyfus publicly resigned on June 10, 1992, at the London Marriott during the annual shareholders meeting. Louis-Dreyfus made no mention of any talks with Adidas, instead telling associates he was toying with taking a year off. In his speech, Louis-Dreyfus conceded he was leaving Saatchi & Saatchi before it had fully recovered. For one, the global advertising markets hadn't bounced back as he had hoped. And there was still a way to go toward his goal of boosting the company's operating margin from 2.8 percent in 1991 to between 10 and 12 percent. In his usual self-deprecating manner, Louis-Dreyfus said he would stay on an additional year "to take the heat" for any earnings disappointment and not spoil Scott's first year at the helm. At the time, he said he would leave in June 1993, although he would actually depart March 31, 1993.

He told reporters that appointing Charles Scott as his successor should be read as a clear signal that the company's future, at least for the time being, was in the hands of a money man and not an advertising executive. Publicly, Maurice Saatchi agreed. "That's a fair assessment," he said. "We expect Charlie to be CEO for a long time." In Chicago, Herro was pleased because he had respect for Scott and what he had accomplished with Saatchi & Saatchi.

At around the time Louis-Dreyfus was announcing his resignation, David Herro was doing the same from the State of Wisconsin Investment Board. By the summer of 1992, Herro had cemented his reputation as an astute investor, and he began receiving offers. One that interested him in particular was from Harris Associates L.P. in Chicago. "I wanted a crack at a partnership," Herro said, "and Harris had emerged from a rough period and was willing to give me that chance." He started an international fund at Harris in 1992 and by 1993 it was one of the fastest growing funds in the country.

While at the State of Wisconsin, Herro had each year increased the stake in Saatchi & Saatchi Company PLC, to 7.97 percent of the company in 1991 and 8.99 percent in 1992.

Herro was visited at Harris Associates by Scott and Tim Jackson in the fall of 1992. "I still liked the stock," Herro said later. He started investing in Saatchi & Saatchi again in 1993, with Harris holding 9.64 percent of the company. The State of

Wisconsin remained an investor as well with 8.11 percent. In 1991, another U.S. company, General Electric Investment Corp., also began investing in Saatchi & Saatchi with an initial stake of 4.84 percent.

In August 1992, Saatchi & Saatchi posted a first-half pretax profit, its first since June 1989, of £11.1 million compared to a restated loss of £32 million in the year-earlier period. The improved earnings resulted from cost-cutting and not from a recovery in advertising spending. The cost-cutting measures improved Saatchi & Saatchi's operating margin to 5.5 percent, up from 2 percent. The company's £11.1 million pretax profit included an extraordinary gain of £1.8 million on the sale of a portion of Saatchi & Saatchi's art collection. The financial statement allowed Louis-Dreyfus to facetiously comment, "Somebody recently told me that this year we've made more money from art than Christie's."

Adidas A.G. announced in mid-February 1993 that Robert Louis-Dreyfus would become its president. A group, including Louis-Dreyfus, had acquired a controlling stake in Adidas from Bernard Tapie, a French investor and politician, for $370 million. Adidas was ailing on several fronts, including relentless competition from Nike and Reebok International. Adidas was being outspent and outmaneuvered in terms of marketing by its competition. Louis-Dreyfus's blueprint for a recovery by Adidas—slashing debt and expenses and trying to increase profit margin—wouldn't be enough. It would need a clever advertising campaign and Louis-Dreyfus, a generous individual, immediately looked to his soon-to-be-former employer, Saatchi & Saatchi.

It was a well-intentioned gesture Louis-Dreyfus would soon regret.

CHARLIE SCOTT assumed the office of chief executive at Saatchi & Saatchi Company PLC on April Fool's Day, 1993. He faced a number of challenges, including reducing the company's $273 million debt. There was also the sensitive and vexing matter of the holding company itself, which cost £20 million annually. That figure had hardly been touched by Louis-Dreyfus.

Before he departed from Saatchi & Saatchi, Louis-Dreyfus

had some advice for his successor: "Watch your back, Charlie. They're going to try to get the business back. It's very, very important you have the board on your side. Control it and you won't lose any battles you have with Maurice."

When Scott took over from Louis-Dreyfus, the Saatchi & Saatchi Company PLC board consisted of ten members, equally divided between executive directors and non-executive directors. The executive directors were Maurice and Charles Saatchi, Charlie Scott, Jeremy Sinclair, and Wendy Smyth. The non-executives were Louis-Dreyfus; Ted Levitt, the Harvard business professor; Tom Russell, former IMS chairman and ally of Louis-Dreyfus; Stuart Cameron, a chairman and chief executive of Gallaher Ltd., a longtime Saatchi & Saatchi Advertising client; and Clive Gibson, an executive director of St. James's Place Capital PLC.

Maurice, his critics said, had placed Stuart Cameron on the board for no other reason than he was an unabashed fan of the brothers. Gallaher, a division of American Brands, manufactures Silk Cut cigarettes and, even in 1996, it remained Charles Saatchi's pet account. Silk Cut suffered an image problem: it wasn't considered a masculine product and Saatchi & Saatchi's assignment when it first got the account in 1984 was to strengthen the brand's perception. Charles did it by inserting a cut into a piece of silk, usually with scissors, in all Silk Cut ads, a design still used in 1996. Cameron was a strong supporter of Maurice and Charles, but would retire from the board voluntarily in September 1994 when he turned seventy.

St. James's Place Capital PLC had a 3.94 percent stake in Saatchi & Saatchi when Clive Gibson was appointed to the board in May 1991. Gibson was viewed as one of the most influential board members and was well liked. Although he was fond of Maurice, he didn't hesitate to oppose him and support the board in matters concerning the chairman and his role in corporate governance and fiduciary responsibilities.

The other major shareholder who joined the board in May 1991 was Edward S. Lampert, a Dallas businessman whose ESL Partners held a 5.8 percent stake in the company. Lampert's tenure would be unusually short, however. He resigned in October 1991, saying he wanted to devote more of his attention to researching new investment opportunities. In reality, the board was relieved that Lampert chose to resign. He pushed for sweeping changes within Saatchi & Saatchi in order to achieve a swift return on his sizable investment, changes the board felt were too drastic. His abrasive manner was also deemed too direct for the British directors.

Scott did little to heed Louis-Dreyfus's advice about minding the board. Instead, Scott did what Scott always did: he avoided clients and proceeded to bury his head in a pile of numbers and bar charts. In May 1993, he pushed through one of his conditions for taking the job: a rights issue. It wasn't as much as investors, such as David Herro, would have wanted, however: a £73 million rights issue with an offer to shareholders of ten new shares for every twenty-seven old shares held at 130 pence per new share. Approximately £36.5 million was used to reduce the bank debt; £19 million was used to acquire minority interests in European advertising subsidiaries; £10.5 million was invested in strengthening media buying businesses and to develop businesses in Asia, Latin America, and Eastern Europe; another £7 million was used to acquire new information technology. At the time of the rights offering, which was underwritten by S.G. Warburg and UBS Ltd., 50 percent of Saatchi & Saatchi's shareholders were in the United States, 40 percent were in the United Kingdom.

Nineteen ninety-three marked a milestone in Saatchi & Saatchi's acquisition bender: it was the final year of major earn-out payments, the runaway system the brothers used to obtain their worldwide empire. Remaining payments at the end of 1993 were £12 million, a 52 percent decrease from 1992's payments of £25 million.

In 1993, there were changes within Backer Spielvogel Bates, which was having problems with client defections as well. In April, Scott gave Michael Bungey, president and chief operating officer of Backer Spielvogel, additional responsibilities as chairman and chief executive officer of the agency's Americas region, which includes the United States, Canada, and Latin America. Bungey, fifty-two years old, was the Saatchi & Saatchi Company PLC executive who could be mistaken for Michael Caine. Gregarious, handsome, and not someone who would be accused of breaking a sweat when working, Bungey was greeted with suspicion at Backer Spielvogel headquarters at the landmark Chrysler Building on Lexington Avenue in Manhattan. For one thing, Bungey was yet another import from London who was going to tell these American slackers what was wrong with the advertising business. Shortly after he was given additional responsibilities, he addressed a meeting of Backer Spielvogel Bates executives from around the world who gathered at the Versailles/Louis XVI room at the St. Regis Hotel on East 55th Street in Manhattan. He warned them the agency was in danger of becoming a "Division II" shop, a reference to a British football classification for inferior teams. The speech did little to endear him to the American executives, but that didn't concern Bungey. He didn't care whom he crossed, even if it meant alienating Carl Spielvogel, the agency's chairman and co-founder. By the time Bungey assumed his new role at Backer Spielvogel, it was no longer ranked among the top ten agency companies.

Bungey began his career in the research department at Nestlé in the United Kingdom in 1961 before moving to the agency side. He worked at Crawfords and then moved to S.H. Benson, which would become Ogilvy & Mather. In 1971, Bungey started his own agency, Michael Bungey & Partners, which went under in 1984 after a client's business, a record company, failed. The agency was sold to Dancer Fitzgerald Sample, which eventually became Michael Bungey DFS. It was merged with Dorland Advertising, which, in turn, was combined with Backer Spielvogel Bates in 1987.

Not long after Bungey received his promotion, Bill Backer retired as vice chairman and worldwide creative director at age sixty-seven. Backer wrote "I'd Like to Teach the World to Sing" for Coca-Cola and created such campaigns as "Soup Is Good Food" for Campbell Soup and "Tastes Great, Less Filling" for Miller Lite.

Bungey tapped a fellow Briton, Andrew Cracknell, vice chairman and executive creative director at BSB Dorland in London, as Backer's successor. Cracknell would never warm to New York and would quit less than a year later.

But the setback caused by Cracknell was a blip in an otherwise calm year. "Things were going pretty well," Scott said of 1993. But things going well at Saatchi & Saatchi Company PLC meant that things weren't a total disaster.

Saatchi & Saatchi Company PLC and its ad agencies were not making news, which was a mixed blessing. Not making news meant Saatchi & Saatchi Advertising and Backer Spielvogel Bates were not winning new business. It had net losses of $41 million in billings. In the last three months of 1993, Saatchi & Saatchi began reverting to its own version of normalcy; in other words, setbacks and chaos.

Usually, the reason a client fires an advertising agency isn't complicated or ambiguous, but nothing involving Saatchi & Saatchi was routine. Chrysler Corp. had been a longtime client of a highly respected Minneapolis advertising agency, Campbell Mithun Esty, a Saatchi & Saatchi shop. Campbell Mithun had been purchased by Ted Bates Worldwide prior to Saatchi & Saatchi's acquisition of Bates. In 1988, Saatchi & Saatchi merged it into another agency it had bought along the way, William Esty.

In September 1992, Saatchi & Saatchi hoped to launch a third ad agency network, separate from Saatchi & Saatchi Advertising and Bates Worldwide; to do so, it merged Campbell Mithun Esty in the United States, with $1 billion in annual billings, with KHBB in London, which had $100 million in billings. It used the slogan "Hub and Spoke" to introduce what the company boasted was a new structure to the international ad arena. The agency would be based around a group of full-service, or "hub," offices that would provide clients with strategic planning and execution. "Spoke" locations would adapt the strategic themes to local market requirements. It marked the first time in years the company was in a growth, not retreat, mode.

CME KHBB handled the domestic and Canadian advertising for Chrysler's Jeep/Eagle division, worth $135 million. In 1993, Chrysler decided to consolidate its account to two agencies, with BBDO as the second. Such moves were increasingly popular along Madison Avenue. It had been commonplace for a client with a large account to spread it over several agencies, but in order to achieve what the client believed was cost efficiency, ad accounts began to be bundled into one agency. Chrysler chose Bozell Worldwide, a unit of Bozell, Jacobs, Kenyon & Eckhardt. However, the automobile manufacturer didn't want to lose the talented services of CME KHBB, so it told Bozell to buy the agency, including the 280 CME KHBB employees. Bozell's offer to Saatchi & Saatchi was $15 million. It was described by one Saatchi & Saatchi executive as "a gun-to-the-head" takeover.

Saatchi & Saatchi suffered twice: it lost the Chrysler business as well as the talent within the agency to perhaps win another automotive account. "I did my best to negotiate the best deal," Scott said. "But if I kept the people and ultimately didn't get another car account, I would have had to fire all of them. I had to think of the employees and what was best for them."

Two months later, in December 1993, Saatchi & Saatchi Advertising in New York was forced to resign from Helene Curtis Industries' Finesse, Salon Selectives and Vibrance Shampoo, and Degree antiperspirant accounts with combined billings of close to $90 million. The agency created ads for Curtis brands in the United States, Australia, and New Zealand. But it still handled the advertising for Procter & Gamble, a Helene Curtis rival, and its brands Head and Shoulders and Vidal Sassoon shampoo in Europe and Asia. Procter & Gamble had recently dethroned Helene Curtis from the top spot in the $4.5 billion shampoo and conditioner business. Procter & Gamble was not comfortable with one of its flagship ad agencies handling a competitor's business. And agencies tended to listen to Procter & Gamble, the world's largest advertiser. Although the ads created for Procter & Gamble products didn't win awards for creativity—the Cincinnati giant didn't want to jar its customers, which it felt were conservative housewives—they did pay the bills.

Procter & Gamble accounts were coveted, highly serviced, and protected. Maurice Saatchi took great pride in reminding one and all that he was a close confidant to Edwin L. Artzt, Procter & Gamble's outspoken chairman until 1995.

Charles Scott had a clear understanding of the division of power between the chairman and the chief executive officer at Saatchi & Saatchi. Scott, as chief executive, would tend to the operations and balance sheet; Maurice, as chairman, would tend to the clients and whatever glad-handing that required. So, Charlie Scott was surprised and a little more than disturbed when he was given the word from Cincinnati: re-sign Helene Curtis or lose the Procter & Gamble account. He was then told that this was not the first time Procter & Gamble had registered a complaint. Scott was also informed that Procter & Gamble was told the situation would be taken care of. "I was horrified when the client came to see me in person to tell me all this," Scott said. "I thought Maurice was seen as the great client man. Did I go back and confront the person at the company [who was responsible for clients]? What was the point?"

Scott felt let down by Maurice. Wasn't his closest client in the United States Procter & Gamble? How could Maurice let this happen? Typically, Scott chose the route of not confronting an uncomfortable situation. "It is my belief that I cannot be blamed for Helene Curtis or Chrysler," Scott said. "In fact, I was seriously disappointed that Maurice appeared never to have been near Chrysler or Helene Curtis. I was working on the assumption that this was his job. I confess I hadn't been near them. But I had to deal with the fucking problem when it came up." Instead of speaking to Maurice about the situation, Scott decided to change the way he worked. He would now have to be involved with clients. "Maurice," Scott said, "wasn't interested in being a client man."

In its annual report, Saatchi & Saatchi Company PLC noted that the losses "in neither case [were] due to the quality of our work." Nevertheless, the damage from Chrysler and Helene Curtis would have a profound negative effect on the company's 1994 results.

Scott needed to embark on yet another serious cost-cutting program. "Anyone not pulling their weight had to be addressed," he said. Immediately, Scott picked up the baton that Louis-Dreyfus had dropped. Berkeley Square was costing Saatchi & Saatchi millions of dollars each year, even though the offices were a virtual ghost town, except for Maurice, Charles, and their small support staff of ten. Scott wisely decided that if he, like Louis-Dreyfus, couldn't address the brothers on the subject of leaving Berkeley Square, he would place the taboo topic on the agenda of the next board meeting, which was scheduled for early in December at the Berkeley Square offices.

Scott had a perfect excuse—as if the chief executive needed any—for introducing Berkeley Square at the meeting. The board had asked Scott to prepare a strategic paper outlining the direction of the company. Even Maurice got deeply involved. He approached Scott and asked him to examine a number of different options. Would it be better for the company, Saatchi wanted to know, if Backer Spielvogel Bates and Saatchi & Saatchi merged to form a single giant agency, or if one of the agencies was sold entirely? In other words, a merger or a demerger?

There was nothing new in what Saatchi had to say; he had been asking the same question for seven years. Each time, the answer was that neither would be best for the company. The structure should be left as it was; the company would be best served by winning new accounts and getting new business from existing clients. But Saatchi wanted one of his options adopted because it would solve the nagging problem of the holding company's name. If Backer Spielvogel was swallowed by Saatchi & Saatchi, there would be the need for only one name. Or, if Backer Spielvogel was sold, there would be no need for a holding company. Prior to the board meeting, Scott told Maurice that his strategies for the company were "unacceptable."

Maurice had previously thought he had enough support from the board to do virtually anything he wanted, but the makeup of the board was beginning to trouble him. A new board member, handpicked by Maurice, was joining in January, but the showdown over Berkeley Square was coming weeks before the new year. The newest board director was Sir Peter Walters, former managing director and chairman of BP and former chairman of Midland Bank PLC (after the Saatchis' attempted acquisition). The announcement was made in November 1993. Immediately some thought Maurice was trying to stack the board with his supporters.

Maurice defended the selection of Walters. He said he was merely trying to add individuals who were appropriate for the worldwide company. "I was very keen to have people of class on the board," Saatchi said later. "Having the board consisting of Russell and Levitt as our star non-executive directors was not high-class enough for what I thought was a high-class company. We are a starry company, so why shouldn't we have a very starry board?"

On December 3, 1993, the board met at Berkeley Square. It was an awkward situation; Maurice was the chairman of the board and was chairing the meeting but much of the discussion was about him and how much he and his brother were costing the company. Addressing the board, Scott said, "We don't have an alternative. The company must leave Berkeley Square. We just lost two serious accounts. This move is critical for the company. We can't afford any surplus costs."

Maurice then spoke of the need to remain at Berkeley Square. It was an office fit for client meetings. Unknown to virtually all of the board, Maurice had been lobbying Bill Muirhead and fellow board member Jeremy Sinclair. "Berkeley Square isn't being used properly," Maurice would tell them. "You should hold all your client meetings here. Bring your clients around." Muirhead and Sinclair believed that Berkeley Square was the last place to bring clients. One look at the luxurious surroundings and clients might conclude a Saatchi & Saatchi Company PLC–owned agency was overcharging in order to meet the lavish expenses.

In the meeting, Sinclair was, as usual, analytical and articulate. Although he didn't relish the position he was placed in, he sided with Scott and against Maurice. It had become clear that it was time for the brothers to leave Berkeley Square. It was an onerous symbol and reminder of a time that had passed Saatchi & Saatchi Company PLC. "It's fair to say Maurice didn't like this," Scott said.

Scott also addressed the continued tenure of Charles Saatchi as a board director. Since Saatchi & Saatchi had become a public company, Charles had attended only one board meeting and had never showed up at a shareholders meeting. "When they decided to get Charles," Maurice Saatchi said later, "they didn't realize he was a very, very willing victim. He never wanted to be on the board. The only reason he stayed was because I begged him." Maurice described his brother as his "companion and supporter. Without him I would have been lonely and surrounded by them. It was a lonely and hostile atmosphere."

Charles Saatchi was voted out as a board director. He received instead the ridiculous face-saving title of honorary president. Charles would still receive his substantial £312,000 a year salary. The event may not have even caused a ripple. But a remarkable coincidence then took place once the board meeting adjourned that would set off a seismic chain of events.

The brothers' evacuation of Berkeley Square and getting Charles Saatchi off the board were hardly anticlimactic. Ted Levitt and Tom Russell, who had become allies in their disdain for Maurice's work ethic, retired to Lou Pescadou, an obscure restaurant on Old Brompton Road in South Kensington, to celebrate. Louis-Dreyfus knew the owner and had suggested it for dinner. Louis-Dreyfus would join them shortly.

Levitt and Russell were seated at a corner table when Louis-Dreyfus eventually showed up. With wine flowing, the three toasted the events that unfolded earlier in the day. Surely the shareholders will be pleased with the cost-cutting measures. And, hadn't it been easy to get rid of Charlie Saatchi? A lot easier than any of the three ever imagined. The trio was having a pretty good time of it.

Seated at the next table in this out-of-the-way restaurant happened to be one of Charles Saatchi's best friends, Sir David Puttnam, chairman of International Television Enterprises Ltd. since 1988, who was dining with his wife. Instantly, the couple suspended their conversation and began listening to everything their dining neighbors were saying.

On the way home, Puttnam agonized to his wife. Should he tell Charlie what he had heard, or should he stay out of it? Charles was an adult who could take care of himself, Puttnam said. Don't be foolish, Puttnam's wife said. Charlie must be told. As soon as he arrived home, Puttnam telephoned Saatchi. "Are you out?" Puttnam asked. "Have you been sacked?" He then gave Saatchi chapter and verse of the dinner-table conversation. Charles Saatchi exploded. He had been a quiet victim, going willingly, a good corporate soldier. Now he was being ridiculed. He called Maurice and told him what Puttnam overheard. Watch out, Charles told his brother, as if he needed to be warned.

All of this was quite humiliating. They were being dressed down by an accountant, someone the brothers viewed with disdain. Instead of being in the driver's seat, they were being driven. They quickly decided they would become proactive in getting back their company. There were two ways of achieving this lofty goal: Maurice and Charles could buy Saatchi & Saatchi Advertising in a management buyout (they hadn't wanted Backer Spielvogel Bates anyway), or they could scheme to rid the company of Charlie Scott, their chief nemesis, and Maurice could appoint a chief executive to his liking.

Raising the money would pose a problem. The brothers were still poison in the City. Charles told several friends that he could always raise capital anytime by dipping into his vast art collection.

To alert outsiders that trouble was yet again brewing within

Saatchi & Saatchi, the brothers returned to their favorite method: they called an ally in the press, this time Rufus Olins of the *Sunday Times.* On December 12, 1993, a story appeared that said Maurice and Charles "are understood to be attempting to raise funds" for a buyout of Saatchi & Saatchi Advertising. "They are expected to contribute more than 10 million pounds of their own funds . . . valuing Saatchi & Saatchi Advertising at about 200 million pounds." Olins and others dutifully reported that Charles Saatchi had not been dismissed from the board, he had resigned. Maurice Saatchi had actually turned against Charlie Scott long before. On November 10, 1993, he sent a memorandum to the Saatchi & Saatchi Company PLC board detailing the company's falling revenues. Never mind that revenues are precisely what Maurice Saatchi was supposed to be overseeing. The memo said that Charlie Scott, who became chief executive in April 1983, should be up to implementing the "new group strategy." Implicit was the chairman's skepticism that Scott would be able to do so.

While the brothers were deciding what to do, Saatchi & Saatchi Company PLC gave them ammunition: three days after the board meeting that moved Maurice and Charles out of Berkeley Square, the company issued a profit warning during an annual presentation in New York at the PaineWebber Media Conference. The 1993 revenues, Charlie Scott told analysts and reporters at the McGraw-Hill Building, would be "broadly flat," but redundancy provisions would reduce profits. Furthermore, 1994 revenues were likely to be "adversely affected as a result of preliminary indications from clients, particularly in the U.S. and continental Europe, of their likely level of expenditure." Saatchi & Saatchi planned to find £10 million of additional savings.

The news stunned analysts. Saatchi & Saatchi's share price fell 23 pence to 157 pence that day, and within days it dropped to 135 pence, erasing nearly 30 percent of the company's value. Maurice thought Saatchi & Saatchi had once again become a company out of control, but this time it was neither he nor his brother who was in control.

That, Maurice vowed, would soon change.

CHAPTER
NINE

$\mathbf{M}$AURICE SAATCHI needed a blunt instrument in order to cripple the administration of Charlie Scott and it didn't take him long to find one in Robert E. Kennedy. In January 1994, Bob Kennedy, fifty-two, was the chairman and chief executive officer of Saatchi & Saatchi Advertising North America, which was exactly the wrong job to have at that moment. The agency's North American operation was performing poorly, particularly the New York office, and Kennedy's long run at Saatchi & Saatchi was about to come to an abrupt end.

Kennedy had been vice chairman and chief financial officer at Dancer Fitzgerald Sample when it was acquired by Saatchi & Saatchi, having been with DFS since 1961. After the mergers of the agencies that Saatchi & Saatchi had acquired that led to the formation of Saatchi & Saatchi Advertising Worldwide, Kennedy was named chief financial officer of the North American unit. Robert Louis-Dreyfus had named Kennedy chief operating officer in February 1992 after first firing Richard Humphreys in London and appointing Ed Wax as worldwide chief executive officer. Kennedy was then promoted to chairman of Saatchi & Saatchi North America, second in command behind Wax in 1993, with an annual salary of $1.3 million.

But Kennedy's string was about to run out. Louis-Dreyfus had left the company and Scott and Kennedy didn't get along from the beginning. Nor did Kennedy ingratiate himself with executives in London, such as Bill Muirhead, who felt Kennedy's inability to win new business in New York was harming the worldwide network.

Scott was particularly appalled at a budget presentation by Kennedy in London in late 1993. Usually, Muirhead, the head of the U.K. operations, would be asked to leave during the North

American presentation, but Scott asked him to remain in the room. The numbers were alarming: traditionally, 50 percent of the agency's profit came from North America, with the balance equally divided between Europe and the rest of the world. But, Kennedy said, that equation had been completely turned around. Fifty percent of the profits were in Europe while the New York agency was actually losing money. The Helene Curtis fiasco was one reason for the poor results. But, Wax said much later, the agency was also hurt by having the same name as the holding company. Clients were leery about placing accounts with Saatchi & Saatchi, since that name was synonymous with mismanagement and instability. Executives inside Saatchi & Saatchi Company PLC, including Jeremy Sinclair and Bill Muirhead, also advocated changing the name of the holding company.

Over dinner in London, Scott told Wax the obvious: "We have to make changes in North America. What are you going to do?"

"Bring over Bill Muirhead," Wax said. (Muirhead insisted Wax had nothing to do with his appointment.)

As it turned out, Maurice and Louis-Dreyfus had already approached Muirhead about coming to the United States to infuse the New York operation with some gusto and creativity. Wax then spoke with Muirhead on January 5, 1994, over lunch at Tres, Tres, Tres, an Italian restaurant near the company's New York headquarters on Hudson Street.

Maurice was keen on having a close associate in New York. "Have they asked you yet?" Maurice would ask Muirhead in frequent phone calls. "Will you do it?"

Muirhead set two conditions: he must be named chief executive and it must be understood that he would succeed Ed Wax when Wax retired. Once those terms were met, Scott had to fire Bob Kennedy, who was nothing if not a shrewd negotiator for Bob Kennedy. In the regime preceding Louis-Dreyfus and Scott, Kennedy had managed to secure a new, long-term lucrative contract. It was bulletproof: Saatchi & Saatchi had to pay Kennedy $6 million to leave, which it did. The company announced on January 18, 1994, that Kennedy was "retiring," effective March 1. "We've downsized, restructured, and streamlined. That's what I've done," he said at the time. "Now it's time for the people who write the ads and sell them to develop more revenue. It's all very amicable."

Although Saatchi & Saatchi was a public company, it had no legal obligation to disclose the details of settling an employee's contract, but the terms of Bob Kennedy's settlement would find their way into the British press. On February 15, 1994, the *Evening Standard* stated that the "patience of Saatchi & Saatchi shareholders will be further tested by news" of Kennedy's " multimillion dollar payoff." "At this stage in the corporate and economic cycle," the article continued, "Saatchi should be moving steadily forward. It is not." Then, in prose that would usually be reserved for the editorial pages, the *Evening Standard* wrote, "Just as a different management style was needed to secure retrenchment, so it is that a new management approach is required to secure recovery which is so far proving unnecessarily elusive.

"The time is approaching for Maurice Saatchi, who has played a detached role as chairman, to become more active in directing strategy."

The Guardian weighed in on February 26 with a column headlined "Maurice Sets Out to Fill the Sails of the Becalmed Saatchi Yacht." Saatchi had willingly taken a back seat, the article said, "but he has become increasingly frustrated with the role of business-getter and client-soother. It is not hard to see why. . . . And when, last December, Saatchi was obliged to put out a profit warning after the loss of two big U.S. accounts, the chairman decided it was time to act."

As if the dustup in the press wasn't enough, it was preceded by an ominous event. In early January, Maurice Saatchi was feeling that he "wanted to get out of the vise-grip that the IMS brigade"— which included Charlie Scott and non-executive board members Robert Louis-Dreyfus and Tom Russell—"had on the company."

When Sir Peter Walters came on the board, Saatchi believed he had found his wrench. Saatchi's first move was made during a meeting, fittingly one of the last to be held in the palatial Berkeley Square offices. In attendance were Maurice, Charlie Scott, Peter Walters, and David Scholey, chairman of S.G. Warburg investment bank. Maurice wanted Walters to conduct a review of the company's salary structure, including Maurice and Charlie Saatchi's five-year contracts. He also wanted Walters to investigate whether it made business sense to merge Saatchi & Saatchi and Bates, or whether one of the agencies, presumably Bates, should be sold. It was precisely what Saatchi urged Scott to examine only three weeks earlier, and what the board had rejected at that time. "Peter, being new, should have a fresh look at the company." Maurice said later. "I wanted someone outside to review the company. This was taken very, very badly by the IMS band. It was taken as a criticism of the Scott and Dreyfus legacy. The myth was the company was completely turned around. That wasn't true."

The press picked up on the Walters study as well. It was all ugly, quite unprofessional, and damaging to the company. Clients want their agencies to make advertisements, not news. They want their agencies offstage, and the message and product in the spotlight.

The British media were having loads of fun with the latest episode in the Saatchi & Saatchi soap opera. The *Mail on Sunday* in February reported that the Kennedy payoff "fuelled a row" between Scott and Walters. The *Sunday Times* reported the Walters study "could lead to a boardroom shake-up and the return of Maurice Saatchi in a more active management role." *The Independent on Sunday* noted the company "continues to be wracked by board-level rows." *Adweek*, the trade publication, brought the latest Saatchi & Saatchi crisis to the attention of U.S. readers by writing, "to those who have endured the circus-like atmosphere that has surrounded Saatchi . . . the current round of press has the trappings of a power struggle" between Maurice and Scott.

"It was clear to me that Maurice was organizing a press campaign to get rid of me," Scott said. He never confronted Saatchi with his justified suspicions "because the way these things were done, he would never admit it."

For his part, Maurice Saatchi said the quiet period ended when "I got fed up. The IMS brigade was doing its work and fixing the company. But I started to take the view that it wasn't working. Somehow, it all got into the press." Saatchi said he does not recall how the press war began. He did remember believing that a spokesman for Saatchi & Saatchi was conducting "negative briefings about the chairman" to journalists. "I know all these journalists," Saatchi said. "They're friends of mine."

Although Maurice Saatchi insists that he did not fire the first salvo in the press war that ensued, he is more than capable of launching potent counterattacks. "I started to be more assertive," Saatchi said. "The company was going nowhere. Revenues were going down. All the IMS brigade was doing was managing costs." (Of course, it was precisely Maurice Saatchi who was in charge of reversing revenues and looking after clients.)

Meanwhile, in Chicago, David Herro was reading it all. It didn't take much investigating on Herro's part to deduce that Maurice Saatchi was behind most of the damaging leaks to the press. "I was pissed off," Herro said. "The company is finally turning around, good things are happening, and now this guy is rocking the boat." Herro was clear in his thinking: "A chairman of a PLC should not be waging a press war against the chief executive officer," he said, "especially given the image nature of the advertising business. It was completely unforgivable." Herro believed that if Maurice thought Scott was the wrong person, then Maurice should formally approach the board and cite the reasons. If the board agreed, then Scott would be gone. "If not," Herro said, "then shut up."

Herro placed a call to Tim Jackson, Saatchi & Saatchi Company PLC's director of investor relations, shortly after seeing the piece in the *Times*. If Maurice and Charles Saatchi were such believers in the company, Herro asked Jackson, then why didn't they put their money where their big mouths were and invest in their company?

Then, Herro made an odd offer: if Charlie Scott ever needed help defending himself, then he should call Herro. He told Jackson he would be happy to help in any way he could. Scott was told of the offer, but never placed a call to Herro.

Instead, Herro decided to become involved on his own.

On March 1, 1994, the board of Saatchi & Saatchi received a two-page single-spaced letter on Harris Associates L.P. stationery from David Herro. With the exception of Charlie Scott, chief financial officer Wendy Smyth, and Tim Jackson, the company's liaison with its investors, no one had ever heard of Herro. Herro's nationality was also an issue. Who, some board members thought, did this upstart American think he was, barging into the business of a United Kingdom company?

The letter's subject: "Adverse Publicity." Herro wrote that although internal disagreement and thorough debate are healthy, "public disagreement is destructive. Especially given the nature of Saatchi's image-related businesses, negative publicity is more damaging than it would be for other types of business.

"The most distressing aspect of this, however, is the possibility that the source of this publicity has been from Saatchi board members. It seems possible, if the above is true, that the fiduciary responsibility the board members have to the shareholders of the company has been taken less than seriously.

"I urge the Board to take this matter seriously and act to end the negative publicity."

The reports of Maurice and Charles Saatchi trying to hobble a management buyout of one of the advertising agency networks had also reached Herro. In his letter he wrote, "any board member who may be interested in a purchasing from or selling to transaction is expected to relinquish his position due to the potential for conflict of interest."

Copies were sent to executives at General Electric Investments and Herro's former colleagues at the State of Wisconsin Investment Board.

On March 4, Maurice responded in a letter with the company's Berkeley Square address: "Firstly, let me assure you that, to my certain knowledge, every one of our Board Directors, both Executive and Non-Executive, take their fiduciary responsibilities to the shareholders . . . very seriously." Saatchi went on, writing that he agreed "debate should not take place in public. All the Board have been concerned about this adverse publicity and at our next Board Meeting . . . we will be reviewing our procedures in this area."

Addressing the rumors of asset sales and purchases, Saatchi wrote, "I know of no Director who has any interest in a purchasing from or selling to transaction with this Company. . . ."

Saatchi concluded by writing, "I am glad that we have made this contact and I look forward to meeting you when you are in London."

Around this time, unknown to anyone, Maurice, who needed no advice in dealing with the press and his public image, quietly sought such counsel from an associate, David Burnside. The two had known each other since 1984 when Burnside was the public affairs officer for British Airways. Burnside had a notorious past; he was the executive who took the fall for the so-called dirty tricks campaign launched against Richard Branson and Virgin Atlantic Airways, a British Airways rival. During that period, individuals had hacked into a Virgin computer, accessed their mailing lists, and contacted customers offering cheaper deals to fly British Airways. Burnside resigned from British Airways in 1993 and opened his own public relations firm.

At the time of Maurice's arguments with Scott, Burnside was serving as an outside public relations adviser for Saatchi & Saatchi Company PLC, although several senior company executives said Burnside really only worked for Maurice Saatchi. Specifically, though, he was helping to organize the festivities planned around Saatchi & Saatchi Advertising's twenty-fifth anniversary to be held in 1995 at the Saatchi Gallery. Burnside was also helping Bill Muirhead arrange a similar gala at the Guggenheim Museum in New York. And Burnside was working with a public relations firm in New York that would help place positive stories about Saatchi & Saatchi Advertising North America in the mainstream and trade press in the United Kingdom.

Burnside read the press reports of the latest unrest at Saatchi & Saatchi and was shaken. He was a huge fan of Maurice and Muirhead and thought the media war was severely damaging the company. Friends of both Burnside and Maurice, including (Lord) John King, the former chairman of British Airways, privately suggested that Burnside might be the individual to help Maurice make his case that a change in management was needed.

Burnside told Maurice to be careful in his criticism because the outside world may say "a plague on both your houses." Burnside believed that a change was in order and what it should be was obvious: "Saatchi," he told friends, "is the biggest name in advertising internationally." It was clear who Burnside thought should be shoved aside.

Burnside's brief association with Saatchi & Saatchi became a symbol of Maurice Saatchi's audacity. When Burnside submitted a bill for £25,000, it included charges for the London party, his work for the New York agency, and one amorphous item: "work for the chairman's office." Although two-thirds of Burnside's bill related to work in the United Kingdom, Saatchi told Muirhead in New York to pay it.

At the time Maurice was arming himself with Burnside, Scott called in executives from Grandfield Rork Collins Financial, a London public relations company. They placed articles in London that criticized Maurice's salary. The *Times* weighed in during March 1995, writing, "The board of Saatchi & Saatchi is expected shortly to tackle the vexed issue of the generous remuneration package enjoyed by Maurice Saatchi." Scott also gave an interview to *The Guardian* in which he said that for the first time since he joined the group he was happy with the top management of all the operating companies. For those who didn't get the message, *The Guardian* wrote, "in other words, he was not happy with the people appointed by Maurice Saatchi." Scott also took a shot at Maurice's five-year contract. Although the amount was not out of line, he said, "I don't believe [the length is] in the best interest of the company. [It is] to the benefit of the employee." It was an emotionally grueling time and Scott, an avid newspaper reader, decided not to pick up any papers for a while.

It was about 10:30 A.M. on Sunday, March 20, 1994, and Charlie Scott was out for a stroll, waiting outside Hyde Park for a traffic light to change when David Kershaw happened along. Kershaw, a whimsical forty-year-old with a passion for dining at the Ivy and Caprice, two superior London restaurants, had joined Saatchi & Saatchi Advertising in London in 1982. He had risen through the ranks as an account executive and had replaced Bill Muirhead as chairman and chief executive of the U.K. agency when Muirhead went to work in the United States.

Kershaw was walking leisurely, listening on his Walkman to *The Archers*, a soap opera, on BBC Radio 4.

The conversation was purposely brief because Kershaw did not want to miss any of his favorite radio program. "Read the papers this morning, Charlie?" Kershaw asked. Scott had no idea what Kershaw was talking about. Kershaw said another negative article about the company was in the *Sunday Times* and, although Kershaw didn't go into details, Scott imagined the worst. "This is just devastating to our clients," Kershaw said before returning to his walk.

Upon returning home, Scott picked up the *Times,* slumped into a chair, and began reading a 2,450-word story plastered across the front page of the Business section. "Saatchi Isn't Working," blared the headline over the article written by Jeff Randall and Ivan Fallon, the author of a 1986 biography of the Saatchis called *The Brothers.* The article was a horrible indictment of the incompetence of Charlie Scott. It opened with an enticing scene: a meeting between Scott and Tim Jackson, the company's investor relations executive, that Maurice happened upon. Scott waved Maurice in and he reviewed slides that Jackson had prepared for a presentation to financial analysts. The *Times* piece said, "[Saatchi] paused at one cost-cutting, which showed that, in the past three years of deep financial trouble for Saatchi, the group spent £37 million on redundancies and got rid of 2,000 people. In his role of devil's advocate, Jackson dropped his bombshell. 'Why,' he enquired, 'are staff costs higher now than they were before all the redundancies?' "

Randall and Fallon reported that "alarm bells were ringing in Maurice Saatchi's head as he headed back" to Berkeley Square.

Maurice Saatchi's attitude toward Scott changed "overnight," the *Times* reported. Of course, Saatchi had always viewed Scott with disdain. The *Times* said Maurice told his brother, "It's a double whammy. We've lost market share and good people and we've spent £37 million for nothing."

Ivan Fallon penned an editorial that was published the same day. He called Scott a "good-natured and guileless accountant who probably never should have been put in to run an advertising group." "It is clear to me," Fallon wrote, "that Saatchi and Scott cannot long remain in the same company, and one or the other will eventually have to depart. Although the Saatchis now own less than 1 percent of the company, they still have their names above the door and Saatchi & Saatchi without one or both of the founding brothers is hard to imagine. It will probably be Scott who leaves."

Worse, just in case the article had not been seen by Saatchi & Saatchi and Bates clients in the United States, the article was picked up by U.S. newspapers, including the *New York Post,* under the headline "Civil War at Saatchi & Saatchi."

Scott stared at the newspaper in disbelief. "Bloody hell," he thought to himself. "This is amazing. There is no doubt about what is going on here."

Scott recalled what company executives such as Jeremy Sinclair and Bill Muirhead had counseled: "Please don't fight this in the press, Charlie, because this is very bad for our business. The clients wouldn't want open warfare in the press."

The *Times* didn't let up. Two days after its Sunday blowout, the *Times*'s financial column, called Pennington, wrote, "Scott would appear to be on difficult ground if, in the end, the board has to choose between him and Saatchi."

If one desired effect of Maurice's press campaign was to rally his loyal executives against Scott, it badly backfired. Muirhead was camped in New York, having arrived only three weeks earlier on March 1, when he began receiving by fax all the negative articles on Scott and the company. His reaction was to telephone Maurice. "That's it," Muirhead told Saatchi. "You're going to get fired for this."

Saatchi was his usual unflappable self. "Oh," he responded, "do you think it's really stupid?"

Then he telephoned David Burnside and yelled louder. "This is dangerous," Muirhead said. "You've put Maurice in a position where he could get fired." Sinclair told Saatchi that it was "bad for a communications and image company to wash its laundry in public." He also told it to Scott.

For his part, Maurice would not even confirm it was he who fired the first volley. "I found myself in the middle of a serious press war. It was an ugly situation. I fought my corner. Put aside who started it." But the company had no doubt it was all the work of Maurice Saatchi and David Burnside. If Scott and Grandfield were involved, it was only with defensive maneuvers. Wendy Smyth, the chief financial officer, thought the press war was "appalling. . . . All the bloody chairman was doing was sitting in his ivory tower. No one had any doubts it was Maurice." Saatchi would submit expense accounts with reporters' names shortly before a negative article written by that reporter was published. "Then

Maurice would deny he ever spoke with those reporters," Smyth said. "Charlie and I stopped telling Maurice anything because it would wind up in the press."

In the midst of the growing civil unrest, David Herro came to lunch with Maurice Saatchi in his office in Berkeley Square on March 25. They were joined at the beginning by Tim Jackson. Saatchi is at his best when his back is against the wall; he was charming and unflappable. But Saatchi had rarely run across someone such as Herro, an individual immune to the Saatchi charm. In a way, Saatchi was ill-served by years and years of getting away with anything with only a wink and a smile. Virtually everyone who had ever come in contact with Saatchi had forgiven him.

Saatchi began the lunch by doling out compliments to Herro. What an astute businessman Herro was, Saatchi said. Thank you for being so diligent and caring about the company. Thank you for having so much faith in the management and the growth potential. Then, Maurice unveiled a suspicion he had harbored in regard to Herro since he had first received Herro's letter: Herro was acting on orders from Robert Louis-Dreyfus. "He put you up to this," Saatchi said.

That was a sentiment shared by Maurice, Charles, and Saatchi & Saatchi executives such as Jeremy Sinclair and Bill Muirhead. Maurice called Herro Louis-Dreyfus's "puppet." Charles Saatchi told friends he was convinced that Herro was "Robert's stooge." Charles never formally met David Herro, but he told close associates that he believed Louis-Dreyfus "wanted to kill Maurice" and enlisted Herro to aid in the plot.

Charles told friends he was baffled as to what Louis-Dreyfus's motives could be. "At the time, we tried to understand his motivation," Charles told friends. "When we brought him in, we gave him the company with the understanding that Maurice would look after top-level clients and I would look at the top creative work."

The Saatchis had two requests before relinquishing the company: they didn't want the name changed from Saatchi & Saatchi and they didn't want to leave Berkeley Square. Charles Saatchi said he and his brother presented a bleak picture of the company's finances to Louis-Dreyfus, something Louis-Dreyfus does not deny.

Indeed, Louis-Dreyfus blamed himself for not understanding how close Saatchi & Saatchi was to bankruptcy.

But Maurice thought Herro was acting as Louis-Dreyfus's proxy in a complex battle over money earned by the Saatchis in an investment in Adidas, an investment made at the invitation of Louis-Dreyfus. The payout to the brothers was close to $40 million, but to get it the Saatchis had had to go to court against Louis-Dreyfus. Maurice Saatchi thought Louis-Dreyfus was using Herro as a weapon for revenge.

That was ludicrous, Herro responded. He said to Saatchi, "Maurice, personally, I think it's very inappropriate for a chairman of a public company to be conducting a press campaign and also talking about a buyout. If you want to make a bid for the company, fine. But you should resign from the board and then make your bid. As long as you're on the board, you have a fiduciary responsibility to the owners of the business to do what is best for them."

"I couldn't believe he would confirm something as damaging as trying a buyout while he was chairman," Herro said later. Not only did Saatchi not deny the press campaign against Charlie Scott, he confirmed that he and Charles Saatchi had attempted a buyout, but "we couldn't get bankers to go along."

Every few minutes, the conversation would be interrupted by a gentleman with short hair and no tie. He would open the door and peek in. Maurice would look up and acknowledge the individual, but never invite him in. Herro later found out it was Charles Saatchi.

"What about the press campaign?" Herro asked Maurice when the two were alone.

"Oh," Maurice said evenly, "that was a terrible thing. But we had to do something about expenses."

By this time, lunch was over and fine cigars were offered. Maurice lit his and began bemoaning the fact that he and his brother would soon depart from Berkeley Square. "It was ironic," Herro said later. "Here we were, in the most expensive real estate in London, and this guy is talking about out-of-control expenses."

The conversation between the two continued. "Where do you think things went wrong?" Maurice asked his luncheon guest.

"My question to you, Maurice," Herro said, "is why did you

make all these acquisitions [through the 1980s] at such inflated prices?"

"You know," Maurice said, "the City and [Wall] Street was expecting growth out of us. If we wanted to maintain our strong market rating, we had to" continue the company's acquisitions.

"There is another way to maintain market rating," Herro shot back. "You could have issued stock buybacks, you could have made wise acquisitions."

"We never thought of that," Maurice said without a hint of irony. "Where were you eight years ago?"

Herro suggested that Maurice might want to take a more active role and purchase more shares of Saatchi & Saatchi Company PLC.

"Oh no," Maurice said dismissively, "that is too risky."

When the meeting was concluding, Maurice walked Herro to the elevator. "The next time you're in London," Saatchi said, "we should visit the Saatchi Gallery. And I'll be sure to see you when I'm in the United States."

Herro left Berkeley Square for his next appointment: Charlie Scott at Whitfield Street. Scott was noticeably uncomfortable. "There is a board meeting next week and I'm unsure what is going to happen," Scott said to Herro.

Asked to elaborate, Scott said, "I think my job is in serious jeopardy. I could resign, Maurice could resign."

Herro was shocked. "I didn't think things had gotten this bad," he said, even though he knew that Maurice wanted to chase out the management. "I thought if we lose Charlie Scott, the company will be in serious trouble," Herro said later. "The board has to know we can't lose this guy."

Herro asked to meet with Peter Walters prior to the regularly scheduled board session at the Langham Hilton in London on Tuesday, March 29. However, Maurice had already debriefed Walters on the lunch with Herro. Predictably, Maurice believed the meeting had gone extremely well and that Herro was "great." He thought he and Herro "could have a great relationship." Walters was stunned when Herro's opinion of Saatchi was 180 degrees opposite that of Saatchi's recollection. "I began by stating my displeasure about Maurice," Herro said, "and I added that the board 'dare not touch Charlie Scott.' "

Although he was a close friend of Maurice, Walters was simmering in his anger. "That was damn foolish for Maurice to be involved in the press campaign," Walters told Herro.

"This isn't the way a chairman of a public company should act," Herro said. "The board must act."

In case Walters had trouble understanding what Herro wanted, he presented Walters with two letters. One was from Herro himself, which he had dictated by telephone to his assistant in Chicago on March 28, and which was given to every board member; the other was written by John Nelson, the investment director of growth equities at the State of Wisconsin Investment Board. Both communiqués were devastating to Maurice Saatchi. Nelson wrote, "I strongly support Charles Scott as CEO. . . . I believe that whoever serves as Chairman . . . should be fully committed to aiding Charles Scott. . . . If this requires replacing the current chairman, Mr. Saatchi, then it should be done." Herro wrote that "it has become obvious that changes are needed in the management. . . . Specifically, the Company needs a Chairman who will be more complementary to and compatible with the Chief Executive. Through my investigation and observation, it is clear that the current chairman, Maurice Saatchi, does not fill this need."

Herro advised the board to act as soon as possible and his letter included a portentous fact: for the first time, Herro stated that he had spoken with other major shareholders, representing over 30 percent of Saatchi & Saatchi shares, and they were in total agreement.

Around this time, Martin Sorrell initiated a secret discussion with David Herro. Sorrell telephoned Herro, congratulated him on having the courage of his convictions, and asked to have dinner with him at the Post House in New York. Over dinner, Sorrell said, "You're the spokesman for the disgruntled shareholders. I wish to have an option to buy your stock and the stock of the entire group."

"First of all," Herro replied, "I only speak for myself. And second of all, why would I do anything as foolish as let you buy all the shares? Why don't you make a bid for the whole company and the company will examine your bid."

"What's a fair price?"

"Three hundred pence." At the time of the dinner, Saatchi & Saatchi shares were trading at around 170 pence.

Sorrell said that if he gained control of the company, he would install a manager, perhaps Sir Peter Walters, to shake things up.

"Martin," Herro said slowly, "I fail to see anything here that is a benefit to shareholders."

"Look, if I have control, I can put in good management."

"Management is fine."

Sorrell snapped at Herro's assessment; Charlie Scott, he said, was a bean counter, Wendy Smyth was not up to the job, and Jeremy Sinclair was irrelevant.

After Herro initially rebuffed his offer, Sorrell never mentioned it again.

CHARLIE SCOTT was right to be concerned about his job; Maurice believed the company was off balance again and wanted Scott to pay for it with his head. Maurice was hoping the board would fire Scott at this meeting, which was scheduled to begin at 10 A.M. Herro had spoken with Walters at 9 A.M., and now the full board meeting was suddenly postponed.

"We're going to have a serious discussion involving a serious assessment of Maurice," Ted Levitt told the board, "and where do we go from here." It was Levitt who suggested that the non-executive directors meet separately prior to convening the full board.

The non-executive board members, Clive Gibson, Ted Levitt, Louis-Dreyfus, Tom Russell, and Peter Walters, wanted to speak separately with the two adversaries—Scott and Saatchi—and asked Scott to come in and Saatchi to wait outside in the lobby of the Hilton. Saatchi was furious. It galled him that individuals such as Levitt and Russell were ordering him about.

In the meeting, a lot of old ground was plowed over and old wounds reopened. Scott was surprisingly blunt in his assessment of the situation. He could no longer have his credibility undermined by a chairman who was scheming to get him out.

Peter Walters and Jeremy Sinclair had an audacious suggestion to solve the unpleasantries: Scott should step down as chief executive and become chief financial officer. It was a position he was better suited for anyway, Walters said.

Scott listened with disbelief. Wasn't he, not Saatchi, the one being defamed in the press? Scott told Walters and the others, "If it is your desire that I step down, I will be happy to do so." Then, he added, "I will stay long enough for a replacement to be nominated and then I am leaving the company." He then got up and walked out. Scott's session was concluded in about an hour.

The room's atmosphere immediately changed. The board couldn't afford Scott's resignation. He had the credibility in the City and on Wall Street. If he left, who would the company be left with? Maurice Saatchi. That was no bargain. It was a lose-lose situation.

Maurice was then summoned and confronted about his recent missteps, including waging a battle in the public arena. The result was unsatisfying, another inconsequential session of Maurice bobbing and weaving and not answering questions directly.

By the time Maurice left, it was late in the day and everyone was too exhausted to go on to a full board meeting. That session would be held the following day at a ground-floor conference room at Saatchi & Saatchi Advertising on Charlotte Street.

The non-executives, feeling the full weight of Herro's letters, decided to bring in Robert Sutton, a partner at Macfarlanes, the company law firm. He began advising the board of its duties to shareholders and to Saatchi & Saatchi, the company, and on whether Herro and other shareholders could dislodge Maurice as chairman.

At the full board meeting on March 30, a session that Maurice chaired, Peter Walters began by attempting to introduce a draft of an announcement that would soon be sent to the media: Maurice Saatchi would be named a non-executive chairman, Charles Scott would continue as chief executive, but a new chief executive would be recruited, after which Scott would become chief operating officer.

Scott stood up and said that was unacceptable. Hadn't the board heard anything he had said only one day earlier?

The meeting quickly dissolved into chaos. Saatchi and Scott and the other executive board members were asked to leave the room. It became clear that Maurice had lost the majority of the non-executive board's support. Walters backed away from the Saatchi-dictated press release and conceded, "If it is between Maurice and Charlie, Maurice has to go."

Maurice Saatchi was fired from Saatchi & Saatchi Company PLC.

All that remained was to take a formal vote on the proposal to ask Maurice for his resignation and inform him of the news.

Then, Jeremy Sinclair knocked. He hadn't been invited to address the group. "I have to speak," he said. "You don't know what you're doing. You're wrong. All of you know nothing about our business. Neither Maurice nor Charlie Scott have to go. It is unacceptable for either of these two to leave. You have to dismiss that possibility from your minds. Maurice's name is on the door, for heaven's sake. And Charlie Scott is as good as you're going to get when it comes to monitoring the numbers. He's straight. When he says it's six, you know it's six. I plead with you to make one last attempt at peace between these two." Sinclair, the creative genius, then showed he had a knack for the dramatic. He closed his soliloquy by covertly warning of what would happen if the board remained on its selected path: "If you fire Maurice, the damage to this company is incalculable. You cannot imagine the damage this man could do to this company."

When Scott, Saatchi, and the other executive board members were brought back in, Scott was told he had Saatchi by the throat and could continue to strengthen his grip. He was told of Sinclair's dire prediction. It was Scott's choice, the board said.

Scott decided to make peace and gave Maurice back his professional life. "He did so for reasons that to this day I don't understand," Tom Russell said later.

Walters suggested that Clive Gibson, Saatchi, and Scott retire together to a separate room and not return until the chairman and chief executive hammered out their differences. The bizarre session was awkward at best for Charlie Scott, who was finally facing his accuser in a controlled environment. It wasn't easy for Maurice Saatchi, either. He acted humble, while not admitting any wrongdoing. "I need certain assurances as to what is going to happen from this day forward," Scott said. "I mean, it's pretty unsettling for our clients and staff to keep reading all this shit in the newspaper. I want some ground rules laid down. I want this to be run as a proper company."

Maurice, predictably, agreed with everything Scott said. The bad will in the place had festered too long and only rival advertising agencies were benefiting from the civil war.

"Then everyone will agree to shut up?" Gibson asked.

Both men nodded and shook hands. Peace was declared.

The following day, March 31, Saatchi & Saatchi released a cryptic two-paragraph statement that said it was in the best interests of the company for both Saatchi and Scott to remain. It also said "action will be taken to recruit a senior advertising and marketing executive . . . whose main function will be to guide and direct the revenue development of Saatchi."

In truth, Saatchi & Saatchi had no intention of ever filling that position. It was concocted to give the company an appearance of being proactive. Tim Jackson, for one, held his breath when the release was distributed to the media and to shareholders: "What was this job description? It made no sense," he said. Almost everyone involved in the peace-making process viewed the ceasefire as nothing more than a charade. In an uncharacteristic departure, Saatchi kept his word, however, and did not contact the press. "Scott and I could have worked in theory," Saatchi said. For his part, Scott said, "From that meeting with Gibson until the day Maurice left, I don't believe there was acrimony between us."

Nagging problems remained, however, most having to do with Maurice's compensation and his duties. Also around this time, Maurice and Charles Saatchi finally moved out of Berkeley Square and to the sixth floor of the Whitfield Street complex. They weren't pleased about doing it, but they weren't despondent either. The brothers were allowed to take over the top floor of the building and, at great expense, proceeded to re-create their Berkeley Square offices. Further, Maurice and Charles were able to enter the facility on Howland Street, which ran perpendicular to Charlotte and Whitfield Streets. They closed off the entrance to all but themselves, and their contact with other Saatchi & Saatchi employees was minimal.

Maurice Saatchi was not apologetic about the separate entrance. Using the Charlotte Street entrance of Saatchi & Saatchi Advertising was unacceptable, he said. "To have me sitting in Saatchi & Saatchi Advertising pretending that I was even-handed in my view between Saatchi and Bates was ridiculous. I was seeing clients from [both agencies]. Why would I bring in Bates clients to the Charlotte Street advertising agency reception?"

Saatchi was even more emphatic about the Whitfield Street entrance of the parent company: "I made it crystal clear that I would never ever bring a client into Whitfield Street. It's a dump. It's a total dump. They were trying to save money, and they liked the idea that it looked tacky. It was a benefit. They took the view this was good for the analysts and shareholders who would come and visit and see the place was worn and no paint on the wall and the chief executive sat in a shabby tiny office with shabby furniture. The shareholders would think this is a buttoned-down, no-waste type of company. That was the theory.

"That wasn't my target audience. I was with the clients. I said in board meetings that I would never take a client into Whitfield Street. I thought we would never get business and that entrance might cost us business. The compromise was [the separate entrance on] Howland Street. It wasn't going through the agency and it wasn't going through the dump."

ONCE ON THE TOP FLOOR, Maurice and Charles each retired to their separate offices, painted a blinding shade of white. There was also a huge boardroom. Scott and other executives of the holding company worked one floor below in cramped, antiquated facilities.

Meanwhile, Peter Walters wrote to David Herro, detailing the events that led to the Saatchi-Scott handshake. On April 5, Herro responded, writing that he continued to be concerned that Saatchi "may continue to influence" the company "in a way counter to the interests of the shareholders, employees and clients. . . . It is hoped that the Board will remain extremely diligent in monitoring this situation and consider the chairman's past record when determining compensation and expense budgets." Plainly, Herro wanted Saatchi kept on a short leash with a new contract that would nullify his existing five-year deal.

Herro was nothing if not impatient. He telephoned Tim Jackson on April 13. During the conversation, Herro inquired about the mechanism for putting a resolution to shareholders. It seems that if the board didn't continue to watch Saatchi's salary and movements, Herro was prepared to initiate a shareholder-led revolt to vote Saatchi out of office. The annual meeting was scheduled for June 9 at the Queen Elizabeth II Conference Room opposite Westminster Abbey. Saatchi was up for reelection, which meant getting rid of him at an annual shareholders meeting was actually quite simple. Herro also requested a conference call between some of the major shareholders and the non-executive board directors. Finally, he told Jackson that although he did not wish to take any action in public that would harm Saatchi & Saatchi, he would do so if he felt it would benefit the company in the long term.

The following day, Herro sent a polite, but nonetheless threatening, letter to Saatchi, in which he thanked the chairman for lunch in March. But, Herro said, based on their discussion as well as talks Herro had had with individuals inside and outside the company, "I have become extremely concerned about your role as Chairman. . . . This concern stems from my belief that your interests do not appear to be aligned with the interests of the shareholders. . . ." Herro recalled the luncheon conversation in which Maurice said he would not purchase additional shares in the company because it represented a risk and confirmed that he and Charles had been speaking to the City about the brothers buying back part of the company.

Herro wrote he hoped Saatchi would continue to play a "very prominent role . . . but at this point, as I stated in the letter to the full board . . . it does not appear that this role is as Chairman given your past record."

Maurice Saatchi had sat still for this shareholder from Chicago long enough. Saatchi wasn't used to dealing with anyone but the very top person on the corporate ladder at any company. Surely Herro must have a boss. That is whom Saatchi would contact and charm in the way he delighted dozens of other hard-as-nails executives. So Saatchi called Victor Morgenstern, president of Harris Associates. He tried to persuade Morgenstern to lean on Herro to stop his meddling in the affairs of Saatchi & Saatchi. But Saatchi failed to grasp that Harris Associates was a partnership and Saatchi & Saatchi was specifically Herro's business.

Still, on April 18, a conference call was arranged among Morgenstern, Herro, and Mike Welsh, Herro's associate, in Chicago and Saatchi, Scott, and Jackson in London. Maurice wanted the situation sorted out; he felt he was being unjustifiably persecuted by Herro. But Herro would not be swayed; he wanted "firm evidence" why Maurice should be believed when he said he was working hard with clients. And from the voice-box that hooked in the Chicago delegation, those on Whitfield Street heard the same old song about Maurice's infractions.

"What are the solutions to this?" Scott asked finally.

"The solution to this," Herro said, "is for the chairman to align himself with the company, for the chairman to make a financial investment in the company, and for the chairman to accept a variable pay scheme."

"We're going to institute a revenue committee," Saatchi said without being specific. "The business is on the way back."

Several times, Herro had to cut Saatchi off. "Let's get back to where we were, Maurice. Let's cut to the chase."

The conversation petered out and ended with neither side feeling satisfied and no promises made. Saatchi followed up with a brief note on April 25 to Morgenstern: "Just to say thank you for your timely and constructive intervention—which has put us on a positive track." For Herro, the only thing the conference call accomplished was to heighten his anxiety about Saatchi as chairman and to strengthen his resolve.

On May 5, David Herro made a one-day trip to London— "The only time I've gone out of my way for an unscheduled trip," he said. He was accompanied by Richard Hughes, director of the United Kingdom desk of M&G Investment Management, a unit of M&G Group PLC, a major shareholder in Saatchi & Saatchi Company PLC. Their purpose was to meet with the non-executive board members at Clive Gibson's office at St. James's Place Capital. Stuart Cameron and Peter Walters attended and John Nelson of the State of Wisconsin joined on a conference call from the United States. Ted Levitt from Harvard did not participate.

Herro ran through the list of reasons to fire Maurice. Gibson's reaction was not encouraging: "Maurice is Maurice," he said. The implication was Maurice Saatchi could get away with virtually anything because of his easygoing charm and seductive smile. Walters agreed that, if everything Herro said about Saatchi were true, it was a bad situation. And Walters said he had already spoken quite sternly with Saatchi. "We're all on the same level now," Walters said. But Herro had heard all this before and he had had enough of what he thought was a gutless board. Again, nothing was settled. But this time, Herro was not going to leave unsatisfied.

"Fine," he shot at the board, "nothing is settled. So we'll settle it. Maurice is on the ballot next month. Thirty-five percent of the shareholders will not vote for his reelection."

Even for a company that had become accustomed to nonstop turmoil and negative press, the prospect of Saatchi & Saatchi Company PLC having its chairman voted out of office by institutional shareholders woke up the executives. An emergency board meeting was held on May 14 at the Grosvenor House Hotel with Maurice Saatchi in attendance.

It was a tense six-hour session that began at 10:30 A.M. The company's financial advisers and attorneys were asked what would happen if a vote was taken at the June annual meeting. The concise response: Maurice would be voted out. Maurice was then asked to leave the meeting. The discussion turned to what to do: have the chairman voted out at the meeting, or have the board remove him prior to the meeting? Usually, once the chairman loses the confidence of shareholders, he will quit or be fired. The board decided that there was only one thing to do: fire Maurice.

Then, Jeremy Sinclair spoke. Sinclair, the deputy chairman who had saved Maurice's job once, decided he could repeat the impossible: "Okay, I will lead a delegation to Chicago and persuade Herro not to do it," Sinclair said without a trace of hubris. "And I want the former chief executive and the current chief executive to come with me." Sinclair was told that if he couldn't work his verbal magic, Maurice would indeed, finally, be fired. But the board wasn't united; Ted Levitt, for one, thought the shareholders, not the board, should force the issue of Saatchi's dismissal.

Nevertheless, it was an amazing and audacious gamble for Sinclair. "I wasn't prepared to fail," Sinclair said later. "This had to be done."

Robert Louis-Dreyfus declined the invitation, so Stuart Cameron, the diplomatic and most liked board member, was recruited.

On May 18, Sinclair, Scott, Cameron, and Jackson met in Herro's office at Harris Associates in Chicago; John Nelson from the State of Wisconsin attended via a conference call.

Sinclair mustered all the persuasive talent he had honed over two decades of pitching campaigns to a potentially abusive Charles Saatchi and skeptical clients. Sinclair spoke for close to three hours. He used Herro's letters to the board as props, examining each of Herro's concerns and what action the board or the company took. Sinclair said Herro's demands were escalating in each subsequent letter and this, in turn, worried Sinclair. When would Herro be satisfied?

"And now, the final point," Sinclair said. "You say that unless the board pulls the trigger on this guy, you're going to vote against him at the annual general meeting? Fine, but you should know the consequences of such an action."

Sinclair next read quotes from major clients, including Sir Colin Marshall, chairman of British Airways, and John and Forrest Mars of the giant Mars company, which endorsed Maurice Saatchi and warned they might fire the Saatchi & Saatchi agencies if a move was made against Saatchi. "I can't guarantee there wouldn't be defections from major clients nor senior people in the company," Sinclair said.

To Herro, this was another egregious misstep. Herro said later he was offended by Saatchi getting clients involved with the company's internal problems. "Is this the action of a man concerned about his company?" Herro said. "He was trying to pit clients against chairman. This was a form of extortion."

Sinclair finally pledged that Maurice Saatchi had changed, that he would work hard with clients and attract new business.

"I don't feel good about this," Herro said. "He has reneged on things in the past. Sure, he'll change. He'll change until June when there is a reelection. Then he'll get reelected and there is no touching him for another five years when there is another election."

Suddenly, John Nelson, who had been silent throughout the discussions, spoke: "Why don't we have an annual election just for Maurice?"

"Done," Sinclair said, seizing the unexpected opening.

"No," Herro said, "let's have an annual election for the entire board." Herro had told associates privately that he feared Maurice would stack the board with cronies who would rubber-stamp whatever mandates Maurice wanted. The Cadbury rules of conduct for corporate governance specifically said that outside board members should be diverse and independent.

"We'll give him one last chance," Nelson said, with one key condition: Maurice must sign a new contract with a revised, lower salary. Maurice's annual pay was slashed to £200,000 annually, a figure that Herro initially resisted as too generous. This time, Charlie Scott spoke up: "Look at it from Maurice's point of view. He has a contract for five years that pays him £625,000 and you're asking him to cut it down to virtually nothing. Now why is he going to do it? I wouldn't advise him to sign this as one human being to another. But let's get on with it already."

Within fifteen minutes, a new contract was drawn up for Saatchi to sign. The details of the contract were critical; for the first time, Saatchi's salary bonus and stock options would be tied to the company's performance.

Jeremy Sinclair planned to present it to Saatchi as soon as he returned to London, and he left Chicago almost immediately after the meeting.

That evening, Herro, Scott, and Jackson had dinner at a hamburger pub in a low-key celebration. "We thought it was finally over," Herro said. "We linked Maurice's compensation with his output. He needed the money, so maybe he'll actually work for it."

The shareholders declined an offer from the company to place one of their own on the board. Herro maintained his position that he wanted to continue as a passive investor: "This wasn't a personal vendetta. We wanted what was best for the company. If we could get Maurice to work energetically for the company, that would be best. We would have our cake and eat it, too."

Later that week, the formal letters from Colin Marshall at British Airways and the Mars brothers arrived at the offices of Peter Walters and Saatchi & Saatchi Company PLC, respectively. Marshall wrote that Saatchi "has been the driving force and key lynch-pin behind the relationship. . . . In the event that Maurice should no longer be in a position to direct our advertising strategy we would have to consider our own position as well as [recommending the agency to Qantas Airways]." The Mars brothers, who placed their account at Backer Spielvogel Bates, addressed their letter to Maurice and were more combative: "we insist that our agencies have their top people involved in our business. . . . We are pleased that you have been able to do this and believe that if you were not fulfilling that role our service would suffer significantly. In fact we might and probably would have to transfer our business to your competitors.

"Your leaving would be a major factor in a decision to let such a move take place. Charles Scott has never bothered to meet us, one of his major clients. He has no relationship with us and shows no desire to have one."

On May 19, shortly before a board meeting to review the events in Chicago, Herro telephoned Sinclair with a demand that Herro said he had forgotten to raise face-to-face: changing the name of the holding company from Saatchi & Saatchi to, well, anything. Herro did not care whether it was Acme Advertising, just as long as the brothers' name was erased. Sinclair promised to raise it at the board meeting, but, privately, this call concerned him: "This is out of the blue," Sinclair said later. "What does Herro know about a brand name?" Sinclair assumed someone from Backer Spielvogel Bates had planted the idea of a holding company name change in Herro's mind. "Bates always believed it was the unfortunate relation," Sinclair said. "Bates said it didn't have the family name, but it had all the family problems."

In reality, the suggestion came from someone close to the chief executive's office at Saatchi & Saatchi Company PLC. This individual was furious that the State of Wisconsin had unwittingly provided Maurice Saatchi with a new life as chairman and that Jeremy Sinclair had seized upon it. Shortly after the Chicago meeting, this individual telephoned Herro and expressed his disappointment. Herro must keep up the pressure, Herro was told. One more issue Herro should raise, the individual said, was the holding company's name. Unknown to Sinclair, Herro did this reluctantly, believing that the debate that would result would only distract from the main issue of Maurice Saatchi's behavior. Herro also took offense at Sinclair's allegation that he was ignorant as to why the holding company's name should not be Saatchi & Saatchi. "There are no products with the name Procter & Gamble," Herro said. "A holding company isn't a brand. A brand is what is within the holding company. A holding company is a financial entity."

In a letter to Herro dated May 19, Sinclair recapped what was discussed. He wrote: "The Board believes that changing the Company name is a critical operational issue which will be considered carefully in the context of a comprehensive review of the options."

Sinclair may have thought that his toughest assignment was to convince Herro and the other shareholders to grant Saatchi a pardon. He was wrong. Convincing Saatchi to sign the new contract, one with a much tighter noose, would tax Sinclair's patience and persuasiveness. There were endless meetings between Saatchi, his attorneys, and Sinclair. Every time Saatchi would begin protesting, Sinclair would silence him with a wave. "This is the best I could do," Sinclair said. "This is the offer that's been negotiated with Herro. Do you want the job? Yes or no? It's an easy sale. If you want the job, sign the paper." It was an uncomfortable task for Sinclair. Although he was with the company before Maurice arrived, Saatchi was nonetheless the chairman. To help him speak sternly to Maurice, Sinclair kept reminding himself that he was addressing Charles Saatchi's kid brother.

The shareholders grew exasperated at Maurice's resistance and finally said that if his signature wasn't on the document by May 24, a proxy process to remove him would begin. Saatchi signed on May 24.

The five-year contract was replaced by a three-year pact, effective July 1, 1994, with an annual salary of £200,000. It also included a stock option scheme that would grant Saatchi options valued at £5 million if the stock reached agreed-upon levels within three to ten years. The details were to be worked out at a later date by the board's compensation committee, the chairman of which was Peter Walters, Saatchi's ally.

An uneventful annual shareholders meeting was held on June 9 with only a small inner circle of Saatchi & Saatchi Company PLC executives knowing the tumultuous events of the preceding months.

Maurice was still pouting, however. Charles Saatchi berated his younger brother for buckling under shareholder pressure. But Charles did not have an alternate plan to save his brother's head from the chopping block. And Maurice remained unhappy with the company's structure. Again he began pressing for a strategic review by an independent outsider. Charlie Scott and the board, embracing a spirit of reconciliation, agreed.

Maurice Saatchi would vastly underestimate the integrity and backbone of the individual he handpicked to conduct the strategic review. He believed this individual could be browbeaten and manipulated like so many others under the Saatchi spell.

More than almost anyone, this individual would lead to the undoing of Maurice Saatchi at Saatchi & Saatchi.

CHAPTER
TEN

As A TENSE AND WOBBLY TRUCE began at Saatchi & Saatchi Company PLC, Bill Muirhead set about recasting the faltering Saatchi & Saatchi Advertising North America in his own image. Although Muirhead is an account handler with few peers, there is a bit of the dramatic showman in him. He chose David Kershaw's fortieth birthday party, held on February 26, 1994, at a private box at the Kempton Park horse racetrack, to inform colleagues he was being exported to New York. Unknown to virtually anyone else, Muirhead already had told Maurice Saatchi and the board that he wanted Kershaw as his replacement at Charlotte Street and Nick Hurrell and Moray MacLennan to become joint managing directors.

The only person Muirhead couldn't reach on his executive board was Alan Bishop, vice chairman of the agency and one of Muirhead's closest associates. Bishop, tall and lanky with dark black hair and a bright white smile that rarely dims, joined Bates in London as a trainee in 1974 and worked on such accounts as Pedigree Pet Foods and Mars. He joined Saatchi & Saatchi Advertising in 1985 to run Ross Foods and Anchor Foods and was appointed group director to lead the United Kingdom team for the European launch of M&Ms in 1987. He became the group director in the United Kingdom on the Procter & Gamble account in 1988. It was difficult to find anyone who did not adore Alan Bishop.

When Bishop arrived at the racetrack, Muirhead pulled him aside to inform him privately of the changes, none of which included him. When told of Hurrell's and MacLennan's promotions, Bishop turned ashen and returned to the races, saying nothing to Muirhead. After a few minutes, Bishop approached Muirhead and said he was resigning. "I don't want to work for Nick and Moray," Bishop said.

"Look, Alan," Muirhead said, "you've only thought about this for about a half hour. You're not going to resign." But Bishop would not be moved.

Muirhead next spoke with Kershaw and the two pounced on an obvious solution. Bishop should accompany Muirhead to New York to fix Saatchi & Saatchi Advertising. Bishop immediately agreed. He was named chief operating officer of North American operations.

Saatchi & Saatchi Advertising in New York was a mess. The agency produced lackluster commercials for clients such as General Mills, Johnson & Johnson, Procter & Gamble, and Sara Lee. While the agency was not known for its creative output, those clients did not encourage cutting-edge advertising. But worse for Saatchi & Saatchi, its new business record was abysmal. It had fallen from the number-four-ranked U.S. agency to number seven in 1993. Clients felt they were treated like second-class citizens and were ignored. Part of the problem was that Saatchi & Saatchi in North America was never a true independent agency with roots. It was an amalgamation of Dancer Fitzgerald Sample and Compton and executives protecting their own turf.

Muirhead wanted free rein to dismantle the North American operations. He called Peter Walters on the board of Saatchi & Saatchi to describe the dreary situation. "I can't wave a magic wand to fix America," Muirhead said. "You can't sell a bad product and we have a very bad product. It'll take two years to fix this and I want you and the board to know this."

It did not take long for Muirhead to fixate on one problem he could easily solve: Harvey Hoffenberg, the forty-three-year-old chairman and chief creative officer of the New York operation, had to go. This was no surprise to anyone, least of all Hoffenberg. In April, one month after he arrived in New York, Muirhead stripped Hoffenberg of the chief executive title just six months after Hoffenberg was named to the position. Hoffenberg was dismissed from the agency entirely on June 3, 1994, along with Richard Pounder, the vice chairman.

The two firings did not upset other executives at the agency, who viewed the pair as aloof and uninspiring, but there was a fear that the agency would become another beachhead for non-American executives, specifically those with British accents. Unknown to Saatchi & Saatchi employees on Hudson Street, Muirhead planned another major import from across the Atlantic Ocean. He held long dicussions with Peter Cullinane, chief executive of Saatchi & Saatchi Advertising in New Zealand. The agency dominated New Zealand and produced some of the best creative work outside the legendary Charlotte Street office.

Everything was set for Cullinane to come to America, but when he arrived he told Muirhead that while on the airplane to New York he had changed his mind. Cullinane had recently been divorced and wanted to remain in New Zealand to stay close to his children.

Muirhead next turned to Michael Jeary, forty-six, the chief executive of Saatchi & Saatchi Advertising's San Francisco office, to be chief executive of New York. Jeary, diminutive and handsome with bright blue eyes and a good nature, began in advertising in 1972 at Young & Rubicam as an account coordinator. In 1975, he joined Dancer Fitzgerald Sample, working on such accounts as General Mills, Yoplait yogurt, and Western Union. Bishop and Jeary took an instant dislike to each other, yet, in 1996, they both remained at Saatchi & Saatchi, although Jeary was moved aside from the North American operation and named head of new worldwide business development.

Muirhead also brought in Stanley Becker, fifty-nine, vice chairman and chief creative officer of Saatchi & Saatchi DFS Pacific in Los Angeles, to restructure and regenerate the creative department. Becker enjoyed a stellar reputation as a creative executive, having worked in the Saatchi organization for close to a quarter-century. He helped create the "You asked for it, you got it" strategy for Toyota. Becker also possessed a hair-trigger temper. He once threw a chair across a room that impaled itself in the wall and another time he punched a hole in a wall. He said he did it for effect: "I had to establish myself as someone who didn't take garbage."

Becker was visiting New York on family business when he decided to stop by the Hudson Street offices. He met Muirhead, who asked him where he sat. "About three thousand miles away," Becker replied. Muirhead and Becker spoke for two hours and Muirhead decided he needed Becker to jump-start the faltering agency. When Becker left Muirhead's office, he shook his head and said to Muirhead's secretary, "He has no idea who I am."

Another individual whom Muirhead had in his cross-hairs was Michael Keeshan, president and chief operating officer of the New York office and the son of Bob Keeshan, the beloved star of *Captain Kangaroo,* a top-rated children's television show that aired on CBS from 1950 through the 1980s. Son closely resembled father, and it was difficult not to warm up to Mike Keeshan. But Muirhead had little knowledge of Captain Kangaroo. He fixated on the poor creative output of the agency and thought it was natural to fire Keeshan. The two had dinner with a senior executive from General Mills on June 3, the night Muirhead fired Hoffenberg and Pounder. Keeshan arrived late, not knowing that Muirhead was being "mauled" by the General Mills client. Then Keeshan showed up and took control of the conversation, saying that now that Muirhead was in charge, General Mills and all Saatchi & Saatchi clients would begin seeing changes. The agency would become more responsive to the needs of its clients. The poor relationships would be turned around. Muirhead warmed up to Keeshan—"I actually wanted to kiss him," Muirhead said—and his job was saved.

Muirhead also wanted the agency to abandon its infuriating policy of not pitching against Backer Spielvogel Bates. A Mars executive called Muirhead to welcome him to the United States and Muirhead used the call to invite the official to the agency for a sales pitch. But Michael Bungey, chairman of Backer Spielvogel, discouraged Muirhead from getting involved. Maurice Saatchi called Muirhead from London and gave his approval for Muirhead and Bishop to visit Mars executives in New Jersey. Muirhead said he hoped to snag Mars business not from a Saatchi & Saatchi–owned agency, but from another Mars agency, such as Grey Advertising.

Meanwhile, changes were percolating at Backer Spielvogel Bates. Bungey thought the agency's name was a tongue-twister and confusing outside the United States. To be sure, Backer Spielvogel was well known within the United States. Elsewhere, Bates was far stronger. Therefore, he wanted the name to be Bates Worldwide everywhere. The idea was not new. Robert Louis-Dreyfus had ordered a worldwide study about a name change in his last days as chief executive of the holding company. Charlie Scott agreed with his predecessor: "We should definitely have worldwide branding for the agency," he said. "I don't want to be in one part of the world and see one name and then go off to another part and see another."

Carl Spielvogel, whose name would no longer be hung on a shingle along Madison Avenue, officially declined comment. Privately, he would tell anyone who would listen how insulted he was and what a bad idea it was. His relationship with Bungey, while never warm, was virtually nonexistent after the agency's plan to change its name was made public in April. It was officially changed to Bates in June. Spielvogel resigned on October 19, 1994, and defied everyone's predictions that he would enter public life, presumably as an ambassador. Instead, Spielvogel would wait an entire month to announce his next venture: he and a partner said they would purchase and operate large automobile dealerships around the country under a company titled United Auto Group Inc. United Auto would quickly become a success and issue an initial public offering in October 1996.

DUSTUPS INVOLVING INDIVIDUALS considered inconsequential to the future of the organization, such as Spielvogel, did not concern Maurice Saatchi, who now had to work if he wanted his large payday. And, according to his associates, he did work. "The rainmaker was making it rain," Jeremy Sinclair said. "Maurice was reenergizing the business. The carrot was attractive." In fact, Sinclair said he received a note from Herro in August 1994 thanking him for his efforts and noting that things seemed to be improving. Sinclair, not one to miss an opportunity to lobby for Saatchi, replied to Herro and agreed that events had taken a turn for the better, "but we'll need your help to get the [share option scheme] through."

Scott remarked publicly that he now had a "fantastic" relationship with Saatchi. "I have worse disagreements with my wife . . . and I've only been married four weeks."

In May 1994, Saatchi & Saatchi Advertising in London won

the £35 million Camelot Group account for the United Kingdom's first National Lottery. It was believed to be the United Kingdom's biggest account for a single product. It brightened an otherwise gloomy new business record for Charlotte Street and Saatchi loyalists immediately seized on it as an opportunity to credit the recent infusion of Maurice Saatchi.

The summer continued on an upbeat note, even though by then Saatchi & Saatchi Company PLC had slipped to the fifth-largest ad group in the world with annual billings of $6.5 billion; between June 9 and August 8, the Saatchi & Saatchi share price rose 31 percent to 176 pence from 142 pence. Newspapers called the much-improved interim profits for the company the first peace dividend. Margins were improving as well during 1994, to 5.7 percent from 4.7 percent, although Charlie Scott said he would not be satisifed until margins were 10 percent. The outlook remained poor in the United States in 1994, however, with revenue falling to £159.1 million from £179.5 million; operating profits in America fell to £6.1 million from £10.7 million. By August, Saatchi & Saatchi had seen its American Depositary Receipts plummet from a peak of 343 in 1987 to $7\frac{1}{8}$, a 98 percent drop in value.

Bates also won several coveted new pieces of business. One was Warner-Lambert, which had once fired Bates. The other account win would have reverberations for the holding company and both agencies. In August, Compaq computer selected Bates Europe to handle its account, valued at £33 million, for Europe, the Middle East, and Africa.

Some periodicals incorrectly credited the win to Saatchi & Saatchi; after all, Bates is owned by Saatchi & Saatchi Company PLC, so the mistake was understandable. However, Saatchi & Saatchi Advertising was the agency for Hewlett-Packard, a Compaq rival. This was a lose-lose scenario: Bates was upset because it won the account and did not receive the proper credit; Compaq was upset because its selection was ignored; Saatchi & Saatchi Advertising was upset because it did not want the credit; and Hewlett-Packard was upset because its agency was now incorrectly identified as the Compaq agency.

The incident further justified changing the name of the holding company, while Maurice Saatchi again told anyone who would listen: "I will not be the chairman of this company while its name changes." Bill Muirhead embraced the idea of changing the name. "We have the brand name, so we won't lose anything," he said. Unfortunately for Muirhead, he made his comments at a meeting attended by Maurice. Afterward, Saatchi telephoned Muirhead and yelled. "I won't stay in this company," Saatchi shouted.

"Grow up," Muirhead said. "Don't be so fucking sensitive. The name is famous because of advertising. It hasn't been a great stock for a long time."

Around that time, during the summer, Muirhead also met at the Park Avenue Cafe in Manhattan with Charlie Scott. Muirhead listened as Scott confessed he was puzzled about something: "Why is Jeremy so loyal to Maurice? Maurice probably wouldn't be as loyal to Jeremy." Muirhead said Jeremy recognized Maurice's character flaws, but "he sees the positive part of people and is loyal to that. Jeremy magnifies everyone's good side."

In Chicago, David Herro was beginning to hear noises from London he did not like. Through a source Herro developed on the board, a source who shared Herro's low opinion of Maurice Saatchi, he discovered that Saatchi was planning to name a new nonexecutive member to the board. Saatchi's choice did not thrill Herro.

Sir Paul Girolami was an old acquaintance of Maurice; Girolami, sixty-eight, was about to retire as chairman of Glaxo, the giant pharmaceuticals company. Girolami was to replace Stuart Cameron. Agitated, Herro again cited the Cadbury Commission's rules on corporate governance. Non-executive board members are supposed to be a diverse and independent group. With Peter Walters of SmithKline Beecham, Saatchi & Saatchi already had a member who was affiliated with a pharmaceuticals company. Why did it need another? For Herro, the worrisome answer was that Maurice Saatchi was trying to stack the board of directors with his old pals.

On August 25, Herro wrote a brief letter to Cameron, chairman of the nominating committee. "After reviewing the Cadbury Commission's recommendations on board selection and composition, I am curious as to what the Saatchi board's policies are concerning this issue. Especially given what has transpired in the past, I and other institutional holders will be watching this very closely to ensure that in the event of any changes, these policies are strictly adhered to. We would also be interested in being kept informed as to future board member considerations. . . ." This time, Herro's wishes were brushed aside. Girolami was formally nominated in September and placed on the board October 3.

Girolami would become the most vocal anti-shareholder board member. He said the shareholders should not have so much information about the company's inner workings. Why is the company taking this group of troublemakers so seriously, he wondered. And, these shareholders are so young. Do their bosses know what they're doing?

It was another victory for Maurice Saatchi in what was shaping up to be a positive second half of 1994. He had the board in his grasp, business was picking up, he was credited for the upswing, and the share option scheme that would pay him millions was about to be approved. Saatchi's summer brightened even more when Suzanna Taverne was ushered into his Whitfield Street office one day in early July. Taverne came highly recommended to conduct an independent review of Saatchi & Saatchi Company PLC's structure.

Although he did not know it at the time, when Saatchi shook hands with Taverne, he had finally met his match.

CHAPTER
ELEVEN

ONE OF THE FIRST THINGS that registered to Maurice Saatchi about Suzanna Taverne, other than her model good looks, was her last name: Taverne was the thirty-four-year-old daughter of Dick Taverne, the well-known former Labour leader. Taverne had worked at S.G. Warburg for eight years until 1990 and was familiar with Saatchi & Saatchi, having done a little work on the Europreference deal. She then moved to newspaper publishing and *The Independent* as finance director, but Taverne left when *The Independent* was effectively taken over by the Mirror Group.

The break was well timed. Taverne, tall with short dark hair and a warm face with chiseled features and a dazzling smile, had recently had a baby and began thinking about a new job in June. Former Warburg colleagues suggested she meet Maurice Saatchi, who was casting about for someone who could conduct a strategic review. In their first session, Maurice told her that Peter Walters had recently joined the board and he was "determined to do a review of our structure."

Maurice said he had a long-held belief that the structure wasn't right. Does it make sense to merge Bates with Saatchi & Saatchi? If not, can we de-merge the two? "Find us a way out of this straitjacket," Saatchi told Taverne even before she officially accepted the position.

A week later, she met with Maurice Saatchi, Charlie Scott, and Peter Walters. Scott reluctantly went along with hiring Taverne. She was signed to a three-month contract. "She wasn't hired on my behalf," Scott said later. Scott did not feel her presence was necessary because he had already made a strategic review only months earlier, coming up with a plan that the board had overwhelmingly approved. "I did it in the spirit of compromise," Scott said.

Taverne moved into her fifth-floor office on Whitfield Street on August 1 and spent two months talking to senior management in the parent company and the two major agencies. What she discovered was disturbing: first, everyone was surprised she was bothering to explore these issues, since it was assumed the matter was settled. Second, everyone agreed that merging the two major agencies would be harmful: there were too many client conflicts and both agencies ran the risk of losing major accounts. Of course, Maurice thought his agencies were immune to such threats. It did not take long for Taverne to develop a theory as to why Maurice wanted to merge Saatchi & Saatchi and Bates Worldwide. She told friends that a merger was another way for Maurice to achieve his goal of becoming the biggest ad agency in the world. Taverne wanted to convey the conclusions in a way that was so compellingly persuasive that they would never be explored again.

Taverne would meet with Maurice several times in August and September and was surprised at how little interest he took in the detail of her arguments or the process she was using. Saatchi was only interested in the bottom line: can the company manage to merge the two advertising networks? His approach was in stark contrast to that of Charlie Scott, who, although he hadn't wanted to hire her, nevertheless threw himself into the process and went over everything she did in detail.

Taverne was scheduled to present her conclusions during a major two-day meeting of Saatchi & Saatchi Company PLC executives, including senior officials from the ad agencies and the entire divided board, at the Oakley Court Hotel near Windsor outside London beginning October 18, 1994. Two weeks before her presentation, Taverne separately presented her conclusions to Saatchi and Scott. Saatchi's ears, of course, perked up when Taverne began speaking of the need to change the name of the holding company. "One of the things that stopped the company from growing was that the holding company has the same name as one of the parts of the business," Taverne told Saatchi.

She reminded Saatchi that the twenty-fifth anniversary of Saatchi & Saatchi Advertising on Charlotte Street was to be celebrated in 1995 and that Saatchi had told Michael Bungey that he expected clients of Bates Worldwide to attend the festivities.

Bungey refused the invitation. "This isn't the twenty-fifth anniversary of anything relevant to me," Bungey had said to Saatchi. "I'm not going to take clients to a dinner under the name of a rival agency."

Taverne also repeated to Saatchi what others before her had said: the holding company's name was "endlessly problematic" to Saatchi & Saatchi Advertising because it was confused with a holding company that had deep financial problems and that was perceived as being unstable. "It is an issue that is oozing out of the walls," she said. Saatchi sat passively until Taverne showed him a slide she planned to present at the Windsor meeting that clearly explained why there should be a new holding company name.

"You're wrong," Saatchi began. "The name shouldn't change. It's one of the great brand names. Mars has one. Philip Morris has one."

"There are difficulties," she said.

"I don't care whether your arguments are right," Saatchi shot back, "the name won't change. I will not be the chairman of this company while its name changes. It's a great name. It's my name."

Saatchi then paused. Taverne told friends that he looked at her, daring her to say anything, assuming the threat was so horrifying that no one would venture beyond that point.

"I'm sorry," Taverne said. "The arguments are strong and it ought to be discussed." She offered to rewrite the slide to include arguments for and against the name change. "If you like, I won't express my view," Taverne said.

"No," Saatchi said. "I'm not having it raised. You won't bring it up. If you're going to merge the two agencies or de-merge the company, then there is no point in raising this incredibly sensitive subject, which is definitely going to lead to a row."

Saatchi much later defended his orders: "It was completely logical. It was my meeting. I called it. I was the chairman. No one else initiated this strategic review. Only if we were stuck with the status quo were we going to address the difficulty of the status quo, [part] of which was the name."

To Saatchi, there was another, more important, matter: what the purpose of the holding company was. Saatchi said the advertising agency executives thought the holding company was a waste. And Saatchi thought Saatchi & Saatchi and Bates were vulnerable to a takeover if they continued operating as separate agencies because they were midsize shops competing in a world where clients overwhelmingly favored large agencies. Bates, Saatchi said, had only one true international client, Mars. And Saatchi & Saatchi had more, but he described it as an agency with a "very patchy network that was number one in Britain, but not in the United States or very many other places."

Then Saatchi said the existence of the holding company itself was "ludicrous" in the first place. Even after his salary reduction and the vacating of Berkeley Square, Saatchi & Saatchi Company PLC was costing 30 percent of the operating profits, three times what it should have. "Having created the holding company structure," Saatchi said later, "I viewed it as a relic of a completely different imperial past. When this was a company making acquisitions every five minutes and had profits of £100 million, having a big holding company is one thing." Of course, the end of the holding company, Saatchi said, would mean the end of jobs for Charlie Scott and Wendy Smyth. "They hated me for bringing it up," Saatchi said.

Saatchi's critics said ridding the world of Saatchi & Saatchi Company PLC was a desperate and somewhat clever way not to change the holding company's name. Saatchi said he would have been happy with Saatchi & Saatchi Advertising and for Michael Bungey to have Bates. "We were no longer a giant empire," Saatchi said. "I was happy not to preserve the status quo." In fact, the company was saddled with so much debt, the banks would not have accepted Saatchi's plan, the so-called de-merger.

To Taverne, the web spun by Saatchi, while interesting, was off the point and avoided addressing a topic that needed immediate attention. She said she wasn't happy about the situation and wondered aloud what she should do. Saatchi confided to her that the boardroom with its warring factions and the involvement of Herro "is a very difficult place now." He suggested that Taverne speak to Peter Walters. Taverne told friends she agreed to do so partly because he was the only board member she knew at that time and partly because if she was going to be forced to exclude part of her report, she wanted to pin it on someone in addition to Maurice Saatchi.

Once Taverne explained to Walters the need for the name change and Maurice Saatchi's steadfast position of not including it in her presentation to the board and senior company executives, Walters confessed he had not understood the severity of the situation. "There is a group on the board who are out to get Maurice," Walters said, naming Robert Louis-Dreyfus, Tom Russell, and Ted Levitt. The trio had a long-held belief that Maurice Saatchi may have had something of value to contribute to the company, but it was not in the role of chairman. Louis-Dreyfus and Russell were shaken by a disturbing sight during their first annual shareholders meeting in 1991. After the session, a lavish buffet lunch was served, as had become the custom. While chatting near the buffet table, Louis-Dreyfus and Russell witnessed elderly Saatchi & Saatchi Company PLC shareholders covertly stuffing sandwiches into their pockets. "A lot of these people had put money into the company," Russell said later. "When the dividend was wiped out, there went some of the money they were relying on to live." Russell said it was one thing for institutional shareholders to be damaged ("That isn't right either," he said, "but they're big boys"), but it was far more sobering to watch pensioners sneak food.

Walters, however, saw his mission as saving Maurice Saatchi, and in that way he was isolated from a majority of the board. "We need stability." Walters gently suggested she drop the matter.

"Shareholders also want the name changed," Taverne then said.

Walters did not want responsibility for this sensitive matter. He told Taverne to see the executives at S.G. Warburg.

The advice of Mark Nichols, a senior managing director at Warburg, was concise: "We don't want any more rows with the board. This isn't the moment to raise this issue, so leave it for the time being."

Much to her deepening anger and resentment, Taverne revised her presentation and mentioned the name change only in passing by saying there is a "perceived bias of the holding company." She later told associates, "it was there to whoever wanted to see it."

In Windsor, Taverne was the second speaker on the first day of the conference. Management, morale, and momentum were the three major issues facing the company, she said in her seventy-five-minute presentation. Although she was plagued by a bad cold, Taverne's presentation impressed virtually everyone who heard it. Tom Russell told her that he hoped she could do some work for him someday. Bill Muirhead offered her a job on the spot in New York.

After her formal presentation, Levitt was the first to speak. "I want you to know that I was opposed to the process upon which you were selected," Levitt said, "and I was opposed to you. What's more, these are issues that have been dealt with already. If you're going to hire someone, then you should hire a respectable consulting firm. Notwithstanding that, I am very impressed."

Taverne elaborated on her presentation, saying the reason the company's performance was poor was because all the relationships were either "corrupt or disharmonious." Further, there was a level of distrust between shareholders and the parent company. Saatchi & Saatchi Company PLC's employees thought the senior executives of the operating companies were flaky and had failed dismally in getting the businesses to perform. Conversely, the senior executives were resentful of the holding company because its acquisition spree had left them with a crushing debt and a load of negative publicity. The relationship between the agencies and their clients was considered poor because the agencies were losing market share.

Unknown to most involved with Saatchi & Saatchi Company PLC at the time, Levitt telephoned Taverne once he returned to Cambridge, Massachusetts. The two agreed that what was preventing the company from developing and growing was Maurice Saatchi as chairman.

Levitt thought Saatchi was an incompetent and ineffective executive and believed he had the evidence to support that opinion. In the early summer of 1994, Saatchi had telephoned Levitt's office at the Harvard Business School. Saatchi had finished an article about Coca-Cola and he wanted Levitt to arrange a meeting with Donald R. Keough, president of Coca-Cola. Levitt was working as a consultant for Coke and told Saatchi he would be glad to help, but first he needed to know the basis of the conversation. "I needed the reason," Levitt said later. "I value my business relations and I don't want to capitalize on them." Saatchi responded that he wanted to lecture Coke on the importance of brands. Levitt was taken aback; Keough and Coke wrote the book on brands. Then, Saatchi let it slip that he had already been to Coke and had seen senior executives but was politely rebuffed. Levitt said that he would not circumvent Coke executives. "Also, Maurice didn't indicate any knowledge of the situations facing Coke," Levitt said. "You have to understand the local problems and distribution systems and the power of local Coke franchisers. Maurice didn't do his homework."

While Levitt and Taverne were communicating, Saatchi and Scott concluded that, despite all the fuss over her presentation, she had done a good job and should be signed to a second contract for another six months. The second time around, Taverne was sponsored by Scott rather than Saatchi. She attempted to talk to Scott about the growing dissatisfaction among shareholders, but all too often the discussion would be interrupted or Scott would not even sit still to hear what Taverne had to say. As was typical with Scott, he avoided confrontation and unpleasant tasks. He had a head-in-the-sand quality about him. He was not interested in getting involved in a situation that, yet again, pitted Maurice Saatchi against himself.

IN NOVEMBER, Charles Saatchi's grim prediction that the shareholders would be back with a vengeance came to pass. This time, the shareholders, again led by Herro, were protesting Maurice Saatchi's super-option scheme. The plan favored Maurice Saatchi and no one else.

As proposed, the package would provide him with £5 million in three years if the company's share price doubled in that period. Other senior Saatchi & Saatchi executives had option packages, but theirs were tied to stock performances over five years.

On November 17, 1994, the board received another letter from David Herro that said that once he had received a copy of the super-option scheme, he spoke with other shareholders as well as with employees of Saatchi & Saatchi Advertising and Bates. Herro wrote that he was dissatisfied not only with the plan, but with how it was crafted. Herro had learned that Maurice Saatchi had attended meetings of the compensation committee, the board members who were the architects of his share option package. "It is a no-no for an executive to sit in on non-executive meetings," Herro said later.

In his letter, Herro wrote that it "appears" the plan was not formed in a "fair and objective manner. . . . The plan seems to also be very destabilizing to the employees of the operating companies, for they see it as another example of extravagance at the holding company level."

Herro also reminded the board that it had promised to analyze a name change for the holding company and "yet it remains obvious that no action has been taken."

Herro concluded, "These issues all point to a problem that seems to linger with the board. There continues to be actions taken that are in the interest of the Chairman, and are contrary to the interests of clients, employees, and shareholders of the company. I urge the board to once again reexamine the issue of the company management, as well as the holding company name."

Taverne had kept in constant contact with Tim Jackson, the meticulous director of investor relations. And Jackson told her of the growing storm the shareholders were threatening to create. At one point in November, Taverne and Scott debated what would be the effect if Maurice Saatchi left the company involuntarily. "Although that might be the right thing for the company in the long term," Scott said prophetically, "it will be terrible in the short term. Maurice won't go quietly. He will do maximum damage."

Then Taverne gave the most valuable advice of her brief tenure at Saatchi & Saatchi, advice that was foolishly ignored: "If you know all this, then you can be prepared. See the major clients and prepare the press. The board and you, Charlie, should realize you have to go for sudden death. Don't give Maurice any chances. He is the kind of negotiator who enters a negotiation without knowing what he wants to get out of it. Instead, he looks for an opening and once he finds it, he pushes and pushes until he gets a new, stronger position. He exploits each situation." With the knowledge that the board may not have any choice but to fire Maurice, Taverne counseled Scott, all your efforts should not go to putting your head in the sand, but to working out how to deal with it.

David Herro's letter of November 17 accomplished something that other events had not been able to. It provoked Charles Saatchi into action. Until then, he was focused mostly on his go-carts, his art collection, his wife and young daughter, Phoebe, and his social life. He dabbled occasionally with clients such as British Airways and Silk Cut cigarettes, but little else. On November 28, Charles telephoned David Kershaw, the chairman of Saatchi & Saatchi Advertising in London, and asked him to come to the hallowed sixth floor on Whitfield Street.

Charles Saatchi handed Kershaw the latest missive from Herro. "This is fucking outrageous," Kershaw said.

"Herro consulted the senior people from the group, including Bungey," Saatchi said.

"Well, he didn't fucking consult me," Kershaw said. "I'm going to write to Herro and tell him exactly what I think."

"Do what you want," Saatchi said. "I'm not telling you what to do."

On December 5, Kershaw faxed a three-page, single-spaced letter to Herro. He defended Maurice Saatchi's super-option scheme, adding that the plan was "designed and promoted by Sir Peter Walters, a hugely respected figure in the UK...." The management and employees of the Charlotte Street agency have responded "enthusiastically" to the plan as well, he added.

Kershaw, clearly taking a risky stance that only seemed to be backed by the Saatchi brothers, supported keeping the holding company's name as is. "I am absolutely certain that if the Holding Company name were to change," Kershaw wrote, "it would have a negative effect on our clients, our prospective clients and our employees. From the situation now where the Holding Company is not an issue, it would once again raise it to the top of the agenda. The natural response would be—why are they doing this? what is going wrong again? and are they ashamed of their heritage. As someone responsible for delivering profit to the shareholders, I urge you strongly not to advocate this course of action."

Kershaw then praised Maurice Saatchi as a "major contributor to the success of this Agency in terms of the quality relationships he has with the senior management of our most important clients and his input in development of new business is critical.

"There is not a corporate door in this country that, subject to conflict, Maurice Saatchi cannot get his foot into. . . ." Kershaw ended the letter by writing that it was not sent "out of a sense of emotional loyalty to Maurice Saatchi."

Kershaw showed a copy of his letter to Jeremy Sinclair and Charles Saatchi and sent a blind copy to Charlie Scott. Maurice Saatchi was shown the letter by his brother and was touched. Having committed what he believed was a proper act, Kershaw left for a business trip in Hong Kong and got rather drunk at an awards dinner. When he stumbled into his hotel room, his message light was flashing. He had six messages, all the same: call Bill Muirhead immediately.

Muirhead was furious. Charlie Scott had called Muirhead upon receiving the blind copy of Kershaw's letter to Herro. Scott and Wendy Smyth had gone ballistic. "But David doesn't work for me," Muirhead had told an agitated Scott. "Don't yell at me."

Muirhead told Kershaw that Scott had said, "That letter was counterproductive." To Scott and Smyth, the Kershaw letter sounded as if it had been dictated by Maurice Saatchi. And to Herro, Scott said, it exemplified how manipulative Maurice could be. Kershaw's defense was that he was forty years old and could write anything he wanted whenever he wanted to.

Muirhead, the consummate corporate politician and survivor, did not believe that communicating with Herro was the most effective approach. But Muirhead did not know how much power Herro possessed when it came to actually booting out the chairman of a public company. Instead, Muirhead thought the way to go was to write a confidential memorandum to Charlie Scott and try to persuade him again to support Maurice Saatchi.

Muirhead was a rarity in the top echelon in the corporate world. He loved his job and did not plot or scheme over anyone else in the company. In many ways, he was the most focused of all the Saatchi & Saatchi Advertising executives. If a client loved opera, Muirhead would work at liking opera and, indeed, become an expert. That is not to say he would not think twice about firing someone he felt was not doing a good job. Muirhead wanted the company to succeed, even if that meant losing a friend. To Muirhead, success at Saatchi & Saatchi, the holding company and advertising agency, meant keeping Maurice Saatchi. Muirhead had other problems, such as repairing the North America operation, and he had scant time to fixate on some shareholder from Chicago he never spoke with. That is one reason Muirhead's memo to Scott was so elementary and brief. "Maurice has told me about the letter you have received from Mr. Hero [sic]. . . . I understand that the thrust of the letter falls into three areas. 1) Maurice's remuneration package; 2) The name of the Holding company and 3) Whether Maurice makes an important contribution to the company." If Saatchi were to leave the company, Muirhead wrote, "we would be severely damaged as a business. . . . He is close to many of the senior people in the agency, including myself. Perhaps, more importantly though, he is the human face of what is now a large, multi-national advertising group, without whom we would lack an obvious figure-head."

Muirhead summed up Herro's other two concerns by writing: "I thought they had been previously agreed." It would be a shame to see the latest mess at Saatchi & Saatchi played out in the press again, Muirhead said. The only benefactors would be Saatchi & Saatchi and Bates competitors, who would "rub their hands with glee and make great capital out of the situation; and prospective clients would not even bother to see us—life is hard enough, especially over here. Please could you tell the Board and Mr. Hero [sic] my view."

Muirhead also checked around Saatchi & Saatchi Advertising to see whether anyone had spoken to Herro. No one had—at least no one would say so publicly. Then he telephoned Michael Bungey, the chief executive at Bates Worldwide. Why yes, Bungey said, he had spoken with Herro and, in fact, had found him to be quite nice and sensible. That is interesting, Muirhead thought—so Bungey had "stuck his boot in this." Of course, Bungey favored a de-merger. Then he, in all likelihood, would become chief executive of Bates Worldwide with no parent company. He would run the show himself.

In London, the situation again had reached a crisis pitch.

Herro was not going to back away from his demands regarding Maurice Saatchi's bonus and the renaming of the holding company. Incredibly, the situation had not been played out in newspapers, the usual location for squabbles within Saatchi & Saatchi. The reason: Maurice Saatchi had nothing to gain by going public now. He would be portrayed as a greedy, ineffective chairman who wanted to regain control of a company whose ruin he once oversaw. On the other side, Charlie Scott continued to be astonishingly naive when it came to using the press toward his own end. Not heeding Suzanna Taverne's advice, Scott thought the whole sad, ugly episode with Saatchi would somehow evaporate. Nor did Scott have an inner circle of advisers who could counsel him on the benefits of getting his side out to the public. And Herro wanted the matter settled internally; he continued to believe that if the board was presented with evidence that Saatchi was doing more harm to the company than good, the board would do the right thing and dismiss the chairman.

With both sides keeping quiet about the mutiny of major shareholders, few individuals knew the significance of Maurice Saatchi's trip to New York on December 5, 1994. On the surface, Saatchi's unusual sojourn served two purposes: he would, for the first time, and at the insistence of Bill Muirhead, address the employees of Saatchi & Saatchi Advertising North America on Hudson Street. He would also, for the first time, deliver remarks at PaineWebber's annual media conference. The conference was a well-attended four-day affair in the auditorium of the McGraw-Hill Building on Avenue of the Americas where analysts and reporters heard from chief executive officers and chief financial officers speaking on the status and the outlook of their companies, ranging from Time Warner to Times Mirror to Interpublic Group.

But Maurice Saatchi had a more urgent mission when he crossed the Atlantic with Charlie Scott, Wendy Smyth, and Tim Jackson. The four were to meet, yet again, with the non-executive board directors and the major shareholders, including Herro, at Bates Worldwide headquarters in the Chrysler Building. The issue of whether Maurice Saatchi would be allowed to continue as chairman was to be settled once and for all.

If Saatchi was concerned, he did not betray it. On December

6, he made his unprecedented appearance at PaineWebber, choosing to speak after Scott and Smyth delivered their financial news. Saatchi's remarks were widely anticipated for the logical reason that he was rarely seen by those in the audience. He rose to speak to a receptive early morning crowd: "I want to talk to you about the word 'global' in relation to advertising."

Saatchi badly misjudged his audience. It did not care one iota about theories of global advertising. Saatchi droned on, however. "Look at the sphere that is closest to advertising and that is art," he said. "Think of a painter like da Vinci or Mozart, Shakespeare, the Rolling Stones, Van Gogh, Picasso, all masters of their own field. None of these artistic luminaries could be described as producing work which is the lowest common denominator. It is the best. Yet it appeals to people all over the world. . . . The quality of great art, painting, drama or literature is it transcends all barriers and can touch people in any country. . . . In great advertising as in great art, simplicity is all. Simple logic, simple arguments, simple visual."

Saatchi was feeling pretty good after the speech, and his next stop was Hudson Street. Saatchi did not want to make this appearance. He was nervous about having to meet the entire agency because he knew that he was unpopular in America. There was lingering resentment about a foreigner buying an American agency and, worse, because once Saatchi had made his acquisition, he appeared to have no interest. But Muirhead was insistent. "Your name is on the door," Muirhead told him. "No one here has ever seen you." Muirhead also wanted Saatchi to establish an office in New York and visit it frequently. Charles Saatchi had also agreed to become more involved as well; he promised Muirhead that he would loan Hudson Street several pieces from his art collection.

For Maurice's appearance, Muirhead called the entire advertising agency staff to a gigantic reception area that was under construction. There was a magnificent view north of the Hudson River, clear to the George Washington Bridge and beyond, and south to the Statue of Liberty.

It was another command performance by Maurice Saatchi. This time, he abandoned any references to the Rolling Stones or Picasso or global advertising. Saatchi had something special and profound in mind for his North America employees. He told them a bedtime story: Once upon a time, there was a frog and a scorpion sitting by a river. The scorpion, wanting to cross the river, asked the frog for a ride. "But if I let you ride on my back, you will sting me and I will die," said the wise frog.

"Not so," replied the crafty scorpion. "If I sting you, then you will die and sink and I will drown since I cannot swim."

The frog invited the scorpion onto his back. Halfway across the river, the scorpion pricked the frog with his stinger. Mortally wounded, the frog looked back at the scorpion and said, "But now you're going to drown. Why did you do this?"

The scorpion stared at the frog and said, "Because I'm a scorpion. And that's what scorpions do."

Saatchi left it to the audience to conclude why he told such a baffling story. "I don't think anyone understood," Muirhead said later. "God, I didn't understand it."

It could be surmised that Saatchi was making a comparison between the scorpion and himself. Saatchi is compelled to do what he does—advertising—as if it were preordained. Of course, critics would make less flattering comparisons between Saatchi and a scorpion. Saatchi, others would say, is compelled to stab people in the back and watch them sink; he is unable to consider the consequences.

After the curious show was over and everyone returned to work, Saatchi and Muirhead had another pressing problem to tackle. Burger King, known throughout the advertising industry as the client from hell because of its habit of firing agencies after a short period of time, was making noises about pulling an account from Saatchi & Saatchi. The Hudson Street agency was responsible for the children's advertising for Burger King. Because the fast-food chain has an impressive Kids Club and the most successful tie-ins with major movies, including *The Lion King,* and other Walt Disney Co. releases, the account was coveted. Saatchi and Muirhead as well as executives from the separate children's unit of Saatchi & Saatchi met with Burger King officials. This time, the Saatchi charm failed and Burger King pulled the account. It was awarded to Ammirati Puris Lintas, the Interpublic Group–owned agency that also handles the main Burger King advertising.

■

MAURICE SAATCHI had one additional formal function to perform prior to the meeting with the non-executive board members and the shareholders on December 8. On the eve of that crucial meeting, Saatchi would host a relaxed dinner in a private room at Mortimer's, a trendy restaurant on Manhattan's Upper East Side.

Although Saatchi did not know it at the time, the after-dinner conversation took a sinister turn against him. Even though a considerable amount of wine was consumed, several attendees were quite lucid and were weighing the potential damage to the company if Maurice Saatchi was indeed fired.

CHAPTER
TWELVE

MORTIMER'S OPENED IN 1976 and was an instant hit with the chic crowd. The restaurant is dark and serves acceptable if not exceptional food and is often the setting for book publishing parties. On the night of December 7, 1994, executives from Saatchi & Saatchi Company PLC and its agencies and its companies gathered there for dinner. It was a well-attended event with even Milton Gossett, the chairman emeritus of Saatchi & Saatchi Advertising Worldwide, present as well as executive and non-executive board members.

Maurice Saatchi delivered yet another speech, this time with a self-deprecating tone. He described himself as the Willy Loman of advertising, making the comparison to the tragic hero in the Arthur Miller play *Death of a Salesman* because now Saatchi was traveling around the world in search of new clients. In a gracious gesture, he also thanked Charlie Scott for saving the company.

At around 9:30 P.M., when some of the diners began to leave, a small group formed at the far side of one table, away from Saatchi. The group consisted of Bill Muirhead; Michael Bungey; president of Bates New York Frank Assumma; Charlie Scott; and non-executive board members Clive Gibson, Ted Levitt, and Tom Russell. Other non-executives, Peter Walters and Paul Girolami, remained near Maurice and departed when he did. Wendy Smyth, one of Saatchi's staunchest critics, did not attend the dinner, opting to take her daughter to the Big Apple Circus at Lincoln Center.

Russell had invited the advertising executives to join the board members away from Saatchi. The board members had already been in a lengthy discussion about the meeting with shareholders the next day and what appeared to them to be the inevitable solution to the Maurice Saatchi problem. Now, Gibson,

Levitt, and Russell wanted to hear details from those with intimate knowledge of the advertising business: "Tell each of us," Russell said, "what will happen if we fire Maurice? What about fallout from the clients?"

Muirhead's response was immediate. "Maurice has been my mentor," he said. "I owe the man a large part of my career. I am loyal to Maurice. To answer your question specifically, I do not believe that Procter & Gamble will leave. Nor do I think British Airways will leave. But you will lose Mars without question." Muirhead thought British Airways would remain a client because the team that serviced the airline account was not being fired, only Maurice was.

Bungey was more optimistic in his assessment: firing Maurice "will be very good, a very positive thing for Bates. Maurice makes no contribution at all. In fact, he is an impediment. If Maurice is no longer in the company, Bates will do even better. I don't think you'll lose Procter & Gamble and I don't think we'll lose Mars."

Bungey yielded the floor to Frank Assumma, who was close to several clients, including Miller Brewing and Mars. Assumma insisted that Mars would not fire Bates if Saatchi & Saatchi fired Maurice. He conceded that Mars might "punish" the agency by pulling some of the Mars brands, but that was as far as the censure would go. "Mars may be cruel," Assumma said, "but they're not stupid. We're too important to Mars." The association between Mars and Bates had spanned nearly four decades. (Others said Assumma hardly spoke and Bungey made the comments about Mars.)

Much later, Tom Russell said that the predictions of Muirhead and Assumma gave the board further confidence to fire Saatchi.

Muirhead reflected upon the after-dinner discussion and thought that Russell, for all his business brilliance, and other board members for that matter, failed to ask Muirhead one critical question: What will *you* do if Maurice leaves? In early December, Muirhead was in New York having a telephone conversation with Jeremy Sinclair in London. Sinclair was recounting the latest developments involving David Herro and his relentless attack on Maurice Saatchi. When he got off the call, he did two things: he wrote a memo to Charlie Scott and telephoned Sir Colin Marshall, the chairman of British Airways. Marshall was a hero to Muirhead and the two had developed a close working relationship through the years. Muirhead wanted to hear Marshall's assessment of the crisis facing Saatchi.

In London, Marshall answered his own office telephone. "Bill, it's interesting you should call me now. In May, I wrote a letter to your board to say it would be unwise to get rid of Maurice. Now I read in the papers that Herro hasn't taken my letter seriously. It seems Maurice is in danger again. I don't understand it, Bill, when a company like yours doesn't listen to its customers." British Airways was a signature client and was apparently being ignored. To Muirhead, the ultimate client man, what the board of Saatchi & Saatchi Company PLC was doing was "stupid beyond belief."

That was when Muirhead began to think that if Maurice Saatchi were forced from the company, then he might leave as well.

BATES WORLDWIDE is accustomed to having executives of major corporations shuttling through its wood-paneled modern offices, but nothing prepared anyone for the parade of heavy-hitters that appeared on December 8. The board of Saatchi & Saatchi Company PLC, including its chairman, as well as David Herro and other major shareholders, were gathering for one of the most important meetings of Maurice Saatchi's career.

The non-executive board members met alone first and decided that they would tell the shareholders that they were there to listen only. Ted Levitt did not agree. He said he wanted to speak and had a lot to say. To others, it appeared as if Levitt came well prepared to document any indictment he would deliver on Saatchi's capability as chairman. In front of him were stacks upon stacks of papers.

In another room, the shareholders—David Herro along with Rosemary Sagar and Mike Solecki from General Electric Investments and James Lyle from Tiger Asset Management—were conducting their own meeting. John Nelson from the State of Wisconsin was present through a telephone hook-up and Richard Hughes from the M&G Group in London appeared via video hook-up. Together, these shareholders held approximately 35 percent of Saatchi & Saatchi stock.

The shareholders then joined the non-executives. Maurice

Saatchi was not invited to attend; instead he was asked to remain in a Bates office.

Clive Gibson said the board was aware of the shareholders' concerns, but it now wanted to hear the complaints. Before that took place, Herro wanted the shareholders to meet alone as a group to make sure they were unified. Herro, who heretofore had never displayed any penchant for theatrics, said that before any shareholder spoke, he had a "special guest," someone he wanted the board to hear for itself. He then opened the door and asked Suzanna Taverne to step in. Herro had seen Taverne in New York several days before and requested her presence here. Taverne, in turn, had asked permission from Charlie Scott to speak before agreeing to come. Herro led her through a concise question-and-answer session, asking how was she hired and what her conclusions were. None were positive for Maurice Saatchi.

Next, the company secretary, Graham Howell, who had only recently been hired by Maurice, said he was concerned about the poor corporate governance. He said that at his previous company, he had been impressed that the chairman would remind the board at the beginning of every meeting, "Remember, we have widows' money invested in us." That chairman, Howell said, was "very cognizant" as to what a chairman should be doing. He believed Maurice was not acting in a similar manner.

Then the shareholders spoke. Herro gave his reasons why Maurice Saatchi should be removed, ranging from his poor record for corporate governance to the share option scheme that favored him over any other Saatchi & Saatchi employee. To Herro's astonishment, when it came time for the non-executive members of the board to speak, the vast majority said that although Saatchi was not a good chairman, they still had many concerns about firing him. Maurice could wreak havoc on the company just as the advertising agencies were recovering.

Herro responded that it was not the intention of shareholders to rid the company of Maurice entirely. "As shareholders," Herro said, "our only concern is to remove him from the board. What you do with him then is your business. We don't want to micromanage." Taverne left the room before the non-executives joined the discussion.

Russell and Gibson agreed, but said the time was not right to dismiss Maurice. "Why rock the boat?" Gibson asked.

Peter Walters, who disliked Herro intensely, grew impatient with the rebellious shareholder. The stock price is up, business is coming in, Maurice is moving the business forward, Walters said, so what is your beef? Saatchi agreed to all of your terms, he said to Herro, and now it is you who are reneging.

Herro quickly recovered, redirecting the conversation to the fact that the details of Saatchi's bonus scheme were not agreed to by the shareholders.

Herro next polled Robert Louis-Dreyfus, who joined the meeting two hours late. By December 1994, the relationship between Louis-Dreyfus and the Saatchi brothers had deteriorated into insults and lawsuits over a $10,000 investment Maurice and Charles had made in Adidas, the company Louis-Dreyfus left Saatchi & Saatchi to head. The investment had netted the brothers $38 million. The suit arose because Maurice and Charles said their agreement included an option to purchase, with Louis-Dreyfus and Tom Russell, Adidas at a low price. When Louis-Dreyfus proceeded without the Saatchis, they sued to stop him and won. Louis-Dreyfus paid them $38 million to back away from Adidas. He then issued a press release that said: "I very strongly feel that having been offered a free lunch, the Saatchis then demanded the restaurant."

"Should we get rid of him?" Herro asked Louis-Dreyfus. Despite the Adidas affair, Louis-Dreyfus replied, "No. The best job for him would be to run the Saatchi advertising network."

That was quite a generous recommendation considering Louis-Dreyfus recruited Maurice and Charles Saatchi to pitch the Adidas advertising business. Louis-Dreyfus first approached Maurice and Charles about investing in Adidas in the winter of 1992–93 in large part because he thought Charlie Saatchi was one of the great creative geniuses in advertising. He wanted Saatchi & Saatchi to devise a marketing and advertising campaign for Adidas. As a measure of good faith, Louis-Dreyfus, who along with partners owned 15 percent of Adidas through Ricessa, a small Luxembourg holding company, allowed the Saatchis in on the investment. The individuals owning the remaining 85 percent of the company granted Ricessa the option to buy out their shares at a fixed price on or before January 3, 1995.

Then, Maurice and Charles, along with Jeremy Sinclair,

showed Louis-Dreyfus and Adidas executives the proposed campaign. Because this was a pet project of Charles Saatchi and Sinclair, the entire creative and marketing resources of the Charlotte Street agency were utilized.

"We thought it went rather well," Sinclair said after the pitch.

"It was appalling," Louis-Dreyfus confided later.

There were several parts to the proposed campaign: the new slogan, as proposed by Sinclair, was "Do It Right," a cheeky reference to the highly successful Nike campaign with the tag line "Just Do It." One commercial tried to convey that, more than its rivals, Adidas was the true athletic shoe. More Olympic Games gold medals were won with Adidas than with any other shoe. The commercial Sinclair and Charles Saatchi devised included footage of Jesse Owens, the African-American track star, at the 1936 Summer Olympics: a close-up of his Adidas running shoes, and then Owens winning a gold medal. Then the screen suddenly filled with a disgusted Adolf Hitler.

Privately, several high-ranking Saatchi & Saatchi Company PLC and Advertising executives had viewed the commercial with skepticism. First, it is always risky to place Hitler in any advertisement, and secondly, Jesse Owens does not resonate as a heroic icon with teenagers in the 1990s.

A second proposed commercial featured the slogan "Thank God for Sport." The idea was that in a world filled with so many horrible events, thank goodness there remains something as wholesome as athletic competition that can be celebrated. The problem was in the execution: intercut with footage of inspiring athletic events, such as high-jumping, were stomach-turning shots of things such as baby seals being clubbed to death.

At the time, Louis-Dreyfus told his former colleagues that he would vote for them despite his private opinion that the campaign was unsuitable. But the agency was not hired. Louis-Dreyfus said he endorsed Saatchi & Saatchi to Adidas "out of friendship." Louis-Dreyfus ordered Adidas to reimburse Saatchi & Saatchi the full amount, $300,000, it said it spent on the presentation. "I didn't want them to be out any money," Louis-Dreyfus said. But associates of Louis-Dreyfus said he was deeply hurt by the sloppiness and ineptitude of the Saatchi & Saatchi presentation. Some believed that it was this unpleasant incident that led to the unraveling of the relationship between the Saatchis and Louis-Dreyfus.

Two weeks after Louis-Dreyfus promised to vote for the Saatchi agency, Adidas faxed a two-line note of rejection to Peter Levitan, the Saatchi & Saatchi account executive assigned to Adidas. Less than a month after that, the brothers learned that Louis-Dreyfus was buying out some other Adidas investors. The Saatchis felt their opportunity to cash in on Adidas was undercut.

There were lawsuits filed and finally a peacemaker was brought in. The Saatchis were bought out for $38 million. The cash went directly to Maurice and Charles Saatchi, although some company executives wondered whether the money did not belong to the agency.

THE FINAL PERSON to speak at the Bates meeting was Ted Levitt. At first, he appeared nervous, but then he warmed up to the process and spoke eloquently for a half hour. "First of all, I agree with everything David Herro has said," Levitt began, before addressing Peter Walters directly. "And I have to question your independence on this, Peter, because of your close friendship with Maurice." Levitt then delivered what amounted to a closing summation of why Maurice Saatchi should be fired. Levitt said the shareholders were correct and that Saatchi was damaging to the business. He piled on evidence of how Saatchi flaunted his disregard for the Cadbury principles of corporate governance—Saatchi would attend compensation committee meetings, for example. Even worse, Saatchi was no longer in touch with the advertising industry. He was not an effective advertising executive. He was not a good chairman. Levitt concluded: "We have no choice but to remove this malignant body from the corporation."

Those in the room sat in silence. Later Russell said, "It was a well-documented performance that ripped into Maurice's lack of quality of leadership and all of his character flaws. But it was not done out of meanness. It was done out of the company's best interests."

Levitt's inspiring and sobering speech "sealed the shareholders' resolve to go to war against Maurice," Russell said.

The shareholders had not even been aware of everything Levitt spoke about. When shareholders left the meeting, they told the non-executive board, "We request you do something about Maurice, and if you don't, we will."

There were only four executive board members, compared with six non-executives. Neither Saatchi nor Jeremy Sinclair was invited in. Scott was asked to come in after Levitt had spoken. Some shareholders left convinced that the board would fire Saatchi, thereby sparing the shareholders from beginning the arduous process that would amount to impeachment proceedings. Herro, on the other hand, was not so sure. "I left the meeting skeptical," he said later. "Maurice has nine lives and the board, frankly, was not a strong board. Some were very much afraid of Maurice. He had pressure points on these people."

It fell to Peter Walters and Clive Gibson to inform Maurice Saatchi of what transpired at the remarkable meeting. The duo planned to deliver some humbling news. The bonus package would have to be revised, the name of the holding company would definitely have to change, and there was still a discussion as to whether he could remain as chairman. But Walters and Gibson were not given a chance to tick off the latest conditions. Maurice Saatchi, composed and even-tempered, stood upon their arrival at a Bates office and said, "Before you say anything, please have a look at this. What you are about to see might change the situation."

Saatchi removed a piece of paper from his pocket and presented it to his friends. Walters and Gibson were staring at an offer to buy Bates Worldwide. The interested party was Richard Humphreys, the former president of Saatchi & Saatchi Advertising Worldwide who was fired by Robert Louis-Dreyfus in 1992. Humphreys and his Korean millionaire partner in Adcom, W. Y. Choi, controlled Ayer, the oldest advertising agency in the United States.

Humphreys had kept close tabs on his former company, and in mid-1994 he grew to suspect that things were going off the track again. "The company was still lacking a strategy," he said. Humphreys came to believe that he was the solution to sorting it out. The best remedy was to sell Bates to Adcom, move any possible client conflicts to the Saatchi & Saatchi Advertising network, install Maurice as chairman, and get rid of the holding company.

In other words, do precisely what Maurice himself had been advocating.

Humphreys offered $300 million, plus an additional $75 million based on whether certain profit criteria were achieved. Saatchi & Saatchi Company PLC had spent over $500 million in its ill-conceived acquisition of the agency, once payments to the agency and its former chairman, Robert Jacoby, were made.

The offer should not have come as a surprise to some in the holding company. Humphreys had written to Charlie Scott earlier in the year, but did not receive a reply. He then telephoned Scott, who did not speak with him. Instead, Scott sent Humphreys a one-line note that thanked Adcom for its interest, but Bates Worldwide was not for sale. "I thought that I was getting nowhere with Scott," Humphreys said, "so I'll write to Maurice."

Upon receiving a communiqué from Humphreys, Saatchi, who thought selling Bates was a wonderful idea, had a few covert meetings with Humphreys's merchant bankers without informing anyone, including Scott and the board. Saatchi was convinced Humphreys's offer was legitimate, so he then presented it to the board.

The board decided it could not act on Maurice nor the Bates offer immediately, so it adjourned and said it would meet in London on December 16.

After the meeting at Bates, Saatchi entered Bungey's office. "I will never resign from this company," Saatchi said. He then asked Bungey to write a letter to the board in his support. Bungey had no qualms because he thought it would be a good idea if Maurice remained with the company and headed up the Saatchi & Saatchi Advertising network. "It never entered my mind that Maurice should leave the company entirely," Bungey said later. "That was out of my hands anyway since I wasn't going to be at the board meeting."

Interestingly, Bungey's counterpart at Saatchi & Saatchi Advertising Worldwide, Ed Wax, was not contacted about drafting a letter in support of Maurice. "I guess they knew my answer," Wax said. "They [Maurice and Charles Saatchi] should have been thrown out in 1989 when the stock crashed."

The Bates offer from Humphreys and Adcom was seriously considered by the board. Saatchi & Saatchi Company PLC brought in its investment bankers and cash flow charts were prepared. The offer was ultimately rejected because it was considered vastly undervalued. The surprise in Maurice Saatchi's dramatic presentation of the offer at Bates was that Maurice had managed to pin Humphreys down with a firm offer.

At another point in the Bates offices on December 8, 1994, Louis-Dreyfus met with Saatchi and Sinclair. "You think I'm the instigator," Louis-Dreyfus said to the duo. Indeed, Maurice Saatchi told friends he came to believe that Louis-Dreyfus pushed Herro into calling for Saatchi's dismissal because of the Adidas mess. Although there is no evidence to support this thesis, Maurice told friends he was convinced Louis-Dreyfus and Adidas were the reasons for his dismissal; he cited as evidence an event that took place in the early days of the Adidas battle. As the Saatchis were seeking the injunction againt Louis-Dreyfus and his investment partners in Adidas, a meeting took place in Paris between Louis-Dreyfus, Maurice Saatchi, and Edward Stern, the head of Lazard Stern, who was acting on behalf of the brothers. At one point, Louis-Dreyfus and Stern spoke privately, after which Stern said to Saatchi, "Are you in a strong position in your company, Maurice? Robert said to me that if you go further with this litigation, he will use his position on the board to damage you. He said he has a lot of friends on the board and, if pressed, he would use that position to get his revenge."

Later, in December at the private meeting at Bates in New York with Saatchi and Sinclair, Louis-Dreyfus said he knew Saatchi believed he was the catalyst behind the entire movement to displace Saatchi. "I'll tell you what," Louis-Dreyfus said. "If you want me to resign from the board, I will. I have had my disagreements with you and with the others. I think you behaved like a shit on the Adidas affair. But I don't think you should leave the company. I think you have something to contribute.

"I won't vote against you. But if you prefer not to have my vote because you don't trust me and you think I will vote with the others, then I will resign."

Saatchi was momentarily speechless. Then he said he would think about it.

Later, Louis-Dreyfus said he was amused that Saatchi thought he "created" Herro to avenge the Adidas affair. He said he did contemplate revenge on the brothers at the time. "But my revenge would have been physical," Louis-Dreyfus said. "I would have punched them."

Again, none of the unusual and highly significant events—the Mortimer's dinner and the Bates meeting—found their way into newspapers on either side of the Atlantic Ocean. The company, it appeared, had dodged yet another public relations disaster. Nevertheless, Saatchi & Saatchi Company PLC and its board received more pressure from the shareholders on December 12. David Herro sent another letter to the board: "This is to inform the Board that subject to Board action this week, an Extraordinary General Meeting will be requested by shareholders during . . . the week starting December 18th. . . . The EGM agenda will include, but will not be limited to, a resolution which removes the current chairman from the Board of Directors. It is understood that a press release will accompany this requisition."

Everyone was aware of the significance of the last line in Herro's letter. Company bylaws are such that there must be a seven-week waiting period between the time an EGM is called and when it is held. Herro was clearly stating that the public would be made aware of the EGM and why it was necessary. What would likely follow would be a month-and-a-half press war unprecedented even by Saatchi & Saatchi's standards.

The board and senior company executives correctly feared that clients would flee such a mess to avoid getting wounded in the crossfire of negative publicity. The momentum was building for the board to finally remove Saatchi as chairman on December 16.

Three days prior to the meeting, on December 13, the story finally became public when Robert Peston of the respected *Financial Times* published a story detailing the entire dilemma engulfing Saatchi & Saatchi. "Maurice Saatchi's future as chairman . . . hangs in the balance following an explosive row between the company and leading shareholders over a proposed five million pounds [$7.8 million] option package. . . . Shareholders controlling a third of the group's shares, led by Harris Associates . . . were so angry to learn of the so-called 'super option scheme' that they last week put three proposals to the company's board." One option: "that the company consider whether [Saatchi] should stand down from the board altogether, to work instead for the operating subsidiary."

Peston further reported that the board was scheduled to meet within days to consider the proposals. The leak to the press was a clever maneuver to ensure that the board could not straddle the fence any longer. With the issue before the public, the board had to take clear action supporting or finally rejecting Maurice Saatchi.

Although many people were suspected of leaking the story, much of the suspicion, through a process of elimination, began to center on Suzanna Taverne and David Herro. Taverne and Peston knew each other socially and she was in constant contact with Herro. Others who knew intimate details, such as Charlie Scott and Tim Jackson, did not ever whisper in the ears of reporters. And board members thought such behavior to be untoward. However, the following is known: someone within Saatchi & Saatchi Company PLC telephoned Herro in Chicago to talk of concern that, despite the call from shareholders for an EGM, the board was "dancing around" firing Saatchi. After some prodding, Herro agreed to speak to a reporter. The individual within Saatchi & Saatchi suggested the *Financial Times* because it would have the most impact in London. The Saatchi & Saatchi person telephoned Peston, who in turn called Herro.

Much later, Herro said that even the *Financial Times* misunderstood the nuance by placing too much significance on Saatchi's bonus package. "It was Maurice's basic behavior of putting his own self-interest ahead of the company's," Herro said.

The shareholders were aware that calling for an EGM might be dangerous—that as a result clients might fire Saatchi & Saatchi and Bates. But Herro said he had no choice. "Do you allow yourself to be extorted?" he asked.

Events were moving quickly as Jeremy Sinclair predictably and admirably began to circle the wagons. He drafted a detailed, three-page letter to the non-executive board members in support of Maurice that the executive board members—Saatchi, Scott, Wendy Smyth, and Sinclair himself—hopefully would sign. That week, Charlie Scott came down with a bad case of the flu and was not in the office. He was somewhat groggy when Sinclair telephoned him at home and asked whether he would sign such a letter. "That depends on the contents," Scott wheezed into the telephone. Sinclair said he would compose the letter and get back to him.

Meanwhile, Saatchi and Sinclair informed Wendy Smyth of their plans to send the letter. Smyth's reply was identical to Scott's.

Sinclair then drafted the letter: "The Herro group of shareholders have indicated that they would like the Board to replace the Chairman of the Company. We thought it might be useful if you knew our views on this." Sinclair said that, once "properly motivated and incentivized," Saatchi could make useful contributions. To that end, Saatchi's contract was replaced with one that included a "high performance related scheme. Since then, the Company's position has stabilized. Press and analyst comment has been favourable." The letter listed seven examples, including 1994 results in line with market expectations; the 1995 budget showing a "significant revenue increase for the first time in four years"; and the share price rising 17 percent.

It continued: "Since the new arrangements with the Chairman, he has been promoting the development of the Company by visits to the company offices, meeting existing and prospective clients, making speeches to staff, speeches to conferences, new business projects, chairing the Revenue Committee, the Executive Committee, and the organisation of a successful Strategy Conference for the Board in October. . . .

"Therefore the question that we have asked ourselves is why we should recommend the change now.

"In our view going back on this agreement arrived at unanimously by the Board would be to jeopardize unnecessarily these hopeful signs of progress.

"Therefore if a resolution is put to the Board demanding the Chairman's dismissal we could not in the best interests of the shareholders, support it."

Scott later described a debate with himself over whether to sign it. It was the most difficult dilemma of his life, he said. Saatchi was accused of well-known abuses that had to stop. On the one hand, the shareholders were making a convincing case that Saatchi was not a suitable chairman of a public company. Scott said he could not disagree with that. It was clear to anyone who cared to see that the company was not run properly until Robert Louis-Dreyfus arrived. On the other hand, Scott thought, he knew what some of the clients wanted, which was for both Saatchi and Scott to remain. In the end, Scott based his decision on what he thought was best for the company. He had to do what the clients wanted.

Wendy Smyth thought the letter was fine and accurate until, she said, "the last bit about how it was in the best interest of the company for Maurice to remain as chairman." In a final meeting in Maurice Saatchi's office with Sinclair, Maurice, and Scott, Wendy Smyth was asked to sign the letter. "No. I can't," she said. "I don't agree with the statement about it being in the company's best interest to keep Maurice as chairman. I'm sorry."

Smyth said she did not think Maurice should leave the company entirely. Instead, he should be chairman of Saatchi & Saatchi Advertising Worldwide, a position already held by Ed Wax in New York. Maurice and Sinclair accelerated the verbal pressure on Smyth by asking questions such as did she know what would happen to the company once Maurice left? How could the company allow a thirty-four-year-old "kid" from Chicago to have so much influence?

Finally, Scott interrupted. "If you keep pressuring Wendy, I might change my mind about signing it."

The letter was finally sent, signed by the curiously aligned trio of Maurice, Scott, and Sinclair.

Smyth, who thought Saatchi was continuing to run a public company as if it were a private, family business, did not think there would be a calamitous fallout if Saatchi was pushed out. She assumed that Jeremy Sinclair would leave with Saatchi, but she was not concerned because Sinclair had moved away from intimate involvement with the creative output. Indeed, none of the other senior executives said, "If Maurice goes, I'll go," so Smyth assumed very few would follow Saatchi.

Saatchi and the board received additional letters in support of the chairman prior to the December 16 meeting. When David Herro found out about one in particular, alarm bells again went off. The author of the letter, written to Saatchi directly, dated December 13 and marked private and confidential, was Ali E.

Wambold, chief executive of Lazard Frères & Co., a specialist in corporate advice and mergers.

"Directors of a public company, in both the US and UK, have a fiduciary duty to act in the best interests of the company as a whole, not of any particular group of shareholders. . . .

"If as a result of indulging the wishes of such a shareholder, the performance or share price of the company suffers, the Directors could be subject to serious reproach . . . in the US at least, this could mean legal action by shareholders not in the dissident's group."

What upset Herro, upon learning of the so-called confidential letter from his sources inside Saatchi & Saatchi, was that Wambold was more than an ardent supporter of Maurice. Wambold, it turned out, had been asked by Maurice to join the company board only one week prior to sending the letter. He was scheduled to become a non-executive board member January 1, 1995. To Herro, this again smacked of behavior not befitting the chairman of a public company because, Herro said, Saatchi was trying to wrest control of Saatchi & Saatchi by stacking the board in his favor.

The board that week also heard from a former member, Stuart Cameron. He wrote that Herro knew the details of Saatchi's bonus package verbally and in writing around the time of the Chicago meeting in May. "Jeremy performed brilliantly at that Chicago meeting," Cameron wrote, "and in particular emphasised the importance of Maurice's continued contribution as Group Chairman. I wholeheartedly endorse that view."

Sir Colin Marshall of British Airways wrote an ominous letter directly to Herro on December 15. "I wrote to Sir Peter Walters . . . telling him the importance of Saatchi's work for BA and of the fact that Maurice Saatchi had been the driving force and key lynch pin behind the relationship between our two companies." Marshall went on to say that in the event Saatchi was no longer with the company, British Airways would consider whether it wanted to remain with Saatchi & Saatchi, and indicated "astonishment" that his views were not being taken seriously.

David Montgomery, chief executive of the Mirror Group of newspapers, also weighed in with strong support for Maurice and concerns about the "continuing public attacks" by militant shareholders and some board members.

Sir Paul Girolami, the newest board member, would be unable to attend the December 16 meeting in person, instead communicating on a squawk box from the Hassler Hotel in Rome. In case there was a communications snafu, Girolami faxed the board a handwritten letter in which he said he was unhappy about the way the company was discussing "vital issues affecting the management and future of this company with institutional shareholders whose only claim to privileged treatment is that they have a controlling vote."

Girolami did not support abandoning any proposal for the special option scheme for Maurice and added that although he was opposed to changing the holding company's name, he would go along with it, and concluded, "I believe it is against the long term interests of the company and investing shareholders to remove the Chairman."

On the other side, David Herro was emphatic in an interview with the *Wall Street Journal*, published the day of the board meeting: "We are very firm that he must stand down as chairman. He may continue to work for the company and we think he is fine with marketing, but not as chairman."

Two days earlier, the *Journal* published another damaging blow to Saatchi; it was the first to report on the contents of *Architectural Digest*'s January 1995 issue. Although the eleven-page spread profiled Saatchi's wife, Josephine Hart, the real star of the piece was Old Hall in Sussex. Hart told the magazine, "Old Hall to me *is* M. [her nickname for Maurice], the perfect expression of his particular soul and psychology—the gentle persistence of the gardener and the commitment to the future." The article could not have hit the newsstands at a worse time for Saatchi. In Chicago, Herro, reacting to the *Journal* story, received a fax of the *Architectural Digest* piece and fumed about Saatchi's exorbitant life-style. Employees within Saatchi & Saatchi Advertising and Bates Worldwide shook their heads and seethed with resentment. Again.

WITH THE WHEELS set in motion on what he believed was an inevitable course, David Herro flew south from Chicago on December 15 to the Cayman Islands to scuba-dive in the warm waters of the Caribbean. Herro was turning thirty-four years old on December 17 and he wanted to celebrate someplace far warmer than Chicago in mid-December. Anything that transpired at Saatchi & Saatchi on a cold gray London afternoon and evening during the December 16 board meeting could easily be relayed to Herro as he sat poolside sipping beer.

CHAPTER
THIRTEEN

AT PRECISELY 2 P.M. on December 16, 1994, the board of Saatchi & Saatchi Company PLC filed into the starkly decorated conference room on the sixth floor of the Whitfield Street offices. The board was accompanied into the room by a dozen attorneys and financial advisers from S.G. Warburg and the United Bank of Switzerland. Paul Girolami was present on a speakerphone from a hotel in Rome. One non-executive board member was missing: Robert Louis-Dreyfus. Maurice Saatchi, the chairman, remained in his office nearby, accompanied by his brother Charles.

Louis-Dreyfus and the Saatchis were the only three who knew precisely why Louis-Dreyfus did not attend. One week after Louis-Dreyfus told Maurice he would resign if that was Saatchi's wish, Saatchi took him up on the offer. When Louis-Dreyfus did not submit his resignation immediately, Saatchi became nervous that he would renege and kept calling to ask when he would resign. Finally, Louis-Dreyfus called Saatchi and said he would fax a letter of resignation during the board meeting on December 16. But Saatchi did not want to leave anything to chance. Saatchi was convinced that Louis-Dreyfus would not resign, and instead would vote against him, siding with the shareholder revolt. No matter that Louis-Dreyfus assured Saatchi directly that he wouldn't. "It shows something about the difference in people's characters," Louis-Dreyfus said later.

Saatchi telephoned Henri Filho, vice president of investment banking at Crédit Lyonnais, an investor in Adidas. Filho had been the peace broker between Louis-Dreyfus and the Saatchis in the Adidas affair. Filho contacted Louis-Dreyfus. "Maurice doesn't believe you will resign," Filho said.

"Fine," Louis-Dreyfus said impatiently. "I'll fax you my letter of resignation and you can fax it to Maurice yourself."

It was Louis-Dreyfus's wicked idea to resign during the board meeting because he wanted the board to be shaken by the resignation, to be forced to think about why he was suddenly quitting. He also did not want board members to ask him to explain his abrupt action: "I didn't want to be in a position to say the brothers were great, nor did I want to say they were lousy."

The meeting, chaired by Clive Gibson, had only one item on the agenda; that piece of business—whether to fire Maurice Saatchi—was to some a foregone conclusion and to others a highly debatable option.

The board had to consider many angles. It was receiving legal advice, for instance, on whether it had to do what the shareholders wanted. It had the letters from Mars, British Airways, and Mirror Group theatening that the high-profile and valuable accounts would be in danger if Saatchi walked the plank. The letters proved ineffective; a majority of the non-executives thought Maurice had coerced the letters as a desperate last-minute bid to save his neck.

Several times during the marathon eight-and-a-half-hour meeting, Peter Walters left the room to provide the Saatchis with brief updates.

At any point, several board members said, Maurice could have stopped the proceedings by merely popping his head into the meeting and saying words to this effect: "I have seen the error of my ways. Let me try and speak with Herro." Several board members told Saatchi prior to the board meeting that he should seek a rapprochement with Herro, be prudent on expenses, and be more reasonable on salary demands. Saatchi was offended. He had compromised so much; he felt taken advantage of.

The board, in the end, was looking for a way out, one that spared it from making the heavy decision. But, increasingly, the walls were closing in and the options becoming fewer. The two financial consultants, Warburg and United Bank of Switzerland, delivered sobering news: they had conducted a poll of the major shareholders and concluded that a majority wanted Saatchi fired, and if the board did not do it, they would do so six weeks hence.

Only 2 to 3 percent of those polled favored Maurice remaining as chairman.

Maurice Saatchi would long harbor doubts that a poll was ever formally conducted. He said much later that several major shareholders were not contacted. And if any institutional shareholders were polled, Saatchi did not believe they were given a complete assessment of the situation, including the letters supporting Saatchi from clients such as British Airways and Mars.

In fact, an informal poll was taken by Richard Hughes, a director of M&G Investment Management, a major shareholder in Saatchi & Saatchi Company PLC. According to an individual close to the process, Maurice went to see Hughes close to the time of the December 1994 board meeting. "Maurice wanted M&G to put its reputation on the line and come out against the American who wanted to oust him," this individual said. "In the end, M&G wasn't willing to do that." Hughes then contacted a number of large institutional shareholders to ascertain whether they would be willing to back Saatchi. None were, except for Alastair Ross Goobey, chief executive of Hermes, formerly Postel Investment Management, who held only 1.7 percent of Saatchi & Saatchi Company PLC shares, rendering his endorsement quite ineffective. Goobey later recalled that he would have preferred an Extraordinary General Meeting to the events in the boardroom in December 1994 that led to Maurice's ouster. "I know Maurice quite well," he said, "and it didn't take a genius to know the kind of damage this would do to the company. It was better to have him in the company."

"This was a terrible possibility," said Tom Russell. "Between now and the EGM, not only would the company be dragged through the mud, but so would our clients. And they wouldn't stand for it."

Some board members believed that it would be best for the company to fire Saatchi and hire a veteran advertising executive to run Saatchi & Saatchi Company PLC with Charlie Scott.

From Rome, Girolami spoke up with what were rather naive questions at this point: "What exactly is the problem with Maurice? What are the accusations you have against him? This is all rubbish. You couldn't put someone on trial like this if it were a kangaroo court."

Again, the details of shareholders' complaints were plowed

over: the reluctance by Saatchi to change the name of the holding company, the astronomical costs of refurbishing the brothers' Whitfield Street offices to duplicate the extravagant Berkeley Square facilities (that was a nonstarter, since Charlie Scott approved the bill without a complaint), the ugly press war against Scott by Saatchi, and, front and center, the bonus package.

Sinclair informed the group that Saatchi wanted that issue off the table. Prior to the board meeting, Saatchi agreed to a share-option scheme that was identical to that offered to Scott.

There was a great deal of grumbling about the Adidas money taken by the brothers. Tom Russell said the money was paid because of work Saatchi & Saatchi had performed for Adidas. Therefore, the $38 million belonged to the company.

Then Jeremy Sinclair spoke. Carefully, evenly, and without raising his voice much beyond a well-controlled whisper, Sinclair addressed the meeting: "You are about to do something you know is wrong. You are going to do this because if you don't, Herro will. Let me tell you. You are not responsible for other people's actions. God will only judge you on what you do, not on what Herro does. You are not his conscience. This is wrong. Do not do it. There is no justification. The shareholders and advisers say there will be six weeks of bad press. How many weeks of bad press will there be once Maurice is gone? You all have had the fear of God put into you by Herro. The easiest thing is to get rid of Maurice."

Tom Russell replied that, contrary to the Saatchis' belief, the non-executives had no "rancor" toward the chairman. There was a way out of this lunacy where everyone could benefit. Maurice, said Russell, should present a "reasonable offer" to purchase Saatchi & Saatchi Advertising Worldwide. Others at the meeting thought Maurice truly wanted to be fired, so he could then wreck the company from the outside, drive the share price down, and purchase Saatchi & Saatchi Advertising at a deeply depressed price.

Girolami spoke again. "Maurice should stay. Now which of the non-executives share my point of view?"

The answer was somber: none. "Ah, well," Girolami said to no one in particular, "then I can't help you."

Saatchi's death knell sounded when senior representatives from Saatchi & Saatchi's two law firms, Macfarlanes and White &

Case, declared that, given the circumstances, the board had no choice.

Then the board began tackling the question of what to do with him. "Despite all the criticism, the board recognized that Maurice's name has pulling power," Wendy Smyth said later. "He could open doors, even if he didn't do much once they were open. He could get to people no one else could see. In that way, he and his name were a genuine asset." Charlie Scott suggested Maurice could be the chairman of Saatchi & Saatchi Advertising Worldwide.

Earlier on the day of the board meeting, Scott telephoned Ed Wax, the chairman and chief executive officer of the Saatchi advertising network in New York, to feel him out about the plan. It was fine with Wax. "To keep peace, we need stability," Wax said. "It would have been sweet for him not to have the chief executive stripes." The board agreed to present Saatchi with Scott's proposal; it also offered Sinclair, who had been with Charles Saatchi since the beginning, the role of acting chairman.

Peter Walters delivered the news to Maurice along with the other non-executive board members. "You have to go as chairman of the PLC," Walters said. A brief discussion ensued with the board telling Saatchi that he was fired because Herro could outvote the nine-member board. Saatchi was then presented with the alternative plan that would let him remain with the company and told of Sinclair's ascension to acting chairman.

Saatchi was in his office with his brother when Sinclair entered. Predictably, he gave Sinclair two conditions before he would accept the offer: Saatchi told Sinclair he'd rather "his old mate," referring to Sinclair, not be chairman. "It would look like I approved of the board's action," Saatchi said. He also did not want any noncompetitive restrictions placed on a new contract. Put simply, Saatchi wanted the ability to walk away a free man in case Herro came back with more repressive demands. And, he wanted his salary to be identical to Ed Wax's and Michael Bungey's.

Sinclair returned to the boardroom, its twenty or so occupants taking in Saatchi's conditions. "Well, have you worked out your plan?" Sinclair asked impatiently when no response was immediately forthcoming. "Have you done your homework?"

The board and others collectively shrugged their shoulders and answered with a sheepish "No." After a few minutes, the board readily agreed to offer Saatchi a contract with no competitive restrictions. Then, it inexplicably debated the salary.

Sinclair later said the board should not have agreed to Saatchi's demand of not including noncompete clauses in a new contract: "To allow a man as resourceful as Maurice to walk away with no strings, that is lethal.

"The board should have agreed to the money on the spot. Why didn't they? They were scared about how it would appear publicly. Maurice's salary would have doubled to £400,000 and they were worried that he would present this in the press as a victory."

Sinclair wanted Saatchi to take the job: "I didn't want him to go. I've known these people as long as I've known my wife, longer than I've known any of my children. I didn't want to upset it."

Saatchi waited for twenty minutes and when no one came back with an answer, he appeared in the doorway of the boardroom for the first time in over ten hours. He recalled they all looked up and appeared "quite ashen."

"I'm not ready to decide," Saatchi said. "I have given my life to this company. And you're asking me to make a difficult decision after a difficult day. I can't do it. I need more time."

Can you decide by Monday morning? he was asked.

No.

How long do you need?

Until after Christmas.

Okay, you have until January 3, 1995.

"It was the humane thing to do," a surprisingly patient Levitt said later.

Late on December 16, the company released a curt, three-paragraph press release: "Maurice Saatchi . . . ceased to be Chairman and a Director of the Company. . . . Jeremy Sinclair . . . will be acting Chairman . . . pending the appointment of a successor Chairman."

At the Radisson Hotel in the Cayman Islands, where it was late in the afternoon, David Herro returned from diving to find a message from London waiting: "He's gone, but it's not official.

Don't say anything yet." Not long afterward, the hotel's fax machine spit out the official Saatchi & Saatchi Company PLC press release. "I was happy it was all over," Herro said. "In a way, it was anticlimactic."

In Switzerland, Louis-Dreyfus did not even bother to place a telephone call. Nor did anyone contact him. He read about the events in the newspaper on Saturday. "I was surprised they gave him two weeks," Louis-Dreyfus said. "I would have given him ten minutes."

With the release of the company statement late in the evening of December 16, Maurice Saatchi called Jet Cars, a private service, and was taken by Arthur Greenaway (nicknamed by the company "the mouth of the south"), a driver, to Bruton Place, where he picked up Josephine Hart and went off to dinner at Poissonnerie de l'Avenue on Sloane Avenue. After dinner, he and Hart left for Old Hall.

On Whitfield Street, the board members and company advisers trickled out of the office. Jeremy Sinclair passed the boardroom and saw Charlie Scott slumped, his head in his hands. "What's the matter with you?" Sinclair asked with a tinge of resentment.

Looking up, Scott said, "I know what's ahead."

DAVID KERSHAW, the chairman of Saatchi & Saatchi Advertising in London, was dining at Launceston Place in Kensington when his mobile telephone rang. It was Greenaway, the company driver, who had just dropped off Saatchi and had gone to Covent Garden to pick up Bill Muirhead from the opera. Kershaw was not surprised at the news. After he arrived home, he telephoned Saatchi at Old Hall. "He sounded really despondent," Kershaw said. "He sounded punch-drunk. I told him he should stay, accept the job, and get the fuckers from within. I wanted him to get those bastards."

Bill Muirhead and his wife, Jeanne, were being entertained by executives from Spencer Stuart, the executive headhunting firm, as the board was tossing out Maurice Saatchi. He had gone off to the opera with few concerns because he had spoken with Saatchi earlier in the day and was told not to worry; throwing out a chairman because of shareholders was virtually unprecedented.

But when Muirhead strolled out of the opera, after a charming evening in a private box, Greenaway greeted him and said, "They've topped him," a Cockney expression for the poor soul who has had his head chopped off.

Muirhead and his wife were in the Toyota Camry when the car phone rang. Saatchi was calling from Old Hall and sounded as if he were crying. Muirhead hardly recognized the voice of the man he had worked closely with for close to a quarter-century. "They've done it, they've done it," Saatchi kept repeating. "They want me to take Ed Wax's job. I can't. I can't."

"You must take it," Muirhead answered, "and fight from the inside."

Then Kershaw called Muirhead in the car; Kershaw was in tears. Muirhead reached Sinclair at home and they agreed to speak again Saturday morning and include Kershaw in the conversation.

There was another call Muirhead needed to make. Saatchi & Saatchi Advertising North America was throwing its office Christmas party in the fourteenth-floor cafeteria on Hudson Street when Alan Bishop, the agency's chief operating officer, was summoned to the phone. Bishop had imbibed a great deal when he received the call from Muirhead, who quickly ascertained Bishop was drunk and incapable of carrying on an intelligent conversation. It ended quickly.

ONE PERSON who was monitoring the events on Whitfield Street throughout the day was Tim Bell, who had been the so-called third brother in establishing the Saatchi advertising empire until he was usurped by Martin Sorrell and had his role diminished by the brothers. A sober and far happier Bell was now one of the leading public relations executives in Great Britain, with two tastefully decorated brownstone offices off Shepherd's Market.

The Saatchis had rekindled their relationship with Bell in early 1994. When Maurice Saatchi decided he could no longer stand Charlie Scott as chief executive, he and Charles Saatchi met with Bell at the Berkeley Square offices and asked him to return. "We've had a falling out with Scott," Maurice told Bell. "We think the best thing for the company to do is for Scott to go back to being finance director and you should come back as chief executive."

But Bell's public relations firm, Lowe Bell Communications, was about to become a public company and Bell had signed a contract to remain five additional years. One solution was for Saatchi & Saatchi to purchase Bell's company and merge the public relations companies. The discussions involving the acquisition of Bell's company went as far as to involve Charlie Scott in the fall of 1994. Maurice called Bell two weeks after the meeting with Scott and said the negotiations had become too protracted and Saatchi & Saatchi was halting the discussions. Nonetheless, Bell would become involved with trying to save Maurice Saatchi's professional life.

After the first *Financial Times* story appeared on December 13, Maurice called Bell and said he wanted to get his side of the story across. Bell arranged for the reporter, Robert Peston, to meet Maurice privately, but the session did not go well. Peston believed that Maurice had behaved badly and, although he was impressed with Maurice's charm, he was not persuaded by his argument. Bell told Maurice this much in a telephone call following the meeting with Peston. "If you're so concerned," Bell said, "why not let me help you?" After the board meeting, Charles Saatchi telephoned Bell and asked him to help with subsequent announcements.

OF COURSE, it was humane for the board to allow Maurice Saatchi two weeks to decide whether to accept a lower, figurehead position. It was also ill-advised. "I was pissed off that we didn't nail it," said Wendy Smyth. "We should have nailed him that day for an answer. It was a huge mistake to give him time." Scott conceded that the board could be criticized for "not being ruthless enough, but here was a man the board wanted to stay with the company. We didn't want any rash decisions." It was Saatchi & Saatchi's blatant ineptness in preparing for the possibility that Maurice Saatchi would try to destroy the company once he left that was so infuriating to the few savvy people in senior management.

One of those people was growing increasingly frustrated with Charlie Scott. By signing the letter supporting Maurice Saatchi, Scott hoped to have it both ways at a point in time when it was too late. If Scott truly believed that it was wrong for Saatchi to go, he should have taken that position earlier and gone off to see the shareholders himself. He should have said, "I, as chief executive, believe for the following reasons that you are embarked on the wrong road." Instead, Scott foolishly sent conflicting signals. And, at the very end, when what was needed was some sense in the press that Saatchi's departure was in line with the company's desires as well as those of the shareholders, he signed a letter supporting Saatchi.

The board, too, acted imprudently. It should have formulated a specific offer for Saatchi and made him answer immediately. And it should have played hardball; after all, it had the damning details of the shareholders' complaints. "That's it, you're out," the board could have said. "If you call a single client, we're going to release information to the press that is damaging to you." Louis-Dreyfus for one was puzzled as to why the board did not act aggressively. "I'm ruthless," he said. "I would have tapped every fucking phone on December 17. I would have called the newspapers, the clients. How can you be so naive? The only excuse I can think of when this happened was it was around Christmastime and they didn't want to be bothered."

THE TELEPHONE at Old Hall in Sussex began ringing at 7:30 A.M. on December 17 and continued all weekend. Saatchi's spirit was buoyed by what he heard: dozens of calls supporting him, telling him the company should go to hell and he should rain havoc on it.

As important, he was not crucified in the weekend press. That led Saatchi to believe that he could emerge as the persecuted victim and position Saatchi & Saatchi Company PLC as the hapless loser in danger of being torn apart by warring factions.

In truth, Maurice Saatchi was a man battling internal conflict. "I was quite tempted to stay," he said. "If it hadn't been for Herro, I could have been talked into it. My fear was if I accepted it, it was his aim to get me out. In six months' time, Herro would have been back, checking on my expenses, asking why I was flying the Concorde. He would have drummed up another reason to fire me." Also, Josephine Hart was opposed to Saatchi staying because she, too, did not trust Herro.

Over the weekend, Saatchi received one call in particular

that should have been impossible to ignore. A senior executive from Procter & Gamble said, "I see you're considering this offer. I don't want you to be in any doubt on where Procter & Gamble stands. We'd like you to stay. If you go, there will be a civil war. This could be destructive to our business." Saatchi recalled it was a "realistic" conversation. He confessed he had no idea what he was going to do, that leaving the company entirely was a possibility. But he promised to let Procter & Gamble know his decision before it was made public.

Meanwhile, in London, Sinclair, Muirhead, and Kershaw, the trio whom the press would soon dub the three amigos, met in Sinclair's office on December 18. The ostensible reason for the meeting was to compose letters that the agency's employees and clients could read the following morning.

As always, Sinclair led the conversation. "I'm leaving the company if Maurice leaves," he said without showing any emotion. "I can't work for a company that will be run by this man Herro who can't be trusted."

Muirhead said he could not imagine working anywhere without Sinclair. "Maybe we can open our own agency," Muirhead said.

It was not a new idea. The two had contemplated doing so in 1985 along with an executive from the renowned Leo Burnett agency in Chicago, but the plan never got far.

Kershaw did not want to be left out and vowed he would leave as well.

In the middle of the intense discussion, Maurice Saatchi, who had tried to reach Sinclair at home, called the Whitfield Street office. The three read Saatchi the notes they planned to leave for employees and clients. "What happens if I don't stay?" Saatchi asked.

"The preferred option is that you stay," Sinclair answered. "But the three of us are thinking of setting up our own business."

"That is terribly interesting," Saatchi said. "Let me call you back."

The three instantly knew what Saatchi was doing: he was calling his brother seeking advice. He then called back and asked more questions about the plan the three were hatching. Saatchi was clearly interested in latching onto anything the three talented executives were constructing. But Muirhead was emphatic on one point: the new agency would be vastly different from anything Saatchi had been involved with; it would be a partnership. "I wasn't interested in being a serf again," Muirhead said. Further, the money to open the new agency would be advanced by Maurice and Charles Saatchi. The brothers could use the tens of millions they earned from the puny Adidas investment.

The trio was cocky toward Maurice for a reason: for the first time, he needed them far more than they needed him. They had jobs they loved and that paid extremely well. There was no reason, other than emotional, for them to leave. Further, if they chose to resign, the three could open an agency more easily than Maurice could. They were close to clients and were all diligent workers. Saatchi was incapable of launching a new agency without the help of such finely tuned executives.

One major stumbling block, however, was that they were each under contract, which meant they could not work for any other advertising company, or client of Saatchi & Saatchi, for a minimum of one year.

With their contracts weighing heavily on their minds, the three had a brief meeting December 19 with Charles Smallwood, Maurice's attorney, who told them he could not give them any advice because it would have amounted to a conflict of interest. Saatchi was still supposed to be considering the company's offer. He could be in serious legal trouble if he instigated discussions about opening a rival agency. On December 20, the three retained their own attorneys, Julia Palca and Jonathan Goldstein, who told them that any agreement they made with Saatchi "must be contingent on your contractual duties with Saatchi & Saatchi . . . and would be in effect when you are free to do so. . . ."

By December 22, the agreement between Maurice Saatchi and the three amigos was hammered out, signed, and placed in escrow. It was assumed that Charles Saatchi would resign in short order and join them. Saatchi and the three amigos took off for vacations in far-flung places. Saatchi returned to Old Hall, Sinclair went skiing in Switzerland, Muirhead took his family to New York and then headed to Vail, Colorado, to ski, and Kershaw went to Mexico with his charming and attractive wife, Claire.

Before leaving for Switzerland, Sinclair was in the Whitfield Street office and saw Scott. "He advised me to change the name of the holding company immediately," Scott said later. "He said I should do anything that would distract people from Maurice Saatchi."

In New York, Muirhead, his wife, and three sons spent Christmas Eve at Ed Wax's Gramercy Park home singing holiday carols. Wax recalled that Muirhead appeared "preoccupied," but Muirhead did nothing to betray what was planned.

MAURICE SAATCHI began 1995 a very busy man. On January 2, he faxed a draft of his letter of resignation from Saatchi & Saatchi Company PLC to Sinclair, Muirhead, and Kershaw at their various vacation locales. In Vail, Muirhead did not sleep soundly. "It began to dawn on me that this is so sad," he said. "This is going to be a civil war with families killing one another and a lot of innocent people getting hurt." In Mexico, Kershaw's reaction was succinct: "Oh, Christ," he said to Claire upon receiving Saatchi's draft resignation letter, "this is for real."

CHAPTER
FOURTEEN

MAURICE SAATCHI telephoned Procter & Gamble on January 2 and said he would not accept the lower position his company offered. To his relief, the Procter & Gamble executive said he and the company respected Saatchi's decision. On January 3, Saatchi delivered his resignation to a company that was largely on vacation.

There were actually two resignations; one, submitted to Graham Howell, Saatchi & Saatchi's corporate secretary, was written by Maurice alone: "Please inform Mr. Herro that I do not accept his offer. It was kind of him to consider me for the position."

The second, written on Saatchi & Saatchi Company PLC stationery and distributed to company employees, clients, and the press, was composed by Maurice with help from Jeremy Sinclair. Saatchi said it was with "sadness" he would not accept the board's offer. "Saatchi & Saatchi has been taken over," he said. "No bid for the Company has been announced. No offer has been made. No premium has been paid. No shareholder vote had been taken. But, make no mistake, Saatchi & Saatchi is under new control.

"The new 'owners'—a group of shareholders owning around 30% of the shares—have found a simple, if crude, method of controlling the Company. By threatening the Directors with an Extraordinary General Meeting—at which they could outvote others—they have given the Directors their orders: 'Take your Chairman into a corner and shoot him quickly—we don't want the fuss of a public trial.'

". . . And, for the first time in 25 years, [I] found myself in an advertising company where the term 'advertising man' was being used as an insult.

". . . How could I reassure you of your critical importance to the Company, when the views of so many of the most respected among you have been ruthlessly brushed aside.

"This enforced parting grieves me deeply.

"Yet I look forward to 1995 with great anticipation. Because, as we have always believed at Saatchi & Saatchi . . . Nothing Is Impossible."

JANUARY 2 WAS A BANK HOLIDAY in London. It was not illogical, however, to believe Saatchi & Saatchi executives would forgo the extra day off to prepare for whatever Maurice Saatchi's answer would be. Incredibly, Charlie Scott and Wendy Smyth, the two senior managers of a company that was now under siege by its former chairman leveling charges, were nowhere to be found. "There wasn't a lot of preparation and there should have been," Smyth said later. "This isn't an excuse, but everyone was so exhausted by the whole Maurice Saatchi business that everyone wanted to put it behind us. This was wrong. We should have been working away since December 17 with the press."

The lack of response puzzled many at the company. It was particularly vexing to some that Saatchi used company employees to distribute his resignation, which was printed on company stationery and copied on company machines. Instead, the only muffled noise from Charlie Scott that day was an uninspired statement thanking Saatchi for the "valuable contribution he has made. While Maurice will be missed, I have every confidence in the many other outstanding employees of this Group whom I am certain will continue to service clients to the highest possible standard."

BILL MUIRHEAD returned to New York from Vail, Colorado, on Saturday, January 7. Landing at John F. Kennedy Airport at nine o'clock in the morning, Muirhead telephoned his secretary to request a meeting in his office in two hours. He then called Alan Bishop and told him to come to Hudson Street at noon.

Muirhead presented his secretary with a handwritten letter of resignation, which he had composed on the airplane. He asked her to type it and make thirty copies, while he began writing by hand notes "to people I felt I wanted to explain my action to." The resignations of Muirhead, Sinclair, and Kershaw were to be distributed on Monday at a predetermined time. Therefore, Muirhead's secretary was told to keep the letters on her until he telephoned from London.

When Bishop showed up, Muirhead took his personal files, including a bank statement, pictures of his wife and three sons, and two bottles of red wine, and stuffed them into a green shopping bag from Harrods, the famous London emporium. The two walked through the ornate marble lobby and, because Muirhead's arms were stuffed with his belongings, Bishop signed the weekend security log for both of them. Their exit from 375 Hudson Street, including Muirhead clutching the Harrods bag, was dutifully recorded by the building's security camera. That footage would become critical to Muirhead before too long.

It was while sipping a beer at the Grange, a pub near Saatchi & Saatchi's downtown New York office, that Muirhead told Bishop he was resigning, effective Monday, along with Jeremy Sinclair and David Kershaw. Bishop said later he was "shell-shocked" by the news, although he should not have been.

Muirhead's departure was foreshadowed in a call to Bishop on January 4 when he asked Bishop to attend a meeting at Bates Worldwide with Forrest and John Mars, Michael Bungey and Ken Rogers of Bates, and Charlie Scott. "I can't break up my vacation," Muirhead said disingenuously.

"Bill, use common sense," Bishop said. "If you don't turn up, it will be taken as a sign that your loyalties are elsewhere."

Bishop reluctantly attended what amounted to several unpleasant hours of listening to the Mars brothers bawling out Bates executives, who basically repeated Maurice's position, including the untrue allegation that the shareholders were running the company. Their treatment of Bates was not unexpected. On December 21, 1994, Mars quietly placed a portion of its $1 billion worldwide account in review, a stinging rebuke of Saatchi & Saatchi's disposal of its chairman. Mars's billings at the Bates and Saatchi agencies were $400 million. The agencies handled such brands as M&Ms, Snickers, 3 Musketeers, Kudos, and Sunburst.

Charlie Scott responded that he respectfully believed the Mars brothers were incorrect. "The interests of our clients are paramount," he said.

The meeting ended and Forrest and John Mars declined the invitation to join Bates and Saatchi & Saatchi executives at a luncheon catered by Bates. Instead, the two walked onto Lexington Avenue and indulged in Sabrett hot dogs from a sidewalk vendor.

As BISHOP WAS SIPPING his beer at the Grange and absorbing the seismic moves that would take place two days hence, Muirhead said he wanted him to join Sinclair, Kershaw, and himself. Bishop was confused; he was unclear whether the resignations were a part of a half-baked scheme to pressure the company into reversing itself on Maurice Saatchi. Equally unknown was whether Muirhead and the others believed their resignations would be permanent. He remained noncommittal.

The three amigos met again on Sunday, January 8, at Kershaw's London apartment in Kensington before leaving for Maurice Saatchi's house off Berkeley Square to speak with the brothers. Over white wine and spring rolls prepared by the Saatchis' housekeeper, three of the five partners of a yet-to-be-announced new advertising agency discussed the resignations with two attorneys retained by the three amigos as well as a lawyer representing Maurice.

The participants recalled that the meeting's overall mood was one of elation. A draft agreement was signed, but not before Maurice laughed and said he would control half the company. Sinclair quietly responded, "Maurice, you're not listening. Our days of serfdom are over." At one point, there was talk of giving Kershaw less than an equal share because he was the newest member of the team, but Sinclair vetoed that as well, saying it would not be right. In the end, the agreement delineated a new agency owned equally by five partners.

The trio hired Financial Dynamics, their own public relations firm, to handle the news of their resignations, opting not to use Maurice's designated hitman Tim Bell. They reserved a room at the Langham Hilton and arranged to meet Financial Dynamics representatives at 12:30 P.M. By chance, Sinclair had scheduled a meeting with Scott at noon on Monday, January 9, ostensibly to discuss company business moving forward in the wake of Maurice's resignation. They did not expect the session with Scott to take very long.

Prior to speaking with Scott, the three met at Cranks, a health food restaurant around the corner from the Charlotte Street agency, and swapped resignation letters.

At noon, Sinclair, Muirhead, and Kershaw entered Scott's office and presented him with what amounted to three stinging indictments.

"The Company is in the grip of people who do not understand the business and seem prepared to ignore the advice of those who do," wrote Jeremy Sinclair. ". . . I never intended to leave the Company, but it seems the Company has left me."

"I no longer feel that the people who control our company understand what we really do," wrote Bill Muirhead. "I warned you and the Board, and anyone else who would listen to me, of the damage Maurice's removal would cause the Company. I now feel totally compromised by Mr. Herro and the Board's decision, particularly as it was against the express wishes of several of our most important clients, including a number I am personally close to.

". . . As far as I am concerned, when you don't listen to your clients you've lost the plot."

"I cannot continue to work for a company which no longer cares about its clients or staff and is apparently so utterly ignorant of the advertising business and how much client relationships and agency morale matter," wrote David Kershaw. He said his letter to David Herro, along with other letters from Saatchi & Saatchi colleagues, were "treated with contempt and totally ignored."

In all, more than sixty years of employment with Saatchi & Saatchi was walking out the door.

Scott read the letters and went ashen. His first reaction was to attack Maurice Saatchi. "He is a man of no integrity," Scott said.

At that point, Sinclair began to speak with his chin pointing outward, a telltale sign he is angry. "Don't you talk to me about integrity," Sinclair said. "You signed a letter in support of Maurice."

Muirhead sat quietly, privately hoping the whole ugly episode would somehow be reversed. Maurice had worried that Scott would offer the trio a huge raise as an inducement to stay. Surprisingly, money did not come up, although Scott said, "If I resign, will you stay?" The answer from Sinclair, who was acting as a group spokesman, was no. Much later, Muirhead said he wished at that moment that Sinclair had responded affirmatively.

Scott has a different version and said at no point did he offer to resign: "I said that if this was about me, we should talk about it," Scott said. "I was seriously concerned about doing what is best for the company. They said their minds were made up and that the reason they were leaving wasn't me."

Oddly, Scott asked for Muirhead and Kershaw to recommend their replacements. Muirhead named Alan Bishop for North America and Kershaw suggested Nick Hurrell and Moray MacLennan, joint managing directors, for Charlotte Street.

With their business with Scott complete, the three left the office to go to the Langham Hilton and began speaking with reporters with their public relations handlers present. Before they left, Sinclair said to Scott, "Now, you are going to put this on the screen, aren't you?" The reference was to a wire service watched by the City. Scott never gave them a direct reply; he was too absorbed with the ramifications from the earthquake that was soon going to rumble beneath Charlotte and Whitfield Streets and extend to Hudson Street across the Atlantic.

As word began to circulate that three senior Saatchi & Saatchi executives had resigned, the stock plunged 10 percent, closing at 125 pence, down 14 pence. But the news was not official yet since the company was silent on the matter. Only at 4:28 P.M. in London did Saatchi & Saatchi release the devastating news to the screen. Two minutes later, the *Evening Standard* hit the stands with the headline-making story.

One major shareholder was unable to sell even a single share during that critical day when Saatchi & Saatchi shares were being dumped: Jeremy Sinclair could not make a move since he was an insider; he had to wait until the news was officially released by the company.

Scott's tepid, predictable announcement on the resignations contained a final foreboding paragraph: "The Company intends to accept the resignation of all three employees from their management positions with effect from the end of their notice periods. All three have restrictive covenants in their contracts relating to clients and staff."

In a long overdue move, Saatchi & Saatchi Company PLC

finally named two advertising executives, Ed Wax and Michael Bungey, to its board.

The five partners—the Saatchi brothers and the three amigos —had a plan: let the news of the resignations simmer in the newspapers for at least a week before the next official announcement. Columnists and reporters could only speculate that the five would form a new advertising agency. Charles Saatchi had not even announced his resignation. As far as anyone was concerned, he remained Saatchi & Saatchi Company PLC's president-for-life.

Scott, Smyth, Bungey, and Wax held a teleconference with financial analysts in Europe and the United States on January 10 as the share price continued its free fall. "With regard to Maurice Saatchi's departure," Scott said, "the board took a long time to reach its conclusions because it was aware that Maurice might seek to damage the company if he were no longer chairman." The board voted Saatchi out because it decided "it was better to suffer any damage immediately rather than to undergo some weeks or months of guerrilla warfare only to end up with the same conclusion.

"Since [his departure] it is clear that Maurice has used his formidable skills as a professional communicator to cause as much damage as he can to this Company while apparently claiming concern for its clients and staff."

Scott was only partly right; Saatchi was interested in the well-being of the Saatchi & Saatchi employees, at least those he wanted to lure away. Saatchi & Saatchi was planning to take Kershaw's advice and name Hurrell and MacLennan as his replacement. But late on January 10, the two went "AWOL," Wendy Smyth said. The reason became apparent soon enough.

The Charlotte Street agency was rocked again on January 11: four additional senior executives said they were leaving—Simon Dicketts and James Lowther, creative directors, as well as Nick Hurrell and Moray MacLennan, joint managing directors.

The company moved quickly and immediately announced their replacements, which included naming Tamara Ingram, group director and a ten-year veteran of the agency, and Adam Crozier, vice chairman and executive media director, who had been with the agency for seven years, as joint chief executives.

Many of the Charlotte Street agency employees streamed into the Pregnant Man, the on-site pub, following news of the latest resignations. Ingram and Crozier delivered rousing speeches and the mood quickly turned ugly toward the former Saatchi & Saatchi executives. One group wanted to change a public service poster in the parking lot from "One in every eight people who walk past this poster was abused as a child" to "Every eight people who walk past this poster were abused as employees."

Maurice Saatchi chose that day, on which his former colleagues were reeling from the latest news, to deliver a new blow: he announced the establishment of The New Saatchi Agency.

There was great debate among the five partners over the agency's name, with agreement on only one matter: the name Saatchi would be included. "We spent twenty-five years building up Saatchi as a brand name," Jeremy Sinclair said. "We didn't need our names on the shingle." But other, better names were batted about, including Saatchi Partners. It was Charles who wanted to position the new agency as something exciting and up-to-date; every time someone mentioned The New Saatchi Agency, it would place Saatchi & Saatchi as old and, therefore, dated and less desirable to potential clients.

The brief announcement said that "in due course" Sinclair, Muirhead, and Kershaw would join Saatchi as partners "at a date to be agreed."

As if to affirm that bad things do happen in threes, British Airways released a statement that same day saying it would begin searching for a new advertising agency, a process known in the industry as conducting a review. Mirror Group, which publishes the *Daily Mirror* and *The Independent*, Dixons, an electronic retailer in the United Kingdom, and Gallaher, which produces Silk Cut cigarettes, also placed their accounts in review.

Saatchi's announcement about starting a rival agency finally shook Saatchi & Saatchi Company PLC and its advertising agencies out of their complacency and defensive position. "The mood changed at once," Smyth said, "to fuck the bastards. They dumped us in the shit. We'll show them what we're really made of."

The next day, on January 12, the company did just that. It filed against Maurice Saatchi and the three amigos alleging "damages against all of them for a conspiracy to injure the business of the Group and against Maurice Saatchi for soliciting the other three." The suit also sought to prevent Sinclair, Muirhead, and Kershaw from joining Maurice Saatchi or from soliciting clients. There were also rumblings that Saatchi & Saatchi Company PLC —now dubbed Old Co. by Maurice and his cohorts—was considering suing the Saatchi brothers for the $38 million payment they had received from Adidas.

On the same day, news editors received an unusual two-page communiqué from Saatchi & Saatchi Company PLC: it conceded there had been a great deal of confusion about the company's affairs. It sought to set the record straight on everything from the value of client accounts to the staff resignations.

To savvy observers of the advertising industry, Maurice Saatchi and The New Saatchi Agency faced greater obstacles than lawsuits in launching their fledgling business. The New Saatchi Agency had to get two elements in place before it could be taken seriously by potential clients: a worldwide network to provide services ranging from creative to media buying for clients, and employees.

When The New Saatchi Agency was first announced, Maurice and his partners said they would open offices in London, New York, and Sydney. But there was immediate skepticism that this small venture could handle clients such as British Airways, which needs a sophisticated global network to react to the cutthroat nature of the airline business.

It is fair to assert that the five partners were mismatched to start such a mammoth operation. In truth, there were four working partners; Charles Saatchi had yet to resign from Saatchi & Saatchi Company PLC, where he was honorary president. He had not worked a full day in years and no one was expecting him to help greatly in starting an agency from scratch again. Charles did not walk out of Saatchi & Saatchi Company PLC simply because there was no compelling reason for him to do so.

The other four were going to work, to be sure, but few expected them to work at the new agency with the same gusto as they had when Saatchi & Saatchi Advertising was an embryonic operation setting out to conquer the world and achieve number one status.

And, with the youngest of the five—David Kershaw—being forty-one years old, the five were set in their ways. Early on, they held frank discussions on the expensive habits they were unwilling to break. Maurice loved flying on the Concorde, with a one-way ticket costing in excess of $4,000; Charles relished go-cart racing and buying art; Jeremy smoked fine Cuban cigars and retreated several times each year to teach philosophy; Muirhead cherished his Ferrari automobile; and Kershaw loved to eat at the Ivy and Caprice, two pricey restaurants. The five were used to the company paying for many of these extravagances; now, they were the company and there were occasional arguments over, say, whether Maurice would be allowed to fly on the Concorde.

As important as working out their differences, The New Saatchi Agency needed young blood to do most of the heavy lifting. Instead of luring employees away from rival agencies he admired, Maurice stayed with those he knew. Maurice had to do the soliciting, since the three amigos remained in the murky area of continuing to be under contract to Saatchi & Saatchi.

On January 9, Maurice held court at his London home for approximately forty Charlotte Street employees, told them his new agency was going to handle British Airways advertising in the near future, and offered jobs to one and all. Saatchi's actions were basically nullified four days later when Mike Batt, a senior British Airways marketing executive, visited Saatchi & Saatchi Advertising and said the airline had reached no such decision. For Charlie Scott and Saatchi & Saatchi, it was a rare reprieve.

Several employees from Charlotte Street did defect, however, to join Maurice. Unquestionably, the most crucial exit was that of Tim Duffy, a well-regarded, intelligent, hardworking account planner who worked on the British Airways business. When Maurice Saatchi resigned, Duffy knew immediately that he, too, would quit. "It was absurd not to know that [Maurice and Charles] were the heart of the company," Duffy said. On January 9, Maurice summoned Duffy to Bruton Place and told him of his plan to open a rival agency, but omitted the fact that Sinclair, Muirhead, and Kershaw would join him. On January 11, Duffy wanted to resign, but there was no one in his line of command to resign to; all his superiors had quit as well. The atmosphere at the Charlotte Street agency was so tense and chaotic that Duffy's new superiors, no doubt because of frustration and fatigue, angrily told Duffy to get out of the office at once when he said he wanted to quit. He was fired and free to work with Saatchi on pitching the British Airways account.

In establishing his new outfit, Maurice Saatchi did not stray far from his London home nor his old beloved office on Berkeley Square; Saatchi rented a modest office on Davies Street on the opposite end of Berkeley Square where he placed a label over the street buzzer that read "Dress Rehearsal Ltd." Those who entered the office were greeted with the antithesis of Maurice Saatchi's studied, urbane, cool persona: the place was a hodgepodge operation of young men and women scurrying across a tacky, stained dark blue carpet. Telephones rang incessantly and there was cheap, rented furniture.

In mid-January, Saatchi received an unexpected telephone call. A senior executive from Procter & Gamble was not pleased by the events that had taken place over the past month or so. "We told you this was going to be bad and it was," the executive told Saatchi.

"That's true," Saatchi answered. "It's an ugly civil war."

"There is only one solution. You'll all have to go back. Herro's shares will have to be bought out. The clock will go back to December 16, the company will make you an offer to be chairman of Saatchi & Saatchi Advertising Worldwide, and this time you will take it. Herro won't be around anymore, so you can't use the excuse that you'll fear Herro."

"What makes you think Herro won't ignore you? He ignored Mars and British Airways."

"We're Procter & Gamble. Maurice, you must stop this war."

"I won't."

"Maurice, it is said the tallest tree bends the most."

Maurice mentioned this extraordinary conversation to his brother Charles, who in turn placed several events in motion. He called Ali Wambold, a partner in Lazard Frères, over the weekend of January 14 to tell him of the Procter & Gamble development. Wambold, who abandoned his intention to join the Saatchi & Saatchi board after Maurice was thrown off, approached Derek Higgs, chairman of S.G. Warburg's merchant banking operations, who told several board members. Most important, Charles Saatchi telephoned Charlie Scott on January 16 to propose that Maurice accept the offer to run Saatchi & Saatchi Advertising Worldwide. Charles also suggested that the Saatchi advertising network break away from its parent company within two years, at which point Maurice could operate the Saatchi agency as an independent company.

Charles Saatchi also called Wendy Smyth with the same appeal. By happenstance, Alan Bishop was visiting Saatchi & Saatchi Company PLC's headquarters at the time Charles Saatchi was trying to weave his spell. Bishop was told of the odd call and his reaction was swift.

"The whole agency turned against Maurice once he announced his new agency," Bishop told Scott. "It created an atmosphere of 'Fuck 'em.' Charlie, the agency won't take him back now. We won't be able to sell this to the employees. They don't want him back anymore."

Indeed, the offer was discussed the next day during a three-hour Saatchi & Saatchi board meeting in London and rejected. At the same time, Sir Peter Walters, a close friend of Maurice, spoke publicly to the *Wall Street Journal* and the *Financial Times* for the first time since Maurice's ouster. He told the *Financial Times* he "could not conceive" of Saatchi's return. "What Maurice has done [since being ousted] is a great personal disappointment." Addressing Saatchi, he said, "How you are regarded and respected is in your hands." To the *Journal*, he said, "I am, in a personal sense, saddened that Maurice did not accept this situation with a greater sense of dignity and tolerance. He has not been very considerate of the people who are left behind."

Shortly after the board recessed, Maurice told the *Wall Street Journal*, "Though the board was aware of the identity and magnitude of this client [who asked me to return to the company], it has chosen yet again to ignore the wishes of a major client and the devastating consequences that could follow."

Procter & Gamble moves carefully and deliberately. Therefore, it did not retaliate against Saatchi & Saatchi Company PLC for shrugging off its desire for Maurice to return to his former company. And, in its first months of operations, The New Saatchi Agency did not receive any Procter & Gamble business.

ON JANUARY 24, 1995, The New Saatchi Agency received expected but nevertheless welcome news: it was one of four finalists in the competition for the British Airways account. The others were Saatchi & Saatchi Advertising; Bartle Bogle Hegarty, a London agency with a well-deserved reputation for producing spectacular creative work; and J. Walter Thompson, a sleeping giant owned by WPP Group. British Airways asked the agencies not to produce any creative work, only strategic plans for the airline as it entered the twenty-first century.

The shoot-out, as competition among agencies vying for an account is known, amounted to a bizarre homecoming week for Maurice Saatchi. He was, in Saatchi & Saatchi, competing against his former agency; in Bartle Bogle Hegarty, he was competing against, among others, John Hegarty, one of the early talented art directors recruited by Charles Saatchi; and in J. Walter Thompson, he was competing against an agency controlled by Martin Sorrell, Saatchi's former finance director.

For The New Saatchi Agency, there was great urgency to identify and establish an affiliation with a worldwide agency network. British Airways needed to be convinced that The New Saatchi Agency had the resources to service its demanding account.

The assignment to coordinate the candidates for an alliance fell to David Kershaw, who was stationed in a temporary office with Jeremy Sinclair and Bill Muirhead on Sackville Street. The three were still drawing their salaries from Saatchi & Saatchi Company PLC and, because of the legal dispute involving their contracts, were temporarily prohibited from working in The New Saatchi Agency offices. It was an understandable but ridiculous situation. It was impossible to monitor exactly what the three executives were doing every day and it was foolish to believe they were showing up at the Potting Shed to shoot the breeze.

Maurice Saatchi's supporters were correct when they said the Saatchi name remained a door-opener. Once Saatchi said he would launch a new agency, calls poured in from those interested in exploring an alliance. Kershaw and Saatchi began considering potential candidates in early January.

Saatchi's first choice was D'Arcy Masius Benton & Bowles, a respected, privately held worldwide agency that counted Procter &

Gamble among its many clients. DMB&B had offices around the world, with 5,500 employees and annual billings exceeding $4 billion, but the firm had hit a rough patch and lost high-profile accounts. Its creative work was on the skids and an alliance with The New Saatchi Agency might be a welcome jolt. Saatchi would produce the creative work for any client it attracted and DMB&B would provide the services of a worldwide agency.

Saatchi held discussions with Roy Bostock, DMB&B's gravelly-voiced chairman, in London in early January. Bostock was widely respected and well liked throughout the advertising industry and was known as an incredibly strong personality who would not have stood for a shred of nonsense or corporate misbehavior from Maurice Saatchi.

As any prudent advertising executive would do, Bostock contacted executives at DMB&B's prized client, Procter & Gamble, shortly after speaking with Saatchi. Though no one will specify which Procter & Gamble executive reacted, everyone concerned agreed the response was succinct: if DMB&B held further discussions with Maurice Saatchi, DMB&B was placing its relationship with Procter & Gamble in jeopardy.

The inference was clear to everyone: Procter & Gamble was upset with Maurice's behavior since leaving the company. Further, it was disturbed when it heard that during the meeting Saatchi held at his London home with forty of his former colleagues, he implied that if they left to join his agency, Procter & Gamble would come as a client.

Saatchi spoke with a senior Procter & Gamble executive who, Saatchi said, ultimately sanctioned a DMB&B–New Saatchi Agency alliance. By then, however, DMB&B was too shaken by Procter & Gamble's initial objection and the matter was dropped.

Other than DMB&B, New Saatchi had discussions with Grey Advertising, a publicly traded agency; Chiat/Day, a privately held agency; and Lintas:Worldwide, a unit of Interpublic Group. Grey was a button-down agency and it was quickly clear that the cultures of the two organizations would not mesh. Chiat/Day, cofounded by Jay Chiat, one of the giants in advertising in the 1980s—his agency created the famous "Big Brother" ad for Apple Computer, which was shown only once, during the 1984 Super

Bowl—was experiencing a tough losing streak and its network was weakened. Chiat/Day would soon be sold to Omnicom Group and merged with another Omnicom agency, TBWA Advertising, in one more example of an independent midsize agency being swallowed by a giant holding company.

The three amigos found Lintas appealing because of its strong network. It, too, was in disrepair, having lost major accounts, including IBM and Diet Coke, but its worldwide organization was potent. Lintas's primary client, however, was Unilever, the giant packaged goods manufacturer and Procter & Gamble's major competitor. Lintas, in fact, was originally founded as an in-house ad agency for Unilever and was later spun off as an independent agency. Sinclair, Muirhead, and Kershaw were "uncomfortable" with any connection to Lintas, Kershaw said, "because we thought it would look like an aggressive act against Procter & Gamble." If New Saatchi teamed with Lintas, any hope of winning even a sliver of Procter & Gamble business would be gone.

The list eventually shrank to Publicis SA, a large French agency. One of the first individuals to contact Maurice Saatchi about an alliance early in January was Maurice Levy, Publicis's chairman. A major selling point in Publicis was Optimedia, a powerful worldwide media buying service in which it owned a stake. Publicis had 180 offices in fifty-six countries and would handle media buying as well as logistical and technical services. New Saatchi would also gain coverage in Japan and Asia through Daiichi Kikaku, an agency with equity ties to Publicis.

But Publicis had problems of its own: a previous seven-year-old alliance with True North Communications' Foote, Cone & Belding ad agency, from which it was trying to extricate itself prior to any interest in New Saatchi. Publicis alleged that True North was not interested in expanding as aggressively around the world as Publicis wanted. The two sides were so interwoven, it was hard to negotiate a separation. In 1996, True North and Publicis would still be in negotiations to settle their differences.

The situation with True North did nothing to dissuade Maurice Saatchi from forging an alliance. He and Maurice Levy met for a private dinner in early January and liked each other immensely. Levy, like Saatchi, is tall, thin, and elegant, with dark hair and a taste for the finer things in life. He dresses elegantly and has a reputation among his detractors for being hard-nosed and a tough taskmaster. Like Saatchi, Levy is a savvy manipulator of the press. When he spoke to reporters, Levy, like Saatchi, generally preferred to talk off the record. Cynics were surprised the two Maurices got along, even though there were reports of minor, and predictable, ego skirmishes.

ON THE RAINY EVENING of January 18, Jeanne Muirhead was home alone in Kent, outside London. That was not unusual. Her husband, Bill, often ate dinner in London and was busy with clients. The Muirheads live in an area not unlike a tony suburb such as Short Hills, New Jersey, with expansive homes next to one another. The sweep of the Muirheads' home is somewhat deceptive from the front. In the rear is a tasteful Japanese garden complete with a tiny foot bridge, a swimming pool, and a large guest house, all of which the Muirheads inherited from the previous owner.

Jeanne Muirhead, an attractive, intelligent blonde, was watching television, awaiting her husband's return, when she began hearing noises outside. Alarmed, she went to the window and saw a man and a woman peering through. They shouted in order to identify themselves. The pair were lurking about to serve Bill Muirhead with papers for a lawsuit that Saatchi & Saatchi Company PLC had filed against him. The suit, asking $50 million in damages, accused Muirhead of breach of contract, breach of fiduciary responsibilities, and misappropriation of confidential and proprietary documents. In everyday terms, this meant the company believed Muirhead stole company documents from Hudson Street on the day he met Alan Bishop and finalized his resignation letter.

It was the only one of the slew of Saatchi & Saatchi suits to be filed in New York State, which enabled company attorneys to depose Muirhead immediately, something that could not be done in a timely manner in London because of differences in legal procedures.

The suit puzzled even some senior executives within Saatchi & Saatchi. Of the five partners, Muirhead had the least money. In fact, when Muirhead began worrying whether he did the right thing by resigning, Charles Saatchi told him, "Don't be concerned, Bill, of course you did. You will be paid in perpetuity."

The suit against Muirhead appeared to many to be nothing

more than a nuisance action. It did accomplish one thing, however. It infuriated Muirhead, who justifiably felt libeled. After all, Saatchi & Saatchi was publicly labeling him a thief. The suit also underscored how aggressive Saatchi & Saatchi was suddenly becoming toward Maurice and his partners. Others felt the company was merely flailing about, seeking revenge wherever it could.

At times, the suit sounded comical. One potential witness against Muirhead was an elevator-service operator who was working in the building the day Muirhead departed with Bishop. He told company officials that he saw Muirhead leaving the building with files under his arm. Muirhead's attorneys from Paul, Weiss, Rifkind, Wharton & Garrison said the elevator operator was married to a Saatchi & Saatchi Advertising North America vice president who works for William H. Cochrane, the company's chief financial officer.

Asked about this witness, a company spokesman said, "I assure you, we have considerably more evidence than just a lift man." Additional evidence was never presented.

WHILE LAWSUITS WERE FLYING back and forth in London and New York, Maurice Saatchi met the press en masse publicly for the first time since his dismissal. The date was February 8 and the occasion was a luncheon at the Foreign Press Association. Saatchi was delivering a speech he entitled "Reductio Ad Veritas: The Search for Truth in Advertising."

It was an odd scene. Everyone was whispering and staring at the guest of honor. Maurice Saatchi stood at ramrod attention with a slight smile, remaining quietly stationary and soaking in what was being said to him and around him. He frequently nodded politely and spoke softly.

The much-anticipated appearance soon degenerated into a shouting match when it became apparent that Maurice did not want to adhere to the organization's tradition, which called for an on-the-record question-and-answer period following the prepared remarks. The journalists hurled demands at the president of the Foreign Press Association, who was ill-prepared for the crowd and the ensuing revolt. As it was explained, Saatchi would speak and then he and a select group would retire to an off-the-record lunch. Everyone else would be asked to leave.

After a great deal of shouting—during which Saatchi patiently and silently sat amused by the fuss—and whispering between Saatchi and the association's head, a compromise was struck. Questions could be asked, but the responses could not be attributed directly to Saatchi.

It was a ludicrous solution that was made even more offensive since virtually all of the reporters agreed to the absurd guidelines. Dozens of supposedly independent journalists would dutifully report to their readers quotes from "a person close to Maurice Saatchi" instead of attributing quotes directly to Saatchi himself.

The speech was a retread of the boring address he delivered in 1994 to the PaineWebber media conference. This time, however, he added a postscript: "In the late 1980s, when we deviated from the simple objective of producing advertisements and strayed into other areas of business life, serious problems resulted. The same lesson can be learnt from more recent experiences. The simple objective of the owners of advertising agencies—the shareholders —is to invest in shares which go up.

"When a small group of shareholders of Saatchi & Saatchi deviated from that simple objective, and strayed into areas of client relationships, and personnel, similar problems ensued."

Saatchi's address coincided with the opening round in London's High Court in which Saatchi & Saatchi Company PLC asked for injunctions to stop Maurice and the three amigos from setting up a competitive agency. On February 13, Justice Jonathan Parker of the High Court denied the request for the injunction against Maurice Saatchi. "It is plain to me that this motion represents an attempt to obtain relief against Maurice Saatchi by the back door with a view to preventing him setting up competition with the group," Parker wrote. "But the back door is in my judgment firmly closed." Additionally, Parker called the company's arguments "fundamentally misconceived" and ordered Saatchi & Saatchi to pay legal fees amounting to £100,000.

Saatchi responded with predictable glee: "For Old Co.'s part, I hope they will now acknowledge that legal action is not the way to stop competition. You can't put the toothpaste back into the tube. Clients have the right to choose."

There was no ruling on the three amigos. They were left in limbo to tend to their alleged bucolic existence on Garden Leave on Sackville Street in the Potting Shed. A trial to sort out that mess would begin in the spring.

MEANWHILE, BURIED in the documents filed in High Court on February 8 and almost lost in the back-and-forth rhetoric was a critical fact: Charles Saatchi, who officially remained as honorary president-for-life of Saatchi & Saatchi Company PLC, was identified as the "backer" of The New Saatchi Agency.

CHAPTER
FIFTEEN

O<small>N</small> T<small>HURSDAY</small>, F<small>EBRUARY</small> 16, 1994, Charles Saatchi finally resigned, but, saying he was being forced out, he sued Saatchi & Saatchi Company PLC for constructive dismissal. His position as lifelong president was made "intolerable" because Saatchi & Saatchi had named him in legal actions. The company responded in a terse statement that said it accepted his resignation and "totally rejects any suggestion of unfair or constructive dismissal."

Now, Saatchi & Saatchi was truly dissolved. After all, Sir Tim Bell, who was knighted in 1990 and who thought of himself as the ampersand in Saatchi & Saatchi, was long gone. Saatchi's resignation followed by two days the company's latest suit against the brothers, this one going after the $38 million the Saatchi brothers received from the investment in Adidas. The company was investigating whether the settlement with Robert Louis-Dreyfus was actually payment for marketing advice and the failed advertising campaign devised by the brothers and other Saatchi & Saatchi employees. The brothers answered the suit by characterizing the investment as "personal."

Meanwhile, the day before Charles resigned, The New Saatchi Agency delivered a counterblow to Saatchi & Saatchi: Mirror Group Newspapers and Gallaher awarded their accounts to New Saatchi.

W<small>HILE</small> S<small>AATCHI</small> & S<small>AATCHI</small> Company PLC was trying to stem client losses and attempting to keep employees from defecting to its former chairman, it also set out to cease being known as Saatchi & Saatchi. The company was finally free to change its name. The assignment was given to Siegel & Gale, the corporate identity company that Saatchi & Saatchi had purchased in 1985. Some executives, including Ed Wax, facetiously believed Siegel & Gale's participation was unnecessary. The new name was preordained: ABS, initials signifying Anything But Saatchi.

Siegel & Gale immediately went to work to establish criteria: the name, it said, should be substantial and not frivolous like AdMinisters; it should be understandable, not obscure like Syzygy; it should be proud, not subject to ridicule like Cosmic.

In the first-round confidential report given to Charlie Scott on February 1, Siegel & Gale recommended: Momentum Communications ("a force; influence; ability to sustain progress"), Prisma Communications ("suggests 'prism' and a full spectrum of capability"), Constellation Group ("group of stars . . . a collection or gathering of excellent, splendid and radiant things or people"), Cordia Group ("heart or center of things . . . sustaining, empowering and vital"), Envision Communications ("able to visualize the future"), ComQuest ("combination of communications and quest, suggesting a strong communications mission"). Scott received another report on February 15 with more possibilities: ComQuest Group, Comcor Group, CorQuest Group, Cordiant Group, ComCordia Group, and QuestCom Group.

ComQuest was the recommendation from Siegel & Gale. "It was focused, committed, and idealistic," said Alan Siegel. "I thought it was the best."

Scott, however, did not like the capital "Q" in the middle of the word. Nor did it strike his ear pleasantly. "I had to make sure I was not embarrassed when I was introduced as the chairman of so-and-so," said Scott.

For reasons he had difficulty articulating, Scott gravitated to Cordiant, a wholly made-up word. Siegel explained it was derived from "accord" and the Latin word *cordia*, for heart. Siegel said it suggested "harmony, agreement and a shared mission." Siegel & Gale also designed a logo that, Alan Siegel said, would be "elegant and eminently professional. The Cordiant workmark joins the letters 'R' and 'D' with a ligatured swash that adds an element of informality and a touch of cohesiveness to the organization. The formal serifed type connotes stability, sincerity and confidence."

Cordiant was announced to the press and the London Stock Exchange on February 20. It was a significant accomplishment for

Siegel & Gale, which had received the assignment only two months earlier; usually, the company requires six months to achieve a list of viable new names.

Cordiant did not have an easy entry into the world. The name hit the ear oddly. Cordi-what? was the general reaction. Cordiant executives dismissed the guffawing. The name of a holding company ultimately did not matter. How often was Interpublic or WPP spoken? The important mission—ridding the holding company of the Saatchi moniker—was accomplished.

The company may have acquired a new name, but otherwise it was business as usual. Or, more accurately, it was losing business as usual. One day after Cordiant was introduced to the world, Mars dealt Cordiant, Bates Worldwide, and Saatchi & Saatchi Advertising a devastating blow by firing the agencies. Combined, the agencies handled $400 million of Mars business; the dismissal ended a relationship that spanned forty years.

The loss was financially crushing: Mars contributed approximately $45 million in revenues to the parent company; Cordiant's 1994 pretax profits were about $45 million. Saatchi & Saatchi Advertising lost about 4 percent of its annual revenues of $1.2 billion, or $47.4 million; Mars accounted for 6 percent of Bates's total billings of $5.2 billion. In some Bates offices outside the United States, Mars was the only major client. Of the major Mars defection, Wendy Smyth said, "We didn't actually believe they would've taken all the business away."

The decision to jettison Bates came swiftly for Mars. Bates officials, including Michael Bungey and Ken Rogers, gave a three-hour presentation to Mars executives, including John and Forrest Mars and John Murray, a staff officer for Mars, at the company headquarters in McLean, Virginia, on February 17.

Mars's chilly reception caused Bungey to believe that his original assessment, told at the fateful Mortimer's dinner in December 1994, was horribly incorrect. Although Bungey was on target when he thought he had the support of several senior Mars executives, that support evaporated during the pitch because of several missteps by the agency. By March, the Mars loss resulted in Bates firing 3 percent of its staff, or 150 employees.

Pointedly, when Mars divvied up its plum assignments to

agencies including BBDO, Grey Advertising, D'Arcy Masius Benton & Bowles, and a well-respected yet tiny agency, Merkley Newman Harty, The New Saatchi Agency was not on the roster. Its exclusion was not unexpected since the agency's ability was unknown.

NO MATTER what it was called, Cordiant or Saatchi & Saatchi, there was little good news emanating from the company. The steam in the Saatchi & Saatchi international engine remained Charlotte Street, since the U.S. operation continued to need nurturing and massive rebuilding.

Ed Wax, chairman and chief executive of Saatchi & Saatchi Advertising Worldwide, felt a particular hatred for the Saatchi brothers, specifically Maurice. To Wax, their business practices stymied growth. Wax has a well-deserved reputation of being the ultimate client man. In that way, he and Muirhead are quite similar. Both would do virtually anything legal if a client requested it.

Wax was vacationing on the Caribbean island of St. John in late December as Maurice Saatchi was contemplating the company's offer. "My wife said the only pressure you're going to have is to get up at seven-thirty every morning for beach chairs," Wax said. "She knew it was going to be crazy when we got back and she wanted me well rested."

Wax and his wife, Carolyn, returned to New York on January 3, Wax's birthday and the date Maurice resigned. When Wax called his office, his assistant, Deanna Goldowsky, said, "You have to call Procter & Gamble. All hell is breaking loose." Procter & Gamble demanded to know why Wax had not informed the company of Saatchi's resignation prior to its receiving a memo from Saatchi himself. "That's when I got upset," Wax said. "Maurice cleverly informed clients before he told us." Wax became further incensed a week later when he was showering in his apartment and his wife came to the door holding the telephone. Charlie Scott was calling to say that Sinclair, Muirhead, and Kershaw had resigned and had already released the news to the media before he had an opportunity to tell the company employees.

Wax wanted to hit The New Saatchi Agency hard and the best way to do so was to ensure the continued strength of the Charlotte

Street agency. To that end, in late February, Wax reached back to the glory days of Saatchi & Saatchi and contacted Jennifer Laing. Laing would prove to be a most vexing opponent to Maurice Saatchi and his partners.

AT FIRST GLANCE, Jennifer Laing does not appear to be much of a threat to anyone. Scratch the surface and a complex woman whose good nature can quickly turn to steel is found. In fact, she is more popular with clients than she is with her subordinates. Even after women's liberation swept much of the world, Laing remained coquettish about her age. "I'm forty-six-ish," she would often say in 1995 when she began making headlines for returning to Saatchi & Saatchi Advertising and Charlotte Street as chairwoman, assuming the position vacated by her close friend David Kershaw.

The daughter of a Scottish plastic surgeon and an Irish mother, Laing was raised in Salisbury and attended Salisbury College of Technology before receiving a degree in business studies from Northwestern Polytechnic in northwest London. She began her career in advertising in 1969 at Garland-Compton as a graduate trainee working with clients such as Rowntree Mackintosh and Schweppes. With the reverse takeover by Saatchi & Saatchi, she was promoted to the board after several Compton Garland executives above her level resigned. The Saatchi contingency, she said, included "the most exciting group of people, especially Charles Saatchi." The Saatchi executive she worked most closely with was Tim Bell.

Laing resigned in 1979 to join the Leo Burnett advertising agency as group account director. It is part of advertising folklore that Bell and Maurice Saatchi enticed her back two years later with a red Ferrari and the job as Bell's management assistant. She was married to John Henderson, a television director, but divorced by the time she was thirty due to her workaholic tendencies.

During her second stint at Saatchi & Saatchi Advertising, which lasted seventeen years, Laing was eventually promoted to vice chairman of the Charlotte Street agency. She resigned a second time in October 1987, eight months after her latest promotion, to become chief executive officer of Aspect Hill Holliday Group, a fledgling London agency that was a spinoff of a Boston agency, Hill, Holliday, Connors, Cosmopulos. Laing purchased the agency from the Boston parent a year later and it eventually became Laing Henry. One of the principals in Laing Henry was Tony Dalton, a former Saatchi & Saatchi executive from its days in Golden Square and a former chairman of Ted Bates and Foote, Cone & Belding. Dalton was also Laing's long-standing live-in companion, a position he holds to this day.

Laing was profoundly saddened by the events at Saatchi & Saatchi in the winter of 1994–95. She had stayed in close contact with many of her former colleagues and felt resentful of the executives that were throwing the place into turmoil, especially Maurice Saatchi. Laing would tell friends it was painful to see him destroying what she worked so hard to build and maintain.

Laing was surprised to hear from Ed Wax in late February 1995. He was going to be in London and wanted to pick her brain, he said. The two met at the Stafford Hotel, not a locale frequented by the advertising industry. Bluntly, and not too far into the conversation, Wax popped the question: would Laing be interested in going back to run Charlotte Street as chairwoman? "We need someone who understands the culture, the employees, and the clients," Wax said.

Although Laing was flattered, she was also conflicted. Her private life was settled. She was well respected and successful with her own agency, the headquarters of which was called the Toffee Factory because it had formerly been a Callard & Bowser candy plant. She had a slew of outside interests: for example, Laing was a co-owner of a race horse named Western Legend.

She told Wax she would think about it. The next day, Charlie Scott called Laing and the two agreed to meet discreetly behind a pillar at the dining room of the Stafford. At their meeting, Scott told Laing that the problem she had mentioned to Wax—that she was a major shareholder and owner of Laing Henry—was not a problem at all. Scott suggested Saatchi & Saatchi purchase Laing Henry.

Over the next few weeks, there were several secret meetings between Laing and Scott. In the interim Laing also spoke with John Foster, Laing Henry's finance director, who said it made sense for the forty employees to merge into the larger Charlotte Street agency.

The most difficult conversation Laing initiated involved Max Henry, her partner and creative director. Saatchi & Saatchi already had three creative directors and was not looking for a fourth. Ultimately, Henry decided not to be part of the acquisition. "I like being an entrepreneur," he told Laing. Nor did he stand in the way of the others who wanted the deal completed.

On March 13, Saatchi & Saatchi Company PLC purchased Laing Henry for £1.2 million and signed Laing to an initial two-year contract worth £175,000 annually. Laing also received a company car: a Lexus, manufactured by Toyota, a Saatchi & Saatchi client. Not a Ferrari, to be sure, but no slouch of a car, either.

Laing immediately set the record straight about the state of affairs on Charlotte Street, something Scott and others appeared unable to do. And Laing did it with gusto, a refreshing change from the static propaganda distributed by Saatchi & Saatchi. In her initial interviews with the British press, Laing went on the offensive: "Only 11 people have left Charlotte Street; there are 600 left. That's not exactly a mass exodus," she told the *Sunday Telegraph* in London. Others said the number hovered near 60.

As far as The New Saatchi Agency was concerned, Laing told the *Sunday Express*, "Of course, they're a threat, but so are the other 300 agencies here."

When Laing was at the Toffee Factory, she had not been a passive observer of the turmoil within Saatchi & Saatchi; she, her mother, and Tony Dalton were all shareholders in the company and saw the stock price collapse.

"Maurice should have stepped down sooner than he did," she said in late 1995. "He was a good ad man, a good client man, but not a good chairman of a public company."

Laing provided the company with backbone, something it heretofore was missing. Later in 1995, when Saatchi & Saatchi Company PLC and the five partners of The New Saatchi Agency were laboriously negotiating a peace settlement to put aside the spate of lawsuits and other less formalized charges, it was Laing alone who resisted giving Maurice and the others what they wanted.

SAATCHI & SAATCHI Company PLC officially changed its name to Cordiant PLC on March 16 at an Extraordinary General Meeting held at the (Whitbread) Brewery on Chiswell Street in London after the change was approved by shareholders. Although the management team wanted to put the whole sorry Maurice Saatchi episode behind it, the shareholders used the meeting as an opportunity to blast Scott and the board. One former Saatchi & Saatchi employee, Catherine Simmonds, questioned the board's handling of Maurice. "To lose one Saatchi brother may be misfortunate," she said, paraphrasing Oscar Wilde, "but to lose two looks like carelessness."

On the day of the holding company's name change, Cordiant shares closed at 87 pence on the London Stock Exchange. They had been trading at £1.5 in December prior to the shareholder and board mutiny. At Saatchi & Saatchi's zenith in 1987, its shares traded at £53.

A day earlier, the company released its 1994 financial results, in which it posted a 69 percent profit gain. However, it warned that the departure of Maurice Saatchi and other senior executives considerably diminished the outlook for 1995. Saatchi & Saatchi's 1994 profit was £32.4 million, up from £19.2 million a year earlier.

Around the City and throughout the advertising industry were persistent rumors that Cordiant was exploring the sale of CME KHBB, which the company had hoped would be a third worldwide network to coexist alongside Saatchi & Saatchi Advertising and Bates. CME began as Campbell Mithun, which was founded in 1933 and purchased by the Saatchi brothers' empire in 1986. Two years later, it was combined with William Esty Co., a Bates subsidiary. In 1992, CME was combined with KHBB, which Saatchi & Saatchi purchased in 1986.

The impetus for the sale was not an insatiable hunger for cash, however. Charlie Scott once again needed to please a demanding client, Procter & Gamble. In September 1994, CME scored a major victory, winning the $100 million Dow Brands account. Procter & Gamble objected to a competitor within the Saatchi & Saatchi stable and Scott responded by promising the situation would be resolved to Procter & Gamble's satisfaction.

Quickly, Interpublic Group made known its interest in CME KHBB. But CME KHBB's senior management team did not want Cordiant to sell 100 percent of the agency. Bill Dunlap, the agency's chief executive and president, and Howard Liszt, its chief operating officer, pushed for, and won, a partial management buyout. In the end, Interpublic purchased 50 percent of CME KHBB for $40 million. By the second quarter of 1995, Cordiant's advertising agencies were pared to Saatchi & Saatchi and Bates.

MAURICE SAATCHI was true to his word. He had sought to destabilize his former company and he had worked hard at it. But revenge only goes so far. So, other than scheming against the company he had co-founded and against the ad agency that still included his name, how was Saatchi spending his days? Few who knew Saatchi found the description to be credible: Maurice Saatchi worked.

No matter what was said publicly, The New Saatchi Agency needed to win the British Airways pitch in order to go forward. Airline accounts are time-consuming and some agencies steer clear of such accounts, deeming them not worth the trouble. An airline is basically a flying retail store whose major selling point is the price of a ticket. It is a cutthroat and highly competitive industry; once one airline lowers its fare, others follow suit. That means overtime for the ad agencies involved, which must rig up new, unimaginative commercials and print ads to get the message of a fare war out. But, while agencies do not usually weep over losing an airline account, such accounts are high-profile. In an industry where perception is reality, it is not beneficial for an agency to make news for being fired by an airline.

For Maurice Saatchi and his partners, British Airways amounted to a critical game of bragging rights. If The New Saatchi Agency did not win, it would become the subject of intense ridicule from the advertising industry. Losing would have raised an unsettling question: why didn't it win? After all, the team was basically the same group that had produced the successful batch of ads for years, and the chairman of British Airways had aggressively lobbied the Saatchi board and David Herro not to move against Maurice Saatchi. It was one thing for an American company, such as Mars, not to throw his budding agency any business, but British Airways turning its back on Saatchi would be a slap to a fellow Briton.

Legally, the Garden Leave prohibited Muirhead, Sinclair, and Kershaw from doing anything other than prepare to go to work for The New Saatchi Agency. Although the language was wildly ambiguous, it implied that the three had to stay away from the British Airways account. Muirhead was incredulous when told he could not speak to clients who had become close personal friends. "I got into fights with my lawyers," he said. "I told them to get stuffed. If they're going to throw me into prison for talking to a mate, so be it."

And so it was that Muirhead spent hours while on Garden Leave speaking with Derek Dear, general manager of marketing communications at British Airways, and Geoff Dixon, a senior executive at Qantas. He then fed his information to Saatchi and Tim Duffy.

Meanwhile, David Kershaw was exploring global alliances for The New Saatchi Agency, and Jeremy Sinclair, along with Kershaw, house-hunted for the company's permanent headquarters. In addition, the three amigos spent much of their time in conference with their attorneys, preparing for the hearing in London's High Court.

With Muirhead working in the background, much of the preparation for the first of two British Airways pitches, held on April 6, was done by Saatchi and Tim Duffy. The unusual duo—the dapper former chairman and the young, high-strung account planner—spent days at British Airways headquarters at Heathrow Airport outside London peppering the airline's employees with questions. Virtually all were surprised to be visited by Saatchi himself. Saatchi and Duffy learned that the latest slew of ads had been too confusing to the consumers. British Airways had too many messages. The ads had to be clearer and simpler.

Each day, following their sessions at Heathrow, Saatchi and Duffy would return to Davies Street and closet themselves in Saatchi's modest office, which contained only a battered desk, a poster or two, and one of those ubiquitous standing plants that seem to have found their way into virtually every office on the planet.

With the door closed to keep out the chaotic activity, the two began working on a presentation, each word of which was measured. Is that word necessary? Is there a better word? It was an odd circumstance for Saatchi and Duffy. Shortly, they were to appear before British Airways and recommend a starkly new marketing strategy from the approach they had been recently suggesting.

While Saatchi and Duffy were devising a new strategy for British Airways, Charlie Scott was occupied not only with the continued fallout of the company's recent past, but with its uncertain future as well.

Scott was now chief executive and acting chairman. The Saatchi & Saatchi Company PLC board initiated a search for a new chairman. At the time, the company was unsure whether it wanted Scott to be elevated to chairman or remain in his chief executive role.

Immediately after Saatchi resigned, Peter Davis, the former co-chairman of Reed Elsevier, the Anglo-Dutch publishing and information group, surfaced as a viable candidate to become chairman. Davis had resigned from Reed Elsevier in June 1994 following a clash over management styles. But on January 29, Davis let it be known he was not interested: "Peter knows the Saatchis well and would have jumped at it in happier circumstances," one close associate of Davis said. "But he didn't want to be involved in a Bosnian situation."

That was just as well. Davis had one irrefutable strike against him: he was a Briton. "One of the things this company has never done well is perform as well as we ought to in the United States," Scott said. "Business is done differently in the United States than it is in the United Kingdom." To that end, Scott said he was "prepared to get an American chairman or an American chief executive."

Although it was difficult to tell at Saatchi & Saatchi when Maurice was chairman, there is a clear distinction between the roles, especially in the United Kingdom. The Cadbury principles state that the chairman has assigned responsibilities: conducting and being the leader of the board of directors and ensuring that proper corporate governance is followed. That includes leading open and frank discussions, making sure that directors are informed on all issues relating to the company, and forming an assertive, independent board that is well rounded and thorough.

A chief executive is far more hands-on in the company's day-to-day operation, building a staff of executives responsible for running the company. Many chairmen in Britain and some in the United States are non-executive chairmen, meaning they are not even employees of the company.

To help with the search, Saatchi & Saatchi hired Spencer Stuart, a leading corporate headhunting firm. The initial list of candidates was compiled with the objective of filling the chairman's position, but Scott quickly thought the individuals were better suited for the more demanding role of chief executive.

"I was prepared to get an American chairman or an American chief executive," Scott said later. "When I looked at the candidates, I decided we should look more at a chief executive. The first list had about twenty candidates targeted to be chairman. Then, Spencer Stuart produced a list of chief executives, which were much better."

So, Charlie Scott had made a self-liberating decision: he would become chairman, freeing himself of the day-to-day operations of Cordiant, which he greatly disliked. And since he was chairman, why not move from his depressing office to the luxurious surroundings of the chairman's office formerly occupied by Maurice Saatchi? Which was exactly what Charlie Scott did, with a tone of self-importance and self-confidence that many within Cordiant had not previously seen.

WHILE CORDIANT SEARCHED for a senior executive, British Airways and Qantas conducted their combined search for an advertising agency. The first round of meetings between the airlines and the four agency finalists, J. Walter Thompson, Bartle Bogle Hegarty, Saatchi & Saatchi, and New Saatchi, were to take place on successive days beginning April 3.

The account was so coveted that Martin Sorrell, the chairman of WPP Group, owner of Thompson, attended the marathon session, which began at 8 A.M. and ended eleven hours later. British

Airways and Qantas executives left unimpressed. "They didn't demonstrate what the airline business was all about," said one executive who participated in the review. "Though they didn't produce creative work, they described their direction as to get oohs and ahhs out of the audience." The airlines felt they were being lectured to instead of being listened to and did not feel their questions were being answered directly. In all, a frustrating experience.

The next day, Bartle Bogle Hegarty unspooled an impressive reel of commercials, although the potential clients noticed a disturbing theme throughout the ads: virtually all were replete with sexual innuendo. "I can't see sex when talking about an airline," one member of the Qantas team said to John Hegarty. Hegarty agreed and said the agency would create ads that were "unexpected" for the airline industry, but was not specific. Instead, Bartle Bogle said the creative direction was to play up the fact that British Airways was, well, British and that the "British-ness" should be played up in a humorous manner.

Robert Ayling, then–managing director of British Airways, felt Bartle Bogle was a kindred spirit. He saw it as a small London agency, not unlike Saatchi & Saatchi at the beginning when it first began handling British Airways advertising. To Ayling, Bartle Bogle was the next wave, a 1990s Saatchi & Saatchi in terms of energy and creativity. But Bartle Bogle hampered its own chances by steadfastly refusing to open additional offices. Instead, it said it would place an account executive in Sydney, Australia, to handle the two airline accounts. All of the creative work would be produced from London; there would be no Bartle Bogle representative in the United States.

On Wednesday, the airline executives visited Saatchi & Saatchi Advertising. One executive described the session as "atrocious." Several executives, including Jennifer Laing, the newly installed chairwoman of Charlotte Street, basically criticized the airlines' advertising. "In essence, they were criticizing what they had done," said one of the participants. During a mid-morning coffee break, a Qantas executive said to Derek Dear of British Airways, "They not only don't understand the business, but they don't understand how you've positioned your airline."

After the session resumed, Saatchi & Saatchi presented creative ways to get a new message across and the airline teams sat aghast. British Airways is positioned as a quality product. Stunning, then, that Saatchi & Saatchi would suggest that new ads be placed on the backs of doors to toilet stalls, near sinks in washrooms, or on mailboxes. "This was beyond tacky," said one participant.

The agency also spent a lot of time reminiscing. It took the airlines down memory lane and spoke about past ad campaigns. Instead of recalling warm feelings, British Airways and Qantas thought the exercise an utter waste of time. First, virtually all of the advertising executives responsible for the ads had resigned in a public and unpleasant fashion. Second, the airlines did not want to dwell on the past; it wanted exciting proposals for the future.

Saatchi & Saatchi had imported executives from its offices in Sydney, Hong Kong, and New York, but in large part excluded them from the pitch. Instead, London executives ran the show, and they later acknowledged that the pitch did not go well.

When the meeting concluded eleven hours after it began, Saatchi & Saatchi executives asked the airline officials to join them at a nearby pub. The invitation was quickly refused. "These people were clinical, corporate, and not anyone we wanted to get to know any better," said one airline executive.

During the session, Robert Ayling said the decision was primarily his, a disclosure that buoyed Saatchi & Saatchi's hopes. Sir Colin Marshall, British Airways' chairman, was unmistakably aligned with Maurice Saatchi. But Ayling was an unknown. He could be anxious to make his own stamp on the airline and, therefore, make an anti-Marshall choice.

The New Saatchi Agency was a sharp contrast to Charlotte Street. Its presentation was simple, direct, and articulate. Maurice Saatchi apologized for, in part, causing a review in the first place. He spent two minutes on the past and then began speaking about the future.

British Airways and Qantas executives visited the agencies for separate two-hour follow-up sessions on April 25. The New Saatchi Agency's setup at No. 60 Kingly Street, one block parallel to Carnaby Street, looked as if it had been there for months. Charles Saatchi loaned the agency several pieces of art for the day, though some would wonder if he really did New Saatchi any favors.

The artwork was Carina Weidle's *Olympic Chickens*, an odd series of photographs of a plucked chicken—the kind one would place in an oven—performing athletic feats, ranging from swimming to lifting weights to javelin throwing to pole vaulting.

Any hope Saatchi & Saatchi Advertising harbored quickly evaporated even before the second meeting officially began. The agency divided the presentation into two parts and two rooms; in the first room was an assortment of old British Airways ads. Robert Ayling breezed in and in a curt manner said, "We have only two hours exactly. Colin will join us when he can." Colin Marshall, chairman of one of the agency's most important clients, had not even bothered to show up on time.

The presentation ended with Jennifer Laing telling British Airways that it had become too arrogant, too cold to its consumers. Marshall was there in time to hear that and let her have it. "We've been following your marketing advice for years," he said. "In other words, your agency failed." Ed Wax, chairman and chief executive of Saatchi & Saatchi Advertising Worldwide, in London to lend support, sat silently and seethed. "Our agency has failed?" he thought to himself. "You're talking seriously to the assholes who failed you."

One of the intangible factors that is considered when deciding about an advertising agency is the chemistry between the client and the team from the agency. British Airways and Qantas quickly concluded they did not want to work with Saatchi & Saatchi or J. Walter Thompson. They had a positive feeling about working with Bartle Bogle, but were unsure whether the agency's media buying operation carried clout.

As the selection process unexpectedly dragged on, Bartle Bogle and Saatchi & Saatchi quietly negotiated an unusual agreement. Saatchi executives knew it did not stand a chance to win the account, so it offered up the services of Zenith, its powerful and respected media buying subsidiary, to work with Bartle Bogle if it won the creative portion. Prior to coming to an agreement with Zenith, Bartle Bogle also held discussions with two Interpublic Group agencies, McCann-Erickson and Lintas.

During the airline account reviews, The New Saatchi Agency was awarded the account for Dixons Group, the chain of consumer-electronics stores, with more than eight hundred branches in the United Kingdom and with billings of approximately £50 million. Saatchi & Saatchi quickly replaced the account with Comet, another chain of stores with £40 million in billings.

On Friday, April 28, someone connected with Saatchi & Saatchi Company PLC leaked a potentially damaging story about Maurice and Charles Saatchi to the *Sunday Times* of London. The *Wall Street Journal* heard about the leak and, on Saturday, the *Journal's* Advertising columnist called the individual he suspected of being the source. As it turned out, the *Journal* was correct. The individual in London repeated the story in detail.

When Cordiant's annual report was published in mid-May, the *Journal* was told, it would contain an intriguing entry under the harmless heading, "Subsequent events." The company was "seeking legal advice" over pension entitlements that the Saatchi brothers took in 1989. The entitlements amounted to £2.9 million that had been transferred out of the Saatchi & Saatchi pension and assurance plan in 1989 and into a "stand-alone scheme for their benefit." Cordiant said the £2.9 million may have been incorrectly calculated; the brothers entered the company pension plan in 1988 before they reversed that decision a year later when they returned to making their own pension arrangements.

Since it is highly unusual to reveal the contents of an annual report prior to its publication, the objective of the leak was clear: Cordiant wanted to taint the Saatchi brothers and, in turn, The New Saatchi Agency during the delicate period when British Airways and Qantas were deliberating on an agency selection.

The stories hit the papers on April 30 and May 1.

On May 2, British Airways selected The New Saatchi Agency. "The account was the pride and joy of the agency," said Ed Wax of Saatchi & Saatchi Advertising. "It's like one of your children, and it's gone." The following day, Qantas followed British Airways' lead and chose The New Saatchi Agency as well. Said Wax, "We believe this is the last shoe to drop."

On the day following the British Airways announcement, Saatchi & Saatchi Advertising on Hudson Street placed two full-page ads in newspapers in the United States and United Kingdom.

"Who wants to be next world's favourite?" the copy read. The ad included the office telephone numbers of Jennifer Laing and Michael Jeary. The ad's objective was to entice an airline to award its account to Saatchi & Saatchi, and perhaps that airline would receive the same sales boost as British Airways.

In 1996, there were still no takers.

EARLY MAY was a heady time for Maurice Saatchi and his new agency. But there continued to be a nagging psychological and financial drain on him, his brother, and the three other partners. There were still all the legal mine fields strategically planted by his former company with the aim of handicapping the growth of New Saatchi.

So, intoxicated by the account wins spilling his way, Maurice Saatchi began thinking of how he and his partners could be freed from their complex and costly legal entanglements.

CHAPTER
SIXTEEN

THE LEGAL WAR that erupted between Saatchi & Saatchi and The New Saatchi Agency threatened to ruin both businesses and essentially nullify the board's reason for ousting Maurice Saatchi in the first place: to avoid having damaging information, charges, and countercharges from both sides leaked to the press. In preparation of the public trials scheduled to be held in London's High Court, however, the same negative information would be made public. In fact, the trials would likely be worse because the stakes were higher.

Legal fees for both sides were climbing to a combined total of $1 million. Exploring the possibility of an out-of-court settlement would have made sense, except that the two sides hated each other so intensely that few were thinking rationally.

Shortly after Saatchi & Saatchi filed its suit against Maurice Saatchi on January 12, 1995—one day after Maurice announced he would open a rival agency—Charles Saatchi placed a pivotal telephone call to an old and trusted friend. On the other end of the line was Johan Eliasch, a thirty-three-year-old Swedish venture capitalist who had made a fortune by investing in ailing companies that subsequently recovered.

Eliasch, head of Equity Partners, a company registered on the Isle of Man, started in Stockholm as a partner in the Gyllenhamar investment group. He arrived in London in 1985 in part to escape the high income taxes in his native country. Besides Equity Partners, he owned 75 percent of Tufton Oceanic, a London-based shipping investment group, and was the sole owner of London Film Ltd., which holds the worldwide distribution rights to several Walt Disney Co. movies. To relax, Eliasch enjoyed golfing and skiing.

In describing Eliasch, the word "discreet" comes to mind. That was one reason he was such a good friend of the Saatchi brothers. Eliasch was also smart, tenacious, and loyal. Unlike Maurice, however, Eliasch winced on the rare occasion when his name appeared in the media.

Charles Saatchi told Eliasch that he thought the situation with his former company had become ridiculous. Was there any possibility of an amicable settlement between the two warring sides? Saatchi wondered.

The call was not a random search for a solution; instead, it was a trademark Charles Saatchi move, carefully and strategically conceived. Johan Eliasch was one of the few individuals who was a close friend not only to the Saatchi brothers, but to a Saatchi & Saatchi board member as well, the Hon. Clive Gibson of St. James's Place Capital PLC, a major Saatchi shareholder appointed to the board in May 1991.

Eliasch contacted Gibson and several informal meetings between the two took place. When Gibson approached Cordiant about a settlement, the holding company was not initially prepared to discuss the matter.

In early May, Gibson called Eliasch: "Maybe now is the time," Gibson said. On May 11, Gibson put forward a proposal to the board essentially empowering him to negotiate a settlement with The New Saatchi Agency. The board had come to realize that peace was the best strategy. The companies were staring at a June 12 deadline of sorts; that was the date that court hearings were scheduled to commence. Cordiant's annual board meeting was to be held June 13 and company executives were nervous that shareholders might be unhappy with the continued legal maneuvers.

A meeting attended by Johan Eliasch, Jeremy Sinclair, Wendy Smyth, and Clive Gibson took place on May 16 at Spencer House, the opulent headquarters on St. James's Place, where Gibson kept an office. Spencer House is also rented by companies throwing parties, and on the occasion of the May 16 meeting the representatives of Cordiant and New Saatchi passed a bash attended by men in tuxedos and women in long formal gowns. The length and outcome of the meeting were surprising considering the animosity and number of legal issues to be addressed. After only four hours, Cordiant and New Saatchi had the genesis of a settlement.

Smyth was described by Sinclair as "Mrs. Reasonable," someone who wanted the whole legal affair dealt with swiftly. The suit against Muirhead was quickly dropped; executives from both sides privately confessed that they did not know why it was filed in the first place, other than to rattle him. Sinclair was instrumental in resolving the issue of the brothers' pension fund. He pointed out that the pension contribution from the company should have been calculated at the brothers' original salary of £650,000, not the reduced salary. The two sides agreed that Maurice and Charles would not seek additional money from Cordiant for their pension funds and that the company would drop any inquiries into the brothers involving the pension.

The right of the three amigos and others from Saatchi & Saatchi Advertising to join The New Saatchi Agency was also quickly established. Courts in the United Kingdom overwhelmingly favor the employee and his right to earn a living. Lawyers for the trio were prepared to argue that if Cordiant forced the three to sit on the sidelines until their contractual obligations were satisfied, they would be less attractive to potential employers because they had been idle for so long. Cordiant assumed it would not be able to prevent the three amigos from joining Maurice and Charles Saatchi.

New Saatchi cared most about Cordiant dropping its various claims. Cordiant was more interested in stemming the tide of client defections, so it sought a moratorium to prevent The New Saatchi Agency from poaching clients and employees from Saatchi & Saatchi Advertising and Bates Worldwide.

Also discussed was the name of the new agency, with no resolution satisfactory to either side. Both sides examined the proposal, and on May 17 Gibson called Eliasch to request another meeting. Cordiant, and specifically Jennifer Laing, chairwoman of Saatchi & Saatchi Advertising in London, wanted to dictate the name of the breakaway agency.

On May 19, the two sides met again, this time at the offices of Olswang & Co., the attorneys representing the three amigos. The participants were Eliasch, Sinclair, Smyth, Graham Howell,

Cordiant's corporate secretary, and attorneys from firms representing Cordiant and the Saatchi brothers.

The session began at 1 P.M. on May 19 and did not end until 6 A.M. the following day. Once the legal language was agreed upon regarding a majority of the issues, attention returned to the name The New Saatchi Agency. Both sides took a short break on May 20, after the seventeen-hour session, and resumed at 11 A.M.

When Cordiant arrived late, the other side was immediately worried. They assumed—correctly it turned out—that Cordiant was going to fight The New Saatchi Agency on a matter it had agreed to only a few hours before: the name of Maurice's new agency. When the all-night session adjourned, the agreement was for the enterprise to be called MC Saatchi Agency.

More than anyone, Jennifer Laing, who was in constant phone contact through the negotiations, was not willing to compromise on the name. The upstart agency could not use the word "new" nor could it start with the name Saatchi. Therefore, the title favored by the three amigos, Saatchi Partners, was not a possibility. Nor was another name they proposed, New Saatchi Partners. " 'New Saatchi Partners' was pejorative, upsetting, and placed a lot of emphasis on the name Saatchi," Laing said later. If Maurice and his partners were to include Saatchi in their agency's name, then it must have something placed in front of it. Laing was serious; this was a deal-breaker, one that could place both sides back in High Court.

During the final go-around, Smyth and others from the Cordiant side adjourned to an adjacent room to check the "name proposal" with Charlie Scott and Jennifer Laing. The call was made on a speakerphone, which Jeremy Sinclair, Johan Eliasch, and the others were able to hear clearly. Laing said over the phone that she wanted to ensure that when The New Saatchi Agency—or whatever it was going to be called—was referred to in headlines, it would not be confused with Saatchi & Saatchi. If it could not be Saatchi Partners, Maurice and the others reluctantly chose MC Saatchi. Laing again balked.

Johan Eliasch spoke up: "C'mon Jennifer," he said. "We had an agreement. It was to be one of the four names from the list of finalists." The names were MC Saatchi, M&C Partners, M&C Saatchi Partners, and MC Saatchi Agency. Cordiant wanted Maurice

Saatchi Agency or M Saatchi Agency; Laing wanted to personalize the new agency to Maurice.

Laing would not budge. If the new agency was determined to include Saatchi in its title, Laing wanted to ensure there was as much as possible placed before it. Laing was as clever as Maurice and Charles in this instance. If the new agency was called MC Saatchi, headline writers and reporters would undoubtedly shorten it to Saatchi. But, if the name was slightly altered to, say, M&C Saatchi, it might be referred to as M&C. So M&C Saatchi Agency was agreed upon.

The news of the settlement was released on May 22. Cordiant was immediately declared the loser whereas Maurice Saatchi emerged triumphant. The Lex column in the *Financial Times* said the resolution was "rather embarrassing" for Cordiant. "Not only is Mr. Saatchi's rival agency far from vanquished, but Cordiant has dropped a number of actions where it appeared to have a strong case.

"Nonetheless, Cordiant has probably taken a wise course. Protracted legal scuffles . . . would have distracted senior management from the vital task of rebuilding staff confidence and the group's dwindling client list."

Campaign magazine, Saatchi loyalists to the end, characterized the settlement as a "virtual climbdown by Cordiant." *Adweek* in the United States said Cordiant "appeared to have turned on its heels and retreated." In an editorial headlined "Peace in Saatchiland," *Advertising Age* wrote that "Maurice Saatchi has won. Unmistakably. . . . Peppering Mr. Saatchi with lawsuits was a useful tactic for Cordiant. . . . Unfortunately for Cordiant, none of it worked. But it did what it had to do and should not look back." Even the *New York Post* checked in and said the legal dispute ended in a "lopsided truce."

Under terms of the agreement, Cordiant agreed to drop the Adidas-related claim, end inquiries into the transfer in 1989 of a pension plan for the Saatchi brothers that was valued at approximately $4.6 million, and abandon efforts to block the three amigos and others, including Simon Dicketts, creative director of Saatchi & Saatchi Advertising on Charlotte Street, from joining the breakaway agency. They could start working with Maurice on June

1, 1995. Additionally, Cordiant agreed to drop the lawsuit in the United States against Bill Muirhead that sought $50 million. The company said it "accepts that there was no wrongdoing on his part." Cordiant also agreed to pay all legal costs incurred by M&C Saatchi. Of course, it was not a total victory for M&C Saatchi. Although never made public, there were other important details to the settlement. Maurice and Charles Saatchi dropped large counterclaims against their former company for salaries and bonuses. Charles Saatchi, for example, told associates that he had four years remaining on his contract worth £325,000 a year, as well as expenses. Further, the three amigos—Jeremy Sinclair, Bill Muirhead, and David Kershaw—dropped claims for bonuses that were to be based on the performance in 1994 of Saatchi & Saatchi Advertising. Privately, Cordiant said these payments far exceeded the legal fees.

Cordiant made its self-imposed deadline of negotiating a settlement prior to its annual shareholders meeting, which was held at the Queen Elizabeth II Conference Centre across from the Houses of Parliament on June 13. Shareholders had to pass through metal detectors. That did not stop bad news from being delivered verbally. The pact with New Saatchi, now M&C Saatchi, did not placate Cordiant shareholders.

Maurice Saatchi's removal was indeed quite costly: clients who fled, including British Airways, Mars, Gallaher Tobacco, and Mirror Group Newspapers, accounted for 6 percent of Cordiant's revenues. The company, which originally forecast cutting 150 positions after the Mars loss, said it would have to eliminate 470 jobs, or 4 percent of its total workforce of 10,900, with severance costs amounting to about £10 million, or $15.7 million. In addition, there was a noncash goodwill write-off related to the sale in April 1995 of Campbell Mithun Esty.

Charlie Scott told shareholders that the incentive to settle its legal differences with Maurice Saatchi and the others was because clients were growing weary of the prolonged court battles.

The one bit of good news was mixed: Cordiant replaced 3 percent of its revenue, but not with new clients. Instead, it received new assignments from existing clients, including Procter & Gamble and Johnson & Johnson. Although additional assignments from clients already handled by an ad agency are welcome, winning new clients entirely adds to an agency's ability to boast and look more attractive. It is assumed that a client will award additional assignments to its existing agency; if it does not, then that signals there is something amiss and the entire relationship could be in jeopardy.

The shareholders, who were a disgruntled bunch for most of 1994, were, for the most part, a disgruntled bunch in 1995 as well. "We're supposed to be in the PR business and [the Saatchi brothers] won hands down," John Grundy, a former KHBB executive, said angrily to Scott. "We have no confidence in [Cordiant]. The feeling is every move you've made, you've failed. How do you now send a positive message that this cock-up doesn't happen again?"

One answer, Scott said, was that a new chairman or chief executive was about to join Cordiant, in all likelihood an American chief executive with deep experience in marketing. And, for the first time, Scott said publicly that he might ascend to the chairman's office and the search would focus on a chief executive.

IN LATE MARCH, a consortium put together by Robert L. Seelert, a former president and chief executive officer of General Foods Worldwide Coffee & International Foods division, submitted a bid in London to purchase the Tetley Tea business of Allied Domecq of the United Kingdom. On the weekend following the submission of the Tetley bid, Seelert was resting in his New Canaan, Connecticut, home when he received a phone call from Spencer Stuart, the search firm hired to find a new chief executive for Cordiant PLC. He was instantly intrigued by the vague description offered by Spencer Stuart senior director Dick White. In late May, Seelert was introduced to Charlie Scott at Spencer Stuart's London headquarters on Connaught Place near Hyde Park.

Seelert was perhaps the antidote Cordiant needed in the wake of Maurice Saatchi's reign. A bookish-looking executive with no outside displays of pizzazz or humor, Seelert, fifty-two, fit the predetermined mold of what Scott wanted: an American executive whose roots were firmly planted in the corporate, or client, side of the advertising business. Scott's thinking was logical; 40 percent of Cordiant's business was in the United States. And if Cordiant were to know what a client wanted and how a client thought, who better to provide these services than someone who had spent his career as a client? Seelert also oozed stability. He was low-key, grounded, and had been married to the same woman for thirty-one years, having met Sarah Leone Perry, his wife, in high school. He married her in June 1964, the week he graduated from Harvard College with an economics degree.

Seelert liked to play up his former professional life, emphasizing that he had sat "on the other side of the table" for years. "I believe in the power of advertising and marketing communications," he said. "I want to infuse a client's background in this business."

At General Foods, Seelert supervised breakfast foods, beverages, Entenmann's baked goods, and marketed brands such as Maxwell House, Jell-O, and Minute Rice. Seelert said that while he was with General Foods it spent $2 billion a year for over sixty brands with seven different agencies. One of the brands was Country Time Lemonade, a powdered beverage. He was once presented with an internal recommendation to kill Country Time Lemonade because its sales appeared to be in an irreversible slump. But Seelert disagreed and recommended instead that the advertising and marketing budgets be doubled. The powdered product then thrived. Seelert's point was to demonstrate how aware he was of the power of advertising.

He left General Foods in 1989 after it was merged by the Philip Morris Companies with Kraft Inc. "I was the forty-first of forty-seven executives to leave," Seelert said. From General Foods, he became president and chief executive officer of Topco Associates in Skokie, Illinois, a marketing cooperative that was owned by thirty regional supermarket chains and grocery wholesalers. Seelert stayed there for approximately two years before joining Kayser-Roth Corp. in Greensboro, North Carolina, a legwear concern that made socks and panty hose, including No Nonsense and Burlington. After he resigned in January 1994, Seelert spent six months relaxing and "marrying off my two oldest children."

His next business venture was leading the team to buy Tetley Tea; the effort was backed by Citicorp, Candover, Electra, and others, but it failed in June 1995 when Allied Domecq acquired Tetley in a management buyout for £190 million.

Because of his bid for Tetley, Seelert was practically living in

London during the period that Cordiant imploded. He followed the events and characterized them as a "crying shame." He was impressed with the "resiliency" of the company's employees.

Nevertheless, Seelert was not sure he wanted the job; he had concerns about whether Cordiant could ever recover. So Seelert sought the advice of an old friend, Ken Roman, former chairman of Ogilvy & Mather. The two became acquainted when Seelert was an assistant product manager at General Foods. Seelert told Roman he was worried that he did not know enough about the advertising business. "It's a simple business," Roman responded. "Just service the client."

Seelert also wondered whether the instability afflicting the agencies could ever be corrected. "Yes," said Roman, "if someone understood the values of creative product and the values of people." Roman told Seelert the situation was probably not as bad as it appeared because of the "loyalty of the clients, particularly among giants such as Procter & Gamble. Instead of bailing out, they stood by the company. That is the rock on which you will build the future."

Roman had one additional piece of advice if Seelert ultimately was offered and accepted the job: see the clients as soon as possible and do not leave them unattended. Ask the clients what the agencies can do to build their businesses.

Bob Seelert was one of four candidates Spencer Stuart thought fit Cordiant's needs. "Without a doubt, Bob was the best candidate," said Dick White of Spencer Stuart. "Specifically, his depth of background in business building and turnaround and building teams."

Scott and Seelert met three times before Scott decided that Seelert "was the guy." Seelert then met with the members of the Cordiant board with the knowledge that he carried Scott's recommendation. Cordiant executives, including Tim Jackson, the head of investor relations, introduced Seelert to the top managers of Cordiant's U.S. operations. On July 6, Seelert signed a three-year contract with Cordiant in the New York office of his attorney.

The deal for Seelert, an untested executive in the competitive arena of advertising, paid him $800,000 annually. He could earn a further maximum of $640,000 in bonuses if certain revenue and earnings targets were achieved. Seelert also received an executive share options package that built up over three years to provide him with options over shares worth four times his annual salary. His contract also included a clause limiting the compensation he could receive if he was fired. If he was dismissed overnight, he was entitled to $1.68 million; if Cordiant was taken over, the figure climbed to $2.24 million. "I'm being paid as a U.S. industrialist," Seelert said, defending his rich contract.

One day after Seelert signed the pact, he and Tim Jackson flew to Chicago. As a courtesy, Jackson wanted to introduce Seelert to David Herro. Herro, much to everyone's relief, was impressed with what he saw.

Employees within Saatchi & Saatchi Advertising and Bates did not bubble with as much enthusiasm when they heard on July 11, 1995, that Bob Seelert was Cordiant's new chief executive officer. It was not a marquee name, someone with star power. But he passed the ABM test: Anyone But Maurice.

Seelert did not have an immediate corporate strategy, and he did not need one; he needed only to meet with clients and Cordiant employees to assure them of several facts: he was not Maurice Saatchi and he would restore the company's stability. For the first several weeks of his tenure, Seelert recited a mantra: he wanted Cordiant to be the "world's best creative communications resource." It is not important to be the biggest, Seelert said in an obvious swipe at the former chairman; what matters is to be the best. Creativity is paramount in an advertising agency, he said. What else would a client be looking for? Saatchi & Saatchi and Bates must be a resource for the client, not for themselves, he added.

LESS THAN A MONTH after Seelert joined Cordiant, the company released its first-half 1995 results, figures that Charlie Scott said reflected "a particularly turbulent period for this group. . . . The second half results will be delivered against a difficult background, bearing as they will have the full effect of major account losses and the further impact of our cost reduction programme." Cordiant reported a pretax loss of £29.6 million, or $47.7 million, in the first half, compared with a profit of £15.3 million in the year-ago period. The company posted an operating profit of £7.3 million, but incurred a £26.8 million loss on disposals primarily from the sale of Campbell Mithun Esty in the United States and the closing of CME offices overseas. Cordiant was crippled with a debt load of approximately £130 million; net interest payments were £10.1 million.

Cordiant needed cash. Against this background, Kobs & Draft Worldwide, the Chicago-based fourth-largest direct marketing agency in the world, said it was buying itself back from Cordiant. The buyback was initiated "to gain the financial and investment flexibility necessary to set our own priorities for the company's growth rather than be restrained by those of Cordiant," Howard Draft said. The company, with six hundred employees and twenty-nine offices and billings of approximately $500 million, also changed its name to DraftDirect Worldwide. Its clients included Kraft General Foods, Time Warner, Sprint, and Upjohn. Two months after its separation from Cordiant, DraftDirect won four new accounts—Bell Atlantic, BankAmerica, Home Access Health, and NordicTrack—with total billings of $655 million.

Publicly, the buyback was portrayed as smooth and amicable. The road to the deal was far rockier, however. As soon as Howard Draft heard of Maurice's ouster as chairman, he flew to London with the hope of orchestrating a management buyout.

Draft, forty-one, was raised in Chicago and became a philosophy and art major in college. Upon graduation, he looked for a job in advertising because he wanted to be in a profession that changed often. When no one would hire him, Draft chose the next level down from mainstream advertising, direct marketing. He joined Stone & Adler in 1977, and when Jim Kobs left in 1978 he asked Draft to go with him. Kobs & Brady was founded in 1978 with eleven employees and one client. By 1986, when it was sold to Ted Bates, it had a hundred employees, thirty clients, and $86 million in billings. Draft assumed the chairman position in 1988, two years after being made president.

When Saatchi & Saatchi Company PLC acquired Bates, Kobs & Draft, as it was renamed in 1988, was included, but the parent company did not know what to make of this odd company that provided an increasingly important expertise to a client's marketing strategy.

Draft liked and respected Robert Louis-Dreyfus, and when he left he liked and respected Charlie Scott. The two talked and gossiped frequently. In late 1993, Scott and Draft discussed spinning off Kobs & Draft, acquiring ad agencies specializing in the medical field, and creating a second class of Saatchi & Saatchi stock. But after meeting with the potential agencies, Draft decided he did not like any of them, so the plan was abandoned.

In many overseas markets, Kobs & Draft's financials were tied to Bates offices. The problem was that Bates looked down on the services provided by Kobs & Draft while Kobs & Draft resented the occasions when Bates would call and ask the agency to work on a project for a Bates client. Howard Draft and others would say the company does not work solely on a "project."

Howard Draft was in Chicago during Saatchi & Saatchi's tumultuous 1994 and did not know what to make of David Herro. Despite being in the same city, Draft said Herro never bothered to contact him about Saatchi & Saatchi, even though Kobs & Draft was a company that was solid financially and creatively.

Further, Draft was led to believe by Saatchi & Saatchi executives that the company was on the verge of recovery and could make $60 million to $70 million in 1995. Draft believed it was better for the company to put up with the antics of Maurice Saatchi, even if it cost $2 million a year to do so. Draft also felt it was irresponsible for Herro to meddle in a business he knew nothing about, a business in which relationships were paramount.

But Draft also saw opportunity in the chaos that engulfed Saatchi & Saatchi. On Monday, December 19, 1994, he flew to London on the Concorde. The next day, he met with Wendy Smyth for lunch at Il Sorriso, an Italian restaurant across the street from Saatchi & Saatchi Advertising on Charlotte Street.

"You're going to need cash," Draft said. "I don't think we fit into your company any longer and the management of Kobs & Draft would like to buy the company back."

Smyth thought for a moment and then replied, "That's reasonable."

The first offer presented by Draft over lunch amounted to $22 million.

Although Smyth was speaking for Scott, who was not available to attend the lunch, it turned out she did not reflect the board's attitude. The Saatchi & Saatchi board opposed selling Kobs & Draft. Bates France, for example, wanted to keep its association with Kobs & Draft; Bates was hurting from the loss of the Mars account.

Rebuffed, Draft resigned.

The board asked Draft to reconsider and to meet in London with Scott, Smyth, and Ed Wax and Michael Bungey, the chief executives of Saatchi & Saatchi Advertising and Bates Worldwide, respectively. The company offered Draft a solution: merge his direct marketing firm with Saatchi & Saatchi Advertising to create a fully integrated agency. Howard Draft was told he could assume the role of chief operating officer of Saatchi & Saatchi Advertising Worldwide, the number two position to Wax.

"Are you nuts?" Draft said. "I'm a direct marketing guy. This makes no sense."

The plan was tabled and Draft said subsequent negotiations were difficult and tedious until an agreement was finally reached. Kobs & Draft would buy itself back for $27.2 million. Kobs & Draft management, led by Howard Draft, its chairman and chief executive, agreed to pay $13.7 million in cash, $9.5 million in a 10 percent subordinated loan note, and $4 million in redeemable preferred stock in KDA Acquisition, the company formed by management to handle the transaction. Cordiant retained the right to acquire up to 25 percent of Kobs & Draft, which was acquired by Ted Bates Advertising in 1988 for $10 million. Four months later, Bates was purchased by Saatchi & Saatchi.

It had been such a tense period for Cordiant employees, particularly those at Saatchi & Saatchi Advertising on Charlotte Street, they needed to let off some steam. Now there was an excuse. Earlier in the year, it placed an ad in *Campaign* with the headline "1995 Will Be Remembered for the Most Historic Event in Twenty-five Years of Saatchi & Saatchi." The copy said the agency was holding "the biggest party ever" and that anyone who had ever worked at the agency was invited. "We wanted to demonstrate to the world that our spirit was alive and well," Jennifer Laing said.

The party was held on September 2 at the Grey Coat Hospital School, which was converted into Saatchi & Saatchi High School for the evening. Sausages, baked beans, and potatoes were served in what Laing described as a "low-budget affair." One poster featured the past hierarchy; headlined "Head Boys/Girls," it showed that in 1970–74, Charles Saatchi was chairman, Maurice Saatchi was managing director, and Jeremy Sinclair was creative director. Over one thousand past and present Saatchi & Saatchi employees showed up. Laing invited the Saatchi brothers and others from M&C Saatchi; few accepted.

M&C SAATCHI continued winning new business. At the same time Cordiant was announcing its dismal first-half 1995 results, M&C Saatchi, which was nicknamed McSaatchi by some in the advertising industry and the media, won the Courage Best beer account. Once again, Maurice Saatchi acted as if he did not have a care in the world.

Saatchi spoke about executives within his former company and the Cordiant board with contempt. Once, he and his wife, Josephine Hart, were dining at the same restaurant as Peter Walters, a Cordiant board member who supported Saatchi but later publicly criticized him. Walters's wife said, "There's Maurice. Go and say something to him."

Approaching Saatchi, Walters extended his hand and said, "Maurice, this has been very painful for both of us."

Saatchi simply replied, "Yes it has," and, without shaking Walters's hand, turned around and walked away.

Maurice Saatchi later said he felt totally justified in snubbing his former friend. Saatchi said Walters had told him he would quit if the board forced Saatchi out. When the board meeting was over, Saatchi asked Walters why he did not quit.

"They said I couldn't," Walters replied.

"What do you mean?" Saatchi asked.

Walters answered that the board said it was his "duty" to stay on.

Saatchi and his partners loathed the agency's name. Some newspapers printed only M&C after the first reference, a practice that caused great consternation to the partners and Maurice Saatchi in particular. There were constant discussions among the five partners on how to rid the agency of its awful name. A plan was devised, but it was too soon to implement.

During this time, M&C Saatchi moved its headquarters to 9 Marylebone Lane on a crooked artery off Oxford Street, not far from the original Davies Street office.

Saatchi took great satisfaction in knowing that he won the public relations war. Cordiant was seen as the company that could not shoot straight, a bevy of incompetent pencil pushers in the holding company who knew little of the advertising business, while the scrappy and rough-around-the-edges advertising agency that was M&C Saatchi was a burgeoning success.

IN THE LATE SUMMER of 1995, it appeared that each side was doing its best to ignore the other and actually tend to its clients' needs. That is, until the weekend of September 9. This time, it was not Maurice Saatchi who was kicking up damaging mischief. Someone began selectively leaking a harmful story about insider trading at Saatchi & Saatchi during the period of Maurice Saatchi's resignation.

The story reverberated throughout London and New York and threatened the breakdown of the hard-fought truce between Cordiant and M&C Saatchi.

CHAPTER
SEVENTEEN

IT WAS A RARE WEEKEND that Maurice Saatchi and his wife, Josephine Hart, did not flee the bustle of London for the serenity of Old Hall. But not even the palatial gardens and the majestic furnishings could soothe Saatchi as he reached his Sussex estate late in the afternoon of September 8. He was aware that the *Sunday Times* of London and the *Wall Street Journal* were preparing stories about an investigation by the Department of Trade and Industry into stock trading during Cordiant's tumultuous period that began in mid-December 1994 and continued through January 1995.

During that time, the stock of Saatchi & Saatchi Company PLC dropped by approximately 30 percent. On January 3, when Maurice announced he would leave the company, he and his brother Charles sold their entire block of 1.8 million shares of stock, a logical move for exiting executives.

On January 9, the day Jeremy Sinclair, Bill Muirhead, and David Kershaw resigned, there was a delay of about four hours between the time the three amigos resigned in Charlie Scott's office and the time the company placed the news on the screen, the wire service closely monitored by the City. During the delay, approximately seven million Saatchi & Saatchi shares were traded. Sinclair could not trade any of his fifty thousand shares until the news was made public and he stood helplessly by while the value of the shares plunged. An attorney for Sinclair wrote to the London Stock Exchange on or about January 14 requesting an investigation into the trading on January 9.

Word of the investigation began to leak out as far back as March 1995, when a reporter from *The Independent* in London asked the public relations company of Cordiant about a possible probe into stock trading. The spokesman spoke truthfully: he was unaware of any investigation. Then in early September, *The Independent* called again with the same rumor. By this time, Cordiant had learned directly of the DTI investigation. It asked its attorneys what it could say publicly. A statement was released that said Cordiant was aware of the investigation and was cooperating. But someone connected to Cordiant did not want *The Independent* to be the only newspaper to carry a story that was potentially damaging to the Saatchi brothers. Around the same time, this individual connected to Cordiant's senior management informed the *Sunday Times* of the investigation and mentioned that the Saatchi brothers were possibly a central focus of the investigation, which began in June. Further, this individual called the Advertising columnist at the *Wall Street Journal* in New York on Friday, September 8, and told him to be home on Sunday and to expect a telephone call. The person would say only that it was a major story involving the Saatchis. "And don't even try to find this one before I'm ready to tell you," the individual said.

With one telephone call, the *Journal* uncovered the insider trading story and contacted Maurice Saatchi, who was already aware of the *Times*'s story. The *Journal* called the person close to Cordiant and said the newspaper was going to write a story and release it to its worldwide wire service later that day, Friday, two days before the *Times* planned to publish its story. Soon after, a Cordiant spokesman called the *Journal* and said, "Cordiant confirms the existence of an inquiry by inspectors appointed by the Secretary of State in exercise of his powers under Section 177 of the Financial Services Act of 1986 into dealing in securities of Cordiant and confirms also it is cooperating fully with the DTI inspectors. The company has no further comment." Someone also called the *Times* in London and told a reporter of the timing of the *Journal* story; the *Times* then pushed up its version for Saturday, the day when it has its lowest readership.

At Old Hall, Maurice Saatchi was working the phones. He called the *Journal* columnist to say the investigation was not a surprise and it "probably doesn't only focus on the Saatchis. The DTI will look at all stock sales during that period." Saatchi also spoke with Melvyn Marcus, the *Times*'s city editor, who wrote the story, headlined, "Saatchi Share Dealings Inquiry." He told the *Times* that upon resigning, he had "no intention of remaining a shareholder in a company controlled by" David Herro.

On Saturday, Saatchi again telephoned the *Journal* columnist at home with a statement to be included in Monday's edition: "The DTI is, I believe, carrying out an enquiry into all share dealings of Cordiant PLC over an eight-week period, partly at the request of my partners. One of the many hundreds of share transactions during that period was the sale of my remaining shares of 3rd January. . . . In the most public business resignations of recent years I published a letter on 3rd January stating I was severing all my ties with Saatchi & Saatchi Company PLC. After publication of that letter I sold my remaining shares in the company. . . . Wild horses could not have prevented me from selling my shares."

In the selective leak to the press, Maurice Saatchi believed he found an opening to wrest free from the truce preventing his new agency from soliciting Cordiant employees and clients. Cordiant, he said, "has sought to turn this DTI investigation into an attack on myself. . . . This leads me to conclude that the peace agreement signed by The New Saatchi Agency and Cordiant in May 1995 may have been breached by them. The new chief executive of Cordiant has clearly had no impact on the manner in which the company conducts its affairs.

"Therefore I am considering whether I am any longer bound by the moratorium by which I had agreed not to approach their clients or staff until 31st December this year."

The London papers went to town with the story on Sunday, September 10: the *Sunday Times*'s follow-up article said the Saatchi brothers "vowed . . . to clear their names after the disclosure" of the DTI investigation. The *Mail*'s headline was "Tories May Dump 'Inside' Saatchis." The story said, "The role of the Saatchi brothers in the Tories' General Election campaign was in doubt last night" following the news of the DTI investigation. "If the allegations against Maurice Saatchi and Charles Saatchi were proved, they could face up to two years in prison."

It was disclosed that two outside inspectors of the DTI were appointed to head the investigation in June by Michael Heseltine, the president of the Board of Trade. In 1967, Maurice Saatchi worked as a junior assistant to Heseltine and Lindsay Masters at Haymarket Publications.

Clearly one of the motives behind the leak was to create clouds of suspicion around Maurice and Charlie Saatchi that would frighten potential clients away from an unstable agency.

Angry, Saatchi went after Alex Sandberg, chairman of College Hill, a London public relations firm hired by Bob Seelert for Cordiant. Soon after he was appointed, Seelert dismissed Grandfield, Cordiant's ineffective public relations firm, and chose College Hill. Sandberg was a rotund, strawberry blond individual who possessed the same finely honed instincts for battle as Maurice Saatchi.

Sandberg had a characteristic that most journalists found incredibly annoying: he was smug and enjoyed taunting reporters by saying he had information known to only a few people, including the senior executives of the company. Sandberg relished engaging in a media battle with Saatchi. Indeed, both had been at it for years, perfecting the art of schmoozing and whispering to their favorite reporters.

But Saatchi quickly outmaneuvered Sandberg, accusing his new opponent of being the source of the *Times* and the *Wall Street Journal.* If that allegation could be proved, the Department of Trade and Industry could prosecute, leading to a prison term. Sandberg denied he was the source and in interviews accused Maurice of "paranoia." Sandberg went on to say, "Maurice Saatchi issued a fairly hysterical statement [saying] Cordiant had targeted him and set up a media campaign, and named me as the source of the leak. That's absolute rubbish. Cordiant's statement didn't name anyone."

In a way, Saatchi was having fun with Sandberg, and Saatchi soon quieted down. It was as if causing Sandberg to sweat—which he did that weekend—was enough revenge for Saatchi.

MAURICE WAS REBORN after his resignation from the company. He was a regular presence at M&C Saatchi and did not duck responsibility. He no longer had a deluxe office. He was in touch with his employees. More than anything, Maurice Saatchi was a walking example of the opening line in *Damage:* "Damaged people are dangerous. They know they can survive."

Despite all the negative information about him, Maurice Saatchi was still respected and held in awe by the press in London, which continued its favorable coverage. Saatchi appeared liberated in the knowledge that he had dodged the bullet of being maligned in the media. He began to shed his outer, defensive shell and actually began to have fun with his celebrity status.

The most blatant example was heard throughout the United Kingdom on September 24, 1995. At 12:15 on Sunday afternoon, Maurice Saatchi was the guest on the British Broadcasting Corp.'s *Desert Island Discs*, the long-running program that attracts over two million listeners each week. Past castaways included Marlene Dietrich, Orson Welles, Margaret Thatcher, Desmond Tutu, and John Cleese.

Saatchi showed a rare glimpse of his most private life during the broadcast in which guests are asked to share eight records, a book, and a luxury they would most cherish if marooned on a desert island. One of the most moving, and surprising, selections was of Nathan Saatchi singing at the Sephardic Spanish and Portuguese Synagogue in Hampstead. "[The show] was the first really good thing I've done as a son," Saatchi said in February 1996. "I was really pleased I had the courage to do it." There was also a recording of "Poinciana" by 1950s jazz pianist Ahmad Jamal: "It was proof to me of the erotic powers of music. My memory of it is hearing it wafting out of the bedrooms of my two older brothers whenever they had girls in their rooms. So I attribute great magic powers to this track." There was also the Bach Double Violin Concerto and "Surabaya Johnny," a song of unrequited love by Kurt Weill.

Then there was the story behind the third movement of Concerto No. 2 in G Minor, Op. 22, by Saint-Saëns. "My wife, Josephine, had gone to hospital for a minor operation. I made the mistake while in the waiting room of playing this music and it had the effect of causing me to become certain that this was to be the thousand-to-one disaster in which the anesthetic was wrong." Saatchi said he was so nervous that he walked to the operating room. As he stepped onto the elevator, an attendant wheeled in a patient on a stretcher whom Saatchi believed was Josephine. "She was wrapped in a sort of silver foil around her head and was in a very dazed state. As they were wheeling her along the corridor I kissed her a lot and told her how much I loved her. Then, to my complete horror as we came to the room, they wheeled the woman on the trolley past her room and along to another room. I realized that I had been kissing the wrong woman, the wrong patient. It was a moment of horror."

The host of the program, Sue Lawley, asked Maurice whether he planned any revenge against his former company. "The only unfinished business is the name," he said. "It is, I think, one of the great names in advertising. It's hard to see how you can have two agencies competing with each other. At some point that will have to be resolved."

Each guest on *Desert Island Discs* is given the Bible and the complete works of Shakespeare as well as a book of his or her own selection. Nevertheless, Saatchi brought his own dog-eared edition of *Hamlet.* "Hamlet's fatal flaw is his indecision," Saatchi told the BBC. "It is endlessly interesting to try to determine the reason why Hamlet delayed, which is, of course, the fascination of the play. Of his carrying out the revenge which his dead father willed on him?" When asked whether there is a personal analogy to this fascination, Saatchi quickly deadpanned, "I haven't thought of one."

It was near the program's conclusion that Saatchi said his luxury would be a virtual reality headset programmed to display his gardens at Old Hall.

AS MAURICE WAS ENVISIONING life on a desert island, Cordiant was envisioning life as a company no longer burdened by a debt load of £130 million, or $205.3 million. (When Charlie Scott joined Saatchi & Saatchi Company PLC in late 1989, the company had debt exceeding £700 million.) To that end, Cordiant executives, including Charlie Scott, Bob Seelert, and Tim Jackson, in late October began exploring the possibility of another rights offering—generating cash by issuing new shares to be purchased at a discount by existing major shareholders—to pay down its debt.

When news of the rights issue proposal first leaked on October 26, Cordiant shares plunged to 91 pence, far below their fifty-two-week high of 148 pence, and dropped the next day to 84 pence. The fall in share price was attributed mainly to a rumor that Cordiant was in danger of breaching its banking covenants, forcing the company to issue an unusual statement: "The Group is not in breach of any of its banking covenants. As part of its normal financial planning, Cordiant has developed proposals for its financial requirements for the longer term. The Company has put such proposals to its banks and is in the process of obtaining approval. The proposals include raising new equity from the Company's shareholders."

It would be the third rights issue in four years; the first, in March 1991, raised £60 million, and the second was held in June 1993 to raise £73 million. At the time, Saatchi & Saatchi Company PLC said it would not call in its shares until 1996.

Scott believed the timing was right; he wanted to take advantage of the company's recovery since Maurice Saatchi and other senior executives departed. Although it did not make headlines, Cordiant had replaced most of the revenues that had been lost as a result of the client defections based on Saatchi's resignation. "We are effectively back to where we were at the end of 1994," Scott said in October 1995. New accounts for Saatchi & Saatchi included Bell Atlantic, Peugeot, and America West Airlines; account victories for Bates included General Motors Corp.'s Electronic Data Systems unit and Spillers pet food. Bates also held on to the Miller Brewing's Miller Genuine Draft account after months of rumors it would be fired. It was a major vindication for Bates, which had its responsibility on the Miller account reduced through the years.

On November 3, Cordiant announced its 1-for-1 rights issue at a discounted 60 pence a share, which allowed Cordiant shareholders to buy one share, discounted to 60 pence, for each share of stock they currently owned. It was fully underwritten by SBC Warburg and UBS Ltd. The rights issue was quickly fully subscribed to—ultimately 97.1 percent of the shareholders accepted with the balance purchased by Cordiant—and raised £127 million. Reaction from the City was favorable and shares rose to 92 pence. Cordiant would no longer have to pay a crippling £20 million in annual interest payments.

Bob Seelert certainly had an incentive for Cordiant to pay

down its debt: his contract entitled him to a bonus of £100,000 if he completed a long-term debt restructuring during 1995. Seelert made a gesture that few within Cordiant believed Maurice Saatchi would have ever done: instead of pocketing his bonus, Seelert reinvested it in Cordiant in the form of shares in the rights issue. "This is a watershed for the group—putting itself on a solid foundation and wiping out its average net debt. . . . It's a proud moment . . . to be effectively wiping out the average net debt of the group."

Cordiant had a long way to go; its trading margins in 1994 were 5.7 percent, compared with its three worldwide advertising agency holding competitors: Interpublic Group, which had trading margins of 12.2 percent, Omnicom Group, 13.1 percent, and WPP Group, 9.2 percent. The company's Achilles' heel, its U.S. operations, which generated 37 percent of Cordiant's revenues in the first half of 1995, needed to improve in terms of revenues and margins.

FROM THE MOMENT M&C Saatchi won the British Airways account, there were whispers that the relationship was destined to be short-lived. The unsubstantiated reports said that the only reason M&C Saatchi was awarded the business stemmed from the close relationship of Maurice Saatchi and British Airways chairman Sir Colin Marshall. Those not in the M&C Saatchi corner pointed to the one-year contract the agency was given by British Airways as proof that M&C had a lot to prove in a short period of time.

What fueled a lot of these rumors was sheer jealousy that the upstart agency could win such a coveted account. There was a considerable amount of wishing that M&C Saatchi would collapse if and when British Airways left. British Airways was the cement holding the agency together, from both a financial and public relations point of view.

Therefore, there was great delight when, on November 3, British Airways unexpectedly announced that Colin Marshall was stepping down to be replaced by Robert Ayling on January 1, 1996. Ayling, forty-nine, had been managing director of British Airways since 1993, having been recruited by British Airways as legal director in 1985 when it was going through its privatization.

He was company secretary when British Airways was involved with its "dirty tricks" scandal against rival Virgin Atlantic. "Some things happened that we very much regret," Ayling told the *Daily Telegraph* on the eve of his appointment as chairman. "My job is to make sure they never happen again."

Ayling was promoted from company secretary to director of marketing and operations to a main board member. He was trained as a lawyer and, at twenty-four, became the youngest partner in Elborne Mitchell, a law firm specializing in aviation, shipping, and insurance. At twenty-nine, he moved to the Department of Trade and joined the team handling the United Kingdom's entry into the European Economic Community.

Cordiant executives privately liked to say that Ayling was not as open to M&C Saatchi handling the account as his predecessor was. Every so often, word would reach M&C Saatchi, usually Bill Muirhead, about the rumblings on the street concerning the agency's alleged tenuous hold. Bill Muirhead would call Bob Ayling or other British Airways executives, including Derek Dear, and be reassured. Such reassurances meant little in the advertising industry, since a client routinely tells its agency it is doing a great job right up to the moment the agency is fired. But Maurice Saatchi maintained that the good words from British Airways were genuine; he and Muirhead had a particularly close relationship with the client and cited as an example the fact that he had been told of Ayling's impending promotion by Colin Marshall the day Marshall awarded M&C Saatchi the account.

M&C Saatchi continued to press on with its proposals for the airline's advertising, a flagship campaign that would replace the well-received "Island" commercial, in which an entire island was wrapped in material by hundreds of people, or the groundbreaking "Global" ads, in which hundreds of individuals formed an eye, ear, and mouth and then the world. And while M&C Saatchi in London worked on the details of its first campaign, the agency's New York office was hammering out storyboards for British Airways ads that would detail specific services, such as showers in airport lounge areas as well as seats that collapse into flat beds.

By November, M&C Saatchi was performing remarkably well, considering it was a start-up operation. In a survey conducted by

Marketing Week in the United Kingdom, M&C Saatchi was one of the twenty agencies in London most highly regarded by clients. Maurice Saatchi boasted that the agency had 140 employees in four cities, London, New York, Hong Kong, and Sydney, and £160 million, or $248.5 million, in billings. M&C Saatchi wanted to open offices in Dubai and Singapore, which it would in 1996.

M&C Saatchi continued to win new business as well. Account wins were at least partially attributed to old friendships: Alamo, the United States car rental company, awarded M&C Saatchi its $6 million European account, a move orchestrated by Mike Batt, formerly marketing director at British Airways, who resigned in February 1995 to become executive vice president, sales and marketing, at Alamo. Batt was a close friend of Bill Muirhead. M&C Saatchi was also awarded the Head Holdings sporting goods account. Head had recently been purchased by Johan Eliasch, Charles Saatchi's close friend, who had been instrumental in negotiating the peace agreement between the Saatchi brothers and their former company.

But M&C Saatchi was still relying on former employees and clients instead of establishing a new foundation. Eventually, that well was going to run dry and the public and advertising industry might grow impatient waiting to see the Saatchis perform new feats of magic.

The perception that M&C Saatchi was reluctant to compete for totally new clients did not concern Maurice and his partners. In fact, the agency was clamoring for Britain's Tory party, historically one of the stalwart clients in the Saatchi & Saatchi roster. Anticipating that the Conservatives might bolt from Saatchi & Saatchi Advertising, following the settlement of a £500,000 debt by the political party, Bob Seelert of Cordiant made a personal plea to Tory chairman Brian Mawhinney to remain at the agency: "I think that walking out because of some relationship at the top is not a sensible thing."

Seelert's appeal was in vain. On December 15, 1995, the Conservative party said it would no longer use Saatchi & Saatchi; its debt to the company paid, the party said it planned a new strategy for the next election. The advertising assignment would be shared among a cadre of agencies and it was widely expected M&C Saatchi would be at the top of the list.

Saatchi & Saatchi Advertising was invited to be one of the agencies, but Jennifer Laing said no. "This was a professional decision," she said later. "As an agency we do not work in a cooperative with other agencies." Mawhinney said he regretted Laing's decision, but understood her position.

Sixteen days after the Tories broke with Saatchi & Saatchi, a full-page advertisement appeared in the Sunday edition of several London newspapers. The ad, produced by M&C Saatchi, was a personal message signed by Prime Minister John Major. The ad listed "14 irrefutable statements" about the "success" of the economy, including the lowest mortgage rates in thirty years, the lowest basic rate for tax in more than fifty years, and the lowest unemployment of any major European country. It was Maurice's first work for the party since the 1992 election.

For Maurice Saatchi, 1995 was ending quite differently from the previous year. M&C Saatchi was an instant hit. He answered to no one, especially people like David Herro and Charlie Scott, two individuals who Maurice thought were not of his class nor in his league.

The truce with Cordiant was about to end, allowing Maurice to do whatever he wanted in terms of Saatchi & Saatchi and Bates clients and employees.

Maurice was also strutting his stuff as an entrepreneur. On November 30, Saatchi announced his entry into the multimedia business by launching Megalomedia, a new investment vehicle listed in the Alternative Investment Market in the United Kingdom. Megalomedia was the new name for Graduate Appointments Services, a media recruitment agency previously owned by Michael Heseltine's Haymarket holding company; Heseltine sold Graduate Appointments in 1994 to Josephine Hart in exchange for her minority stake in Haymarket. In November 1995, the Saatchi brothers and Hart owned 60 percent of the company.

Saatchi announced on November 30 two acquisitions by Megalomedia; one was a 50 percent stake in Forward Publishing, a contract publishing business. Forward's clients included Westminister Bank and Marks & Spencer. The second acquisition was a 39.8 percent stake in Framestore, a digital special effects company that worked on the 1995 James Bond movie, *GoldenEye.* Megalomedia trading was suspended because of the announcements of the two acquisitions. When trading was halted, it was at 33 pence; when trading was resumed December 5, 1995, it soared to 83 pence.

Yet Maurice was not entirely happy. He was obsessed by his desire to be the only Saatchi in the advertising world. Maurice made it clear to his partners that he would be willing to extend the truce if Saatchi & Saatchi Advertising would rename itself, allowing M&C Saatchi to have sole possession of the Saatchi name.

The first overture from M&C Saatchi came in November when Tim Bell quietly approached Jennifer Laing. To M&C Saatchi's surprise, Laing and Charlie Scott were not concerned about the pending expiration of the peace agreement. Laing said Tim Bell told her "the brothers didn't like the M&C Saatchi name and wanted Saatchi & Saatchi back. I responded that it's categorically and absolutely ours and there's no way we would sell it. They sold their name bloody years ago," she said, "and got a lot of money for it. It takes years and a lot of publicity and effort to get any name established. We're not changing our name. The employees who make up this company wouldn't stand for it."

Charlie Scott said that once the truce expired, he would have to deal "with the realities of life. There will be new competition out there. But there is nothing special about M&C Saatchi. I worry about all the competition."

Stymied, Maurice Saatchi tried to put the best face on the overture's failure: "We're delighted if they continue to use our name," he said. "It's free advertising in fifty countries."

No partner seemed much interested in the name situation other than Bill Muirhead. Charles Saatchi could care less what the agency was called. Nor did the name rankle David Kershaw. And Jeremy Sinclair's response was typical of Jeremy Sinclair. He negotiated the settlement that included the name of the new agency. He felt bound to honor the agreement. And having worked so hard at achieving peace, he told associates he did not have the desire or energy to open old wounds. If others wanted to engage in a new battle, his attitude was "Let them." He was not interested.

Muirhead was intensely interested. On December 14, he arranged an extraordinary breakfast meeting with Bob Seelert at the Hotel Inter-continental on Lexington Avenue in New York. The subject was securing the return of the name Saatchi & Saatchi to Maurice Saatchi and his partners. Seelert used research to justify his response: no.

It became apparent very quickly to Bob Seelert that Cordiant valued the name Saatchi & Saatchi. "The name Saatchi is not a problem," Seelert said in February 1996. "It's a huge asset. It's the most famous name in advertising with tremendous brand-name recognition. It's a very meaningful name in the company."

When Seelert visited Saatchi & Saatchi Advertising in Italy shortly after joining Cordiant, someone asked if he would like to meet the Saatchi brothers. Taken aback, he said okay. An executive went into an adjacent room and emerged with a poster containing dozens of headshots of agency employees. In the center of the poster was the headline "Saatchi Brothers." "The reality is, in today's world this is what the Saatchi Brothers look like," Seelert said. "Thousands of people in hundreds of offices under the banner of Saatchi & Saatchi."

But Muirhead refused to accept Seelert's answer. On December 22, Muirhead called Tony Dalton, Laing's live-in companion, to explore the possibility with him. Muirhead was politely but firmly turned down. Muirhead told his associates that M&C Saatchi should simply start calling itself The New Saatchi Agency. He said Cordiant would not have the stamina to come after M&C Saatchi. Jeremy Sinclair rejected Muirhead's suggestion. If Laing wanted Saatchi & Saatchi so badly, so be it. M&C Saatchi was already working on a way around using the name M&C Saatchi.

THE HOLIDAYS CAME early for Maurice and Charles Saatchi in 1995. The *Sunday Times* of London published a story on December 10 that said that the Department of Trade and Industry investigation into insider trading at Saatchi & Saatchi Company PLC was being "wound down . . . the DTI is unlikely to take further action in either case," the *Times* wrote; other papers, including *The Inde-*

pendent and *The Guardian,* followed the next day. The DTI, these reports said, had uncovered nothing that would give grounds for prosecution.

Privately, Cordiant could not believe it. When the DTI investigation was first leaked, individuals within Cordiant thought that finally Maurice and Charles Saatchi would be properly investigated.

Even as late as January 30, 1996, a Cordiant board member, sipping a Diet Coke in a dimly lit Manhattan hotel bar with a reporter, shook his head in surprise at the thought of the DTI investigation turning up nothing incriminating about the Saatchi brothers.

"I don't believe the investigation is over," the Cordiant board member said. "I think it's still ongoing. But I hear from London it'll just quietly fade away."

CHAPTER
EIGHTEEN

Without British Airways, M&C Saatchi, no matter what the partners profess, may have been stillborn. If that occurred, Maurice could have embarked on a career in politics, Charles would have continued his love affair with the arts and go-carts, and two of the three amigos, Bill Muirhead and David Kershaw, could have continued their careers in advertising, albeit without the Saatchi brothers. But professional life with the Saatchi brothers is all Jeremy Sinclair had known and it is questionable whether he would have wanted to join another advertising agency. However, Sinclair conceivably could have been content to end his tenure in the advertising profession and devote himself full-time to another of his passions, teaching philosophy.

In winning British Airways, M&C Saatchi had set itself up with a formidable challenge: it had to top the airline's spectacular ads the former Saatchi & Saatchi creative team had conceived for the airline since "Manhattan Landing" hit the air.

The main responsibility of crafting British Airways' new flagship advertising campaign fell to Simon Dicketts, one of the agency's creative directors. It was a critical assignment. The ad would run for two years, an unusually long time for a single campaign.

Dicketts, a forty-two-year-old handsome blond with a wide-open, appealing, gentle face, had worked at Saatchi & Saatchi for seventeen years when Maurice Saatchi resigned. At the Charlotte Street agency, Dicketts was paired with James Lowther, age forty-nine, a tall, lanky executive with a scraggly black beard and a wry sense of humor. The two were a close team, able to anticipate each other's thoughts and complete each other's sentences. They ran forty-five creative teams at Saatchi & Saatchi Advertising and their contribution was considerable.

On January 9, 1995, Dicketts and Lowther received a telephone call from Maurice Saatchi inviting them to his mews home off Berkeley Square. The trio then went to Mortons, where Maurice offered them new jobs at his fledgling agency. Dicketts and Lowther did not make an immediate commitment. Instead, they said that whatever decision they arrived at, they would do it together. But the die was cast: Dicketts said he owed a great deal of his career to Jeremy Sinclair and Sinclair's resignation "had a lot of impact on me."

On January 11, Dicketts and Lowther, along with Nick Hurrell and Moray MacLennan, joint managing directors of Saatchi & Saatchi Advertising, resigned to Charlie Scott. Dicketts and Lowther wanted to resign quickly and early in the day, before they saw any of their creative teams. Dicketts drove Lowther to the company's offices and parked the car on Whitfield Street. The meeting with Scott lasted longer than Dicketts expected. For one, Scott did not ask where the duo was going; instead, he launched into a diatribe against Maurice Saatchi, saying he was fed up with all he had been reading. Dicketts felt sorry for Scott, who struck him as a decent fellow. But Dicketts told Scott that he was surprised this session represented their first meeting. Dicketts had a piece of advice for Scott: go around and introduce yourself to the creative teams laboring on Charlotte Street. The meeting ended with an odd invitation: Scott said he would like to have a drink with Dicketts and Lowther when all the dust had settled, an offer Dicketts and Lowther thought would never be realized.

Dicketts and Lowther emerged to find that a clamp had been placed on a tire on Dicketts's car by the London police for a parking violation, creating an uncomfortable scene in which the two executives were forced to wait for someone to come and free the car after a fine of £120 was paid. While they waited, they had to dodge any Saatchi & Saatchi employee who passed on the way to work because the two did not want the news of their resignations to come from them; rather, they wanted to wait for the official company announcement before talking to former colleagues.

After a short stint on Garden Leave, Dicketts and Lowther joined Maurice Saatchi's agency; Dicketts immediately began brainstorming on the creative aspect of the new British Airways campaign.

"British Airways is known for these big commercials and as a big airline," Dicketts said later. "But that loses on personal attention, caring, warm feelings. Some graphs show size and caring are at the opposite end. A big company doesn't care, but a small one does. . . . It's hard work to make size mean caring. If I say we have hundreds of people and all these airplanes, you think it's starting to sound like a corporation [losing the] caring and personal touch." But Dicketts also said British Airways vast size could be turned to an advantage: he emphasized that at any moment during the day, there are fifteen thousand people flying British Airways. Imagine, he said, a large hotel, a huge luxury liner, an island, or a small town. Size, Dicketts told British Airways executives, equals experience and dedication.

Dicketts said he had a second breakthrough thought: he asked British Airways to imagine if someone were to film a meeting between the airline and the agency. "We would find what we're saying quite riveting," he told British Airways, "but it wouldn't be interesting to anyone else." He then went around the room and, pointing randomly at people, said, "He is thinking about his little girl's day at school, he is thinking of his bank balance, he is thinking about screwing her," and so on. "Film that," Dicketts said, "and then you have an interesting image."

Dicketts suggested somehow creating a world that represents the airline. "A place where all your hopes, dreams, ambitions can be and flourish and survive. . . . A landscape [where] somebody may be thinking about being in love or somebody is . . . terrified while reading a book," he said. "All this happens in the same context."

The creative strategy was not difficult to sell to British Airways. With the concept sold, Dicketts and his team set about producing storyboards. When those were approved, Dicketts accompanied the two-hundred-person crew to America, where the commercial was filmed. Locations for the advertisement, with a production cost of approximately $1.5 million, included a ski resort in Utah, a lake near Yosemite National Park, a mountain in Wyoming, and the Sierra Nevada desert.

The so-called masterbrand commercial, which did not emphasize any specific product the airline offered, was shown to reporters in London on January 4, 1996. Robert Ayling, British Airways' chairman, said the airline has an "incredible new campaign which once again sets British Airways apart from the rest and which will do justice to the efforts of the entire British Airways community in taking [the airline] into the next millennium."

The ad began by showing a fully dressed woman frolicking and tumbling backward in a stream. Watching her was her fully clothed lover. The scene switches to a Chinese theater and then to a desert where a yuppie is trying to secure a huge dollar sign to the top of a mountain. A boy is then shown riding on a giant wind-up crocodile toy; he is followed by another male yuppie running through the snow pursued by evil-looking warriors on horseback. It turns out these were all daydreams of various British Airways passengers. The man running away was actually reading a book, titled *The Hunted.* The yuppie with the dollar sign was working on a laptop computer, a businesswoman was dreaming of reuniting with her lover after a trip, and so on.

Reaction among advertising reporters was decidedly mixed: Barbara Lippert in *Adweek* said, "How does this sell Business Class?" The passengers, she correctly said, "could be having the same experience anywhere. . . . Since there is no spoken dialogue, the performers are forced to overact. We get these deep, drinking-in, savoring-the-flavor expressions, better suited for instant coffee."

The commercial did nothing to quell rumors that British Airways's relationship with M&C Saatchi was going to be short lived. Individuals in London and New York continued to spread the story that British Airways kept a dialogue going with Bartle Bogle Hegarty, the runner-up agency in the competition. The reports infuriated Maurice Saatchi and his partners, who routinely called Robert Ayling and Derek Dear at British Airways for reassurances. The agency was told there was nothing to the rumors, although, privately, several M&C Saatchi executives said assurances meant nothing.

Meanwhile, M&C Saatchi in New York developed the first product-oriented ads for British Airways. The best that could be said of these commercials was that they were bizarre. In one, a bald-headed man of about fifty with a mustache is seen lying horizontally in one of the new Business Class seats exclusive to the airline. The man's head then shrinks and is superimposed on the body of an infant, who is rocking gently in his mother's arms. Barbara Lippert of *Adweek* said a woman called her shortly after seeing the ad and, lambasting the commercial, said it was "every man's fantasy and every woman's nightmare." In another spot, a man is taking a shower in a new First Class airport lounge. His head is then superimposed on that of a bird frolicking in a birdbath.

Dicketts said the ads represented a new approach for the airline. "Before, the commercials used to talk about British Airways and how it does this and that," he said. "Now, we want to talk about the people who fly" on the airline.

A second masterbrand spot was filmed in Mexico beginning in the second week of February 1996. This stressed leisure travel and conjured up images of people going on vacations and honeymoons and visiting friends and families.

None of the new British Airways commercials included a jingle composed by Andrew Lloyd Webber, a curious omission since Maurice Saatchi had made much of Webber's inclusion in Saatchi's pitch to British Airways.

M&C Saatchi also devised a clever billboard to show off British Airways' new First Class private cabin service. The billboard, located on Cromwell Road near a heavily traveled thoroughfare on the way to Heathrow Airport, was converted into a stage of sorts where an actor actually lived as if he were in a British Airways airplane. When he wanted to eat, he was served by a stewardess. When it was time to sleep, he reclined as the seat turned into a bed. The slogan: "New First Class Private Cabin. Kindly do not toot your horn." M&C Saatchi planned this for 1997.

On rare occasions, Charles Saatchi would pop into M&C Saatchi's temporary offices on Marylebone Lane and review ads for select clients, principally Gallaher's Silk Cut cigarettes. It is hard to fathom how many executions of the Silk Cut concept—a piece of purple silk with a cut in it—could be conceived over the years, but the M&C Saatchi team, led by Charles Saatchi, flawlessly continued the ad strategy. In February 1996, for instance, a print ad featured the World War I German Kaiser with a pointed hat seated in a tiny car. The roof was made of purple silk and the man's helmet cut through the roof.

Charles Saatchi also assumed a more public presence, although it was not in the world of advertising. Instead, Charles was one of the most visible and prominent members of the go-cart circuit. He gripped the steering wheel of vehicles going 140 miles an hour with the same passion with which he had played tennis in the 1980s. Whereas most go-carters had one or two vehicles, Charles had about a dozen. He employed two full-time mechanics and had a workshop where his engines were rebuilt and a warehouse in Milton Keynes, a town about fifty miles north of London, for the spare parts. He drove not only on weekends, but Tuesday through Friday as well, occasionally paying individuals to compete against him.

While go-carting was Charles's new love, it was not his most cherished. That status was reserved for Phoebe, his daughter born in December 1994. Cooing and attentive, Charles Saatchi surprised no one by being a wonderful doting father. Charles and his wife, Kay, would often discuss whether to have another child, telling close friends that they had so much love and money to give to Phoebe, they wondered if they should not share it with a new baby.

And Charles had not lost his passion for art. On January 25, 1996, the Saatchi Gallery presented an exhibit titled *Young American,* which featured work from artists such as Gregory Green, whose piece titled *Work Station #5 (London)* was a replica of an ordinary room where bombs were built. Two other Green works were suitcase bombs. Another featured artist was Janine Antoni, a thirty-one-year-old New Yorker who created some paintings by draping her dye-soaked hair on the floor and moving her head from side to side, leaving sweeping S-tracks. One art critic said the style was "distinctly reminiscent of giant expressionist brush strokes." Janine Antoni's pieces in the exhibit included *Gnaw,* a 600-pound block of chocolate with bite marks. Next to it was a 600-pound block of lard, also bitten in places.

A truly odd piece at the Saatchi Gallery was *20:50,* a 1987 work from Richard Wilson. One room of the gallery was lined with a steel tank filled with 2,500 gallons of used "sump" or engine oil, which created a beautiful serene black sea that was perfectly still. One visitor at a time could walk through a straight-line passageway in the room, where a security guard cautioned patrons not to dip their hands into the exhibit. A stack of paper towels was placed on the floor just in case.

No matter the abuse Charlie Saatchi heaped upon his younger brother when the two were starting their ad agency in 1970, their love and devotion for each other is unmistakable.

In 1996, Charles Saatchi was no fan of much of the advertising produced in the United States or United Kingdom. "I see very little to get excited about now," he said. "Too much advertising is just weird for the sake of being weird." He had already made millions on smart investments, including his vast art collection, and, having created something special once, he felt no desire to repeat himself. He loved his brother and was unquestionably loyal to those who built the agency empire, including Jeremy Sinclair and Bill Muirhead, but he had no interest in going to an office each day, even if it was to play chess and review ads.

Charles Saatchi has told close friends that his sole ambition in M&C Saatchi is to "see Maurice happy." He described the events subsequent to Maurice's ouster from Saatchi & Saatchi as a "sweet fairy tale. It has been miserable for him and a rough ride. I'm thrilled that with the new agency; fairy tales do come true. For Maurice, 1995 has been the best possible year."

Charles remained protective of his younger brother, especially when Maurice came under attack. Charles told friends that he was appalled when board members, including Ted Levitt, denounced Maurice's expensive and regular practice of hosting lunches twice a week at the Berkeley Square offices. The purpose of the meal was to try to lure potential clients. The lunches were usually attended by the potential client, a current Saatchi & Saatchi Company PLC client (from one of the agencies), a famous actor such as Diana Rigg, a cabinet minister, a newspaper editor, and a television journalist.

Sometimes, the lunches worked like a charm and Saatchi & Saatchi would be invited to pitch an account. Charles Saatchi complained that board members who protested the practice "were only trying to knife Maurice at any costs. Other agencies can't do it. There is nobody in the advertising business who can ring up and arrange these lunches."

AROUND CHRISTMAS 1995, Maurice Saatchi in London received an odd gift: a book on the Chicago Art Museum's exhibit of Claude Monet's works. It was a present from David Herro, who inscribed the book, "Let bygones be bygones." Herro, wishing his former nemesis good luck with his new agency, wrote that he hoped the book would be a piece of Chicago that would serve as a more pleasant reminder of the Windy City. Saatchi, who had little tolerance for humor when it was directed at him, tossed the book aside with barely a thought. His partners examined the present and declared it, at best, a cheap gesture.

The new year passed quietly at M&C Saatchi and Saatchi & Saatchi. Even though the so-called peace accord—prohibiting M&C Saatchi from recruiting Cordiant's employees and clients—had expired, no clients of consequence defected to Maurice Saatchi's camp nor were any employees enticed to resign. There was one hire of note at Saatchi & Saatchi Advertising Worldwide: John Fitzgerald, a forty-eight-year-old chairman and chief executive officer of McCann-Erickson in Japan, was named president and chief operating officer, reporting to Ed Wax. It was widely expected that Fitzgerald would succeed Wax, a job that had been promised to Bill Muirhead before events led to Muirhead's resignation.

Fitzgerald joined McCann-Erickson, an organization that is not known for creative breakthroughs, in 1990 as head of the New York agency. Previously, he was chairman of Ketchum Advertising/ USA with clients such as Heinz, Bell Atlantic, Westinghouse, and the Beef Industry Council.

Fitzgerald's hiring ended a search that had begun in July 1995. Dick White of Spencer Stuart said that shortly after Seelert joined Cordiant, Charlie Scott, Seelert, and Wax "determined that [Wax] needed a partner in the Saatchi organization to help get it moving. It is not a sick company but it hasn't in recent years lived up to its capability of growth in new business or profitability." Fitzgerald fit the criteria for a candidate "who is active and willing to travel the world, day in and day out, and drive the operating part of the business," said Bob Seelert. "One of the things we have in the Saatchi network is a strong cadre of people . . . but they have insufficient experience in running the worldwide business. "So we needed somebody whose experience and credentials would be obvious and compelling." Spencer Stuart searched for an individual who had a reputation for turning around troubled situations in a hands-on manner.

The chief operating officer also needed to "create a vision for the enterprise," White said. "Historically Saatchi has reflected the creative culture of Saatchi in London. [Saatchi in North America] was a combination of DFS and Compton and neither of those were creative dynamos."

Fitzgerald's appointment immediately sparked speculation about how it would affect two Saatchi & Saatchi veterans: Alan Bishop in New York and Jennifer Laing in London. McCann-Erickson is a button-down establishment agency unlike the high-flying flamboyant Saatchi network. It remained unknown how the two would fare under the conservative leadership of Bob Seelert and John Fitzgerald.

Fitzgerald arrived at a time when the agency was receiving both good and bad news: Saatchi & Saatchi in mid-January won the Reynolds Metals account valued at $25 million. However, less than a month later, Hewlett-Packard said it was placing a $50 million portion of its account, handled by Saatchi & Saatchi, in review.

Not all was going smoothly for M&C Saatchi, either. In February, it was defeated by Rainey Kelly Campbell in a two-way creative shoot-out for the Ionica account, valued at £7 million. Ionica was a national digital telephone network. Meanwhile, a major account win in the United States still eluded M&C Saatchi.

M&C Saatchi continued on the prowl for important worldwide clients. Several critics of the Saatchi brothers and their partners were pleased that companies such as Procter & Gamble and Mars initially had not awarded any accounts to M&C Saatchi. Maurice Saatchi privately told associates he expected to win at least one brand from the Mars stable. He also spoke of the possibility of winning business from Procter & Gamble. Saatchi would tell colleagues privately that the venerable packaged goods company would probably not move any account to M&C Saatchi from Saatchi & Saatchi. Procter & Gamble, he thought, would consider such action untoward.

The foundation of Maurice Saatchi's quiet optimism that he could win some Procter & Gamble business was a speech he delivered on November 23, 1995, before the P&G Club at the London Hilton. Saatchi spoke of one of his favorite themes: global advertising. "How do we communicate to lots of different people in all these different countries without being so bland and jellylike that you have nothing real to say?" he asked the audience. "I learned from P&G that ethos is all," he continued. ". . . P&G has experienced again and again that its best brands . . . have almost always been driven by strong advertising. Advertising is viewed as a real source of competitive advantage within the company. . . .

"P&G is one of the very few companies I know where an outside business partner is so fully integrated in a client's operation. . . . P&G is a loyal business partner. They don't believe in short-term hiring and firing of agencies. It is their genuine conviction that it is in the best interests of the company if agencies support them over a long period of time. Even if agencies face tough and troubled times they prefer to help rather than change if at all possible."

Saatchi then launched into a comparison he often makes when speaking publicly: "P&G knows that, in great advertising, as in great art, simplicity is all. . . . P&G would say that if you can't reduce your argument to a few crisp words or phrases, there's something wrong with your argument. So P&G's forms of mass communication are not complicated. . . . They stick to simple themes, simple messages, simple visual images. Not because these are the lowest common denominator, but because they are the highest form of expression of creative talent."

Saatchi's speech was well received within Procter & Gamble. John Pepper, who succeeded Ed Artzt as the company's chief executive, called Saatchi and said he sent a memo to all Procter & Gamble senior managers that included Saatchi's speech and a note that called it "the most brilliant exposition of what is special about P&G that I have ever read."

IN JANUARY 1996 *Adweek*, the respected trade publication, published a lengthy, mostly negative, story on M&C Saatchi titled "Limits of Illusion." The story was a litany of rumors the advertising industry had heard for weeks, but this was the first time they appeared in print. The *Adweek* story, which did not contain one negative comment with attribution, said M&C Saatchi had trouble getting approval from British Airways on the creative aspect of the campaign. Worse, *Adweek* reported that the agency "is barely able to cover its payroll out of operating income."

That simply was not true and rudimentary calculations—the average salaries, the number of employees, and the income from accounts—could have confirmed that fact. By creating doubts about M&C Saatchi's financial stability, the agency said *Adweek* had caused deep damage. What client would want to hire M&C Saatchi if it was not on solid financial footing? M&C Saatchi's attorneys were all over *Adweek* within days with ominous threatening letters.

The *Adweek* reporter called several individuals who were sources for the M&C Saatchi story; not surprisingly, at least one was with Saatchi & Saatchi. The reporter wanted to know if the magazine could count on the sources' support in case a suit was filed. The sources said no; they preferred to remain anonymous.

Two weeks later, *Adweek* published an extraordinary correction, one that caused other reporters and observers to deduce that *Adweek* had barely dodged a lawsuit. "We apologize to M&C Saatchi and its clients for any distress, inconvenience or concern these statements may have caused them," the correction read in part.

Still, M&C Saatchi was not satisfied. It wanted a front-page correction and a two-page ad for the agency placed in *Adweek* free of charge. Once again, M&C Saatchi showed its hubris, though it had to be satisfied with the correction.

M&C Saatchi managed in six months not only to churn out menacing letters to *Adweek*, but also to produce an impressive and amusing series of commercials. One for a medicine called TCP showed a horse standing in front of a bathroom mirror appearing to brush its teeth. The announcer said that TCP "stops you from being hoarse," at which point the horse stops what he is doing and stares into the mirror with a bemused expression.

M&C Saatchi Agency and its 120 employees had rapidly outgrown its headquarters at 9 Marylebone Lane, a modern nondescript building tucked away from the bustle of Oxford Street. The agency had no individual offices, instead opting for large, open spaces. There were tasteful boardrooms for presentations. Jeremy Sinclair, Bill Muirhead, and David Kershaw shared a sizable office, albeit one that was always stuffy with the smell of Sinclair's Cuban cigars, a box of which was always on the large glass desk, available to anyone who wanted a smoke. Only Maurice Saatchi had a separate office, although it was tiny in comparison to what he had known. And it was clear that Marylebone would house M&C Saatchi only temporarily since Maurice had made no attempt to decorate his office and it was as shabby as Charlie Scott's old office on Whitfield Street.

In fact, M&C Saatchi's lease would expire in late June 1996; it then moved to 36 Golden Square, not far from 6 Golden Square, the basement and ground floor of which was the site of the original Saatchi & Saatchi in 1970. Granada Television was moving out of 36 Golden Square and M&C Saatchi believed the building would suit its purpose. In February 1996, designs for the new agency's offices were piled against the wall of the three amigos' office. Charles Saatchi told associates that the move back to Golden Square was a happy accident. It was an appealing building, he told friends. When it turned out to be in Golden Square, he said, it was like someone put on a neon light saying this is the place to set up shop.

The M&C Saatchi partners still were not sure whether they were moving the name M&C Saatchi to Golden Square, too. Someone at the agency had hatched a crafty plan: M&C Saatchi's stationery would directly address the partners' unhappiness with the name. For one thing, the name "Saatchi" would be tastefully printed in large black block letters. "M&C," however, would be placed inside a burst-bubble image, looking not unlike the word "New" when it is placed on a product such as soap. Further, "M&C" would not be printed on the stationery per se. Instead, it would be placed on the paper manually by whoever was sending a letter. The letters "M&C" would be on a stick-on or a Post-it. And, wouldn't you know it, the stick-ons would not have enough adhesive material and would fall off the stationery, leaving only an elegant "Saatchi" remaining.

As if that weren't enough, Bill Muirhead had a dream over the weekend of February 3. The star of the dream was a name to replace M&C Saatchi Agency. On February 5, 1996, a letter arrived on the desk of Bob Seelert on Hudson Street in New York detailing Muirhead's dream.

"In the spirit of our new friendship," Muirhead's letter said, "I am telling you in advance that as of March 1, 1996, we will be changing the name of our operating companies to: London Saatchi Partners, New York Saatchi Partners, Sydney Saatchi Partners, Auckland Saatchi Partners, Singapore Saatchi Partners, Hong Kong Saatchi Partners and Dubai Saatchi Partners."

The letter addressed what Maurice Saatchi believed was the one major outstanding issue between the two companies. "I don't see how [the name conflict] could go on," he said in February 1996. "I really just don't see how you can have two companies called Saatchi. Everyone tells me this is insanity and it can't possibly last. Who is going to win that one? You have a corporation with a total legal right to the name and you have another corporation with a total legal right to the name. One is a corporation, just a corporation. The other is also the family that happens to have the name. So who is going to win? I believe we will win for that reason, sooner rather than later."

It was a brazen move by Muirhead and Maurice Saatchi and it was met with an immediate "Don't you dare" from Saatchi & Saatchi Advertising and Macfarlanes, Cordiant's attorneys. The reaction from Jennifer Laing, the chairman of the Charlotte Street agency, was succinct: keep dreaming.

On Charlotte Street and Whitfield Street in London and on Hudson Street in New York, the name game perpetuated by Maurice Saatchi and Bill Muirhead struck many as amusing at best, pathetic at worst. Bob Seelert said the two agencies could comfortably coexist with both using the Saatchi name. Saatchi & Saatchi Advertising and M&C Saatchi Agency, he said, were "two different entities going off in their own direction and [in their] own way." The advertising industry, he said, is highly splintered, with even the biggest ad company having a small share. Cordiant is a £700 million ($1.1 billion) advertising entity, the fifth largest, with more than 250 offices in eighty countries. "We're geared up to do [big business]," Seelert said. "There are only a dozen or so other companies. That is quite different from M&C Saatchi. They have their own situation, which is dramatically different from ours. It is not good business sense for them. They have to decide what they are going to be. It would be narrow-minded of them to focus exclusively on us."

OF COURSE, Maurice Saatchi is singular in his pursuit of what he wants, whether that is an advertising agency or revenge. Once Maurice Saatchi decides he wants something, he does not rest until he has acquired it or has whittled down his rival to the point where Saatchi receives something close to what he originally sought. Former associates of Maurice Saatchi theorize that he will not be fully satisfied until he replicates the enormously impressive feat he and his brother accomplished in the 1970s and 1980s. To their credit, the Saatchi brothers built the world's largest advertising company from scratch. However, it is unlikely that M&C Saatchi will be anything more than a boutique agency. Whereas being the biggest was previously the brothers' paramount goal, in 1996 stability and surviving debt-free were prime motivations.

M&C Saatchi did not need to embark on another acquisition spree, gobbling up other agencies. For one thing, it has a worldwide network of offices through its agreement with Publicis, the French ad agency holding company. "What is the point of doing exactly what we did last time, which was to borrow large sums of money and put our whole lives at risk again?" Maurice Saatchi said in 1996. "I think this is a nineties way of doing it. We have about five offices in key places and I don't see the point in changing it."

In truth, Maurice Saatchi did see the point in changing it. He had to be convinced otherwise by the three amigos, Jeremy Sinclair, Bill Muirhead, and David Kershaw. For one thing, Saatchi wanted to make a Faustian pact again; he harbored visions of converting M&C Saatchi into a public company. Saatchi conceded he had conversations with his partners about placing 5 percent of M&C Saatchi into Megalomedia. The partners, he said, "talked me out of it. They wanted the agency to be truly private. I said, 'Look, it's only five percent.' They said no and I'm glad they talked me out of it."

Saatchi said brokers had whispered to him that although Megalomedia was a success, it could "really take off like a train" if as little as 5 percent of the advertising agency was tossed into Megalomedia's portfolio. "I tried to convince my partners," Saatchi said. "But they called it a lousy idea. They said we would have all the problems of a public company, like what are your profits and what are the analysts' expectations. They thought it was the worst of all possible worlds and, in the end, they were right."

No MATTER HOW MUCH satisfaction Maurice Saatchi professed to receive from M&C Saatchi, being tossed out of the company he had co-founded by shareholders was a major seismic unpleasant event in his life. Could Saatchi & Saatchi vs. Saatchi & Saatchi have been prevented? Was there another way to have handled the Maurice Saatchi problem other than to spark a damaging civil war?

Simply put, no.

Publicly, Maurice Saatchi said he could have worked well with Charlie Scott once their roles were well defined. Saatchi would have served as the holding company's ambassador, meeting with one chief executive after another. Scott would have continued toiling with the balance sheet. And, in theory, it could have worked. Charles Saatchi has told friends the whole affair could have been avoided "if there had been a willingness on behalf of the board in using Maurice well instead of trying to kill him. I don't think they considered he had any contribution to make."

However, given his history, it is doubtful that Saatchi would have stayed clear of mischief. Sooner rather than later he would have undermined Scott and others at the holding company and the advertising agencies. And he would have rationalized it by saying he wanted to do in Scott before Scott and his supporters had a chance to do him in.

Maurice Saatchi may have also tried to sell Bates Worldwide or merge Bates with Saatchi & Saatchi Advertising Worldwide. There is ample evidence to support this belief. Saatchi hired Suzanna Taverne to study the possibility of a merger or so-called de-merger despite hearing months before that neither could be done.

Even if Maurice Saatchi had been able to stall the company's meek board of directors, he could not have stalled David Herro much longer. Believing he was right about Maurice Saatchi and how a public company should be operated, David Herro did not realize the long-term consequences of firing Maurice Saatchi. Alastair Ross Goobey, chairman of Hermes, formerly Postel Investment Management, and a holder of 1.7 percent of Saatchi & Saatchi Company PLC stock, said: "I know Maurice quite well and it didn't take a genius to know [firing Saatchi] would cause damage to the company. It was better to have Maurice in the company." That remark captured what many who knew Saatchi were saying. But to Herro, Saatchi was a complete affront to corporate governance and to what a chairman should stand for.

To be sure, Herro was ignorant about the advertising business and the importance of personal relationships between ad agency executives and clients. How else to explain Herro's dismissive attitude toward warning after warning from chairmen of companies such as British Airways, Mars, and Gallaher? Herro missed the point when he argued that Saatchi had talked these heads of companies into writing their articulate and threatening letters of support. The point was not who convinced them to write, but that the letters were sent. They simply would not have written what they did not believe in the first place. And everyone underestimated the loyalty of Saatchi's lieutenants; neither Charlie Scott nor the heads of the ad agencies thought the three amigos would bolt.

For Herro, Saatchi & Saatchi/Cordiant proved to be a costly investment. In March 1996, Cordiant announced it lost £34.5 million, or $53.5 million, in 1995, compared with a profit of £32.4 million the year before. Cordiant attributed the loss to one-time charges and said it has restored the revenues it lost from clients who left as a result of Maurice Saatchi's departure. Litigation and other events surrounding Saatchi's dismissal cost £3.3 million, or $5.1 million; the company declined to break down how the money was spent.

"The revenue fall post–Maurice Saatchi was lower than we expected," said Lorna Tilbian, an analyst at Panmure Gordon, who had forecast a 5 percent drop in revenue (revenue dropped 1.8 percent to £761.1 million). "I really think things are looking up." Charlie Scott said 1995 was a "watershed year," and Bob Seelert said Cordiant had "drawn a curtain" on a disastrous year.

David Herro, for one, was optimistic. "If you do your homework right," Herro said in 1996, "you will weather the storm. The question is, is Cordiant a better-run, a better-managed company than it was when Maurice Saatchi was chairman, and the answer is yes. Cordiant is, for the first time, being operated as a professionally run public company, not a privately held company disguised as a public company."

If David Herro had not invested in Saatchi & Saatchi, however, it is likely that Maurice Saatchi would continue to occupy the chairman's office. All of his other opponents were either intimidated or charmed by Saatchi from taking action. And if Maurice Saatchi continued on with the company, it never would have stabilized. There always would have been unrest and uncertainty bubbling below the surface. There always would have been leaks about the company to the press and the source would never have been far from Maurice Saatchi's office.

Even as Saatchi professed that he and Scott would have been an effective team, Saatchi was openly insulting the company's board of directors. He called the caliber of the board as it was constituted in December 1994 "embarrassing," and at the time of his dismissal Saatchi was actively trying to recruit others to (Herro would say "stack") the board. Other than Ali Wambold, who had planned to join the board in January 1995 until Saatchi was fired, Saatchi asked Sir Ian Vallance, chairman of British Telecommunications, and Dennis Henderson, head of ICI, both of whom declined the invitation, and Raymond Seitz, the ambassador to the United States, who said yes.

Under the circumstances, how well and how long could he and Charlie Scott have ultimately worked together effectively?

Clearly, not long at all. Scott would likely not have had the stomach to engage in another ugly public battle. In that case, it would have been Charlie Scott who would have walked out the door and, in all likelihood, taken the company's financial credibility with him. Maurice Saatchi would then have been free to choose a crony to serve as the company's chief executive. Financial instability would have followed and it would have been 1990 all over again at Saatchi & Saatchi Company PLC.

No, Maurice Saatchi had to depart.

It is the departure of Maurice and Charles Saatchi that Charles considers the biggest failure in his life—at least that is what he has told associates. The brothers, he said to friends, wanted to establish a company that would be dominant in their chosen industry for decades, if not well into the twenty-first century. The brothers, Charles Saatchi said, wanted their company to withstand a "dedicated madman determined to destroy" it. And, oddly, Maurice and Charles's company has done just that. Critics of the brothers would readily cast Maurice Saatchi in the aforementioned role. Predictably, the brothers would see it differently: Charles has told friends that Saatchi & Saatchi, now Cordiant, was "a strong enough company that was able to withstand a moronic decision by the board of directors that cost it a lot of business it will never get back."

MUCH TO THE SURPRISE of cynics and skeptics, Maurice Saatchi was still showing up for work daily in 1996, one year after the founding of M&C Saatchi. He was a rainmaker of sorts, someone who opened doors to potential clients for his partners and their subordinates. After all, there was virtually no chief executive in the world who would not pick up the phone when Maurice Saatchi was on the other end. In short, Maurice Saatchi had taken a role he most likely would have assumed if he had accepted the humbling offer in December 1995 to become chairman of Saatchi & Saatchi Advertising Worldwide.

At M&C Saatchi, though, he was a one-fifth equal partner to an advertising agency. Saatchi said he did not miss the chairman's office and, in fact, one is inclined to believe him. "I like being a partner," he said. "I don't feel as I did before, which was everything, the entire total weight of responsibility, rested on me. Now I feel there are other people who can do everything I can do and are willing to. It's great and it only works because it happens to be these people. It is just human relations. There is no agenda, no politics. There are no terrible backdoor conversations."

Some would laugh at Saatchi's suggestion that there was ever a time when the entire weight of the company rested on him.

It would serve everyone's interests if Maurice Saatchi could truly rid himself of his obsession with Saatchi & Saatchi Advertising, if his considerable energies could be directed solely toward building a new agency empire and not tearing down an old one.

Still, it is a wonderful adventure Maurice Saatchi and his partners have embarked on. Visiting the cramped M&C Saatchi offices on Marylebone Lane in June 1996, one sensed the creative energy and enthusiasm of the employees. It was as if the worker bees recognized all of Maurice Saatchi's warts and accepted him nonetheless.

As Bill Muirhead said, "After all these years, his charm is still seductive. He can call you in and say a few choice words and make you feel great. I still fall for it."

Maurice Saatchi was still working hard, hustling for business in April 1996. On April 15, for instance, he had a secret meeting with executives from Mars, who visited the M&C Saatchi offices in London. The possibility of M&C Saatchi snagging Mars's Whiskas cat food account in London from DMB&B, which holds the assignment on a worldwide basis, was discussed. For Maurice, it represents a foot in the door in getting additional Mars business.

M&C Saatchi in New York was also on the move in April 1996. Bill Muirhead never liked the agency's cramped, unattractive offices sublet from Publicis/Bloom on East 45th Street, off Second Avenue. He was thrilled, therefore, when he finally settled on office space in the former Daily News Building on 42nd Street and Second Avenue. Muirhead liked that the building was seen in the *Superman* films and the lobby featured a revolving globe. He was resigned to the fact that M&C Saatchi would not, as he had hoped, occupy space on Madison Avenue itself. But Muirhead couldn't ultimately make a decision in regard to the Daily News Building, even after the *Daily News* headlined the expected move in September 1996. In October, with no firm agreement, Muirhead turned his sights to a possible move to the fashionable Union Square neighborhood of Manhattan.

In April 1996, Maurice Saatchi did not know exactly where M&C Saatchi Agency was headed; for the first time, he was not the captain. He had to share the agency's direction with three others, not including his brother Charles. But Maurice Saatchi just wanted to be along for the ride and have some say in steering the agency toward the twenty-first century.

He could well have been speaking about himself and M&C Saatchi when he delivered a speech before the International Advertising Association in London on February 13, 1996. Reflecting on what global advertising could achieve, he said, "When Christopher Columbus was on his famous voyage, he kept a diary every day. But for the thirty-five days before he discovered America, the diary was blank, except for one solitary entry:

" 'Saw no land. Sailed on.' "

EPILOGUE

THE CELEBRATION WAS lively at the Saatchi Gallery on the evening of June 19, 1996, as over 1,200 individuals gathered on a spectacularly beautiful night to celebrate M&C Saatchi's first birthday. Waiters generously poured Bouvet Champagne, Foster's beer, Hildon mineral soda, and Sub, an alcoholic soda. Trays upon trays of chicken legs, cold lamb chops, shrimp, and egg rolls spilled out of a makeshift kitchen. A delicious vanilla butter cream birthday cake adorned with a rejected M&C Saatchi logo was served later in the evening, along with strawberries dipped in white chocolate and dark chocolate.

It was quite a party, with guests including Prime Minister John Major as well as Auberon Waugh, Evelyn de Rothschild, and members of Major's cabinet, such as William Waldegrave, Michael Howard, and John Patten, maneuvering through unimpressive wood sculptures by Stephan Balkenhol. Michael Heseltine, one of the first individuals to have ever hired Maurice Saatchi, was on hand as well. Maurice and his three partners, Jeremy Sinclair, Bill Muirhead, and David Kershaw, mingled with the guests, many of whom were employees and clients of M&C Saatchi. Predictably, Charles Saatchi was nowhere to be found, opting to stay in character and stay away. He chose to remain at his home on St. Leonard's Terrace in Chelsea, a few doors away from No. 18, where, appropriately, Bram Stoker, the author of *Dracula*, once lived.

Late in the evening, Sir Tim Bell, now fully recovered from his demons, appearing tan and fit, addressed the crowd from a surprisingly cheap microphone with lousy sound. He introduced his old friend and former nemesis turned friend once again, Maurice Saatchi, whose remarks were appropriately brief: "Never before," Saatchi began, "has so much been owed by so many to so few." He ended by quoting W. B. Yeats: "Think where man's glory most begins and ends, and say my glory was I had such friends."

In reality, there was much to celebrate: after only one year, M&C Saatchi boasted worldwide billings of £250 million with a total of 250 employees in offices in London, Hong Kong, New York, Sydney, Singapore, Dubai, and Auckland. Clients included British Airways, with annual billings in June 1996 estimated at £30 million; the Disney Stores, £25 million; Dixons, £25 million; Packard Bell, £30 million; the Mirror Group, £20 million; Silk Cut, £8.5 million; Benson & Hedges, £7 million; and Qantas, £15 million.

The creative output from M&C Saatchi was mixed. Its commercials for British Airways were never well received. (Despite that widespread assessment, the airline renewed its contract for another year.) However, the agency's ads for the £8 million account for Private Patients Plan in the United Kingdom was its best work to date. The commercials featured people falling backward, caught by their shadows. The visuals were mesmerizing. The ads showed the agency's creative potential and should serve as its flagship advertising.

M&C Saatchi had also been retained by the Conservative party, headed by Prime Minister Major. According to a document that had been leaked to *Campaign* and *Advertising Age* magazines and confirmed by the agency, the Conservative party planned an advertising budget of £10 million and a fee of £1 million to M&C Saatchi. That is not a hefty amount considering the resources and time the party had eaten in the past at Saatchi & Saatchi Advertising.

Perhaps most promising of all, M&C Saatchi had, a month prior to the party, finally been awarded an account from Mars, although it was not a major candy brand. Instead, M&C Saatchi was given the assignment to relaunch Whiskas cat food from the Pedigree Pet Food division in the United Kingdom, an assignment worth about £10 million in annual billings. Saatchi's April 15 meeting with Mars officials had paid off handsomely.

Not all was smooth at the self-confident agency, however. Unknown to most people, Maurice Saatchi quietly made a rare trip to the United States on May 21, 1996, specifically to Cincinnati and his former client Procter & Gamble. Saatchi's most stable contact at the giant company, Ed Artzt, had retired as chairman and now he was immersed in untested waters. The sojourn was hardly productive and confirmed Saatchi's worst private fears: that there would be no role for M&C Saatchi to play in Procter & Gamble's advertising strategy. A Procter & Gamble senior executive told Maurice that P&G would do nothing that would harm Saatchi & Saatchi Advertising, which remained a P&G agency.

M&C Saatchi's growth in the United States, arguably the most important region for worldwide acceptance, was, at best, slow. It wasn't until March 1996 that its U.S. operation finally won a piece of business: Packard Bell, a company whose advertising had been dormant prior to naming M&C Saatchi. Cynics from Cordiant and Saatchi & Saatchi Advertising whispered that the only reason the new Saatchi agency won the account was because, in the United Kingdom, Packard Bell is distributed by Dixons, the giant retail chain whose advertising is done by M&C Saatchi.

By mid-1996, Bill Muirhead had tired of transatlantic traveling and the fact that M&C Saatchi was not a major player in the United States. He opted not to move to New York and instead set out to hire a chief executive officer and chief creative officer for the U.S. operation. To some, Muirhead's reluctance to commit himself to the United States was an indication the agency's growth was not going as well as had been expected. Muirhead insisted that was not the case: he would retain control of the U.S. operation; he would just be stationed in London. Nor would he stop traveling back and forth until the U.S. operation was up and running.

On July 1, 1996, Muirhead and Jeremy Sinclair traveled to New York aboard the British Airways Concorde to finalize the hiring of a new executive team. It would be a long and frustrating search with quite a few false starts. One highly regarded candidate was ultimately rejected because he had what M&C Saatchi said was the audacity to involve his attorney in the negotiations. "We hired hundreds of people without hearing from their attorneys," Bill Muirhead said with some disgust in September 1996. Finally, in mid-October, M&C Saatchi announced the appointment of Brent Bouchez, thirty-nine, as president of M&C Saatchi North America and David Page, forty, as executive creative director. Both were five-year veterans of Ammirati Puris Lintas and each had experience with such worldwide brands as MasterCard and Compaq computers. The need for M&C Saatchi to lure a strong leader for its United States operation was obvious. James Dougherty, an analyst at Dean Witter Reynolds Inc. in New York, said in the September 9, 1996, issue of *Business Week* that "M&C Saatchi is a U.K. phenomenon. I don't think they have a realistic chance of being a player outside the U.K. . . . ."

Such a view infuriated M&C Saatchi, especially Bill Muirhead, whose job it was to oversee the agency's efforts in the United States. The agency planned to open a second U.S. office, he said, in Los Angeles. "We're going to grow organically," Muirhead said, echoing what others at M&C Saatchi said. "We're not going to grow through acquisitions."

Meanwhile, M&C Saatchi took no small pleasure in showing the year-to-date results of the respected A.C. Nielsen Register-MEAL, which compiled the rankings of advertising agencies by billings. M&C Saatchi leapfrogged to number fifteen in the period ended June 1996 with billings of £125.2 million, compared with its number sixty-four ranking the previous year. In contrast, there was mixed news at Saatchi & Saatchi Advertising.

Saatchi & Saatchi Advertising was busy putting out the news that the Charlotte Street shop was named Agency of the Year at the forty-third annual International Advertising Festival in Cannes, France. But, even in the south of France, the agency had to share the spotlight with Maurice Saatchi. He was in Cannes accompanying Bob Ayling, the chairman of British Airways; British Airways was named Advertiser of the Year. Ayling stood atop a boarding ramp with his company's logo, flanked by two stewardesses, then descended the ramp to receive the award. It was a grand weekend for Maurice Saatchi, who hosted Ayling at his home in nearby Cap Ferrat. For Saatchi & Saatchi Advertising, the award was one of the only bits of good news, however.

By May 1996, Saatchi & Saatchi Advertising on Charlotte Street lost its status as the United Kingdom's largest ad agency for the first time since 1988, according to *Marketing Week* magazine in the United Kingdom. The agency fell behind J. Walter Thompson, Abbott Mead Vickers BBDO, and Ogilvy & Mather. According to

Marketing Week's survey, Saatchi & Saatchi Advertising's clients spent £232.2 million in 1996's first quarter compared with £325 million in the same period a year earlier. In May 1996, Saatchi & Saatchi Advertising was dealt another blow with the loss of the £9 million British Telecom corporate account after a secret review. A year earlier, it lost BT's global advertising assignment.

Not surprisingly, negative articles appeared from time to time about Cordiant and its agencies and one did not have to devote too much thinking to conclude that M&C Saatchi executives were up to their usual tricks of leaking less-than-flattering news. The *Financial Times* and *Evening Standard* in the United Kingdom and *Adweek* all dutifully listened in May 1996 as someone from M&C Saatchi whispered Michael Bungey's salary as published in Cordiant's annual report. Not that the reporters couldn't discover the salary of Bungey, the chairman of Bates Worldwide, on their own. But M&C Saatchi, as usual, was not taking the chance.

Bungey, the articles said, received a total compensation package of £728,251 in 1995. His bonus was £119,165. Other executives also received bonuses, including Cordiant finance director Wendy Smyth. But, the annual report said, "No salary increases for the other executive directors were considered appropriate." *Adweek* added, "Good thing. Pay and benefits for executive directors cost about 70 percent more in 1995 than in 1994 when Cordiant (then Saatchi & Saatchi) was controlled by Maurice Saatchi. Among the board's complaints when Saatchi was asked to step down? He spent too much money."

One day prior to M&C Saatchi's first birthday party, a far less flashy affair was held in London: Cordiant's annual shareholders meeting. It was so quiet compared with previous years as almost to be a nonevent. Charlie Scott, who looked far younger and more relaxed than at any time since he joined the company, said 1995 "was a year that tested the mettle of [Cordiant]." Cordiant was set to declare its first dividend in seven years in March 1997. One shareholder responded, "Thank you very much for warning us. . . . The shock will now be more acceptable."

In March 1996, Cordiant released its 1995 results: it had a pretax loss of £22.6 million, or $34.5 million, compared with a profit of £32.4 million, or $21 million, in 1994. Still, things were beginning to turn around for Saatchi & Saatchi Advertising—not on Charlotte Street, but rather on Hudson Street in New York. The agency, under the leadership of Alan Bishop, Mike Keeshan, and John Fitzgerald, won such accounts as Bell Atlantic, worth $50 million in billings, as well as Pepcid AC from Johnson & Johnson and Reynolds Wrap.

Though it is highly doubtful, perhaps Maurice Saatchi could take some pleasure in knowing he had had another effect on his former company: Cordiant finally spruced up the entrance on Whitfield Street, the entrance Maurice once accurately described as "shabby." By June 1996, the waiting room contained a large Sony Trinitron television set as well as a handsome sign listing all of Cordiant's divisions. And on the wall leading up to the entrance on the outside were three distinguished silver signs for Cordiant and two subsidiaries. The entrance on Howland Street—which had once served as a private path for Maurice and Charles Saatchi —was shut and grew rusty from neglect.

An odd and somewhat psychologically unhealthy bond remained between Cordiant and M&C Saatchi, though Cordiant executives liked to stress that they had gone on with their lives. Nevertheless, on May 5, 1996, a bizarre dinner took place between Bill Muirhead and David Herro. Muirhead had never met nor spoken with Herro and he wanted to see what made the Chicago money manager tick. Both individuals came away from the lengthy meal more convinced than ever that the other was wrong and a zealot.

Muirhead more than once thanked Herro for creating the situation that made him a richer man at M&C Saatchi than he ever was at Saatchi & Saatchi Advertising. No one believed that, however, although Muirhead insisted it was true.

Herro warned Muirhead to watch himself because he was, after all, in business with Maurice Saatchi. Muirhead later described Herro as "a kind of Billy Graham who believes he is on a crusade." For his part, Herro was amused by the whole incident. The following evening, on May 6, he, Tim Jackson, and Alan Bishop had a good chuckle over the Muirhead dinner in Manhattan.

But Cordiant couldn't walk away from Maurice Saatchi, either. An individual with ties to Cordiant compiled estimates of Maurice's borrowings—in other words, how much Saatchi was in debt—dating back to 1987, when Saatchi was estimated to have debts of £7.3 million. Saatchi's finances grew so bad that in 1991 he was forced by his banks to sell a glorious Italianate mansion, called Lees House, with a mock Elizabethan facade and six bedrooms near Grosvenor Square. The initial asking price was £5.75 million; it finally sold for £2.5 million.

By the end of 1995, Maurice Saatchi was estimated to have debts of £4.1 million; there were whispers that Charles Saatchi actually owned Old Hall, Maurice's estate in Sussex, or at least it was Charles who financed its purchase. But others with knowledge of the brothers said that was simply untrue. And someone else with a Cordiant connection said in July 1996 that Maurice Saatchi had sold three of his Bentleys in order to finance the purchase of a newer Bentley, a fact confirmed by a partner in M&C Saatchi. Appearances are everything to Maurice Saatchi, and now that he had a new agency, he needed to show everything was right within his world.

Demons still plagued Maurice Saatchi, however. In a brief conversation on the morning of June 19, 1996, standing in his cramped, uncluttered temporary office on Marylebone Lane, Maurice listened patiently as the author of this book described his progress: "But you never nailed it," he said finally. "You never connected the dots to Louis-Dreyfus, the Adidas money, and David Herro."

Maurice Saatchi failed to grasp that, ultimately, there was no connection to make. Either he couldn't believe the truth or he chose to ignore it: that his downfall was cleverly orchestrated not by a peer, which is what he considered Robert Louis-Dreyfus, but by individuals he felt were below him and whom, therefore, he did not take seriously, including Suzanna Taverne, Ted Levitt, Saatchi & Saatchi's corporate secretary Graham Howell, and David Herro. As one person with intimate knowledge of the events leading to Maurice's ouster said in June 1996: "Suzanna and Ted supplied the bullets that Herro shot." Herro would not be specific, but one person close to him said, "Don't underestimate what he got from Howell." Graham Howell turned out to be an interesting individual with an interesting perspective; he was hired by Saatchi & Saatchi Company PLC in 1994, shortly after he resigned as director of legal and personnel services at London Weekend Television. Howell was unimpressed with Maurice Saatchi's lack of concern toward shareholders. It was in sharp contrast to his former employer, who agonized over how business decisions impacted on individuals who had invested in the company.

But Howell downplayed his role: "I helped [Herro] in relatively minor terms. I had only been there four or five months. I didn't gossip to Herro about the company. I responded to him as he asked questions as a shareholder. He asked questions such as 'How can we get Maurice out? Can we call a general meeting? What is the United Kingdom practice?' Tim [Jackson, director of investor relations] and I both met with Herro and encouraged him. Suzanna [Taverne] and Ted [Levitt] gave Herro all the dirt." Levitt similarly disputed the significance of his information: "I don't think it's accurate to say I advised him or provided him with bullets. Herro tried to talk to everybody. I didn't violate any norms or rules." Herro, of course, credited Maurice with the result: "There was supporting evidence [I received from Ted, Suzanna, and Graham], but that man [Maurice] was his own worst enemy."

Much of Maurice's speculation amused David Herro, who in mid-1996 remained a respected partner at Harris Associates. He traveled a lot because he was in demand at financial seminars, not because of his notoriety from the Saatchi affair, but because he is considered a savvy investor. In mid-1996, Harris Associates had two of the top-rated international mutual funds.

Maurice Saatchi and the three amigos, in the end, did not topple their former company. Instead, the partners in M&C Saatchi had to derive satisfaction from petty victories: the company logo and stationery, for instance. After much debate, M&C Saatchi executives finally agreed upon a handsome logo for the agency. The name would be spelled out in attractive, huge, bold black block letters. Jeremy Sinclair was pleased to point out that on some literature the agency's name would be divided: M&C would fold into the back, leaving the name Saatchi standing alone.

M&C Saatchi was upbeat as it entered its second year, though others would say the agency would have a rough time as it entered its "terrible twos." Many aspects of M&C Saatchi were unknown: whether Maurice Saatchi, Jeremy Sinclair, and Bill Muirhead had enough fire in the belly to propel the agency into a force to be reckoned with on a worldwide basis, for instance, or whether being a major agency in the United Kingdom was enough, or whether being an also-ran in the United States would dampen the partners' spirits.

Meanwhile, an unexpected event suddenly buoyed the spirits of Saatchi & Saatchi Advertising, which had been hoping for a chance to snare an airline account to replace British Airways. On July 25, 1996, United Airlines suddenly announced that it was placing its account, valued at $100 million in annual billings, in review. The incumbent agency, Leo Burnett in Chicago, had been producing United's ads for thirty-one years; it had created the famous slogan "Fly the Friendly Skies." Still, a new United executive, Mike Howe, a former senior executive at Young & Rubicam who had been recently named head of United's advertising and promotion division, ordered the review, which would include Burnett.

Eight agencies were invited to present their credentials, including, not surprisingly, Saatchi & Saatchi. But on August 19, 1996, Saatchi & Saatchi Advertising was eliminated from the United competition in the first round, along with Ogilvy & Mather and J. Walter Thompson.

The invitation from United coincided with a setback of sorts for Saatchi & Saatchi Advertising Worldwide. During the week of July 29, Charlie Scott let someone close to Cordiant know that he was about to fire John Fitzgerald, Saatchi & Saatchi Advertising Worldwide's president and chief operating officer and heir apparent to Ed Wax, the chairman and chief executive officer. Fitzgerald had joined the agency only eight months earlier, after running McCann-Erickson Japan in Tokyo.

Scott admitted privately that hiring Fitzgerald was a mistake and dismissing him so quickly showed a willingness on the part of Bob Seelert to admit his management errors. Somehow—and logic pointed to a senior executive at a rival to Cordiant or to a partner at M&C Saatchi—a story concerning Fitzgerald's tenuous position found its way into the *Times* in London on August 6 with the headline "Cordiant to Move Saatchi U.S. Chief from His Post." Before the story was made public, Fitzgerald said he had "no idea" of any pending change in his status. And he told the *Times*, "There must be an absolute misunderstanding. I was with Charlie Scott for a successful meeting only a week ago."

Perhaps, but the topic was not likely the bright future of John Fitzgerald at Saatchi & Saatchi Advertising. On August 9, the company released a terse statement saying that Fitzgerald was leaving, effective immediately. "John has made a real contribution," Ed Wax said. "However, following extensive discussions, we have come to realize that we have differing views on the future management of the agency."

Without saying good-bye to anyone, John Fitzgerald left Saatchi & Saatchi. Both the agency and Fitzgerald badly misjudged each other. Fitzgerald, for one, was brought in by Scott, Seelert, and, to a lesser extent, Wax as an "agent of change," according to one person with knowledge of the situation. Fitzgerald also had great pressure put upon him to improve the operating margins of Saatchi & Saatchi Advertising in New York, London, and elsewhere, and fast. He was supposed to complete this daunting assignment within months. To accomplish this, Fitzgerald tore through the agency, leaving himself little time to actually get to know any of the senior executives. Therefore, he was perceived as an arrogant and aloof executive whose only concern was the bottom line, which, of course, it was.

But Fitzgerald was badly served by Seelert and Wax. Neither executive became a mentor to Fitzgerald in the complex world of Saatchi & Saatchi Advertising. One person who knew of these events said that Seelert should have sat in on meetings between Fitzgerald and agency executives. This person added that Wax was out of the office too often, traveling to see clients. There was a management void that proved fatal to John Fitzgerald, whose comfort was in knowing that his salary of approximately $450,000 would be paid for a year.

Fitzgerald's departure left a succession hole at the agency: who would succeed Ed Wax? That was a question gnawing at Charlie Scott and Bob Seelert. Nevertheless, Cordiant would not launch another executive search to replace John Fitzgerald. Not immediately, at least. The company had had enough of outsiders for a while.

As uncertainty involving Saatchi & Saatchi Advertising resurfaced, Cordiant announced better-than-expected midyear 1996 results on August 6, 1996. Cordiant recorded a profit of £9 million in the period, compared with a loss of £36.8 million in the same period a year earlier. Earnings per share were 2 pence, compared with a loss of 12.9 pence in the same period in 1995. Trading margins, a concern of David Herro for so long, improved in the United States to 5.1 percent, compared with 1995's interim results of negative .5 percent. But in the United Kingdom there was a trading margin of 13 percent, a decline of .4 percent. Cordiant noted that revenue growth in the second half of 1996 "is not expected to be as strong as that achieved during the first half of 1996. Revenue for the full year is expected to be similar to that achieved in 1995, after adjusting for disposals." Cordiant was finally receiving some relief from past real estate excesses. It expected further cost savings because it was able to sublet an entire floor in Saatchi & Saatchi Advertising's Hudson Street offices. It was able to sublet space at Berkeley Square in London as well.

Charlie Scott noted that Bates Worldwide "has maintained a consistently successful new business record over 1994 and 1995 and the momentum has been maintained into the current year." Perhaps, but not in its United States operation, which has lacked any significant new business. In fact, in late July 1996, M&C Saatchi was able to win another piece of business away from Cordiant, this time from Bates Worldwide. M&C Saatchi's Hong Kong office won the advertising assignment for Hongkong Bank, one of Asia's top advertisers. Bates had handled the account for thirty-five years.

The atmosphere didn't improve much at Saatchi & Saatchi Advertising on Charlotte Street in late July 1996: at least fifteen employees in the agency's creative department were dismissed, as downsizing and "redundancies" were addressed. The dismissals reduced the creative department to sixty-nine employees from eighty-four, an 18 percent decrease. The agency named Adam Kean, who had been one of three joint creative directors, to take control of the creative department with John Pallant, who was named joint creative director. Kean did not win any new friends when he gave an interview to *Campaign* magazine in the United Kingdom in late July 1996 and said, "Certain people are not right for this agency. We sat down and said, 'Who do we want to give briefs to? Who has the right combination of talent, attitude and passion?' " M&C Saatchi, never missing an opportunity, felt the agency was finally vulnerable and lured away some second-level executives who had worked under Jennifer Laing.

The tension between Cordiant and M&C Saatchi did not subside in the summer of 1996 either. Television and radio commercials for Toyota Motor Sales' New York and New Jersey dealers, produced by Saatchi & Saatchi Advertising in Torrance, California, sounded eerily like ads for British Airways, created by M&C Saatchi, that had begun airing months earlier. In each spot, an individual is frustrated as he tries to reach others by telephone or in person and no one is around. "Where is everybody?" the person shrieks in both series of ads. In July 1996, a British Airways executive, Dale Moss, asked Toyota to take the "steps necessary" to resolve the similarities. (To be fair, the "Where is everybody?" ads were created by Saatchi & Saatchi Advertising and began airing in December 1994, just when Maurice Saatchi was dismissed as chairman by the board. M&C Saatchi argues, of course, that it now employs those who created those series of ads.)

Separately, the British Airways ads from M&C Saatchi continued to struggle to gain acceptance among consumers. On August 5, 1996, *USA Today* advertising and marketing reporter Dottie Enrico published the latest results of the newspaper's Ad Track survey, conducted by Louis Harris. The findings were not encouraging for British Airways. Only 10 percent of consumers polled said they liked the ads. Enrico reported that the work from M&C Saatchi for British Airways was "one of the least popular ad campaigns among more than 60 measured." In its defense, British Airways said the ads might not have appealed to the average Ad Track consumer because they were created for a narrow segment of the audience: upscale international business travelers.

Meanwhile, Maurice Saatchi continued to show his enterprising spirit. His Megalomedia company in July 1996 purchased full control of a digital film and television studio, Framestore, of which it had previously owned 39.8 percent. The deal, financed through a combination of shares, loan notes, options, and cash, is worth approximately £7 million. Maurice Saatchi said, "We believe that digitalization and computer technology will continue to play an increasingly fundamental role in media. We are now well placed to capitalize on the commercial potential offered by such a dynamic sector."

As M&C Saatchi reached its first birthday, it prepared to move out of its undistinguished temporary headquarters on Marylebone Lane. The company's new, permanent headquarters was taking shape not far away in Golden Square, a quiet, charming part of Soho with gardens of ornamental crab apple trees and maple rose bushes, which Charles Dickens chose as a setting for Ralph Nickleby's house.

Construction continued on No. 36 Golden Square, a five-story brick structure that, upon completion, would include a twenty-car garage. Black letters reading "M&C Saatchi" would adorn the building's facade, just as "Saatchi & Saatchi" had once stood over Berkeley Square.

On July 1, 1996, the first phase of the move to Golden Square began, with the entire agency expected to be housed there by January 1997. The estimated cost to M&C Saatchi to renovate its Golden Square offices: £3.5 million. Cynics said that M&C Saatchi was erecting a 1980s building in the 1990s. No. 36 Golden Square, they said, would house an advertising agency mired in the 1980s.

Such criticism, as usual, fell on Maurice Saatchi's deaf ears. Anyone who wondered whether Maurice Saatchi had learned anything from the painful and public lesson the shareholders of his former company had meted out should note that M&C Saatchi, in late 1996, had no plans to go public. Instead, M&C Saatchi would remain a private company, far from the scrutiny of meddling shareholders.

M&C SAATCHI chose the lull in the summer of 1996 to launch what rapidly became the most infamous ad of its brief life. The print ad showed Tony Blair, the Labour leader who was running against Prime Minister John Major, as demonic; his eyes were red and his face had a frightening glare. The caption: "New Labour, New Danger." The Advertising Standards Authority banned the ad on August 28, 1996, and said that the ad violated industry codes against portraying politicians in an offensive way. But the ad had the desired effect. M&C Saatchi had no plans of running it again. It didn't need to; reprints in articles about the ban appeared around the world.

ON AUGUST 21, 1996, Maurice Saatchi became Lord Saatchi. Prime Minister Major had finally rewarded Saatchi for almost two decades of loyal service to the Conservatives with a peerage, one of the highest honors in the United Kingdom. Instantly, his critics seized upon the honor to ridicule Saatchi. A Labour spokesman suggested that Maurice Saatchi be dubbed "Lord of the Lies." If such sniping hurt Lord Saatchi, he didn't show it. He had risen from being the child of Jewish immigrants from Baghdad to a status reserved in the United Kingdom for only a handful. Along the way, he created hundreds of jobs and made more than one employee, including himself of course, quite rich. He had gotten away with a tremendous amount and had almost everything he wanted, with one critical exception.

Cordiant—and Saatchi & Saatchi Advertising—survived.

AFTERWORD

THROUGH THE CONCLUSION OF 1996 and continuing until April 1997, Maurice Saatchi turned his attention and considerable newfound energy to another entity struggling for survival: the Conservative government and the administration of Prime Minister John Major. Almost daily, Saatchi would visit the Prime Minister's residence at No. 10 Downing Street to brainstorm strategy aimed at rattling the seemingly unstoppable Labour party and its telegenic and energetic leader, Tony Blair.

Ultimately many, if not all, of Saatchi's ideas were rejected. Major had grown gun-shy of the advertising executive's proposals. This was an unexpected turn of events because the campaign had started so well, especially with the "demon eyes" advertisement. In January 1997, *Campaign* magazine named it the advertisement of the year. Although a poll found that 64 percent of the population disliked the ad, *Campaign* thought it had achieved its purpose: to raise questions about Blair's character. The Conservative party spent £125,000 to place the ad but scored another £5 million to £10 million of free publicity.

Saatchi, even though he was close to Major and had been instrumental in four previous victorious campaigns for the Conservatives, was becoming unsuccessful in having things his way. In March 1997, for instance, Michael Heseltine, the Deputy Prime Minister, had to resolve a bitter dispute between Saatchi and Brian Mawhinney, the Conservative party chairman. Mawhinney wanted all campaign posters and billboards from Saatchi to be shown to focus groups before being released to the public. To Saatchi, this was an affront. The poster that led to the disagreement was of a lion shedding a red tear. No one liked the lion as an icon of Britain, not even Major. Yet Saatchi would not give in. Eventually, the lion billboard was distributed and was quickly considered a flop. Heseltine declared that all subsequent billboards must be test-marketed in the same way advertisements for consumer products were done.

Still, "Maurice was energized in a way I hadn't seen him in quite a while," said Bill Muirhead in early 1997. Muirhead, too, remained busy, continuing to travel frequently to New York from London to oversee M&C Saatchi's slow progress in the United States. Of the five partners, Muirhead remained the clear workhorse, as if he had to prove his decision to quit the former Saatchi & Saatchi Company PLC in January 1996 was not total folly. In fact, Muirhead earned the most of the five partners. Although M&C Saatchi is a private company, the agency nevertheless is compelled to supply figures to an organization called Companies House in the United Kingdom and did so in January 1997: sales were £15 million for 1995, its start-up year. Also recorded was a loss of £640,000 attributed to start-up costs. M&C Saatchi executives in mid-1997 privately said the business turned profitable and there would be a profit. Muirhead earned a salary of £162,000, a huge drop in what he earned as chief executive of Saatchi & Saatchi Advertising and far less than he would have earned if he had chosen to remain with his former company. Ed Wax, chairman of Saatchi & Saatchi Advertising Worldwide, was planning his retirement and Muirhead had been the clear choice to be his successor.

David Kershaw, a partner with M&C Saatchi, said on the occasion of the second anniversary of Maurice's noisy exit from the company he co-founded: "The spirit of the brand is as strong as ever, but we have been reincarnated. We are a focused ad agency, we are not going to run a bank or a [public relations] agency or try to get into [consultancy] services." In short, two-year-old M&C Saatchi had no plans to be anything other than what it was: a small advertising agency. If Maurice Saatchi harbored any grand ambitions, he didn't tell anyone other than his brother, Charles, or his wife, Josephine Hart. But it wouldn't matter. As Kershaw said: "If [Maurice] had any aspirations to be grand, which he doesn't, we would bring him right back to ground."

Meanwhile, unknown to all but a chosen few, work was being

completed on a plan that had its inception in October 1996 but didn't gather steam until December 1996, when Charlie Scott and Bob Seelert conducted a secret meeting in London with Ed Wax; Michael Bungey, chairman of Bates Worldwide; and John Perriss, head of Zenith Media Services. At the meeting, Seelert briefed the executives on a bold plan that had a disturbingly familiar sound: Saatchi & Saatchi Advertising and Bates would be spun off as separate companies. It was precisely the proposal that had led to the firing of Maurice Saatchi as chairman of Saatchi & Saatchi Company PLC two years earlier.

READERS of the *Financial Mail* in London on February 9, 1997, were greeted with an unattributed article reporting that Cordiant was considering a split into two and that the move could allow Maurice and Charlie Saatchi to buy back the agency that bears their name. As usual, a Cordiant spokesman was not helpful: Cordiant, he said, is "always on the lookout for ways of unlocking shareholder value."

The story of a so-called de-merger—the plan that Maurice Saatchi had asked many advisers, including Suzanna Taverne, to examine, only to be told it made no sense—actually wasn't as earth-shattering as other pieces of significant news from Cordiant in the first quarter of 1997. March 13, 1997, proved to be a turnaround not only for Cordiant but for Saatchi & Saatchi Advertising. For one, Cordiant announced it would pay its first dividend in seven years and was returning to the black after years of woes and red ink. Cordiant's pretax profits for 1996 were £41.8 million after a loss of £22.6 million in 1995. The payment was largely symbolic: one pence payable from earnings of 5.5 pence. Losses in 1995 were 12.8 pence.

Cordiant reported its agencies won new business from clients such as Ameritech, BMW, Campbell, Coca-Cola, General Mills, Gillette, Johnson & Johnson, Kodak, Nokia, Reynolds, and Toyota, among others. It also noted that the agencies lost business, including Miller Brewing, Hewlett-Packard, Ericsson, and Reckitt & Colman.

Such news was overshadowed by the celebration taking place on Charlotte Street in London and on Hudson Street in New York at Saatchi & Saatchi Advertising. It had been awarded the coveted $100 million global advertising assignment from Delta Air Lines. After more than two years, the agency finally replaced the British Airways account, just seven months after it had been quickly eliminated from United Airlines's review. In winning Delta, Saatchi & Saatchi bested Ogilvy & Mather Worldwide and Ammirati Puris Lintas. BBDO, which was the incumbent and was participating in the review, suddenly resigned the account one week before a winner was selected. Delta's decision was quick: on March 11, Saatchi & Saatchi executives delivered a three-hour pitch to Delta officials in a hotel room in Atlanta. Following the presentation, Delta took an informal poll and Saatchi & Saatchi was enthusiastically awarded the business. Saatchi & Saatchi said it would hire additional employees to staff the account and open an office in Atlanta where Delta has its headquarters. One of the architects of the Delta win was Jennifer Laing, who had changed places with Alan Bishop on January 1, 1997. Laing was named chief executive of Saatchi & Saatchi Advertising North America, and Bishop took Laing's place on Charlotte Street. With her new position, Laing supervised accounts with billings estimated at $2 billion out of the agency's $7 billion. That was also more than triple the London office's billings of $650 million. If Alan Bishop objected or felt he was being shunted aside, it didn't show. He was popular no matter where he went. But it wasn't considered a vote of confidence to be sent far away from Ed Wax and the capital of the advertising industry. Thus, observers felt they were justified in assuming Laing would replace Ed Wax to run the worldwide Saatchi & Saatchi Advertising empire. As usual, such thinking was wrong.

Not all was going smoothly at M&C Saatchi. For instance, in March it hired a respected executive, Chris Brooking, to run its new office in Melbourne. At the last minute, Brooking decided to remain with another agency in Wellington, New Zealand. The unexpected action led M&C Saatchi to scramble to service the $20 million ANZ Banking Group account.

But such nuisances didn't bother Charles Saatchi. Granted, he was spending time at M&C Saatchi offices and helping with some campaigns, including the Conservative party and, of course, Silk Cut cigarettes, but the bulk of his waking hours was taken up with doing what he does best: collecting art and go-cart racing. Around the time his former company was declaring a dividend and winning Delta, Charles was acquiring. He paid several million dollars for twenty-eight realistic paintings by a sixty-nine-year-old artist named Alex Katz for the Saatchi Gallery. The purchase of paintings of cityscapes, landscapes, couples, and women (including Katz's wife, Ada) came "out of the blue," Katz told the *New York Observer.* "I got a call [in the summer of 1996] that Saatchi wanted to buy a number of my paintings. I never thought he would be interested in my work. I always thought of him buying minimalists. I have no idea why he decided to do this." At the time the Katz purchase was made public, Charles Saatchi agreed to a rare interview with Catherine Milner of the *Sunday Telegraph* in London. The subject was confined to art, and the reason for the interview was to promote the lending of his avant-garde art collection to the Royal Academy. "The most important aspect of the exhibition is that it will be seen by a much wider audience than we could hope to attract at the Saatchi Gallery." He also touched on his love affair with go-carts. "I have always been hopeless at all sports," he said, "but for some reason I'm OK in my carts." Indeed, Charles has been the Formula A (the equivalent in go-cart racing to the Formula One) champion for the past three years at Rye House, Britain's top club. One year, his birthday cake was made in the shape of a cart helmet. There was one revealing confession from Saatchi in the interview: the regret that his enthusiasm for art did not rub off on the British public. "I think I have failed," he said. "I had rather hoped by now that there would be lots of people out there collecting British art. But there seem to be very few."

Charles was not discouraged, however. In fact, he planned to open a Saatchi Gallery in New York sometime in 1998. Also, in May 1997, Charles Saatchi signed a partnership deal with the family running Hammer Films, one of the venerable movie studios in Britain, to return Hammer to full production. The plans called for Hammer to produce films as well as to operate a chain of restaurants and a theme park. Hammer dates back to the 1920s, but its heyday was between 1957 and 1972 when it produced such films as *The Curse of Frankenstein* and *One Million Years B.C.*, starring Raquel Welch. One of Charles's friends said Hammer was a logical investment since Charles "loves old Dracula and Frankenstein movies."

ON APRIL 21, 1997, what had been rumored for months was finally, officially announced. The empire built by Maurice and Charles Saatchi with hubris, audacity, and solid creative excellence coupled with superb attention to the client was dismantled. In London, Cordiant, which had slipped to the world's sixth-largest advertising agency holding company, said it was splitting into two stand-alone companies, Bates Group of Companies and Saatchi & Saatchi Group. Upon completion of the de-merger, the two agencies would trade separately on the London and New York stock exchanges. One did not have to scratch too far below the surface to see that the plan mirrored one proposed many times by Maurice Saatchi. This time, advocates of the de-merger said, it made sense because the holding company wasn't saddled by mountains of debt the way it was when Maurice headed the company. Such financial handicaps made a de-merger impossible.

Cordiant was going out of business, leaving Saatchi & Saatchi and Bates to divide the spoils. Zenith Media would be jointly owned by Saatchi & Saatchi and Bates. The superior corporate communications firm Siegel & Gale, as well as the Facilities Group —creative and technical services for print, television, and multimedia production—would go with Saatchi & Saatchi, and the floundering Rowland Group public relations firm and HP:ICM—a specialist in conference and exhibition marketing—were to fall under the Bates Group.

Bob Seelert, the Cordiant chief executive who pushed for the de-merger, was named chief executive officer of the Saatchi & Saatchi Group. Meanwhile, Michael Bungey, the head of Bates, got what he wanted: his own agency. He was appointed chief executive officer of the Bates Group. He was finally rid of Saatchi & Saatchi. Further, he stood to gain enormously from a sale of Bates, which many, including several shareholders, assumed would happen sooner rather than in years to come.

Almost as an afterthought, attention focused on Charlie Scott, who had calmly guided the troubled company through its worst period, a period far more ridden with angst than when it was on the verge of bankruptcy and Robert Louis-Dreyfus and Scott were brought in. Scott, who began dressing in expensive and fashionable outfits and looked as if he had reversed his own aging process, said he would become a non-executive chairman of both groups "to facilitate the de-merger process and provide continuity of management during a one-year period." After that, he said publicly, he would relinquish responsibilities from one of the groups. But no one believed he would remain with either Saatchi & Saatchi or Bates. After roughly seven years of intensity he wished on no one, Charlie Scott had had enough of the advertising game. Many expected Scott to rejoin his old friend Robert Louis-Dreyfus, who had accomplished a spectacular turnaround at Adidas.

Cordiant executives privately said that the de-merger was merely correcting what had been a colossally misguided strategy of Maurice Saatchi's in the first place. "The grand plan of the last ten years hasn't worked," said Alan J. Gottesman, who follows the advertising industry as managing director of West End Communications/Consulting in New York. "It didn't seem to be any benefit to anybody to have all these assets co-owned." Gottesman said that no one should be surprised "to see one, or maybe both, snapped up by one of the successful holding companies [such as WPP Group or Interpublic] within twenty-four months."

In Chicago, David Herro, who was told of the de-merger weeks before it was made public, said it was "an excellent deal for everyone." He called the proposal a "dismantling of a holding company structure which was erroneously put together."

For his part, Maurice Saatchi was oddly silent. Even his partners were surprised at Saatchi's self-imposed muzzle. It is incorrect to conclude that he had finally turned a corner and exorcised any feelings for his former company. Instead, his absence from the de-merger coverage was, as usual, self-serving. By suddenly behaving himself, he hoped to prove to potential clients that he was no longer the out-of-control executive who was willing to wage a public war against colleagues and former co-workers, thereby sacrificing what is considered best for the client: having its ad agency put the product, not the agency, in the spotlight. There was one piece of misguided mischief: the *Telegraph* in London incorrectly reported that, following the de-merger, Cordiant "may abandon the Saatchi & Saatchi name." It printed a correction the following day.

The de-merger plan had become a "specific thought" in October 1996. Three months earlier, Cordiant decided to abandon its efforts to buy another ad agency, France's BDDP Group, which owned, among others, Wells Rich Greene. (BDDP was purchased in September 1996 by GGT Group, a little-known British advertising company, for $162.6 million in cash and stock.) "We began to focus on strategic alternatives," Bob Seelert said one Sunday afternoon in June 1997, taking a break from working in his Connecticut garden. "We looked at a merger as well. Everything washed ashore because of conflicts with clients, people, and culture, with the different culture of the two places [Saatchi & Saatchi and Bates] being the most important reason."

But when Cordiant began to consider a merger, it didn't get very far. "One ally said it couldn't be done," Seelert recalled. "Procter & Gamble [a longtime and valued Saatchi & Saatchi client] said that what was a conflict in one network was a conflict for the entire network." Seelert said such an edict had dire consequences for Bates, which was forbidden to compete for any account that could be viewed as having a conflict with Procter & Gamble. (Of course, this is exactly what Maurice and Bungey had said for years, but such frustration went unheard.) Because of Procter & Gamble's insistence, Seelert estimated that approximately 10 percent of worldwide advertising spending was unavailable to Bates. The de-merger would energize both agencies, Seelert said, and unlock their potential, enabling the agencies to accelerate revenue and increase profit margins.

Embracing the idea of a de-merger, Seelert met with Wax, Bungey, and Perriss in London in December and "all three operators thought it was a great idea," Seelert said. As important, the de-merger had the blessing of Procter & Gamble. Bob Wehling, a senior vice president at the packaged goods company, said, "From the client's point of view, we endorse Cordiant's de-merger one hundred percent. Any move by an agency that motivates its staff better and is focused on client service can only be good news for all parties."

Bob Seelert, an articulate, fair-minded, even-tempered executive, said that with the de-merger he had come upon "a big idea, one that history will tell was a great idea." And, he quickly added, six Cordiant shareholders who own 58 percent of the company's stock also thought it was a "great idea." To complete the de-merger, an extraordinary general meeting was scheduled to take place in October 1997, to be followed two months later by the issue of new shares to the new companies.

The news of the de-merger was followed by a "road show," wherein executives traveled and tried to sell the idea to shareholders, analysts, and reporters. On June 12, 1997, for instance, Bob Seelert and Michael Bungey, among others, flew to Chicago from New York to speak with David Herro. Herro was becoming increasingly concerned with what was happening at Bates. During one week in June, Bates lost two major accounts: Compaq Computer Corp. and Texaco Inc., costing the agency approximately $100 million in billings. Also, another client, Foot Locker, a chain of sportswear stores, said it was considering moving its $40 million from Bates. Michael Bungey told reporters that the dismantling of Bates meant that "one of the major jobs I must do is create an ownership culture in the company." His main challenge was to snare a larger share of the American market, which accounted for 25 percent of the revenue, behind Europe (34 percent) and Asia-Pacific (26 percent). His goal was to push Bates's U.S. revenue to 45 percent, and he did not rule out acquisitions of other advertising agencies to reach that number.

Nine days after Cordiant announced its own demise, a lavish luncheon was held on a clear, warm, and sunny day in a private dining room on top of the World Trade Center in Manhattan. The purpose was to preview Delta's new advertising campaign from Saatchi & Saatchi. But when the shades were lowered electronically, blocking the spectacular view, and Michael Keeshan, the Saatchi & Saatchi executive who was given the title chief strategic officer and worldwide account director on the Delta account, introduced the ads, one couldn't help but notice that the tone and look of the spots resembled that of ads from a past client: British Airways. The ads, which used actress Christine Lahti for the voice-over, show a businesswoman sitting alone in the fuselage of an airplane, working on a computer much as she would if she were in her office. Another spot has a man sitting at a restaurant table being tended to by chefs and waiters. Still another has an individual sitting in a plane in which he is the only passenger except for musicians performing jazz. The message is that if one flies Delta's enhanced business class service, one will be treated especially well. The slogan: "On top of the world." The campaign was roundly criticized because it struck many critics as retro; that is, passengers are more interested in an airline's running on time than they are in knowing a select few will be treated like royalty.

A few days after Delta premiered its ads, United Airlines's new campaign from the respected Fallon McElligott in Minneapolis was unveiled. It was considered an instant success: it did everything the Delta ads did not. In one spot, United employees are called to a meeting in an airport waiting room. The person who called them together doesn't show up until after he has kept the group waiting for over thirty minutes. "How do you like being kept waiting with no announcement about what is going on and no one to give you any information?" the executive asks upon finally arriving. Another ad features a man reclining in a luxurious seat, eating a scrumptious meal. The camera is pulled back to reveal he is actually on a soundstage. The headline: "Wouldn't it be great if we all flew commercials?" United Airlines, said critics, was showing it responded to passengers' concerns. Delta was not.

But Saatchi & Saatchi Advertising executives shrugged off any criticism of the Delta campaign. It was back in the big leagues and things were finally running smoothly. Further, within a few months, the agency was not going to have to answer to a holding company in London, a company that had caused it nothing but grief. But things are never calm at Saatchi & Saatchi for too long. Less than one week after the Delta luncheon, Cordiant announced that Ed Wax was, at sixty years old, finally retiring as chief executive officer at Saatchi & Saatchi Advertising Worldwide. But neither Jennifer Laing nor Alan Bishop were selected to replace Wax. Instead, an odd selection was made. Kevin Roberts, a relatively unknown forty-seven-year-old former New Zealand brewing executive, was tapped to replace Wax. Roberts was also named to replace Wax on the Cordiant board of directors. Wax was to remain as chairman of Saatchi & Saatchi until the end of 1997. (Starting in January 1998, Wax was to play a "continuing role" as chairman emeritus.) Roberts was described by former colleagues as aggressive, ruthless, and confident. In short, Kevin Roberts sounded very much like Maurice Saatchi. While president of PepsiCo Canada in 1987, Roberts once placed a Coca-Cola vending machine onstage, picked up a shotgun, and fired, destroying the Coke dispenser. That stunt earned him the nickname Rambo. He also dressed in a commando outfit for other meetings and once brought a lion cub to a conference. He also orchestrated the "World's Largest Barbecue" in Tasmania. At the time of his appointment to Saatchi & Saatchi, Roberts was the proprietor of the Gaults restaurant in Auckland, voted the best in New Zealand. Previously, Roberts worked for Mary Quant cosmetics and Gillette in the United Kingdom, and Procter & Gamble with responsibility in the Middle East and Africa. He was also chief operating officer of Lion Nathan Ltd., a leading New Zealand brewery group that used Saatchi & Saatchi as its agency. That, and his tenure with Procter & Gamble in the 1970s, was how Roberts and Ed Wax got to know one another and became quite chummy. Roberts and Bill Muirhead and their families attended an intimate 1994 Christmas party at Wax's home in Gramercy Park in New York.

The selection of Kevin Roberts struck many within the agency and the advertising industry as puzzling. For one, he had not worked on the agency side of the business; instead, he was a client. He was, in short, exactly what Bob Seelert had been. Many found it peculiar that a worldwide advertising agency would be run by two former clients. But Seelert said in June 1997 that he found nothing wrong with breaking the mold. "[Roberts] was known to Ed Wax, who liked and respected him," Seelert said. "I got to meet him and felt comfortable with him. Then, Ed and I introduced him to the entire Saatchi & Saatchi Advertising board and everyone liked him and he was offered the job. Nothing too complicated." Specifically, Seelert said that Roberts's career "exposed him to the key disciplines essential to our business: marketing and the brand management for major multinationals, a hands-on experience of what good advertising can deliver, and, above all, an entrepreneurial and energetic attitude to management." Peter Cullinane, chairman of Saatchi & Saatchi Australia, told *Advertising Age* that

Roberts "has a very clear idea of what role he has to play to have our network go where we want it to go. He has a clear understanding of the need to be a brand champion at the center and a coach and all-round enthusiast." Roberts did not come cheap. Saatchi & Saatchi paid him a base salary of $700,000 plus pension contributions, bonus payments, and share options; specifically, Roberts was to receive a $300,000 one-time pension payment after three years and was invited to join the company's bonus and share option plan. When asked about the lofty salary by *The Times* in London, David Herro in Chicago gave an answer that struck some as ironic: "It is our policy not to interfere in management issues."

Roberts was finally shown to Cordiant investors, analysts, and shareholders during the second week of June 1997. He told everyone that he wanted the bulk of new business to come from "the biggest source," meaning existing clients. His targets were Procter & Gamble and Toyota, which combined already accounted for a third of Saatchi & Saatchi's worldwide billings of approximately $7.1 billion. Publicly, he had the support of Jennifer Laing and Alan Bishop.

Seelert was clear that neither Jennifer Laing nor Alan Bishop was considered to replace Wax. "They have just signed three-year commitments to their new jobs," he said, "so they could hardly be disappointed."

So much were Cordiant and Saatchi & Saatchi Advertising in the spotlight during the first half of 1997 that one couldn't help but notice that M&C Saatchi, and specifically, Maurice Saatchi, had slipped out of the limelight. It wasn't that Saatchi or his agency craved the attention any less. Rather, quite the opposite was true. It galled M&C Saatchi that it no longer appeared to be the darling of the media. Maurice Saatchi was thrust before the attention of the public briefly, but not for any reason he sought. On May 1, Prime Minister John Major and his Conservative party suffered a humiliating defeat at the hands of Tony Blair and the new Labour party. Of the 659 seats in the House of Commons, Labour won 418, a gain of 146. Virtually all the ridicule was justly reserved for John Major, although Maurice Saatchi did not escape entirely. The *Sunday Times* of London printed a list of winners and losers in the campaign war three days before the election. Of course, Maurice Saatchi was included. It noted that Saatchi had been a Conservative adman on every general election since 1979. "This is his worst," the *Times* wrote. "Now the ultimate nightmare: the 'Lord of Lies' must contemplate the possibility of his first election campaign on the losing side. Verdict: [Saatchi's] last war."

Maurice Saatchi finally broke his silence, if only on the defeat of John Major and the Conservative party, on June 1, 1997, with a verbose opinion piece in the *Sunday Times*. The Conservative party, Saatchi wrote, "needs to set aside its antipathy to planning and overcome its residual distaste for long-term strategy. And there is one more task. The history of the world is built on the precise use of language . . . at the end of the day all that a Conservative supporter wants is a simple signpost in the ground."

The article sounded as if Maurice Saatchi was still pitching the business.

M&C SAATCHI knows how to throw a great party. On May 15, the agency held its first soiree in its new New York headquarters at 895 Broadway. It was far from midtown, but M&C Saatchi's permanent New York offices were in the fashionable Flatiron district. M&C Saatchi was situated in a huge loft space above the Equinox health club. So chic was the Equinox that the joke was you had to work out at another gym first in order to get yourself in shape to be seen at the Equinox. The actress Julia Roberts was a member. And many M&C Saatchi employees were to be members, since Equinox's ad agency was M&C Saatchi. That night, Bill Muirhead was the only M&C Saatchi partner in attendance. He was jovial, chatty, and mingled easily among the several hundred guests. No, he said, M&C Saatchi did not have new business to announce in the United States yet, but stay tuned.

The heat was off M&C Saatchi. The same week the agency was partying, Cordiant continued to make impressive business news, the news that mattered most. Saudi Arabia's billionaire Prince al-Waleed bin Talal purchased more than 3 percent of Cordiant, or 25 million shares. The forty-year-old prince said, "I think the Cordiant management has done a very good job so far to improve the performance of the company." Although the company declined to say how much the prince paid, at the company's share price in May 1997, a 3 percent stake was worth approximately £20 million. His other investments included Euro Disney, Trans World Airlines, Canary Wharf in London, and the Planet Hollywood restaurant chain. "When the world's fourth richest guy makes an investment in your company," Seelert said, "you know what you're doing is a great idea."

OVERALL, the end of Cordiant seemed like a great idea to everyone. The assumption that Saatchi & Saatchi Advertising and Bates would thrive without a holding company may have been overly optimistic, but that strategy was founded on logic. With the death of Cordiant, Saatchi & Saatchi and Bates will have exhausted all excuses for not winning a slew of new business. Much to the surprise of everyone, including themselves, executives at M&C Saatchi, principally Maurice Saatchi and Bill Muirhead, got on with their professional lives and no longer spent days gossiping about their old company. Maurice Saatchi is not a man who is given to public displays of emotion. Therefore, it is impossible to know how he felt about Saatchi & Saatchi Advertising not only surviving, but doing quite well. The company he co-founded in 1970 was being run by individuals—Robert Seelert and Kevin Roberts—with no institutional memory of Maurice Saatchi. No one could have predicted the twists and turns this corporate thriller would have taken, including the fact that Cordiant was not put out of business because of any scheme by Maurice Saatchi, but by a careful business strategy from Cordiant itself. There were no true losers among the principal characters. All are still fully employed. All remain handsomely compensated financially. If there are any wounds, they are psychological. "It's still painful to go back and recall the whole story," Bill Muirhead has often said.

It would be naive, however, to think that there is one piece of unfinished business that Cordiant executives are not looking forward to: when Cordiant's de-merger becomes official, it will be replaced on the London Stock Exchange by new listings of Bates and Saatchi & Saatchi (which will also begin appearing on the New York Stock Exchange). Cordiant executives were privately gleeful in anticipating Maurice Saatchi rising every morning either in his home off Berkeley Square in London or in his mansion in

Sussex, or at his home in the south of France, and being greeted with the name—his name—being traded as a public company once again.

For Maurice and Charles Saatchi, their slogan "Nothing Is Impossible" became less justified in the second half of their lives. In the end, they couldn't get their name back. And, after all the drama of the corporate boardroom, that probably wounded Maurice Saatchi most of all. As he has said on several occasions, "It's a great name. It's *my* name." But it's a name he had to endure sharing with his old nemesis: the company he co-founded. For the foreseeable future, Saatchi & Saatchi Group of Companies will co-exist with M&C Saatchi. That is why it galled Maurice Saatchi that whenever someone spoke of Saatchi and advertising, one question was asked: "Which one?"

ACKNOWLEDGMENTS

THIS BOOK began with a telephone call. On Monday, December 12, 1994, I received one at approximately 8:30 P.M. from an editor at the *Wall Street Journal* where I worked as the daily Advertising columnist. This couldn't be good news. A call at this hour meant there was a story published elsewhere that I needed to follow.

I was told there was an article in the December 13 edition of the *Financial Times* about trouble in London at Saatchi & Saatchi Company PLC, one of the world's largest advertising agency holding companies. Shareholders were calling for the ouster of Maurice Saatchi, the company's controversial chairman, and the board of directors was expected to take action shortly.

The only reliable sources were in London, where it was 1:30 A.M. I quickly decided not to wake Charles Scott, the affable and approachable chief executive of Saatchi & Saatchi, and chose instead to call Tim Jackson, the company's director of investor relations, who spoke to the press and who was always remarkably patient with my questions about the complex financial state of Saatchi & Saatchi. He was neither amused nor helpful when I woke him and his wife.

The story quickly played itself out and my articles resulted in a call from Simon & Schuster asking whether I would be interested in expanding the tale into a book. I didn't hesitate.

Several people led me on the path to writing this book. Judy Klemesrud of the *New York Times* was an early supporter, teacher, and model. I am deeply saddened she is not alive to see her "student's" work. After much coaxing, John Kifner of the *New York Times* finally invited an overeager journalism student to his Cambridge, Massachusetts, home in 1973 and allowed me to be his assistant for three years while I attended Boston University. He taught me to love hard news, how to write on deadline, and how to solidly report a story. There were great stories in Boston during the Kifner era and he generously allowed me along for the ride.

Robert J. Rosenthal and James Naughton of the *Philadelphia Inquirer* gave me chances few others would take. I will always be grateful for their friendship.

Jack Loftus, former television editor at *Variety*, showed me what covering a beat was all about. And what a beat he gave me in May 1983: the news divisions of the television broadcast networks. For the next three years, I worked under perhaps the best editor in the business.

Caroline Miller and Tom Wallace, former editors of *Newsday/New York Newsday*, filled the great void left when Loftus was no longer a *Newsday* editor. They showed patience and humor. When I was leaked a great story—the 1989 internal memo in which Bryant Gumbel criticized the staff of the NBC *Today* show—Miller expertly shepherded it through its editing and publication.

Norman Pearlstine, former executive editor of the *Wall Street Journal*, hired me in the summer of 1989 and endorsed my aggressive, day-to-day coverage of the television industry. He was always supportive, even when network executives called to complain. He urged me to finally write a book and listened endlessly as I spoke with him about it.

At the *Wall Street Journal*, I must thank Dennis Kneale for appointing me Advertising columnist in 1992 and always improving my writing and sharpening my thinking. He never failed to come up with terrific ideas for the column. Any reporter would be lucky to work with him. Thanks must also go to Laura Bird, a first-class reporter who always showed good humor, patience, diplomacy, and restraint while working with me on the column for close to three years.

Patrick M. Reilly and Joanne Lipman of the *Journal* are close friends who listened patiently as I talked about, among other things, this book and never once showed boredom.

Linda Amster lent her considerable intelligence and humor and not only helped with the research, but offered wise editing suggestions as well.

Many thanks go to my radio friends, especially Pete Fornatale, Vin Scelsa, and Jonathan Schwartz, for providing the soundtrack for much of my life and shaping my musical tastes. Thanks also to Roby Yonge.

Arden Ostrander was my contact with the outside world during the writing of this book. I couldn't start writing until I spoke with Arden, a practice I maintain to this day.

Nor could I have written this book without the endless generosity of Robert Marston. For years he was my wise counsel, and his advice was always on target. He is the definition of a close friend.

In London, Penny Rogg and Nic Robertson (along with their two children) opened their home for my seemingly constant visits to report the book. They, too, listened with interest to details involving the Saatchi & Saatchi story, as well as other parts of my life. Penny succeeded me as Kifner's assistant in Boston in 1976. If there was any joy out of that, it is that our friendship endures.

Martin Sorrell of WPP Group and Carl Spielvogel, one of the founders of the legendary Backer & Spielvogel agency, were two individuals who educated me about the advertising business and its personalities. They also showed it could be fun.

Randall Rothenberg, former Advertising columnist of the *New York Times*, took me for a Japanese meal upon the signing of my contract to write this book and graciously told me how he wrote his book on advertising. He has been with me every step of the way since. Thanks, Randy.

This book was greatly helped by several previously published works on Saatchi & Saatchi. Thanks especially to Ivan Fallon and his excellent book, *The Brothers: The Saatchi & Saatchi Story*, published in 1989. He superbly documented the childhood of Maurice and Charles Saatchi as well as the beginnings of their enterprise. Also helpful was *The Saatchi & Saatchi Story* by Philip Kleinman, published in 1987. And I also used Martin Mayer's two thorough books on advertising, *Madison Avenue, U.S.A.* and *Whatever Happened to Madison Avenue?*, as well as *Too Close to Call: Power and Politics, John Major in No. 10* by Sarah Hogg and Jonathan Hill.

Stephen Schiff, who wrote an opus on Saatchi & Saatchi for *The New Yorker* in May 1995, pointed me in several directions I would have missed. He was open with opinions and an early booster of this project.

Thanks, too, to Art Kliner, who wrote excellent pieces on the advertising industry for the *New York Times Magazine*, including a highly accurate and readable account of the Ted Bates acquisition by Saatchi & Saatchi Company PLC. Art was also helpful in several telephone conversations.

I had tremendous help in understanding the contemporary art world and Charles Saatchi's relation to it, including from Phoebe Hoban and David Ross of the Whitney Museum. Thanks especially to Anthony Haden-Guest for his guidance on the telephone and in print, especially for articles in *Vanity Fair* and *Art & Auction*. Thanks also to Don Hawthorne for his excellent May 1985 piece in *Art News*.

This book could not have been written without the main players in the drama itself who were incredibly generous with their time and never sounded annoyed to hear from me no matter how often I called. Maurice Saatchi, for one, never appeared bothered by tough questions, no matter how uncomfortable he may have been. His wife, Josephine Hart, was always in good humor, no matter when or where I called. Bill Muirhead has more patience than any human being I know. If more than a day went by without a conversation with Bill, both of us felt out of sorts. He provided insights and laughs for close to two years. He also opened doors that heretofore had been sealed shut. At M&C Saatchi, James Stuart and Steph Andrews were always helpful in finding individuals who are usually hard to find. Tim Duffy answered endless questions without the slightest hint of being bothered.

At Cordiant, Saatchi & Saatchi Advertising, and Bates Worldwide, Charlie Scott, Ed Wax, Alan Bishop, Michael Bungey, Judy Torello, and Roy Elvove were also patient and generous with their time and did not seem to mind going over old ground, no matter how painful or embarrassing.

Tim Jackson was more than generous with his time and reflections.

Thanks, too, to David Herro, who, beginning on December 13, 1994, answered all my questions with total honesty. He was great company as well and quickly understood my odd radio habits. He never called Sunday nights. Through David, I learned to leave telephone messages not to exceed twenty seconds.

Two close friends were always there either in person or on the telephone to connect me with the world beyond Saatchi & Saatchi: Verne Gay and Joe Rutledge.

I have the world's most indulgent agent, Michael Carlisle of the William Morris Agency. For seven years, he and I spoke regularly about various stories that could be turned into a book. He wisely knew what not to push. And when the call came from Simon & Schuster, he became my biggest champion. He is not merely an agent who is a skillful negotiator; he is a close friend. Thanks also to Arnold Kim at William Morris for never losing patience even after I lost mine.

Having read many acknowledgments, I know now what all the hoopla is about over Alice Mayhew at Simon & Schuster. Thanks for her expert guidance, patience, and support. Thanks, too, to Elizabeth Stein, Alice's associate editor. Liz and I spoke many times a day, via the telephone or e-mail. She never lost her sense of humor, even after the dreaded "template virus" struck our computers. No one could ask for a better and more careful copy editor than Fred Chase. Thanks as well to copy supervisor Steve Messina and to Natalie Goldstein, who did the photography research.

This book would not have been possible without Mark Gompertz at Simon & Schuster. A close friend since 1973, Mark is simply the best and I want to thank him for forgiving.

Of course, a large project is not possible without the support of family and I am lucky here as well. Daisy Blafer, my mother-in-law, showed a deep interest in the book and always peppered me with insightful questions and suggestions.

My mother, Judith, supported whatever I wanted to do at an early age, whether it was writing to Alfred Hitchcock or maintaining a nine-year correspondence with Charles Schulz, who writes and draws *Peanuts*. She and Saatchi & Saatchi shared a common motto: "Nothing Is Impossible." To this date, she remains one of my closest advisers and I am lucky.

My stepdaughter, Joanna, showed incredible patience and good humor as I routinely turned her teenage room into my office late at night.

Having been in her life for a decade, since she was six, I can only embarrass her and tell her publicly what I tell her in private: I am so proud of you. Joanna, you made me realize that if I had a child of my own, I wanted a girl.

My daughter, Alex, became four one month after I finished the first draft of this book. For the previous year, she told anyone who would listen that Dad was writing a book, *The Man on Charlotte Street* (well, I had to make it sound like a children's book), and the main character was "Maur-*ice.*" She is God's gift. And my wife is right: I can't believe I could love anything as much as my daughter.

When I first met the woman who would become my wife, Pam, on a spectacularly beautiful July 4, 1986, I knew I had met a kindred spirit, a soulmate, for life. She is understanding, supportive, and a superb editor. Without ever complaining, she managed the care of two children and my hectic and unpredictable schedule. This is as much her book as it is mine.

Finally, my biggest regret is that my father, Arthur E. Goldman, died without ever knowing his son's accomplishments. He was my closest friend. He was my biggest fan. I think of him every day. He is my model not only as a father, but as a human being as well. A more decent man you could never have met. Daddy, this is for you.

INDEX

NOTE: CS refers to Charles Saatchi; MS refers to Maurice Saatchi; and S&S refers to Saatchi & Saatchi.